ELIZABETH ROSS HAYNES

UNSUNG HEROES

THE BLACK BOY OF ATLANTA

"NEGROES IN DOMESTIC SERVICE IN THE UNITED STATES"

AFRICAN-AMERICAN WOMEN WRITERS, 1910–1940

HENRY LOUIS GATES, JR. *GENERAL EDITOR*

Jennifer Burton *Associate Editor*

OTHER TITLES IN THIS SERIES

Charlotte Hawkins Brown	*"Mammy": An Appeal to the Heart of the South* *The Correct Thing To Do—To Say—To Wear*
Jessie Redmon Fauset	*The Chinaberry Tree*
Zara Wright	*Black and White Tangled Threads*
Maggie Shaw Fullilove	*Who Was Responsible?* *Stories*
Mary Etta Spencer	*The Resentment*
Fanny Jackson Coppin	*Reminiscences of School Life and Hints on Teaching*
Frances Joseph-Gaudet	*"He Leadeth Me"*
Gertrude Pitts	*Tragedies of Life*
Anne Scott	*George Sampson Brite* *Case 999—A Christmas Story*
Mary Church Terrell	*A Colored Woman in a White World*

ELIZABETH ROSS HAYNES

UNSUNG HEROES

THE BLACK BOY OF ATLANTA

"NEGROES IN DOMESTIC SERVICE IN THE UNITED STATES"

Introduction by
FRANCILLE RUSAN WILSON

G.K. HALL & CO.
An Imprint of Simon & Schuster Macmillan
New York

Prentice Hall International
London Mexico City New Delhi Singapore Sydney Toronto

G. K. Hall & Co.
An Imprint of Simon & Schuster Macmillan
1633 Broadway
New York, NY 10019

Library of Congress Catalog Card Number: 96-43477

Printed in the United States of America

Printing Number
1 2 3 4 5 6 7 8 9 10

Library of Congress Cataloging-in-Publication Data

Haynes, Elizabeth Ross, 1883–1953.
[Selections. 1996]
Unsung heroes ; the Black boy of Atlanta ; "Negroes in domestic service in the United States" / Elizabeth Ross Haynes ; introduction by Francille Rusan Wilson.
p. cm. — (African-American women writers, 1910–1940)
Includes bibliographical references.
ISBN 0-7838-1432-1 (alk. paper)
1. Afro-Americans—Biography. 2. Women domestics—Washington (D.C.)—Economic conditions. 3. Wright, Richard R., 1849–1947 4. Afro-American college presidents—Georgia—Atlanta—Biography. 5. College presidents—Georgia—Atlanta—Biography. 6. Afro-American bankers—Georgia—Atlanta—Biography. I. Title. II. Title: Black boy of Atlanta. III. Title: Negroes in domestic service in the United States. IV. Series.
E185.96.H42 1996
920'.00929073—dc20 96-43477
CIP

This paper meets the requirements of ANSI/NISO Z39.48.1992 (Permanence of Paper).

CONTENTS

GENERAL EDITORS' PREFACE

The past decade of our literary history might be thought of as the era of African-American women writers. Culminating in the awarding of the Pulitzer Prize to Toni Morrison and Rita Dove and the Nobel Prize for Literature to Toni Morrison in 1993 and characterized by the presence of several writers—Toni Morrison, Alice Walker, Maya Angelou, and the Delaney Sisters, among others—on the *New York Times* Best Seller List, the shape of the most recent period in our literary history has been determined in large part by the writings of black women.

This, of course, has not always been the case. African-American women authors have been publishing their thoughts and feelings at least since 1773, when Phillis Wheatley published her book of poems in London, thereby bringing poetry directly to bear upon the philosophical discourse over the African's "place in nature" and his or her place in the great chain of being. The scores of words published by black women in America in the nineteenth century—most of which were published in extremely limited editions and never reprinted—have been republished in new critical editions in the forty-volume *Schomburg Library of Nineteenth-Century Black Women Writers*. The critical response to that series has led to requests from scholars and students alike for a similar series, one geared to the work by black women published between 1910 and the beginning of World War Two.

African-American Women Writers, 1910–1940 is designed to bring back into print many writers who otherwise would be unknown to contemporary readers, and to increase the availability of lesser-known texts by established writers who originally published during this critical period in African-American letters. This series implicitly acts as a chronological sequel to the Schomburg series, which focused on the origins of the black female literary tradition in America.

In less than a decade, the study of African-American women's writings has grown from its promising beginnings into a firmly established field in departments of English, American Studies, and African-American Studies. A comparison of the form and function of the original series and this sequel illustrates this dramatic shift. The *Schomburg Library* was published at the cusp of focused academic investigation into the interplay between race and gender. It covered the extensive period from the publication of Phillis Wheatley's *Poems on Various Subjects, Religious and Moral* in 1773 through the "Black Women's Era" of 1890–1910, and was designed to be an inclusive series of the major early texts by black women writers. The Schomburg Library provided a historical backdrop for black women's writings of the 1970s and 1980s, including the works of writers such as Toni Morrison, Alice Walker, Maya Angelou, and Rita Dove.

African-American Women Writers, 1910–1940 continues our effort to provide a new generation of readers access to texts—historical, sociological, and literary—that have been largely "unread" for most of this century. The series bypasses works that are important both to the period and the tradition, but that are readily available, such as Zora Neale Hurston's *Their Eyes Were Watching God*, Jessie Fauset's *Plum Bun* and *There Is Confusion*, and Nella Larsen's *Quicksand* and *Passing*. Our goal is to provide access to a wide variety of rare texts. The series includes Fauset's two other novels, *The Chinaberry Tree: A Novel of American Life* and *Comedy: American Style*, and Hurston's short play *Color Struck*, since these are not yet widely available. It also features works by virtually unknown writers, such as *A Tiny Spark*, Christina Moody's slim volume of poetry self-published in 1910, and *Reminiscences of School Life, and Hints on Teaching*, written by Fanny Jackson Coppin in the last year of her life (1913), a multigenre work combining an autobiographical sketch and reflections on trips to England and South Africa, complete with pedagogical advice.

Cultural studies' investment in diverse resources allows the historic scope of the *African-American Women Writers* series to be more focused than the *Schomburg Library* series, which covered works written over a 137-year period. With few exceptions, the authors included in the *African-American Women Writers* series wrote their major works between 1910 and 1940. The texts reprinted include all the works by each particular author that are not otherwise readily obtainable. As a result, two volumes contain works originally published after 1940. The Charlotte Hawkins Brown volume includes her book of etiquette published in 1941, *The Correct Thing To Do—To Say—To Wear*. One of the poetry volumes contains Maggie Pogue Johnson's *Fallen Blossoms*, published in 1951, a compilation of all her previously published and unpublished poems.

Excavational work by scholars during the past decade has been crucial to the development of *African-American Women Writers, 1910–1940*. Germinal bibliographical sources such as Ann Allen Shockley's *Afro-American Women Writers 1746–1933* and Maryemma Graham's *Database of African-American Women Writers* made the initial identification of texts possible. Other works were brought to our attention by scholars who wrote letters sharing their research. Additional texts by selected authors were then added, so that many volumes contain the complete oeuvres of particular writers. Pieces by authors without enough published work to fill an entire volume were grouped with other pieces by genre.

The two types of collections, those organized by author and those organized by genre, bring out different characteristics of black women's writings of the period. The collected works of the literary writers illustrate that many of them were experimenting with a variety of forms. Mercedes Gilbert's volume, for example, contains her 1931 collection *Selected Gems of Poetry, Comedy, and Drama, Etc.*, as well as her 1938 novel *Aunt Sarah's Wooden God*. Georgia Douglas Johnson's volume contains her plays and short stories in addition to her poetry. Sarah Lee Brown Fleming's volume combines her 1918 novel *Hope's Highway* with her 1920 collection of poetry, *Clouds and Sunshine*.

The generic volumes both bring out the formal and thematic similarities among many of the writings and highlight the striking individuality of particular writers. Most of the plays in the volume of one-acts are social dramas whose tragic endings can be clearly attributed to miscegenation and racism. Within the context of these other plays, Marita Bonner's expressionistic theatrical vision becomes all the more striking.

The volumes of *African-American Women Writers, 1910–1940* contain reproductions of more than one hundred previously published texts, including twenty-nine plays, seventeen poetry collections, twelve novels, six autobiographies, five collections of short biographical sketches, three biographies, three histories of organizations, three black histories, two anthologies, two sociological studies, a diary, and a book of etiquette. Each volume features an introduction by a contemporary scholar that provides crucial biographical data on each author and the historical and critical context of her work. In some cases, little information on the authors was available outside of the fragments of biographical data contained in the original introduction or in the text itself. In these instances, editors have documented the libraries and research centers where they tried to find information, in the hope that subsequent scholars will continue the necessary search to find the "lost" clues to the women's stories in the rich stores of papers, letters, photographs, and other primary materials scattered throughout the country that have yet to be fully catalogued.

Many of the thrilling moments that occurred during the development of this series were the result of previously fragmented pieces of these women's histories suddenly coming together, such as Adele Alexander's uncovering of an old family photograph picturing her own aunt with Addie Hunton, the author Alexander was researching. Claudia Tate's examination of Georgia Douglas Johnson's papers in the Moorland-Spingarn Research Center of Howard University resulted in the discovery of a wealth of previously unpublished work.

The slippery quality of race itself emerged during the construction of the series. One of the short novels originally intended for inclusion in the series had to be cut when the family of the author protested that the writer was not of African descent. Another case involved Louise Kennedy's sociological study *The Negro Peasant Turns Inward*. The fact that none of the available biographical material on Kennedy specifically mentioned race, combined with some coded criticism in a review in the *Crisis*, convinced editor Sheila Smith McKoy that Kennedy was probably white.

These women, taken together, began to chart the true vitality, and complexity, of the literary tradition that African-American women have generated, using a wide variety of forms. They testify to the fact that the monumental works of Hurston, Larsen, and Fauset, for example, emerged out of a larger cultural context; they were not exceptions or aberrations. Indeed, their contributions to American literature and culture, as this series makes clear, were fundamental not only to the shaping of the African-American tradition but to the American tradition as well.

Henry Louis Gates, Jr.
Jennifer Burton

PUBLISHER'S NOTE

In the *African-American Women Writers, 1910–1940* series, G. K. Hall not only is making available previously neglected works that in many cases have been long out of print, we are also, whenever possible, publishing these works in facsimiles reprinted from their original editions including, when available, reproductions of original title pages, copyright pages, and photographs.

When it was not possible for us to reproduce a complete facsimile edition of a particular work (for example, if the original exists only as a handwritten draft or is too fragile to be reproduced), we have attempted to preserve the essence of the original by resetting the work exactly as it originally appeared. Therefore, any typographical errors, strikeouts, or other anomalies reflect our efforts to give the reader a true sense of the original work.

We trust that these facsimile and reprint editions, together with the new introductory essays, will be both useful and historically enlightening to scholars and students alike.

INTRODUCTION

BY FRANCILLE RUSAN WILSON

Elizabeth Ross Haynes was a pioneering sociologist, a talented author of black children's literature, and an activist in black women's clubs, the YWCA, and politics. Her public career spanned most of the first half of the twentieth century and was emblematic of the manner in which educated black women handled the choices and the challenges of career, marriage, and social activism in the early twentieth century. Ross Haynes was a leading member of W. E. B Du Bois's Talented Tenth by virtue of her education, her embrace of the social sciences, and her readiness to assert a progressive viewpoint on social reform. Du Bois published her first book, *Unsung Heroes*. At the same time, she firmly embraced the moral pieties, the nonconfrontational approach to segregation, and the firm belief in economic self-help associated with Booker T. Washington. Washington's wife, Margaret Murray Washington, was a mentor and friend. Her writings often illustrate this dualism, in that they are modern in their structure and methods, but their racial sensibility often reveals a formulaic and conservative approach toward resolving racial discrimination. Her historical writings were based on careful research yet tended to tell the same story. Elizabeth Ross Haynes overemphasized the ability of black individuals to overcome the physical sufferings of slavery and Reconstruction through their faith, hard work, morality, and kindly whites and undervalued collective action and shared values. Her social studies were intellectually rigorous but also undergirded by her firm belief in the importance of religious faith, individual industry, and middle-class social mores as the principal facilitators in the industrialization of blacks.

Elizabeth Ross was born in 1878 or 1879 on a large farm in Lowndes County, Alabama. Her parents, Henry and Mary Carnes Ross, were former slaves, who had become substantial landholders in the heart of the Black Belt. Although blacks outnumbered whites in Lowndes County by more than 8 to 1, most of the black adults in Lowndes County in the 1880s and 1890s were poor, illiterate tenant farmers. Fewer than half of the black children in Lowndes County were enrolled in its segregated schools. Ross's parents' commitment to their daughter's education went far beyond the limited local schooling that was available for black children and they sent her to high school at Alabama State Normal School in Montgomery when she was barely a teenager. As an adult, Elizabeth Ross Haynes often wrote movingly of the many hardships endured by slave parents for their children's future. The struggle of black people for education and personal autonomy before and after emancipation profoundly shaped Ross Haynes's particular vision of Afro-American history and gave her a strong sense of duty to the cause of racial advancement.[1]

Elizabeth Ross was an excellent student and valedictorian at her graduation from Alabama State Normal School in Montgomery. Ross enrolled in Fisk University in 1898–99 where she met her future husband, George Edmund Haynes. The two began an intellectual and romantic companionship at Fisk that spanned fifty years. Haynes, a talented Arkansas native, was assistant business manager and Elizabeth Ross an editor of the Fisk *Herald*. Both were leaders in student organizations, and he was the valedictorian at their graduation from Fisk University in 1903.

Ross began her working life as a high school teacher in 1903 in Galveston, Texas. She also taught high school in St. Louis and became the leading teacher at her alma mater, Alabama State. She took additional summer courses at the University of Chicago for three consecutive years beginning in 1905. George Haynes joined her in 1906 and 1907 and together they met Carter G. Woodson, Monroe Work, Richard R. Wright Jr., and other young black intellectuals who were also studying at the University.

A crucial career shift occurred for Ross in 1908 when she moved to New York City and joined the National Board of the Young Women's Christian Association (YWCA) as their first organizer of student chapters at Negro colleges. This began a quarter century of involvement with the YWCA and other interracial organizations and governmental agencies with programs designed to assist black women workers. At the time of her appointment Elizabeth Ross was among a handful of black women who were college educated social service administrators or social workers. As National Student Secretary for Colored Women, Ross set up about thirty-eight new student branches at southern colleges, dramatically increasing the number of accredited black student YWCAs to over fifty. She also tried to assist black women who had begun their own independent organizations in their efforts to become formally affiliated with the National Board.

Ross found herself in the middle of struggles for black autonomy and against enforced segregation within the YWCA for more than two decades. Since her job was to establish segregated YWCAs, as a practical matter Ross initially was publicly at odds with the official policies of the National Association of Colored Women (NACW) and local black YWCA leaders who often found the national YWCA board's views on racial matters patronizing, controlling, and offensive. In 1910, when the National Board of the YWCA sent her to the biennial meeting of the National Association of Colored Women in Louisville, Kentucky, to explain YWCA policies and to win greater support from black women, Ross encountered suspicion and criticism. Despite Ross's presentation, the NACW passed a declaration of nonsupport of the National Board of the YWCA's racial policies.

Ross attempted to use the militant stance of black women at the NACW meeting to pressure white women on the National Board of the YWCA into establishing more urban branches for black women. She told the National Board that black women doubted its motives in not allowing some black women's associations in the South to bypass segregation in their city YWCAs and affiliate directly with the National Board; she also questioned whether the YWCA was truly "philanthropic and Christian." She felt hampered in carrying out her duties by the Board's actions and explained that her own defense of the Board's policies was not "sufficiently formidable to convince the inquirers of the truth of our sincere interest in them and their work." After some concessions by the National Board, Ross Haynes was able to win the NACW's support for the YWCA National Board's work several years later. Elizabeth Ross had learned to play a skillful mediating role between the competing interests of black and white women.[2]

On December 14, 1910, Ross, then twenty-seven, married George Haynes, in Fisk Memorial Chapel. Haynes was completing a Ph.D. in sociology from Columbia University and had just cofounded the National Urban League. The couple first lived in Nashville, Tennessee, where George Haynes became Fisk University's first professor of Social Science and where their only child, George Jr., was born in 1912.

Elizabeth Ross Haynes resigned from her job with the YWCA after her marriage, but became even more active in national women's groups and political organizations during World War I and throughout the Twenties and the Thirties. After her paid position ended, Ross Haynes continued to get assignments from the National YWCA Board to coordinate the formal affiliation of black YWCA branches. In 1924 she became the first black woman to be elected to the National Board of the YWCA. She was also an active member of the National Association of Colored Women, working closely with her fellow Fisk alumna Margaret Murray Washington during Washington's presidency and eventually serving as chairman of the NACW's Industry and Housing Department.[3] Ross Haynes was a founding member and the first parliamentarian of the National League of Republican Colored Women. An active speaker for Republican candidates in the mid-twenties, Ross Haynes and her husband became horrified at the anti-Catholic and anti-black rhetoric used by Republicans during the 1928 Presidential campaign. She was one of three black women and thirty-one black men who signed "An Appeal to America," which urged thoughtful citizens to reject both religious and racial demagoguery. Ross Haynes met other women of color through her activities in the International Council of Women of the Darker Races. When the Second World War began, Ross Haynes joined the Emergency Committee to Save the Jewish People of Europe.[4]

Elizabeth Ross Haynes moved from Nashville, Tennessee, to Washington, DC, in 1918 when George Haynes was appointed Director of the Division of Negro Economics in the U.S. Department of Labor. She became a $1-a-year worker at the Department of Labor assisting her husband as well as working with the Women's Bureau on matters concerning black women. She researched and wrote her first book, *Unsung Heroes*, while living in Washington, and began to think of herself as a writer and social scientist. When George Haynes's federal appointment failed to survive into the postwar period, Elizabeth Haynes took a job overseeing the placement of domestic workers in the Washington office of the United States Employment Service until her husband found a new position with the Federal Council of Churches in New York. After the family moved to New York City in 1922, Haynes earned a Master's degree in sociology from Columbia University. Her thesis, "Negroes in Domestic Service in the United States," was the first comprehensive study of its kind and formed the basis of her second major publication.[5]

In New York City, Elizabeth Ross Haynes continued her earlier work as an unpaid assistant to her husband but they had quite independent religious and political affiliations. The Hayneses lived in Harlem and Elizabeth soon immersed herself in community and political activities. George Haynes was a Congregationalist and a lifelong Republican. Elizabeth Haynes joined Harlem's Abyssinian Baptist Church and gradually abandoned her active role in the Republican Party. Ross Haynes was among the first national black women leaders to leave the Republican Party for the Democrats. She became co-leader of Harlem's 21st Assembly District's Democrats in 1935, the first year blacks represented Harlem in Tammany Hall.

During the Depression, Ross Haynes supported various efforts of Harlem's professionals to secure state and local jobs. She played a leading role in the 1937 community campaign to ensure that Arthur Schomburg retained his position as curator of the collection of rare books and materials he had donated to the Harlem branch of the New York Public Library.[6] Ross Haynes was the first woman appointed by Democratic governor Herbert Lehman to the New York State Temporary Commission on the Status of the

Urban Colored Population, which analyzed the impact of the Depression on black New Yorkers, held statewide hearings, offered a series of recommendations, and proposed fourteen new pieces of legislation outlawing discrimination.[7] In the 1940s she began a new career in real estate management. In 1952 Ross Haynes completed her second biography, *The Black Boy of Atlanta*. She died a year later. Elizabeth Ross Haynes's full life reflected the themes of family, the importance of a meaningful occupation whether paid or unpaid, and racial pride, all of which are seen in her major and minor written works.[8]

The 1920s were the decade of Elizabeth Ross Haynes's greatest productivity as an author. We have few clues as to how she juggled the demands of an adolescent son, marriage to a prominent figure in race relations, and her own involvement in social welfare reforms and politics with her desire to write. After her marriage, Elizabeth Ross Haynes only worked for a salary during a brief period after World War I. Unlike Georgia Douglas Johnson and Mary Church Terrell, she did not depend on her writing for income. This fact may have freed her choices of subject matter but also may have limited her long-term productivity.

Unsung Heroes, a collection of short biographies of black men and women, was Elizabeth Ross Haynes's first published book. *Unsung Heroes* was among the first attempts to provide black children with historical biographies and was one of a handful of books written specifically for black children in the Twenties. It is possible that Ross Haynes's teaching experiences in the South as well as having a young child at home prompted her to write her first book for children rather than adults. *Unsung Heroes* was written at a time of increasing attention to the pernicious effect of racism on the psychological development of black children. Ross Haynes, W. E. B. Du Bois, and other black intellectuals hoped to counter negative images prevalent in elementary school readers, textbooks, and literature by producing materials specifically designed for black children.

Unsung Heroes and publications such as the shortlived magazine *The Brownies' Book* reflected the heightened racial consciousness of the Twenties and at the same time used a more scholarly approach to historical biography than had most earlier efforts. *Unsung Heroes* and *The Brownies' Book* were both published by the fledgling publishing company Du Bois and Dill, a private business venture of W. E. B. Du Bois and Augustus Dill, the editor and the business manager respectively of the NAACP's official magazine, *The Crisis*. *The Brownies' Book*, a monthly literary magazine "for the children of the sun," began publication in January 1920. Jessie Fauset, literary editor of *The Crisis*, was the creative force in the new venture. *The Brownies' Book* published original poems and stories by Langston Hughes, Nella Larsen, Fauset and other young black artists at the start of their literary careers.[9]

Elizabeth Ross Haynes's article "Benjamin Banneker: A True Story" appeared in the June 1920 issue of *The Brownies' Book*. This was probably her first published children's biography and one of her very first publications. The Banneker portrait carried a notice that alerted *Brownies'* readers to her upcoming and as yet untitled book. A year later, *The Brownies' Book* also advertised *Unsung Heroes*, which at $2.50 was relatively high priced for the time. It was apparently the only book published by the company of Du Bois and Dill, which also advertised and sold other books for black children that were not readily available in bookstores.[10]

Before the publication of *Unsung Heroes* in 1921, most of the small number of books written for black children were in four overlapping categories: Sunday school literature, biographical sketches, inspirational fiction, and school textbooks. Black and white religious presses published Sunday school literature for black children that ranged from simple catechisms and traditional Bible lessons to stories centered around black leaders of slavery and abolition as well as black biblical heroes and heroines. Many religious presses published secular biographies. Benjamin Brawley's *Women of Achievement*, which chronicled the lives of five black women, was published by the Fireside School Series of the Women's American Baptist Home Mission Society. Only one of his subjects was a religious worker, Nora Gordon, a nineteenth-century missionary to the Congo.[11]

Interest in instructional materials on black achievements grew as more and more blacks became public school teachers. However, textbook purchases in Southern schools were controlled by white state officials who were indifferent or hostile to black aspirations.

One turn-of-the-century textbook used in black schools in Virginia and North Carolina, Edward A. Johnson's *A School History of the Negro Race*, was a slipshod, ahistorical mishmash that met segregationists' demands for inoffensive material. A comprehensive black history textbook for children based on historical research did not appear until the Twenties, when historian Carter G. Woodson developed *The Negro in Our History* and *Negro Makers of History* for use in high schools and elementary schools.[12]

The independent publication of fiction and biography for black children was not as explicitly constrained in its content in the same way that textbook content was censored. Nevertheless, very few nineteenth-century authors developed original stories, novels, or poems exclusively for Afro-American juvenile readers. Those who did experienced difficulties reaching a wide audience. One of the most ambitious efforts to produce a children's reader appeared a full decade before the Great Migration and Harlem Renaissance. In 1905 Silas X. Floyd, a Baptist minister and public school principal in Augusta, Georgia, wrote *Floyd's Flowers: or Duty and Beauty for Colored Children*. About a dozen of its 100 short stories dealt with black historical themes. A somewhat edited version of Floyd's book, *The New Floyd's Flowers*, was reissued in 1922 with an updated section featuring ABCs for black children designed to better appeal to the children of the era of the New Negro and the Harlem Renaissance.[13]

Unsung Heroes is made up of biographical sketches of seventeen black men and women. It is unusual among black biographies in the early twentieth century in that a fifth of the subjects lived their entire lives outside of the United States: Alexander Pushkin, Alexandre Dumas, Samuel Coleridge-Taylor, and Toussaint L'Ouverture. Advertised in *The Brownies' Book* as being "told in a way to inspire the children of our time," the most original aspect of the text is Ross Haynes's method of introducing the subject through a vivid depiction of a decisive moment in his or her childhood. Using standard sources of the day as a factual basis for each chapter, Rosss Haynes invented dialogue and offered her young readers access into the inner thoughts of children on the brink of greatness. This technique required a delicate balance between dramatic style and historical accuracy that Ross Haynes did not invariably maintain. Black historians such as Carter G. Woodson deliberately avoided taking quite as many liberties with biographical details, preferring to sacrifice style in order to preserve accuracy. On the whole however, Ross Haynes did not stray very far from the facts that were available to her. When she did stray it was generally in order to emphasize the rugged individuality of her subject.

Ross Haynes's biographies construct characters whose Horatio Alger-like stories stress their individuality, the kindness of most slaveholders, and the importance of morality. Group ideals and collective action, common themes seen in *Floyd's Flowers* and other contemporary materials written for black audiences, were not emphasized by Ross Haynes. For example, much of the dramatic tension in the brief sketch of Reconstruction senator Blanche Kelso Bruce revolves around a mysterious voice that allegedly guided Bruce at critical junctures. Ross Haynes failed to explain fully to the reader the significance of Bruce's election to the U.S. Senate or the consequences of the subsequent disfranchisement of blacks in Mississippi. There is no mention in *Unsung Heroes* of Senator Bruce's lonely championship of black rights while in office.

The facts and persons whom Ross Haynes omitted were as important as those she included. Ross Haynes left out certain vernacular heroes, such as revolutionaries David Walker and Nat Turner; Shields Green and Osborne Anderson, who were at Harper's Ferry with John Brown; and the South Carolina ship captain and Civil War hero Robert Smalls. With the exception of her lively depiction of Harriet Tubman, Ross Haynes omitted recorded incidents that indicated racial militancy or displayed a well-founded contempt for slavery. For example, in her essay on Benjamin Banneker, Ross Haynes described a letter he sent to Thomas Jefferson and reprinted Jefferson's reply without noting Banneker's denunciation of slavery.[14]

Although black children in the Twenties had very limited access to published stories about black men and women, many of the figures chosen by Ross Haynes were not in fact "unsung" in either the folk tradition, popular biographies, or religious publications. All had also achieved at least some recognition by whites for their accomplishments. Familiar figures such as Frederick Douglass, Toussaint L'Ouverture, and Sojourner Truth, whose militancy was often stressed in other biographies by blacks, were depicted as cooperative, earnest children who became important adults. Ross Haynes's basic message to black children in *Unsung Heroes* was to work hard, endure slights, and remain faithful to God and justice would prevail. The story of Josiah Henson, the "real" Uncle Tom, does lend itself to this interpretation, but other stories were adapted to express the same principles. The actions of Crispus Attucks and Toussaint L'Ouverture were presented wholly without any sense of irony and with a curious lack of connection to any sort of mass struggle toward freedom. In the case of Toussaint L'Ouverture, Napoleon was depicted as sending the French Navy to Haiti because he was jealous of L'Ouverture, who was more than content to serve France. There is only a small connection made between L'Ouverture to the cause of Haitian independence. The lessons learned in each story are more in line with Ross Haynes's own views on how blacks endured slavery and Reconstruction than with the biographical writings by other black authors.

Ross Haynes begins *Unsung Heroes* with the unattributed final stanza from Paul Laurence Dunbar's "Ode to Ethiopia" and a description of her pleasure as an adult in reading the biography of Frederick Douglass and her desire to have children experience a similar joy. The order of the first four entries suggests Ross Haynes's personal ranking rather than chronological order: Frederick Douglass, Paul Laurence Dunbar, Booker T. Washington, and Harriet Tubman. The selection of the three black women depicted in *Unsung Heroes* (Harriet Tubman, Sojourner Truth, and Phillis Wheatley) is not out of the ordinary, although Ross Haynes offers a radically transformed interpretation of the life of Sojourner Truth. She is depicted as a long-suffering mother of a ne'er-do-well son and a suffragist, as opposed to an abolitionist, a fighter against segregation, and a women's rights advocate. Sojourner Truth's story was a particular favorite of Haynes and she had previously incorporated Truth's legendary "Ain't I a Woman" speech into a 1920 address to white women meeting with the Commission on Interracial Cooperation in Memphis.[15]

"Negroes in Domestic Service in the United States" is Elizabeth Ross Haynes's best-known work. It is stylistically and materially different from her other publications. This monograph, based on her master's thesis in sociology, was published by Carter G. Woodson in the *Journal of Negro History* in 1923.[16] It was one of the first studies focusing on service occupations and stood for half a century as the most detailed analysis of black domestic workers. Earlier studies of black workers either had concentrated on a single city or examined skilled and industrial workers. Ross Haynes's views were drawn from the tradition of interest in black domestic workers from black women's community organizations and social reformers such as Victoria Earle Mathews, Lugenia Burns Hope, and Nannie Helen Burroughs. Ross Haynes based her methodology on the pioneering studies of blacks in Philadelphia and New York City done by W. E. B. Du Bois and George E. Haynes.[17] She succeeded in creating a multifaceted portrait of the work and personal life of black domestic servants. Elizabeth Ross Haynes adopted the neutral analytical tone of the social scientist, and her personal opinions are much less evident in this study than in the two juvenile biographies in this current volume. The domestic workers study, coming on the heels of her wartime work experiences in Washington, DC, also helped to change Haynes's view of herself. In a petition on behalf of black working women to the First International Congress of Working Women in 1919, signed by two workers and ten black women's club leaders, Elizabeth Ross Haynes was listed as a "working woman" of Fisk University and Washington and as the contact person for communication on issues concerning black women. After the publication of "Negroes in Domestic Service," Ross Haynes described herself in biographical sketches as a sociologist and author.[18]

"Negroes in Domestic Service" combined a straightforward analysis of the occupational censuses from 1900 through 1920 with data gathered by Elizabeth Ross Haynes in Washington, New York, and at least ten other cities between 1918 and 1923. As Du Bois first did in *The Negro Artisan* in 1902, Ross Haynes used survey questionnaires completed by correspondents in distant cities to supplement her own research and the federal census. Ross Haynes was very aware that the occupational categories in the federal census did not always reveal the swift changes in black employment patterns that accompanied the Great Migration. She used data from registration cards that she had gathered while an employment secretary at the United States Employment Service in an effort to characterize these changing patterns more carefully. Ross Haynes was particularly concerned with analyzing studies of employers' assessments of domestic workers, which also was a characteristic of work done by W. E. B. Du Bois, George Haynes, and the National Urban League. However, Elizabeth Haynes was more sensitive to the notion that workers and employers often had radically different perspectives on the same behavior than did most black male social scientists who used similar studies. Employee dissatisfaction with working conditions, particularly in household work, resulted in high labor turnover and a growing disinclination by black women to accept live-in positions. Haynes also briefly sketched the education, training, health, and labor organizations, and the social life of domestic workers.[19]

Ross Haynes's analysis of the federal census occupational statistics for black Americans was competent but she was apparently not fully aware of the inaccuracies in the 1910 occupational statistics in the count of black women workers. Although black social scientists had long complained about various problems in previous census reports on black mortality, health, crime, and other statistics, the implications of the 1910 probable overcount of black female agricultural workers was not immediately observed by Haynes or other scholars. As a result of the 1910 overcount and the subsequent failure to adjust the later statistics, it appeared as if the absolute numbers of black women workers stayed constant between 1910 and 1930 while the proportion of black women in the work force declined. In fact, it is more likely that both the absolute numbers and the proportion of black female workers increased slightly between 1910 and 1920 with significant shifts in black women's occupational categories over the entire thirty-year period. Ross Haynes was perplexed by the census reports, which showed a decreasing proportion of blacks to whites in domestic work but an increasing percentage of blacks in the occupation. However, Elizabeth Ross Haynes's two most important published writings on black workers were researched and written during the economic depression of 1921–1923. The depression, coupled with her personal observations of black women's loss of manufacturing jobs after World War I, undoubtedly accounted for her failure to challenge the accuracy of the census data for black women in agriculture.[20]

Much like her husband and other black social scientists of the New Negro period, Elizabeth Ross Haynes's primary interest was in documenting Northern nonfarm workers. Her thesis neglected detailed descriptions of black domestics and farm workers in the South. Ross Haynes's 1922 article "Two Million Negro Women at Work" gave only a brief paragraph to the one million black women still at work in agriculture in 1920; rather, the article was devoted primarily to descriptions of the impact of the postwar economic slowdown on Northern black women in domestic and manufacturing jobs. Ross Haynes and other black female social scientists such as Sadie T. M. Alexander focused their attention on domestic and manufacturing occupations as the most important for the future of black women.[21]

"Negroes in Domestic Service" attempts to provide a balanced portrait of black male and female domestics but offers more varied and complete information on women's employment in part because Ross Haynes had greater access to contemporary employment data on female household workers. Ross Haynes had personally collected detailed employment data, including employers' attitudes on 9,976 persons employed in Washington, DC, during 1920–1922. Of this number only 202 were males. Ross Haynes's data on wage differentials of black domestic workers in a number of cities are particularly rich. However, the possible problems of incomparablity of the data collected made Ross Haynes shrink from making many comparisons of wages paid between cities. Ross Haynes makes note of the influence of wages on black domestic employment and on the frequent substitution of white workers for black workers when wages rise. She made her most critical comments regarding the displacement of black women after the passage of minimum wage legislation in Washington, a law whose passage Ross Haynes and her husband had protested behind the scenes at the Department of Labor.[22] Ross Haynes was also sharply critical of the role of private employment agencies, which she found overcharged both employer and employee, and all too frequently were associated with vice and crime. Another important finding of this study is its observation of the scarcity of adequate day care for women with dependents. Most cities were without either public or private day nurseries for black children. Boarding children out—a necessity for many domestics, given the long working hours—cost $6 of the domestic's average $9 weekly wage in Washington.[23] Ross Haynes's contribution to the literature of black workers was significant because most of the information on black domestics before her study was anecdotal. Unfortunately, there were very few subsequent studies of either black women workers or domestic service after Ross Haynes's study. The Women's Bureau at the Department of Labor published a few studies of black working women in the Twenties and Thirties, using data on women workers that had initially been collected for George Haynes's Division of Negro Economics and later from materials collected on women workers as a whole at the state or the occupational level. There would be a long wait for another large-scale nongovernmental study of black women workers.[24]

Elizabeth Ross Haynes's final book was *The Black Boy of Atlanta*, a biography of Richard Robert Wright Sr., an ex-slave who became a college president and banker. Like *Unsung Heroes*, *The Black Boy of Atlanta* was designed for juvenile readers, but as the only full-scale biography of Wright to date, it has served as the main source for details of his life. The dramatic elements of Wright's life readily lent themselves to the inspirational themes of hard work, the importance of education, and racial pride and personal commitment that Ross Haynes favored in *Unsung Heroes*. Wright, a small, dark man who was fiercely proud of his African heritage, frequently used his own life to illustrate the perseverance of the freedmen and the fulfillment of the hopes and dreams of generations of enslaved Africans. In the preface to *Unsung Heroes*, the president of Atlanta University, Rufus F. Clement, called Wright, a member of Atlanta's first graduating class, "a little black Aladdin who was something of a Horatio Alger and a Tiny Tim combined in one flaming spirit."[25]

At the end of the Civil War, Wright's mother walked her three children one hundred miles from a plantation in Cuthbert, Georgia, to Atlanta in search of an education for them. Wright's first school was housed in an abandoned boxcar. Wright excelled despite the formidable odds of poverty and less than robust health. When

Wright and his schoolmates were asked by the director of the Freedmen's Bureau, Union general O. O. Howard, what he should tell the children of the North about them, Wright offered the plucky response, "Tell them, General, we are rising." His words were captured in the poem "Howard at Atlanta" by John Greenleaf Whittier, who substituted the word "massa" for "general." As soon as the poem came to his attention in 1869, the youthful R. R. Wright wrote to Whittier with a protest of the word "massa," saying that he had given it up with the end of slavery. Even with his objections over terminology, Wright's reply was widely used to symbolize the freedmen's faith in education and collective uplift, and he had later had cards printed with his picture and the motto "We Are Rising." Wright's story became a staple of black inspirational stories and was recounted again and again in the black press.[26] Wright subsequently became the first principal of the first black high school in Augusta, and the first president of Georgia State Industrial College for Colored Youth in Savannah, among many other "firsts." He founded the statewide black teachers association and edited its newspaper. During the 1880s and 1890s Wright was very active in the Republican Party on the state and national level and was rewarded with an appointment as a paymaster with the rank of major during the Spanish-American War. In 1921, after thirty years in office, Wright resigned as president of Georgia State Industrial College when a study found its educational offerings inadequate. Then in his mid-sixties, Wright relocated to Philadelphia and founded Citizens and Southern Bank and Trust, which survived the Depression and for many years was the most succesful black-owned bank in the North. Wright was a tireless advocate of black business development and a proponent of public commemorations of black history. In his seventies and eighties, Wright started a coffee business with partners in Haiti, tried to popularize airplane travel among blacks, called for the establishment of February 1 as National Freedom Day to commemorate the ratification of the Thirteenth Amendment, led the successful campaign for a postage stamp honoring Booker T. Washington, and participated in the conference establishing the United Nations.

Ross Haynes's version of Wright's life did not stray far from the conservative and individualistic perspective of *Unsung Heroes* and to a large part was faithful to Wright's own version of the instructional uses of his life. Ross Haynes had begun her biography well before Wright's death in 1947 and retained the Wright family's complete cooperation. In the foreword she explains that she chose Wright years before "in a quiet search for an unsung American Negro whose life and solid achievements would be an inspiration to folks irrespective of race."[27]

The Black Boy of Atlanta has two distinct styles. The biography reads as if the first quarter (which deals chronologically with Wright's childhood during slavery and Reconstruction and his young adulthood) was written in the Twenties in much the same manner as *Unsung Heroes*, while the latter sections are quite different in style and tone. In the first section, Haynes uses vivid depictions of Wright's early life as a slave and his struggles to gain an education and woo and win a wife. Ross Haynes draws a sharp portrait of the difficulties of gaining an education in the earliest days after the Civil War. When Wright finally enters Atlanta University, readers are treated to a fascinating glimpse of the educator Lucy Laney as a talented schoolgirl determined not to yield to assertions of male supremacy. As in *Unsung Heroes*, Ross Haynes's literary attempts to draw the reader into the dramatic action often sacrifice essential biographical information and historical context. On the other hand, the mass of details Haynes uses to inform the reader of Wright's career in thematic chapters covering the twentieth century weigh down the imaginative drive of the narrative structure to the point of paralysis. In these chapters Haynes is repetitive and leaps back and forth from the 1890s to the 1930s and from the 1920s to the 1880s with no warning. Surprisingly little is said about the lives and accomplishments of Wright's eight children or his wife. Wright is depicted as an autocratic father who whipped his children publicly to send a message to his students that he was unbending on infractions of the rules, and who had two of his children alter their college and career plans to work for him in his bank. This is a very different person from the idolized father presented by Wright's oldest son, R. R. Wright Jr., in his own autobiography.[28]

Ross Haynes often ignores or understates those aspects of Wright's life that contradict a portrait of a determined person moving from strength to strength. She makes a number of comments indicating that Wright considered himself to be somewhat of a critic of Booker T. Washington, while not being a part of the lighter-skinned black elite either. This is an oversimplification of a very complex life. Wright's life could have been interpreted as an example of the limits of pragmatism under Jim Crow. As an Atlanta University trustee, Wright was an advocate of the rigorous type of college education he had received and claimed responsibility for convincing the rest of the board to hire W. E. B. Du Bois to teach the new discipline of sociology.[29] Wright was instrumental in founding the Atlanta University Conference on Urban Problems and the American Negro Academy. After being rebuffed by a Harvard University summer school instructor for his efforts to learn more about African explorers in the New World, Wright undertook research in the British Museum and published an article on early black and Spanish explorers to the Southwest that was published by a respected journal of anthropology.[30] His efforts as a state college president in an increasingly racialist climate were far less successful. When the Democrats gained full political control in Georgia, Wright was obliged to abandon his public association with the Republican Party and also to limit the academic offerings at Georgia State College. Wright's refusal to endorse a judge's call to repeal the 13th, 14th, and 15th Amendments to the U.S. Constitution led to a suspension of his reappointment as president for a summer, and the aftermath of the mistreatment of his daughter Julia by a white bank employee who struck her after she insisted on being called "Miss" led to Wright's twin decisions to leave the South and to start his own bank. After three decades of compromises, his retirement was forced when federal and philanthropic educational surveys starkly revealed the inadequacies at Georgia State Industrial College that were the inevitable result of decades of deliberate state underfunding and interference in its educational offerings. Ross Haynes does not give these pivotal decisions of Wright the thoughtful interpretation and critical perspective they deserve.

Black children's literature had become far more varied in the thirty years between *Unsung Heroes* and *Black Boy of Atlanta*. Celebrated poets and writers such as Langston Hughes and Arna Bontemps authored beautifully written and illustrated children's books and Carter Woodson had established the *Negro History*

Bulletin in order to offer teachers and children historical biographies and institutional and cultural materials. Shirley Graham Du Bois's children's biographies of Paul Robeson, Benjamin Banneker, and others were written in a fresher, more comprehensible style.[31] However, there was still an enthusiastic audience for Wright's biography. Ross Haynes's good friend, the trade school founder and Baptist Women's leader Nannie Helen Burroughs, felt it was "a vivid story of a great soul, who . . . inspired others to attempt the impossible and make it real." Miss Burroughs, a writer and producer of church pageants herself, suggested that Ross Haynes have a playwright adapt the book for the stage. A reviewer in the *Journal of Negro History* favorably compared Ross Haynes's book to the novelist Richard Wright's *Black Boy* as "a biography which focuses attention not upon the sordid, the vicious, but upon the wholesome, the challenging, and the inspiring aspects of life. . . . ," but urged revisions to correct "the many typographical errors, . . . the loosely constructed sentences and the improprieties in diction."[32]

The Black Boy of Atlanta, published in Elizabeth Ross Haynes's seventy-third year, was a fitting last work of a woman whose own life had been dedicated to the principles she celebrated in Major Wright's: hard work, race pride, and economic self help. While there is ample evidence of her working and public life, surprisingly little is known about Ross Haynes's personal life. Very few letters to or from Elizabeth Ross Haynes have survived. Glimpses of her sunny yet strong personality and its effect on others may be found in collections of the papers of her husband, George Edmund Haynes, at Fisk and Yale universities. Her children's books remain of interest to the historian of juvenile fiction because they offer resilient black heroes and heroines for black children and for their ability to represent a vivid, if not always factual portrait of an African-American child.

The Black Boy of Atlanta is still one of the few published sources on Major R. R. Wright. Ross Haynes's writings on black domestic workers have aged better than her children's literature and continue to offer valuable insights to social scientists. Ross Haynes's self-description as a "sociologist and author" rather than as clubwoman, politician, wife, or mother (reflecting her other interests), foregrounds the importance she gave to the writings in this volume.

I would like to thank Daphne P. Muse and Adrienne Lash Jones for their insights on children's literature and the YWCA; Nataki Goodall for census research; and Ann Shockley and Anne Howse, the archivists at the Special Collections at Fisk University Library. The Graduate Research Board, the Committee of Africa and the Americas, and Sharon Harley, Chair of the Afro-American Studies Program, provided leave and financial support during the wirting of this essay.

NOTES

[1]Francille Rusan Wilson, "Elizabeth Ross Haynes," in *Black Women in America*, ed. Darlene Clark Hine, Elsa Barkley Brown, and Rosalyn Terborg-Penn (New York: Carlson, 1992), 548–9; Ruth Bogin, "Elizabeth Ross Haynes," in *Notable American Women*, ed. Barbara Sicherman and Carol Hurd Green (Cambridge, MA: Harvard University Press, 1980), 324–25; U.S. Census Office, 12th Census, *Population*, "Population of States and Territories by Minor Civil Divisions, 1890–1900," and "White and Negro Population by States and Territories, 1890–1900," 486; *Negroes in the United States* Bulletin 8 (Bureau of the Census, 1904), 42, 69–71, 96, 191; Charles W. Eagles, "From Shotguns to Umbrellas: The Civil Rights Movement in Lowndes County, Alabama," in *The Adaptable South*, ed. Elizabeth Jacoway, et al. (Baton Rouge: Louisiana State University Press, 1991), 212–36. The basic biographical information used in this introduction is from the biographical sketches by Francille Rusan Wilson and Ruth Bogin, cited above, with corrections and additions by the author unless otherwise noted. See also Jessie Carney Smith, "Elizabeth Ross Haynes," in *Notable Black American Women*, ed. Jessie C. Smith (New York: Gale, 1992), 477–79.

[2]Dorothy Salem, *Black Women in Organized Reform, 1890–1920* (New York: Carlson, 1990), 48, 105, 131–32, 251; Cynthia Neverson Morton, *Afro-American Women of the South and the Advancement of the Race* (Knoxville: University of Tennessee Press, 1989), 74–75; Judith Weisenfeld, "'The More Abundant Life': The Harlem Branch of the New York City Young Women's Christian Association, 1905–1945," Ph.D. dissertation, Princeton University, 1992, 86, 201–06.

[3]Elizabeth Ross Haynes, "Margaret Murray Washington" (obituary), *Opportunity* 3 (July 1925): 207–09; Charles Harris Wesley, *The History of the National Association of Colored Women's Clubs: A Legacy of Civil Service* (Washington, DC: NACW, 1984), 69, 93; Emily H. Williams, "The National Association of Colored Women," *Southern Workman* 43 (1914): 481–83; Thomas O. Fuller, ed., *Pictorial History of the American Negro* (Memphis: Pictorial History, Inc., 1933), 169, 187.

[4]"Haynes-Ross," Fisk *Herald* 28, no. 3 (January 11): 4–5; Evelyn B. Higginbotham, "In Politics to Stay: Black Women Leaders and Party Politics in the 1920's," in Louise Tilly and Patricia Gurin, eds. *Women, Politics, and Change* (New York: Russell Sage, 1990), 199–220; minutes of August 9, 1924, National League of Republican Colored Women, Box 309, Nannie Helen Burroughs Papers, Library of Congress. "An Appeal to America Against Making the Negro a Political Issue," October 25, 1928, in Monroe Work, ed., *The Negro Yearbook, 1931–1932* (Institute, AL: Negro Yearbook Company). Elizabeth Ross Haynes's name appears on the American membership list printed on the stationery of the International Council of Women of the Darker Races. See Addie Dickerson to Mary Church Terrell, 19 October 1929, in the Mary Church Terrell Papers, Library of Congress.

[5]Elizabeth Ross Haynes, *Unsung Heroes* (New York: Du Bois and Dill, 1921), and "Negroes in Domestic Service in the United States," *Journal of Negro History* 8 (October 1923): 384–442; David M. Katzman, *Seven Days a Week: Women and Domestic Service in Industrializing America* (Urbana: University of Illinois Press, 1981), 347.

[6]Elinor Des Verney Sinnette, *Arthur Alfonso Schomburg: Black Bibliophile and Collector* (Detroit: Wayne State University Press, 1989), 189. Henry Lee Moon, *Balance of Power: The Negro Vote* (Garden City, NY: Doubleday), 165–68.

[7]New York State Temporary Commission on the Condition of the Urban Colored Population, *Report* 1938 and *Report* 1939. Ross Haynes was not, in fact, the only woman on this committee.

[8]G. James Fleming and Christian E. Burckel, eds., *Who's Who in Colored America* (Yonkers-on-Hudson, NY: Christian E. Burckel, 1950), supplement. Elizabeth Ross Haynes, *The Black Boy of Atlanta* (Boston: House of Edinboro, 1952). Elizabeth Ross Haynes to Nannie Helen Burroughs, 8 January 1953 postcard discussing *The Black Boy of Atlanta*, and undated (October 1953) death notice and announcement of funeral services for Elizabeth Ross Haynes on 19 October 1953 at the Abyssinian Baptist Church, Nannie Helen Burroughs Papers, Library of Congress.

[9]Report on Examination of Records of the NAACP, 31 July 1921, 5–8, reel 10 in the Papers of W. E. B. Du Bois; Report of the Director of Publications and Research and Editor of *The Crisis* for the year 1919, reel

9 Du Bois Papers; Violet Harris, "The Brownies' Book: A Challenge to the Selective Tradition in Children's Literature," Ph.D. dissertation, University of Georgia, 1986.

[10]Elizabeth Ross Haynes, "Benjamin Banneker," *The Brownies' Book* 1, no. 6 (1920): 171–74. Haynes's *Unsung Heroes* was first advertised in *The Brownies' Book* in June 1921. Other books advertised included works by Benjamin Brawley, Mary White Ovington, Paul Laurence Dunbar, and W. E. B. Du Bois. Violet Harris, 269.

[11]Benjamin Brawley, *Women of Achievement* (Nashville: Women's American Baptist Mission Society, 1919). The five women profiled were Harriet Tubman, Nora Gordon, Meta Warrick Fuller, Mary McLeod Bethune, and Mary Church Terrell.

[12]Edward A. Johnson, *School History of the Negro Race in America from 1619 to 1890* (Chicago: Conkey, 1893). There were at least three revised editions of this work through the time of the Great Migration. Carter G. Woodson, *Negro Makers of History* (Washington, DC: Associated Publishers, 1928), and *The Negro in Our History* (Washington, DC: Associated Publishers, 1922).

[13]Silas X. Floyd, *Floyd's Flowers or Duty and Beauty for Colored Children* (Atlanta: Hertel Jenkins, 1905); Silas X. Floyd and Alice Howard, *The New Floyd's Flowers: Short Stories for Colored People Old and Young* (Washington, DC: Hertel Jenkins, 1922). Violet Harris, 275. For an overview of early children's literature, see Daphne Muse, "Black Children's Literature: Rebirth of a Neglected Genre," *The Black Scholar* 7, no. 4 (December 1975): 11–15.

[14]Haynes, *Unsung Heroes*, 17–26, 87–104, 162.

[15]Paul Laurence Dunbar, "Ode to Ethopia," in *Oak and Ivy* (Dayton, OH: United Brethren Publishing House, 1893); Haynes, *Unsung Heroes*, 209–28; Jacquelyn D. Hall, *Revolt Against Chivalry: Jessie Dante Ames and the Women's Campaign Against Lynching* (New York: Columbia University Press), 91–92; Jacqueline Rouse, *Eugenia Burns Hope: Black Southern Reformer* (Athens: University of Georgia Press, 1989), 110.

[16]Elizabeth Ross Haynes, "Negroes in Domestic Service in the United States," *The Journal of Negro History* 8, no. 4 (October 1923): 384–442.

[17]W. E. B. Du Bois, "The Black North," *New York Times Magazine*, November 17 and 24, December 1, 8 and 15, 1901; Du Bois, *The Philadelphia Negro* (Philadelphia: Publications of the University of Pennsylvania, 1899); George Edmund Haynes, *The Negro at Work in New York City* (New York: Columbia University Press, 1912).

[18]Memorial on behalf of Negro Women Laborers of the United States, November 4, 1919, in the *Proceedings of the First International Congress of Working Women* in the National Women's Trade Union League

Papers, Library of Congress. See entries for Elizabeth Ross Haynes in *Who's Who in Colored America*, ed. Joseph J. Boris (New York: Who's Who in Colored America Corp., 1927 and 1929), ed. Thomas Yenser (Brooklyn, NY: Thomas Yenser, 1933, 1937, 1940, 1944).

[19]W. E. B. Du Bois, ed. *The Negro Artisan* (Atlanta: Atlanta University Conference Publications, no. 7, 1902), 20, 94–104, 179–87. Francille Rusan Wilson, "The Segregated Scholars," 79–84. Elizabeth Ross Haynes, "Negroes in Domestic Service," 385–86.

[20]Haynes, "Negroes in Domestic Service," 386–88. U.S. Women's Bureau, *Negro Women in Industry in Fifteen States* Bulletin 70 (Washington, DC: U.S. Department of Labor, 1929), 1.

[21]Elizabeth Ross Haynes, "Two Million Negro Women at Work," *Southern Negro* 5 (February 1922): 64–72; Sadie T. M. Alexander, "Negro Women in Our Economic Life," *Opportunity* 8 (July 1930): 201–03; Helen Brooks Irvin, "Conditions in Industry as They Affect Negro Women," *Proceedings of the National Conference of Social Work*, 1919, 521–24. See also *A New Day for the Colored Woman Worker* (New York: Consumers League of the City of New York, 1919).

[22]Haynes, Negroes in Domestic Service," 394–95, 414–15.

[23]Haynes, "Negroes in Domestic Service," 391–92, 436–40.

[24]U.S. Women's Bureau, *Negro Women in Industry* Bulletin 20 (Washington, DC: U.S. Department of Labor, 1922), and *Negro Women in Industry in Fifteen States* Bulletin 70 (Washington, DC: U.S. Department of Labor, 1929); Jean Collier Brown, *The Negro Woman Worker*, U.S. Women's Bureau Bulletin 165 (Washington, DC: U.S. Department of Labor, 1938).

[25]Rufus F. Clement, Preface to *The Black Boy of Atlanta* by Elizabeth Ross Haynes (Boston: House of Edinboro, 1952), 10; James G. Spady, "Richard Robert Wright, Sr.," in *The Dictionary of American Negro Biography*, ed. Rayford W. Logan and Michael R. Winston (New York: Norton, 1982); Francille Rusan Wilson, "Richard Robert Wright, Sr.," in *Historical Dictionary of Civil Rights in the United States* (Westport, CT: Greenwood, 1992).

[26]This event was emblematic of the determination of the freed persons, and inspired Reverend George C. Rowe to write his own poem, "We Are Rising," about the encounter between young Wright and Howard and how it continued to symbolize the spirit of racial progress. George C. Rowe, "We Are Rising," in J. L. Nichols and William H. Crogman, *Progress of a Race or the Remarkable Advancement of the American Negro* (Naperville, IL: Nichols, 1920), 12. "From Slave to Banker: Major Wright, 91, Most Amazing Living Negro in America Today," *Ebony* 1, no. 1 (November 1945): 43–47. Clarence A. Bacote, *The Story of Atlanta*

University: A Century of Service 1865–1965 (Atlanta: Atlanta University, 1969), 11–12, 37–38.

[27]Haynes, *The Black Boy of Atlanta*, 7.

[28]R. R. Wright Jr., *Eighty-Seven Years Behind the Black Curtain* (Philadelphia: A.M.E. Book Concern, 1965), 37, 98–99, 159, 100.

[29]Haynes, *The Black Boy of Atlanta*, 84; Francille Rusan Wilson, "The Segregated Scholars: Black Labor Historians, 1895–1950," Ph.D. dissertation, University of Pennsylvania, 1988, 37–38; R. R. Wright Sr. to W. E. B. Du Bois, 10 February 1936, in *The Correspondence of W. E. B. Du Bois*, ed. Herbert Aptheker (Amherst: University of Massachusetts Press, 1976).

[30]Richard R. Wright, "Negro Companions of the Spanish Explorers," *American Anthropologist* 4 (April –June 1902): 217–18.

[31]Daphne Muse, "Black Children's Literature: Rebirth of a Neglected Genre," *The Black Scholar* 7, no. 4 (December 1975): 11–15. Shirley Graham Du Bois, *Your Most Humble Servant* (New York: Messner, 1945, and *Paul Robeson: Citizen of the World* (New York: Messner, 1946).

[32]Nannie Helen Burroughs to Elizabeth Ross Haynes, 10 January 1953 in box 37, the Nannie Helen Burroughs Papers, Library of Congress. Saunders E. Walker, review of Elizabeth Ross Haynes, *The Black Boy of Atlanta*, *Journal of Negro History* 39 (1953): 345–46.

UNSUNG HEROES

UNSUNG HEROES

BY

ELIZABETH ROSS HAYNES

NEW YORK
DU BOIS AND DILL, PUBLISHERS
1921

Dedicated

to my

Alma Mater

Fisk University

Nashville, Tennessee

CONTENTS

ILLUSTRATIONS

Foreword

IN casting about for stories to read to a little friend, one day I drew from the Library "My Life and Times" by Frederick Douglass. I knew that the book was written for grown-ups and that it contained many pages, but I did not know that in it was bound up a world of inspiration; for I had never read the book, although I had spent five years in college and university.

This story and the other stories in "Unsung Heroes", telling of the victories in spite of the hardships and struggles of Negroes whom the world has failed to sing about, have so inspired me, even after I am grown, that I pass them on to you, my little friends. May you with all of your years ahead of you be so inspired by them that you will succeed in spite of all odds, that you will

> "Go on and up! Our souls and eyes
> Shall follow thy continuous rise;
> Our ears shall list thy story
> From bards who from thy root shall spring,
> And proudly tune their lyres to sing
> Of Ethiopia's glory."

Washington, D. C.,
April 10, 1921.

THE AUTHOR.

FREDERICK DOUGLASS

Frederick Douglass

Chapter I

FREDERICK DOUGLASS

The Orator and Abolitionist

1817–1895

TUCKAHOE is the name of a plantation on the eastern shore of Maryland. It was once known for its worn-out, flat, sandy soil; for its old, poorly-kept fields and fences, and for its stupid and ignorant people. On one side of this plantation flowed a lazy, muddy river, bringing with it, as some believed, ague and fever.

At some distance from the river bank stood rows of log cabins suggestive of a quaint village whose only streets are the trodden footpaths and whose only street lights are the moon and the stars.

The cabins all looked very much alike except one which stood off to itself. Each one of these cabins had a door but no window, a dirt floor, a fence-rail loft for a bed, and a ladder by which to reach it. And each had a clay chimney with a broad open fireplace and just a block of wood at the door for steps. In this little log-cabin village, called "the quarters" lived the slaves.

Nearly every morning, just at peep of day, the cabin doors were unfastened and people began to stir until "the quarters" were almost like a beehive. Men, women, and children large enough to work were getting ready to go to the fields nearby. Some with their smoking clay or corn-cob pipes in their mouths were jumping astride the bare backs of mules or horses. Some were beginning to ride off without a sound other than that of the jingle of gear and the beat of hoofs. Still others followed.

Now and then a woman hastened to the lone cabin which stood off from "the quarters", pulling by the hand a child or two, or carrying them in her arms. She tarried at this cabin, presided over by "Grandma" Betsy Bailey, just long enough to leave her little children and then hastened on to the field.

Grandma Betsy, an active old fisherwoman, fed the children just as a man feeds his pigs. After placing the mush in a little trough, she set the trough either down on the dirt floor or out in the yard. Then she waved her hand to the children, who made a rush for the trough, each with a little piece of board or an oyster shell in his hand for a spoon. Some of them, without seeming to rush, tried to eat faster than the others, but Aunt Betsy had only to cut a sharp eye at such offenders.

She never thought of trying to call any one of them by name except her own grandson, Frederick Augustus Washington Bailey. Children on the Tuckahoe plantation were not supposed to have names or to know about their ages. Neither were they supposed to know the names of the days of the week or the months of the year, or to know anything at all about time.

Frederick thought much of Grandma Betsy's cabin, of the eating trough, of his bed in the loft by her side, and of the potato hole in front of her cabin fireplace. Little thought of his age or of any separation from his grandma ever entered his mind. Grandma Betsy, however, spent a part of each day thinking especially of his age and the time when he would be separated from her.

She had already begun to picture the circumstances of their separation. One day she said to herself as she sat patting her foot: "Freddie is just about seven years old now. I know old Master will soon be sending some one down from the 'Great House' for him". She waited and looked and listened for days but no one came. She was beginning to wonder where old Master was, when suddenly one Friday afternoon he came down himself and gave orders for Frederick to be carried away the next day. Grandma Betsy simply curtsied, saying, "Yes sir, Master, yes sir".

On this particular afternoon she was engaged

in mending her net for fishing. She finished her task at the close of the day, and early that night she climbed the ladder leading to the bed in the loft of the cabin with tears trickling down her cheeks. She lay down on her bed by the side of Frederick, but instead of going to sleep she lay there thinking, thinking, thinking. Finally the comforting words of an old plantation melody came to her mind. She began singing it to herself just above a whisper:

A little talk with Jesus makes it right, all right.
A little talk with Jesus makes it right, all right.
Troubles of every kind—
Thank God, we always find
A little talk with Jesus makes it right.

Over and over again she sang it until she dozed off into a light slumber. Suddenly the straws on her rail bed seemed to stick her and the hard rails seemed to push up through the rags and hurt her sides. She turned and twisted and opened her eyes, but refused to admit to herself that she was restless until again she began to sing over and over the melody:

A little talk with Jesus makes it right, all right.

The singing finally died away and all was quiet.

The next morning Grandma Betsy rose even earlier than usual and went about her work. Frederick also soon tumbled down from the loft without any thought of a bath or of changing his shirt, for, like the other slave boys, he dressed just once a week and that was Saturday night when he took his bath.

On this Saturday morning Grandma Betsy turned about more rapidly than usual and was therefore soon ready to start on her journey. With a white cloth on her head tied in turban style and the stem of her clay pipe between her teeth, she walked out, pulled and fastened the door behind her and stretched out her hand to Frederick who was sitting on the door-step. "Come, Freddie, we are going away today", said she.

He looked at her and asked, "Where are we going, Grandma?"

She simply shook her head, saying again, "Come on son".

Accustomed to obeying, he arose and grasped her hand but seemingly more reluctantly than usual. Out they went.

After a time Frederick began to stumble along as the journey lengthened, murmuring, "I am tired, Grandma".

Grandma Betsy stopped and squatted down. "Get on my shoulders, son", she said. Freddie stepped behind her, placed his little arms around her neck and with her assistance scrambled up on her shoulders with his legs about her neck. Not another word was spoken. Grandma Betsy rose with her burden and trudged on until Freddie begged her to let him walk again so that she might rest. Finally she squatted down, and Freddie with his tired little limbs almost fell off her shoulders.

Grandma Betsy stretched out both her arms. "Whew!" she said.

Freddie looked at her then and placed his arms around her as best he could, saying tenderly, "Grandma Betsy, was I heavy? Are you tired? I am so sorry".

They continued the journey until they reached the home of Frederick's new master on a plantation twelve miles away. Immediately they went into the kitchen where there were children of all colors, besides Aunt Katie, the cook. The children asked Frederick to come out and play with them but he refused until his grandmother urged him to go. They went out behind the kitchen. Frederick stood around at first as if afraid of the other children. Then he backed up against the kitchen wall and stood there as if he thought the kitchen might run away from him. While he stood there Grandma Betsy tip-toed out unseen by him.

One of the children came up to him and said, "Fred, Fred, your grandma's gone!" Frederick ran into the house as fast as he could and looked all around for her. Not seeing her, he ran a little way down the road and called her. She did not answer. Then he fell down and began to kick and cry. His brother and two sisters who had formerly been brought there tried to pet him, and to coax him to eat some apples and pears.

"No", said he, still kicking, "I want Grandma". There he lay until nightfall, when Aunt Katie came out and told him he must come in. He went in and lay down in the corner, crying and begging to be taken back home. The trip that day, however, had made him so tired that he soon fell asleep.

The next morning he asked Aunt Katie when Grandma Betsy was coming back to get him. She rolled her eyes and cast such fiery glances at him that Frederick understood and hushed. He had thought of asking for ash-cake like that which Grandma Betsy used to make, but her look drove that out of his mind.

Aunt Katie was not long in giving Frederick to understand that he was to drive up the cows every evening, keep the yard clean, and wait on Miss Lucretia, his master's daughter. The very first time Frederick went on an errand for Miss

Lucretia she smiled and gave him a piece of buttered bread. He smiled, too, from ear to ear, bowed and ran off eating and wondering how she knew that he was so hungry. He always ran smiling whenever she called him. And when hunger pinched his little stomach hard, he nearly always crept under Miss Lucretia's window and tried to sing like Grandma Betsy:

> A little talk with Jesus makes it right, all right.
> A little talk with Jesus makes it right, all right.

He knew the next line but scarcely ever had chance to sing it before the window was opened and a piece of buttered bread was handed out to him.

One evening during his first summer on this plantation the rain poured down seemingly in sheets. He could not stand under the window and try to sing and he had in some way offended Aunt Katie. She stood at the kitchen table cutting bread for the other children and occasionally brandishing the knife at Frederick, saying, "I'll starve you, sir". He sat there watching the other children eat, watching Aunt Katie and still keeping one eye on an ear of corn on the shelf by the fireplace. He did not lose his first opportunity to seize it and slip a few grains off the cob into the fire to parch.

While he sat there easing the parched grains of corn into his mouth, to his great joy in walked his own mother with a few cakes for him. She caressed him and asked him several questions. Seeing how nearly starved he was, she shook her fist at Aunt Katie and laid down the law to her. Then she tarried with her child for the last time, and even then just a short while—for she knew that she must again walk the twelve miles back to her home before the overseers came out and the horn was blown for field time.

Aunt Katie, remembering that stormy evening with Frederick's mother, said to him one day, "Come, Fred, and get a piece of bread. Dip it into this pot liquor". He curtsied first, then eagerly taking the bread, he walked up to the pot and dipped it and his hand as well into the greasy broth. For a few minutes he looked as though he would eat both bread and hand but the rattling of the dishes in his master's dining-room attracted his attention. He hesitated a moment, then smacked his greasy lips and bowed himself out of the kitchen and around to the side door of the dining-room.

Just as he reached the door of the dining-room, a big, grey cat slid in. Frederick slid in too. Immediately they began to scramble for the crumbs under the table. As soon as these were gobbled up, Frederick rushed into the yard to get some of the bones and scraps which the maid had just thrown out for "Nep", the dog.

Clad, winter and summer, in just a tow sack shirt scarcely reaching to his knees, Frederick was as scantily clothed as he was fed. On cold winter days he often stood on the sunny side of the house or in the chimney corner to keep warm. On cold nights he crept into the kitchen closet and got into the meal bag headforemost. In addition to these hardships, he often saw his own relatives and others cruelly beaten. Burdened with such experiences, his childish heart began to long for another place to live.

One day, while he was in this unhappy frame of mind, Miss Lucretia called him, saying that within three days he would be sent to Baltimore, to live for a while with her brother and sister, Mr. and Mrs. Hugh Auld. "You must go to the creek and wash all the dead skin off of your feet and knees," she said to him. "The people in Baltimore are clean. They will laugh at you if you look dirty. You can not put on pants unless you get all the dirt off", she added. Frederick made himself busy, spending most of the three days in the creek, and part of the three nights jumping up to see if the boat was ready to go.

The following Saturday morning early, the boat sailed out of the Miles River for Baltimore. It was loaded with a flock of sheep for the market, and a few passengers, among whom was Frederick. After giving the old plantation a last look, as he thought, he made his way to the bow of the boat and spent the remainder of the day looking ahead. They arrived in Baltimore on Sunday morning. After Frederick had assisted in driving the sheep to the slaughter-house, one of the boat hands went with him to the home of Mr. and Mrs. Auld.

Mr. and Mrs. Auld and their little son, Thomas, met Frederick at the door and greeted him heartily. "Here is your Freddie who will take care of you, Tommy. Freddie, you must be kind to little Tommy", said Mrs. Auld. Frederick smiled and nodded his head. Thomas at once took hold of Frederick's hand and seemingly wished to hurry him into the house to see his toys.

The children played until they heard Mrs. Auld begin to read. Frederick stopped playing to listen. Thomas said, "Oh, come on, Freddie, let's play. That is just Mother reading the Bible. She reads it that way every day when Father is away".

"The Bible? What is that?" asked Frederick, looking at Thomas. Little Thomas, surprised because Frederick had never seen a Bible, ushered him into the room where his mother was reading. Thomas knew better than to interrupt his mother while she was reading, but as soon as she stopped, he told her why he had brought Frederick in. Mrs. Auld showed him the Bible, asked him a few questions and sent them both out to play.

Days passed, but not one when Mrs. Auld failed to read her Bible. Frederick became so interested in her reading that one day he went to her and asked her to teach him to read. She paused for a while as if in doubt, then she braced up and gave him a lesson. At the end of the lesson his little heart seemed so full of joy and thanks that he scarcely knew what to say or do.

Mrs. Auld, seeing the situation, said, "Run along now, Frederick. I know you are grateful. Come in at this time every day for your lesson". He made his way out and every day for several days, with beaming face, he went in for his lesson.

One day when Mr. Auld came in and saw his wife teaching the boy, he said to her in great surprise, "My dear, are you really teaching that boy to read? Don't you know he will learn to write? Then he will write a pass and run away with himself". She pleaded for Frederick, but Mr. Auld beat upon the door-facing, saying as he went out, "I will have no more of this nonsense. This must be the end of it". Mrs. Auld dismissed Frederick and seemingly repented of her mistake; but Frederick had learned his alphabet.

Soon he managed to get a Webster's spelling-book, which he always carried with him when sent on errands. After this, every time he went out, he made new friends until the very boys who at first pounced upon him at every corner, now began to help him with his spelling lessons. One day while he was on his way to the shipyard, and just after he had gotten a spelling lesson at the corner, it occurred to him that the boys might also help him to learn to write.

While he was in the shipyard, he watched the carpenters finish pieces of timber for the different sides of the ships and mark each piece. For instance, a piece for the larboard side was marked *L* and a piece for the starboard side was marked *S*. He soon learned for what these letters stood and how to make them. When he went out on the next errand, he said to the boys, "You can't make as good an *S* as I can make". Such a challenge had to be met. They all dropped down on their knees and began the contest by making letters on the pavement. Frederick watched closely and learned to make for the first time many other letters. He kept at it until he learned to make them all.

Then, thinking that he should practice on these letters and learn to make them well, he picked out a flour barrel, without letting any one know what he was doing, and carried it one night into the kitchen loft where he slept. He turned it upside down and propped himself up to it and used it as his desk. Knowing where little Tommy Auld's old copy-books were, he got one out the next day and took it to the loft. That night while the Aulds were asleep he sat in the loft and wrote between the used lines of the old copy-book.

His desire to learn led him into strange paths. One day as he trotted along on his usual errand, with the rain pelting him in the face and over the head, he thought he spied something in the gutter. He stopped suddenly and peeped further into that filthy gutter. There lay some scattered pages of the Bible. He picked them out of the rubbish, took them home and washed and dried them to read.

For days after that, when he went out, he kept his eyes on the gutters for something else to read. Finding nothing there, he bought a box of shoe polish and a brush which he always took along on his errands. Whenever he passed any one with rusty boots or shoes on he said, "Shine, Mister, shine?" By shining boots and saving up carefully, his pennies grew and grew until he had fifty cents. With this he bought a book called the "Columbian Orator", which he read over and over again.

At the end of Frederick's seventh year in Baltimore, news came that he would be taken back to the plantation on the Eastern Shore on account of the death of his old master. This news came as a shock especially to him, Mrs. Auld and Thomas. The three of them, fearing that he might never return, wept bitterly. He was away only one month before he was sent back to Baltimore. Another change, however, soon took place which called him back again to the Eastern Shore, where he remained for two years.

He was now about sixteen years old, and had to work very hard every day and suffer such punishment that he was tired when night came. Yet he wished so much that his fellow slaves might learn to read that he interested a small class of them, which he taught three nights in every week.

He also organized a Sunday-school class of about thirty young men. This he taught under an old oak tree in the woods until three class leaders in old master's church rushed in upon them one Sabbath and forbade their meeting. Later on, however, the class was again secretly begun with more than forty pupils, many of whom learned to read.

Frederick had been reading the "Columbian Orator" which described the cruelties and injustices of slavery. He had also been thinking of how to obtain his freedom; but the pleasant times with his Sunday-school class had delayed his taking any action in the matter. He had not given up the idea, however, for at the beginning of the year 1836 he made a vow that the year should not end without his trying to gain his freedom. He kept the vow in mind and finally told his secret to several of his companions, who agreed to share in a plan to escape.

They met often by night and every Sunday until the day set for their escape was at hand. They were hoping that no one would betray them, but just at the last minute the news leaked out. The boys were seized, dragged to town and thrown in prison, where they remained for some time.

II

For three years after Frederick's release from prison he worked in the fields suffering untold hardships. The following three years he worked in a shipyard in Baltimore learning the calker's trade. During these last three years his mind was constantly running back to 1817, the year of his birth. Realizing how the years were passing, he was always thinking of some plan of escape. At last he hit upon what seemed to be a real one.

With arrangements all made for his escape, he arose early one September morning in 1838, put on a sailor's suit which a friend had lent him and started down to the depot just in time to take the train. He also carried what was called a sailor's protection, which had on it the American eagle. A hackman, whom he knew well, arrived at the depot with his baggage just as the train was about to pull out. Frederick grabbed his baggage, hopped on the train just like a sailor and took a seat. The train moved on slowly until it reached a certain river which had to be crossed by a ferry boat. On this boat there was a workman who insisted on knowing Frederick. He asked Frederick where he was going and when he was coming back. He persisted in asking questions until Frederick stole away to another part of the boat. After a short while he reached Wilmington, Delaware, where he took a steamboat to Philadelphia, and the train from there to New York City.

The wonderful sights of this great city seemed to make him forget almost everything except the fact that he was now a fugitive slave. A few hours after reaching New York, to his surprise he met on the street a man whom he had known in Baltimore. This man, also a fugitive, began at once to tell Frederick that there were men in New York City hired to betray fugitives and that he must therefore trust no man with his secret.

This news so disturbed Frederick, that instead of seeking a home, he spent the night among barrels on one of the New York wharves. Unable to remain longer without food or shelter, the next day he sought out on the streets a sailor who befriended him and then took him to the home of a Mr. Ruggles—an "underground railroad station" —where he was hidden for several days. During these days his sweetheart came on from Baltimore and they were married. On the day of their marriage they set out for New Bedford, Massachusetts, where Frederick as a ship's calker might possibly find work. Their money gave out on the way but a "Friend", seeing the situation, paid their fares for the remainder of the journey.

After reaching New Bedford, a room was soon secured in the home of a very good man who liked Frederick's face. They talked of many things, among which was the wisdom of Frederick's changing his name. The man said, "I have just been reading Scott's *Lady of the Lake* and I suggest that you take the name Douglass, for that grand man, Douglass of Scotland".

"Douglass of Scotland? Who was he?" asked Frederick. The good man began by telling the story of the bravery in battle of Douglass of Scotland. Before he had finished his story, Frederick was eager to take the name of Douglass.

He had now a fine-sounding name—Frederick Douglass—but he had neither money nor a job. He started out seeking work at his trade but was told again and again that the calkers there would not work with him. Finally, he was forced to take whatever his hands could find to do. He sawed wood; he shoveled coal. He dug cellars; he removed rubbish from back yards. He loaded and unloaded ships and scrubbed their cabins until he secured steady work.

While he was at his work one day a young man brought him a newspaper edited by a man whose name was William Lloyd Garrison, of whom Douglass had never heard before. This paper, for which he immediately subscribed, was known as "The Liberator". He read every word in the issue which the agent gave him and waited impatiently for the next one to come. When it came, there was in it an article about a grand convention to be held in Nantucket. Douglass read the article to the home people. He said that he needed a vacation, which might well be taken at the time of this convention. The following issue of the paper told still more of the plans for the convention. He concluded that he must attend it.

He went to the convention without any thought of being known to any one or of taking any part whatever in the meetings. A prominent abolitionist, however, who had heard Frederick speak to his people in a little schoolhouse in New Bedford, sought him out and asked him to say a few words to the convention. When he rose to speak, he was trembling in every limb. He could hardly stand erect.

It seemed to him that he could scarcely say two words without hesitating or stammering, but he went on. As he told of his experiences as a slave, the audience was exceedingly quiet. When he had finished, the people broke into applause and excitement. William Lloyd Garrison, now known as a leading abolitionist, was the next speaker. He spoke with feeling, taking Frederick Douglass as his subject. The audience sat motionless and some people present even wept.

At the close of the meeting, another abolitionist came to Douglass and urged him to become a traveling agent for the Massachusetts Anti-Slavery Society. For two reasons, he did not wish to take such a position. In the first place, having been out of slavery just three years, he was afraid he could not speak well enough to travel in that way; and, secondly, he feared that his former master might hear of him and send for him. The abolitionist, however, unwilling to accept excuses, urged Douglass until finally he consented to travel for three months. Before many days had passed he was on the road as a lecturer against slavery.

One morning he went to Grafton, Massachusetts, and tried to get a place to hold a meeting. But he could not get a hall or even a church. Nevertheless, he was so determined to speak to the people that he went to a hotel and borrowed a dinner bell. Soon he was seen running through the streets like a madman, ringing the bell and crying out, "Frederick Douglass, recently a slave, will speak on Grafton Commons at seven o'clock tonight".

Many came out to hear what such a strange man could say and all left at the close of that open-air meeting apparently more thoughtful than when they came. The next day ministers of the large churches in that town came to him and offered to open their doors for his meetings.

For several years he did nothing but travel and hold meetings. He attended one hundred anti-slavery conventions and spoke at every one of them. During the first three or four months of his travel he told the story of his experiences as a slave. Then he became tired of repeating the same old story and began to show by the manner in which he expressed himself that he was thinking deeply about the whole question of slavery.

"Let us have the facts. Be yourself and tell your story", said his hearers again and again, but Douglass said that he was tired of telling his personal story. He attempted to speak against the injustices heaped upon him and others, but his audiences murmured, saying, "He does not talk like a slave. He does not look or act like one; and, besides he does not tell us where he came from or how he got away; and he is educated, too".

Determined to remove doubt from their minds, Douglass wrote a narrative of his life as a slave and had it published. Now that the story of his life was published, friends like Wendell Phillips, fearing he might be captured and taken back into slavery, advised that he go to Europe. He went and he spoke in all the large cities of England, Scotland and Ireland. In order that he might return home a free man, two women in England, "Friends" they were, started the plan of raising the money with which his freedom was purchased from his old master in Baltimore.

On his return to America, he went to Rochester, New York, and for sixteen years edited there a paper called *The North Star*. So much money was needed for publishing this paper that he even mortgaged his home. For twenty-five years he lived in Rochester. During those years he wrote and lectured and conducted an "underground railroad station" in that city.

Because of the disturbed conditions in his own country at this time, he went to Europe again but returned in six months on account of death in his family. Some of the disturbances which he left behind when he went away had subsided but others had risen. A President of the United States had to be elected. For a long time it seemed that no man was the choice of a majority of the people. Finally, Abraham Lincoln, who had once been a rail-splitter, was elected. Douglass worked hard to help elect Lincoln. He also took part in the terrible Civil War, which had come as a result of the country's disturbances.

As soon as the Governor of Massachusetts issued the order for the many soldiers needed, Douglass enlisted his own sons, Charles and Lewis, from New York State, and took a leading part in raising the Fifty-fourth and Fifty-fifth Massachusetts Negro Regiments. The first of these soon won fame and a name throughout the country because of its brave attack on Fort Wagner in the hour of trial. In that terrible battle at nightfall, the Fifty-fourth was fearfully cut to pieces, losing nearly half of its officers, among whom was its beloved commander, Colonel Shaw. Douglass, with his son Charles as a recruiting officer, worked steadily until the emancipation of the slaves and the close of the war were brought about.

He greatly rejoiced over the outcome of the war, yet a feeling of sadness seemed to come over him. What was he to do? He felt that he had reached the end of the noblest and best part of his life. He thought of settling on a farm which he might buy with the few thousand dollars which he had saved from the sale of his book, called "My Bondage and Freedom", and from the proceeds of his lectures at home and abroad. The question, however, was soon decided for him. To his surprise, invitations began to pour in upon him from colleges, clubs and literary societies offering him one hundred and even two hundred dollars for a single lecture.

One of the literary societies of Western Reserve College invited him to address its members on one Commencement Day. He had never been inside of a schoolhouse for the purpose of studying, therefore the thought of speaking before college professors and students gave him anxiety. He spent days in study for the occasion. Not being able to find in our libraries a certain book which he needed, he sent to England for it. Not long after his address on that Commencement Day, the thought came to Douglass that the Negro was still in need of the opportunity to vote, and thereby become a citizen. He talked about the question and finally set himself to the task of gaining this right for his people.

His first marked step in the matter was to gain for himself and ten other men an interview with the President of the United States. The discussion on that occasion brought the question practically before the whole American public. The next great step in gaining the ballot for the freedmen was taken in Philadelphia in 1866, at a great convention called the "National Loyalists' Convention", which was attended by the ablest men from all sections of the country.

Douglass's own city, Rochester, New York, elected him to represent her. While he was marching in the long procession through the streets of Philadelphia, he saw standing on the corner of Ninth and Chestnut Streets, the daughter of Miss Lucretia Auld, under whose window he had sung as a hungry slave boy. He went to her and expressed his surprise and joy at seeing her.

"But what brought you to Philadelphia at this time?" Douglass asked.

She replied, "I heard you were to be here and I came to see you walk in the procession". She followed the procession for several blocks and joined in the applause given Frederick Douglass as he passed.

In that convention, resolutions were finally passed in favor of giving the freedmen the right to vote. Douglass was called forward to speak. The vote passed by that convention, it is said, had its influence in bringing about the passage of the Fifteenth Amendment to the Constitution of the United States.

After the convention, Douglass went to Washington, D. C., as editor of a newspaper. It was not long before he became what is called Elector-at-Large for the State of New York. As such a representative, the Republican party of that state sent him to Washington to carry its sealed vote which went toward electing Grant as President. Douglass later received an invitation to speak at the monument of the unknown loyal dead, at Arlington, on Decoration Day.

Five years later, when he spoke at the unveiling of the Lincoln Monument in Lincoln Park, Washington, D. C., the President of the United States and his Cabinet, judges of the Supreme Court, members of the Senate and the House of Representatives, and many thousands of other citizens were there to listen to him, to honor the memory of Lincoln and to show their appreciation of such a gift from the freedmen.

Douglass was appointed United States Marshal of the District of Columbia. As Marshal he visited the criminal courts every day to see that the criminals received justice. There were also high social duties attached to this office. President Garfield later appointed him Recorder of Deeds of the District of Columbia, at which post he remained for nearly five years. In this position, he was responsible for having recorded in the public records every transfer of property, every deed of trust and every mortgage made in the capital of the nation.

In 1886, two years after he was Recorder of Deeds, he and his wife—the second Mrs. Douglass—made a tour through England, Scotland and Ireland, where they met many great people besides the children of many of Douglass's old friends. His next and last appointment as a high public official was to the office of Minister to Hayti. President Harrison appointed him to this office. The President of Hayti also appointed him to act as commissioner for that country at the Chicago World's Fair in 1893.

Many boys and girls who have read his books admit that they have been inspired by the life he lived in traveling from the log cabin on the Eastern Shore of Maryland to the high and important offices which he held in Washington. The best one of these books is called "My Life and Times, by Frederick Douglass". After his death on February 20, 1895, at his home in Anacostia, District of Columbia, the citizens of Rochester, New York, erected a public monument to his memory.

His epitaph has been written in his own words: *"Do not judge me by the heights to which I may have risen but by the depths from which I have come"*.

PAUL LAURENCE DUNBAR

Chapter II

PAUL LAURENCE DUNBAR

The Poet

1872–1906

AN elevator boy—Paul Laurence Dunbar—a black high-school graduate—stood for a few moments at the entrance to his elevator. He seemed to fix his eyes on every one entering the Callahan Building.

The Callahan Building was a large structure located in a busy section of Dayton, Ohio. Its quick elevator service in spite of its limited number of elevators was often a subject of comment. The grating of the elevator cables and the thud of the car as it stopped for passengers were constant reminders of the rapid service. Up and down, up and down, went the elevator, and ring, ring, went the bells from morning until night. As the elevator moved upward and downward with grating cables, Paul kept his ear turned as though he were listening to a song.

Apparently unnoticed, day after day he ran his elevator, stopping repeatedly first at one floor and then another until one day a woman entered his car and spoke to him. It was one of his former high-school teachers. After greeting him, she eagerly told him that the Western Association of Writers would soon meet in Dayton. Before the short conversation was finished, she asked him to write a poem of welcome to that association and promised that she would arrange for him to recite it.

Paul's busy days seemed to come and go very rapidly. Yet when the Western Association of Writers met a few weeks later he had composed his poem of welcome for the occasion. The printed programs of the association did not contain his name. The first day of the meeting, however, after being excused from his elevator duties, clad as he was, he hurried to the hall in which the sessions were to be held. His teacher stood in the doorway waiting for him. He entered silently and made his way to the rostrum and began reciting his poem of welcome. Men and women in the audience at first straightened up to look at this swarthy lad. Then, as if suddenly struck by something in the poem, many a one turned his ear and leaned forward to listen. When Paul had finished, the entire audience broke into applause. Some even rushed forward to shake his hand.

At the close of the meeting some of the writers looked for the boy poet but he had hurried back to his elevator. Just at the moment when they were about to give up their search for him they ran across his former high-school teacher. She, with enthusiasm exceeding theirs, told of Dunbar's graduating from high-school in 1891 with honors. She told of his composing the class-song which was sung at the commencement exercises. One of the writers interrupted to ask who the boy was and what he was doing. The teacher, speaking hurriedly as though she had something else important to tell first, said that Dunbar was once editor of their high-school paper. She also told of his writing his first poem before he was seven years old. Then proceeding to answer the writer's questions she said that Dunbar's mother was a washerwoman and that he was the elevator boy at the Callahan Building; and looking each of these writers in the face, she added:

"Dunbar always brings and carries the clothes for his mother".

Three of the men, after inquiring where the Callahan Building was, started in search of it. They found it and soon entered the elevator. Among the first things they saw were a *Century* Magazine, a lexicon, a scratch tablet and a pencil lying on a stool. Dunbar was in the act of starting his car when one of the men said: "No! No! Do not go up for us! We came simply to see you and to tell you how much we appreciated the poem you read this morning".

Dunbar looked at them with great embarrassment. As he began to thank them a ring of the elevator signal came from the top floor. With a modest bow and a request to be excused, he took hold of the power lever and up the elevator went and soon down it came again.

In the midst of the conversation, constantly interrupted by passengers entering the elevator, one of the visitors asked, "What wages are you getting here?"

"Four dollars a week, Sir", answered Dunbar.

"What are you doing with your money?" asked another.

Dunbar, somewhat hesitatingly said, "Well, I help my mother and then I am trying to buy a little home for her, too".

"How on earth —?"

Ring, ring, went bells on different floors. Up went the elevator and then down it came.

Hurrying to finish his sentence, the visitor continued, "How on earth did you start to buy a home on four dollars a week? Where is your father?"

Dunbar, disturbed by so many questions and so many bells, said hurriedly, "I bought the home through the Building and Loan Association. My father was a plasterer but he died when I was twelve years old". As another bell began to ring, the men said goodbye and went away talking about the boy and pledging each other to propose his name for membership in the Western Association of Writers.

Dunbar seemed greatly encouraged by the Western Association members. He had also received promises of help from others. One evening, after a hard day on the elevator, he hurried home, saying to his mother as he entered, "Ma, where are those papers I asked you to save for me some months ago?"

"What, those botany sheets?" she replied. Dunbar failed to answer immediately. She continued, "They are in that box under the kitchen safe". The neighbors had begun to ask Mrs. Dunbar why she was keeping all of those papers piled on the table for so long. Seeing that so many were noticing the unsightly stacks of papers, she had removed them one day from the crowded little room to the kitchen.

With a lighted lamp in his hand, Dunbar went to the kitchen and pulled out the box. There lay his papers, some of which he had not seen for five or six years. He pulled a chair up to the box and began sorting them. When he had finished and given the box a shove which sent it back under the safe, he made known his readiness for his supper.

The next morning as he was leaving for his work he said, "Goodbye, Ma, I'm going to see about publishing a book today". He walked rapidly to the Callahan Building and immediately took charge of his elevator. As soon as his lunch hour came he hurried to a publishing house and asked to see the manager. He was out to lunch but one of his assistants was called in. After looking the manuscript through hastily he offered to publish it for one hundred and twenty-five dollars. Dunbar looked at him and shook his head. Unable to conceal his disappointment, he took up his manuscript, bade him good-day and started out.

The business manager of the firm happened to come in at this moment and saw Dunbar starting out. He noticed the gloom and the disappointment written on the boy's face, called him over to his desk and asked what was the trouble. Dunbar at first, choking with something which seemed to cut off his words, simply handed him the manuscript, repeating as best he could what the assistant had said about publishing it for one hundred and twenty-five dollars. The business manager took the manuscript and read here and there a poem. He questioned the lad at length about his work and his home. Knowing something about Dunbar's high-school record, he said, "You go back to your work; the poems will be published".

He went on with his work, scarcely waiting for the boy to thank him. Dunbar bowed, stepped away lightly and with a broad smile on his face hurried back to his elevator.

The hours seemed to drag and yet he worked away until closing time came. On leaving his elevator he went by leaps and bounds until he reached his mother's door. With his key in hand, he unlocked it and rushed in almost breathless, saying, "Oh, Ma, they are going to print my book!" As he told the story about the business manager he laughed and cried. Mrs. Dunbar laughed and cried too until far into the night.

As the days came and went, Mrs. Dunbar began to listen with unusual interest for the ringing of the door-bell. Finally, one morning as the snow fell thick and fast, there was a knock at the door. Mrs. Dunbar grabbed up her apron, wiped the soapsuds from her hands and hurried to open it. There stood a delivery man with a large package.

"For Mr. Paul Dunbar", said he. "By the way, who is this Dunbar? Is he a doctor, a lawyer, a preacher, or what?"

Mrs. Dunbar responded, saying, "Who? Paul?

Why, Paul is just an elevator boy and a—a poet". The man looked at her with squinting eyes, glanced about at the front of the poor little cottage, then bade her good-day and went his way.

She made a small opening at one end of the package and peeped at the books. Before realizing what she was doing, she threw her arms around the package and knelt down with her head resting on it, offering a silent prayer. When finally she returned to her washtub, she rubbed a garment a while, then wiped away the tears which were dropping into the soapsuds. The wash seemed to hold her unusually long and yet, when she had finished it, the sun was still high in the heavens. She prepared her dinner, did her chores, then sat down to watch and wait. Finally there came a familiar step. She listened for a moment, then rose and opened the door while Dunbar was feeling for his keys.

"See the books, Paul!" she said, pointing to the package. They opened up the package and stood half bent over it while Paul was reading from the little book of poems which he had named "Oak and Ivy". They took it to the dinner table, looked at it, read more from it and rejoiced together.

The next morning, as Dunbar went back to his

elevator, he took along some copies of "Oak and Ivy". These he ventured to show to the passengers who he thought might buy a copy. His supply was soon sold out. Greatly surprised at his first day's success, he took more copies the next day, and still more the following days for over a week. In less than two weeks' time, he walked into the office of the business manager of the publishing house, reached into his pocket and pulled out one hundred and twenty-five dollars. This he placed in the business manager's hands, adding his hearty, humble thanks. He told of his success in selling the books on the elevator and left the publishing-house to see a man who was offering him a minor position in the court-house. After serving notice on the employment manager of the Callahan Building and assisting him in securing another elevator boy, Dunbar left to take up his new duties.

Within the next few days he smiled and rejoiced as he read a review of his poems in a newspaper called *The Toledo Blade*. A few days later he began to receive letters from people who had read this review. Still later, some of these people arranged for him to give readings of his poems.

Among those who wrote him about the review was a Dayton woman who sent a copy of "Oak and Ivy" to a Dr. Tobey of Toledo. Dr. Tobey read a few of the poems and laid the book aside. A few weeks later when he went to Dayton on some business, he discovered to his surprise that even the business men were talking about Dunbar and his poems. On his return home, he took up the book and sat down to read the poems again. He sat there reading and re-reading, occasionally stopping between poems as if he were thinking deeply. When he had finished the book he drew his check book from his pocket, made out a check to Dunbar and enclosed it in a letter asking for a number of copies of "Oak and Ivy".

When Dunbar's letter in reply, expressing his deep appreciation for the check, was received, Dr. Tobey seemed to be deeply moved. He wrote Dunbar immediately inviting him to Toledo to give a reading of his poems. The young poet read the letter to his mother and soon began to prepare for the trip. Night after night, until time to go, he practiced reading some of his poems which had not been published. Even while the train sped along to Toledo, he sat saying over and over to himself the words of some of the poems.

After the reading that night, Dr. Tobey and a Mr. Thatcher, who had also helped Dunbar, shook his hand warmly and asked about the new poems.

Upon learning that the young poet had a second book ready they at once agreed to furnish the money to publish it. Consequently, a second book of poems called "Majors and Minors" was soon published.

The day that Dr. Tobey received a copy of "Majors and Minors" he was called into a consultation which kept him at a hotel that night. He and a friend sat up reading this little book of poems until midnight. Just as they had finished and stepped up to the desk to get their keys, another man walked up too. He was a great actor playing Monte Cristo at that time in Toledo. Dr. Tobey upon being introduced to him said, "I know you actor folks are always being bored by people wanting you to read and give opinions of poems, but I have something here that I wish you would read if you will".

The actor took the crude little copy of "Majors and Minors" and turned its pages. Dr. Tobey asked him to read a poem entitled "When Sleep Comes Down to Soothe the Weary Eyes". He read it at first quietly as he leaned over the counter. Then he read it aloud. With great expression and gesture he read it a third time. He turned to another poem and read that; then to another and another until the clock struck one—

two—three. He took out his watch and looked at it.

"Hello!" he said, "Three o'clock in the morning! Dr. Tobey, I thank you for giving me this opportunity. In my opinion no poet has written such verses since the days of Poe".

Dunbar soon gave up his work and went to Toledo to sell his book. One night after a very discouraging day, he walked into Dr. Tobey's office to tell him his troubles. Dr. Tobey said, "Well, my boy, how goes the battle?"

"Oh, doctor", said Dunbar, with tears streaming down his cheeks, "I never can offer to sell another book to any man".

"Paul," replied Dr. Tobey, "why don't you make up a speech?"

"Oh", answered Paul, "I have tried to do that but my tongue cleaves to the roof of my mouth and I cannot say a word".

The doctor said sympathetically, "You're no good as a book-agent. While I was down town this morning I sold three of your books to three of the most prominent men in Toledo".

Dr. Tobey then advised him to send a copy of "Majors and Minors" to the actor and author of another play which was then being presented in Toledo. Dunbar made several attempts to present the book in person but failed in each attempt. Nevertheless, before leaving Toledo, he saw to it that the book reached the actor. After reading it, the actor wrote Dunbar a most encouraging letter. He also sent a copy of the poems to the novelist, William Dean Howells. This well-known writer in turn sent a full-page review of the poems to *Harper's Monthly*. He described the little book as a countrified little volume in appearance which inwardly was full of a new world. Singular it was that the article appeared in *Harper's Monthly* on the 27th of June, 1896, which was Dunbar's twenty-fourth birthday. After being told of the article by a friend, Dunbar went to a newsstand and purchased a copy of *Harper's Monthly*. As he read the article, he said he knew not whether to laugh or cry, but no doubt he did a little of each. Hundreds of letters from all parts of the world, even from Athens, Greece, began to pour into the office of the publishers. Some were ordering Dunbar's poems, others were asking for his photograph and still others were asking for information about him.

On the Fourth of July, Dunbar and his mother went, at Dr. Tobey's invitation, to Toledo. When they arrived at the meeting place about sixty prominent persons from Toledo and elsewhere sat waiting to greet them. Dr. Tobey, with his arm about Dunbar's shoulder as they walked towards a little ante-room said, "It has all come at once, Paul. Mr. Howells has made you famous. They all want to meet you now. Those who made fun of you because of your color and your poverty are now eager to clasp your hand. This is going to be the testing day of your life. I hope you will bear good fortune and popularity as well and as bravely as you have met your disappointments and your humiliations. If so, that will indeed be a proof of your greatness".

Among the poems which Dunbar recited that day was "Ships that Pass in the Night". The audience seemed especially moved by this poem. The most prominent man in that select group said, "Of all things I ever heard, I never listened to anything so impressive".

That night, after such a triumphant day, Dunbar, sitting alone, wrote these lines:

Mere human strength may stand ill fortune's frown;
So I prevailed, for human strength was mine;
But from the killing strength of great renown
Naught may protect me save a strength Divine.
Help me, O Lord, in this my trembling cause.
I scorn men's curses, but I dread applause.

During these days of public attention, the poet visited some of the eastern cities, giving readings of his works to audiences composed of people from all sections. On almost every occasion, the audience responded with loud applause and often with bursts of laughter.

The following year, when the opportunity to go to England as a reader of his poems presented itself, he took advantage of it. While he was in London, the American Ambassador arranged an entertainment for him at which he read before many of the foremost men and women of London. He was further entertained by prominent clubs and prominent people. Although he was being royally treated, he often ran away from the public gatherings in London to his lodging place to work on his first novel, "The Uncalled".

One day just as he was nearing the end of this novel, he received a letter from a friend in America asking if he would accept a place in the Library of Congress at Washington, D. C. He wrote the friend immediately thanking him for his interest and assuring him that he would be glad to accept the position if offered.

On his return to America a little later, he went at once to Washington, D. C., where he began his work in the Library of Congress. Among the first things he did was to look up a home for his mother. As soon as they were settled in their home, he began to use his evenings and all of his spare time in writing.

For about fifteen months, he sat at his desk nearly every evening until far into the night. One night he wrote a friend, saying, "I am working very hard these days, so if it is only for the idle that the devil runs his employment bureau, I have no need of his services". By such diligence, he soon had published a third book of poems which he called "Lyrics of Lowly Life".

Apparently great joy and a cessation of undue toil took the place of his very busy days for a while. About this time, he married a young woman who also had written some verses. Both she and he appeared to be very happy until he began to be annoyed by a stubborn, hacking cough. The dust from the library books seemed to aggravate it so that he soon resigned his position. Thinking that a change of climate would do him good, he made a tour of the South, giving readings of his poems as he went.

The cough continued to trouble him. Taking the advice of a physician, he began to prepare to go to the Catskill Mountains. However, before he left, another volume of poems appeared which he had named "Lyrics of the Hearthside". The new volume of poems seemed to give him strength. He completed his preparations and set out for the mountains. While there he worked steadily writing poems and stories. Just as steadily did his cough seem to grow worse. After a while, he began to feel that Denver, Colorado, was the place for him. He consulted a physician and was not long in starting out for Denver, accompanied by Mrs. Dunbar and his mother.

The long trip seemed to tire him greatly and yet he reached Denver in safety. After a few days' rest, he did his best at strolling around looking at the mountainous country. One day, as he sat writing a friend, he said, "Well, it is something to sit down under the shadow of the Rocky Mountains even if one only goes there to die".

After securing a little house in a town near Denver, he bought an old mare, which he hitched every morning to his buggy and drove for miles. One day after a long, long ride over the beautiful hills he sat down and wrote a poem about "That Ol' Mare of Mine". Although he could not walk much, he worked for hours each day until he had finished a novel which he called "The Love of Landry".

After spending some months in Denver, he and Mrs. Dunbar returned to Washington, D. C., where they bought a home and apparently settled down. The home, however, was soon closed. He went first to Chicago and then to Dayton, where his mother had returned.

Although his cough was about as bad as it could be, he was working on another volume of poems which came out during the early winter months of 1903 under the title of "Lyrics of Love and Laughter".

During the seven years of his illness, he often received his friends. Sometimes he even served tea for them. Once a friend who had business in Dayton called him by telephone saying that she was coming out to see him. When she reached his home, there he was curled up on a couch for all the world like a small boy. He was writing a poem just to please her. Said he on her arrival, "Just wait a moment, I'm hunting for a rhyme". And sure enough, in just a few moments he handed her a scrap of paper on which was written:

TO A POET AND A LADY

You sing, and the gift of State's applause
  Is yours for the rune that is ringing.
But tell me truly, is that the cause?
  Don't you sing for the love of singing?

You think you are working for wealth and for fame,
  But ah, you are not, and you know it;
For wife is the sweetest and loveliest name,
  And every good wife is a poet!

Dunbar continued to write stories and poems almost to the day of his death, which came on the 9th day of February, 1906. His last poem he never wrote down, but simply dictated to his stenographer.

BOOKER TALIAFERRO WASHINGTON

Booker T. Washington

Chapter III

BOOKER TALIAFERRO WASHINGTON

EDUCATOR, ORATOR, AUTHOR, STATESMAN

1859–1915

I

BOYHOOD AND YOUTH

EARLY one winter morning, about sixty years ago, a big rooster began flapping his wings and crowing—flap, flap, flap—cock-a-doodle-doo, cock-a-doodle-doo. Then a little rooster began cock-a-doodle-doo, cock-a-doodle-doo. Then here, there and everywhere was the sound—flap, flap, cock-a-doodle-doo—until all Franklin County, Virginia, seemed to have wings and crowing apparatus.

In the midst of this flapping and crowing, young Booker awoke, rubbed his eyes and yawned. Then he jumped out of bed, his feet striking the earthen floor and his teeth chattering in spite of the blazing fire before him. The wind, whistling through the cracks in the sides and the roof of the cabin, evidently made the dirt floor very cold to his feet.

He dressed quickly, having only three pieces

to put on—a flax shirt and two wooden shoes. As the coarse shirt began to slip down over his back, it felt so much like pin points or chestnut burrs against his flesh, that he cried "Ouch, Ouch!" as he straightened out the folds of his shirt. Then he sat on the side of the bed to put on his wooden shoes. He pulled at the pieces of rough leather on the tops of them. He twisted and turned his feet until they adjusted themselves as best they could to the shape of the wooden shoes. As he started toward the fire, the sound of his shoes—blump, blump, blump—caused his mother to look around.

She, being the plantation cook, had been so busy getting breakfast for fifty or more plantation hands that she had scarcely noticed Booker until now. "Good morning, son", she said, "run out to the pan and wash your face. Ma wishes you to get out some sweet potatoes."

Booker could not run very fast in his stiff shoes but he went out as quickly as he could, carrying a gourd of water in his hand. He washed his face and soon returned with a field hoe on his shoulder. After removing several boards from the top of the potato hole in the middle of the dirt floor, he began to dig into it with his hoe. First he dug out some of the loose earth and then some of the straw. He dropped down on his knees and pulled out many potatoes with his hands. After clearing a place for them on the hearth, his mother covered them over with hot ashes.

With a long, flat iron she turned the burning coals from the big skillet lids. The smell of the corn-pone and of the roasting potatoes so tantalized the cat that she slid in through the cat hole in the lower right-hand corner of the cabin wall.

Men, women and children hurried from all parts of the plantation to snatch a bite to eat at this little cabin. Many mouths were busy eating corn-bread and molasses. Here and there a crust of bread was used as a knife and fork but many just plunged their fingers into the molasses and bread.

Booker stood like the other children with his tin pan while molasses was being poured into it. He tipped the edges of the pan first this way and then that way so that the molasses might run all over the bottom of it.

Several months later things were all changed. There was no need of a plantation cook, and so Booker's mother was getting ready to go away. One morning as some of those same roosters flapped their wings and crowed for day, a rough little cart rolled up to her cabin door. Booker, his brother John, and his mother hurried around, grabbed up their few bed clothes, stools and skillets and threw them into the cart. "Goodbye, goodbye", they said to their friends. And off they started to join Booker's stepfather in Malden, West Virginia.

For two weeks they traveled, sleeping in the open air and cooking their food out-of-doors over a log fire. One night they started to camp in an old empty log cabin. Just as the fire had gotten well started and their pallet on the floor was made, a large black snake fully a yard and a half long dropped down the chimney and glided across the floor. They ran out of the cabin and later removed their things from it. The next day they continued their journey.

Early one evening, as they began to drive more slowly in search of a good place to stop for the night, a rider came by with his horse in a gallop and bowed to them. Booker called out, "Mister, how far is it to Malden?"

The man did not stop but answered, saying, "About two miles over the hill".

The little cart rolled on until it seemed that they had gone ten miles over the hill instead of two. Finally they heard men swearing and quarreling. They saw men fighting and drinking and gambling. Suddenly a man stepped up and greeted them, "Hello, hello, howdy, howdy". It was Booker's stepfather who had come to Malden several years before.

"Oh, what is that, Pa?" Booker exclaimed, "over there where the light is?"

"That is only a salt furnace", he answered. "There are plenty of them here. I have a job waiting for you in one of them". In a few days, just as he had been told, Booker was at his new job in a salt furnace.

In this part of the town, in that part and all about, people were asking each other, "Have you heard of the school that is to open in Malden? They tell me that the teacher is already here and that old folks as well as children can go to it".

This question was asked young Booker. His eyes sparkled and his face lighted up on hearing such good news. Then he said in an undertone, "Oh, well, I can't go to school anyway for I have to work all day".

When the school began there were many happy faces, old and young. Every night Booker inquired about the school and tried to show his mother and stepfather how he could work and go to school too. After a great deal of talking about it, they arranged one night for Booker to go to work at four o'clock in the morning, work until nine o'clock, then go to school and return to his work after school.

The next morning, at nine o'clock, Booker started off to school on a trot. When he reached the school-room door, panting for breath, all eyes were turned upon him, especially because he did not have on a hat. He hesitated a moment but went in just the same and took a seat.

The teacher was calling the roll. "John Jones", he called. "Present", said John Jones. "Mary Ann Roberts", he added. "Present", said Mary Ann Roberts. And on he went until he came to the end of the roll.

Then he turned to Booker and asked his name. Booker twisted and turned for a few moments and said nothing, because he knew he had no name except Booker. Suddenly he remembered hearing about a great man whose name was Washington. When the teacher asked his name again, he jumped up from his seat, and with one hand raised, said, "My name is Booker Washington". He had found a name for himself that day. That night his mother sewed two pieces of cloth together and made him a hat.

He seemed very happy at school. One afternoon he and his classmates—about fifteen of them

—were sitting on a long pine-log bench, rocking to and fro and singing out their spelling lesson—"b-a, k-e-r, baker; m-a, k-e-r, maker; s-h-a, k-e-r, shaker". There was a knock at the door. Everybody was silent. The door opened and in walked Booker's stepfather. He quietly explained to the teacher that he had gotten Booker a good job in the coal mines and Booker would have to stop school. The next morning Booker entered a coal mine. He hesitated a little at first about working there because of the darkness.

In this mine one day, he overheard two men talking of Hampton Institute. He crept along in the darkness of the mine, close enough to hear what they were saying. One of the men said, "Yes, they tell me that Negro boys and girls can work their way through that school". The conversation continued. Booker Washington eagerly grasped every word; and he made up his mind on the spot to go to Hampton Institute that fall.

That fall, in 1872, with a cheap little satchel of clothes across his shoulder, he started out for Hampton Institute. The journey was long and there were no through trains, therefore stage-coaches were used much of the way. Booker sat back in the stage-coach as the horses trotted along, counting his little money and wondering what he would do when it was all spent. Most of his earnings had been used by his stepfather. When there was nothing left in his pockets, he walked some and begged rides on wagons until he reached Richmond, Virginia. It was late in the night and he did not have a penny left.

He walked and begged for a place to sleep until he was tired out. Soon he spied a high, board sidewalk. After looking around and assuring himself that no one saw him, he crept under it and slept for the rest of the night. For some days he worked in Richmond and slept under the board sidewalk at night.

When he had earned enough to pay his railroad fare on to Hampton Institute, he started out again and reached there with just fifty cents in his pocket. He was tired; he was hungry; he was dirty; he was everything but discouraged. One of the northern teachers looked him over and was not sure apparently that he had come to the right place. While he stood anxiously waiting, he saw others freely admitted to the school.

The teacher finally turned to him, saying, "Well, come with me". He followed her to a recitation room. She said, pointing to the room, "You may sweep that room". He swept the room three times. He moved every piece of furniture and swept. He swept every closet and corner. He dusted everything four times. He dusted the wood-work around the walls. He dusted every table and table leg. He dusted every bench.

Then he returned to the teacher and said, "Well, I am through with that job".

She went to the door of the room, walked in and looked into every corner and closet. She took out her handkerchief and rubbed it over benches and wood-work. Unable to find one bit of dirt anywhere, she said, "I guess you will do to enter this school".

His first two nights at Hampton Institute were somewhat trying ones. Although he was thirteen years old, he had never used a sheet on his bed; and now there were two sheets on his bed. The first night he slept under both of them and the second night he slept on top of both of them. However, with the help of older boys he learned the right way. He paid his expenses that year by working as a janitor. He brought in coal. He made fires. He removed ashes. He swept and dusted class-rooms.

Summer time came and Booker Washington had nothing to do. He scratched his head as he thought of selling his coat or of trying several other plans, none of which, he feared, would work.

A hotel job opened up to him. He took it and by working hard that summer and washing his own clothes, he saved all the money which he earned.

Several more summers and winters of hard work came and went. Finally one June morning in 1875, the Hampton teachers were busy decorating the little chapel for the commencement exercises. People began to gather. The students took their places. The choir began to sing. The graduating class marched in and at the head of the line marched a young man who was calling himself now Booker Taliaferro Washington. He had learned that his mother had named him Booker Taliaferro when he was born.

II

Educator: Tuskegee Institute

One evening just six years after Booker Washington's graduation from Hampton Institute, he and General Samuel Chapman Armstrong, the founder and principal of Hampton Institute, were walking to the railroad station. General Armstrong was talking earnestly, shaking his head and making gestures now and then. He was telling Booker Washington why he had asked him instead of any other boy to go to Tuskegee, Alabama. Washington was listening without saying a word. Just as they reached the station, the sound, t-o-o-t, t-o-o-t, rang out up the road. Then, clang, cling, cling, chuff, che-e-e was heard.

The train stopped with a sudden jolt. Booker Washington grasped General Armstrong's hand. They shook like warm friends and bade each other goodbye. The former, with his bag in his hand, stepped upon the platform just as the bell rang and the train began to move. He glanced out of the window at the General, waved his hand and sat down.

Apparently he tried to look out of the window and forget everything but he kept thinking of what General Armstrong had said about his work —of his two years of teaching at Malden, his night school, his debating club with one of his big, brawny boy debaters waving his hand and saying, "Most honorable judges, I have proven to you that the pen is mightier than the sword". He reached into his bag and took out a picture of the little library which he had started for the school. He looked at it a long time, then he brought forth a letter which a friend had written him the year he was studying at Wayland Seminary, Washington, D. C., and read that.

He placed his things back into his bag, stretched

himself a little, yawned and fell asleep. Before the break of day he awoke and read several other letters telling of some of his experiences at Hampton Institute: for instance, his teaching the new Indian boys how to brush their teeth, how to comb and brush their hair, how to wash their hands and faces. One of the letters described Booker Washington's work in organizing the Hampton Institute night-school and teaching in it.

Just at that moment, the train gave a sudden jolt which seemed to shake him out of his deep reverie. He straightened up and began to plan what he would do when he reached Tuskegee. He traveled on for nearly two days listening to the porter call out the names of the many towns and cities as the train reached them. At last he heard the call, "Tuskegee, all out for Tuskegee!" He caught up his bag and hustled out.

He looked all around; but seeing no one looking for him he went ahead making inquiries about the building in which he was to open his school. He looked here and there for several days but the only buildings he could find for his use were an old, dilapidated church and an old shanty with an old chicken-house nearby.

After making arrangements for the use of these

old buildings and hiring an old mule and a little wagon to take him over the country, he set out and visited the country people for miles around. He ate with them in their little log cabins. He often used the one and only fork on the table and passed it on to somebody else. That person used it and passed it on to the next person. Around that fork went until everybody at the table had had a chance to use it. He often slept with a family in its one-room cabin when there were so many in that family that he had to go out of doors to undress and dress. Still he kept on visiting for several months until he had seen what the people needed, and had advertised his school.

On the morning of July 4, 1881, the doors of the old dilapidated church in Tuskegee were pulled as wide open as the sagging walls would permit. An old cracked bell was rung, and in walked thirty pupils, some of whom were forty years old. Not one was less than fifteen years old. Every one worked hard and things went well until one day a hard rain came. Water streamed in upon Mr. Washington so that a pupil had to hold an umbrella over him while he heard the recitations.

Six weeks of such teaching passed and then another teacher, Miss Olivia Davidson of Ohio, came to assist Mr. Washington. She taught school and gave festivals and suppers in order to raise five hundred dollars to pay for a school farm. All of the people for miles around wanted to help the school. Some brought five cents; some brought stalks of sugar cane. Others brought quilts.

One old lady about seventy years old, clad in just clean rags, hobbled in one morning on a cane. She said, "Mr. Washington, God knows I spent the best days of my life in slavery. God knows I am ignorant and poor; but I know what you and Miss Davidson are trying to do. I know you are trying to make better men and better women of my race. I haven't any money, but I want you to take these six eggs which I've been saving up, and I want you to put these six eggs into the education of these boys and girls".

Mr. Washington and his assistant worked very hard to raise the five hundred dollars and to get the school started well. He knew how much the farm would mean to the school. He knew also that the students did not like clearing the land and working the field, and so one day he planned what he called a "chopping bee". With his ax swung across his shoulder he led the students out to the farm and made a challenge to outchop any of them. The old ones chopped and the young ones chopped. The boys chopped and the girls chopped. All of them chopped but none out-chopped their teacher, Booker Washington.

Boys and girls who look at the picture of Tuskegee Institute as it is today will probably say: "My! Can this be the school for which the old lady brought the six eggs? Can this be the school for which the 'chopping bee' was held?"

It is really that same school. Booker Washington and his assistants worked so faithfully and well that Tuskegee Institute has received not only the six eggs but hundreds of thousands of dollars. The gifts had increased so that when Tuskegee Institute was thirty-four years old it owned two thousand four hundred acres of land, with one hundred and eleven buildings on the grounds. In addition to this, Tuskegee Institute had about twenty thousand acres of land given it by the United States Government as an endowment. The number of students in thirty-four years had increased from thirty to about two thousand and the number of teachers had increased from one to two hundred.

In the early days the school had a dark basement dining-room but now there is a large dining-hall on the campus. In the early days the few knives and forks had to be passed around among the students almost continuously during a meal; but now there are sufficient knives and forks for all. Once upon a time the students used rough boxes and stools for dining-room seats but now there are dining-room chairs for all. In the early days Tuskegee Institute had no kitchen. Blazing fires were made out of doors upon which pots and skillets were set for cooking. Many a time a girl would step on a live coal, throw down the skillet lid and hop away to nurse her burn for a moment; now there are modern kitchens at Tuskegee Institute.

Perhaps you have already begun to think that Tuskegee Institute with about one hundred large brick buildings must look like a little city. It really does. All the buildings and the grounds are lighted by the school's own electric plant. Many industries such as domestic science, carpentry and blacksmithing are taught.

The brick-making industry at Tuskegee Institute is an evidence of the fact that Booker Washington believed in the saying, "If at first you don't succeed, try, try again". He and his students of the early days made their first brick kiln for burning bricks, but the kiln would not work. They made a second kiln and that was a failure; a third brick kiln with about 25,000 bricks in it fell in the middle of the night just when the bricks were nearly ready to be taken out. This seemed like hard luck, but it appears that Booker Washington was never in all his life wholly discouraged at anything. He started a fourth brick kiln with the $15 which he secured by pawning his watch. To-day 1,200,000 first-class bricks are manufactured in one season by the students of Tuskegee Institute.

Every day in the year visitors go to Tuskegee Institute from all parts of the world. They go to the shops where the boys are busy making wagons, buggies, cabinets and all sorts of things. They go to the trades building where the girls are cooking, sewing, making hats and doing laundry work. They go to the hospital, to the library, to the classrooms, to the dining-hall and other buildings. They go to the farm, to the piggery, to the dairy farm. They go to the chapel. They hear the students sing and see them march out. Now and then at chapel exercises they see a girl or a boy called out of a long line because a button is off, or shoes are not polished, or clothing is not neat and tidy.

These visitors go away saying to their friends that Booker Washington was certainly a great man. Some go to their homes far away and start schools like Tuskegee Institute. Other visitors have been there, studied the school and gone away to do honor to Booker Washington.

III

Orator, Author, Statesman

In 1896 Harvard University, one of the greatest colleges in the country, honored Booker Washington. He spoke at the University and was later given the degree of Master of Arts. Five years later, another great institution, Dartmouth College, invited him there and gave him the degree of Doctor of Laws.

Wherever he spoke, people came from far and near to hear him. He spoke once in Essex Hall in London, England, and once at Bristol, England.

Just after the Spanish-American War, he was the peace-celebration speaker at the Chicago Auditorium. In the auditorium that day there were thousands of people, among whom was the President of the United States. And many thousands were on the outside trying to hear Booker Washington speak.

In the middle of his speech he said as he walked across the platform, "Nobody should help a lazy, shiftless person". Then he smiled, opened his eyes wide and said, "Let me tell you this story: Once there were two men seeking to cross a river by means of a ferry boat. The fare across was three cents. One of the men, who seemed to be shiftless and lazy, said to the other, 'Please let me have three cents to cross the ferry; I haven't a penny'. The other man said to him, 'I am sorry not to accommodate you, boss, but the fact is that a man who hasn't three cents is just as bad off on one side of the river as he is on the other' ". The audience laughed and applauded.

He said further: "But let me tell you, my friends, everybody is not like the man who did not have three cents. Early one morning not long ago, I was out watching my chickens and pigs. A pig I think is one of the grandest of animals. Old Aunt Caroline came striding by with a basket on her head. I said to her, 'Where are you going, Aunt Caroline?' She replied, 'Lord bless you, Mr. Washington, I've already been where I was going' ". The audience laughed again.

The singing that day lifted one up and made one feel like marching and humming. Some of the poor people present wept for joy, and at the close of the meeting Booker Washington shook hands with many of them. He seemed to understand them and to know their needs. When he wrote his book, "Up from Slavery", much of which was written on the train, he told how poor he himself was once.

Dr. Washington traveled all over the North, East, West and South. He traveled in a special car through Arkansas, Oklahoma, Mississippi, Tennessee, South Carolina, North Carolina, Delaware, Texas, Florida, Louisiana, parts of Alabama, Georgia, Virginia and West Virginia.

His friends began to say, "Dr. Washington looks tired. Let us send him and his wife to Europe on a vacation". They gave his school a large sum of money. Then they talked with his wife, Mrs. Margaret Murray Washington, who was a graduate of a great college called Fisk University. She had helped Dr. Washington for some years in his work and knew how tired he must be. These friends talked and urged until she agreed to go too.

All arrangements for the trip were completed. Dr. and Mrs. Washington bade goodbye to their friends, sailed across the ocean, and for three months went here and there through Holland, Belgium, France and England. He crossed the ocean a second time and then a third time. On these trips kings and queens entertained him and honored him. In his own country, presidents of the United States called him in to talk over important matters.

Following one of his trips abroad, he wrote a book called "The Man Farthest Down", in which he told many sad stories about the poor and ignorant of Europe. He wrote about the women whom he saw in Europe hitched with oxen ploughing the fields. Among his other books are: "The Future of the American Negro", "A History of the Negro" and "Working with the Hands".

He worked hard and seemed to hammer out success in everything. No one called him conceited and yet he had great confidence in himself even to the last. When the doctors in New York told him that he had but a few hours to live, he said, "Then I must start now for Tuskegee". He was a very sick man and could hardly walk when he reached the station but he refused to be carried to the train in an invalid's chair. For many hours the train sped southward before it reached Cheehaw, the junction station for Tuskegee. A smile came over his face as he drew near the school.

However, he did not live many hours after reaching home. It had been his custom to rise early every morning, and so early in the morning on the 14th of November, 1915, Booker T. Washington, the chieftain and the servant of all peoples, rose and departed to the land of the blessed.

For the next few days, the Tuskegee Institute grounds, even as large as they are, were almost packed with people from near and far. The poor, uneducated people, black and white, from the cotton fields of Alabama were there. Statesmen, scholars, editors, professional men, business men and just men were there. His wife, his two sons and his daughter were there. Many of those who were present said that the mind of the thinking world was there, for Booker Washington was regarded as one of the greatest men that ever lived.

HARRIET TUBMAN

SHE TOLD HER HEARERS THRILLING STORIES.

Chapter IV

HARRIET TUBMAN

The Moses of Her People

1820–1913

ABOUT one hundred years ago, people in every civilized country were talking about the "underground railroad" in the United States. The "underground railroad" was not really a railroad under the ground, but a secret way by means of which slaves escaped from their masters in the South and reached free territory. Reaching free territory sometimes meant escape from this country into Canada. Passengers, those seeking to escape to free territory, on the "underground railroad" were led by very brave and daring conductors. Among these conductors there was a woman whose name was Harriet Tubman.

When Harriet was born in Dorchester County, Maryland, in 1820, she was named Araminta Ross. After she grew up, she called herself Harriet. When she became a woman she was married to John Tubman and was called Harriet Tubman.

Harriet almost died with the measles when she was six years old. Soon after she recovered from this, her master threw a heavy weight at her and injured her skull. For years she suffered from pressure on her brain which caused her to fall asleep at any time, wherever she was, whether she was seated on a rail fence or in a chair. It also caused her to stagger sometimes as she walked. No one except her African mother seemed to care for her or to pay any attention to her.

Early one morning a lady came driving up to the home of Harriet's master, who met her at the gate and inquired what he could do for her. She asked for a slave-girl to care for her baby, but offered very low wages. The master shook his head, saying, "I can not furnish you a girl for that". As the lady pleaded with him, he stood looking on the ground and knitting his brow. Suddenly he lifted his head and said, "Yes, I have just one girl whom you may take; keep your eye on her because she may not have all that is coming to her". Harriet was called, placed in a wagon and driven away to the lady's home.

The first thing the lady gave her to do was to sweep and dust the parlor. Harriet cautiously tiptoed into this wonderfully fine room, amazed at everything she saw. She finally began to sweep in much the same way as she had swept her mother's cabin. As soon as she had finished sweeping, she took the dusting cloth and wiped off the chairs, the table and the mantel-piece. The particles of dust, still flying here and there over the room, soon settled on the furniture again.

About this time, Harriet's new mistress stepped in and began to look around. The dust lay on the table, the chairs and the mantel in such a thick coating that she spoke very harshly to Harriet and ordered her to do the work all over. Harriet swept and dusted just as she had done before. The dust, having no other place to go, settled again on the furniture. The mistress entered the parlor again, bringing with her this time a whip. With this she lashed Harriet with a heavy hand. Five times before breakfast that morning Harriet swept and dusted the parlor.

Just as she had gotten her third whipping, her mistress's sister, who had been awakened from her morning slumber, opened the parlor door. "Why do you whip the child, sister, for not doing what she has never been taught to do?" she asked. "Leave Harriet to me for a few minutes and you will see that she will soon learn how to sweep and dust a room."

The sister ordered Harriet to open the windows first, to sweep the room and leave it a while until the dust settled, and to return then and wipe the dust from the furniture.

Harriet looked strangely at the big window, went to it and raised it inch by inch until it was high enough to fasten by a latch. She set in again and swept, and while the dust was settling, she went out and set the table for breakfast. Then she returned and dusted the parlor.

That night she was ordered to sit up and rock the baby. The baby's cradle and Harriet's chair were placed near her mistress's bed. Occasionally Harriet's eyelids dropped and her head bobbed this way and that way. The cradle kept on rocking because her foot was on the rockers. Once in a great while, the cradle would stop and the baby would begin to cry. The mistress would pick up her whip and give Harriet a cut across the head and shoulders which would make her jump and almost knock the cradle over.

Under such treatment, Harriet became so worn and thin that the lady sent her back to her master saying that she wasn't worth a six-pence. Harriet was turned over to her mother, who nursed her until she was again strong enough to work.

She was then hired out to a man who made her plow, drive oxen, lift a barrel of flour, and sometimes cut a half cord of wood a day. Soon she became ill again. She lay on her sick-bed from Christmas until March. Day after day she prayed, saying, "Oh, Lord, convert old Master; change that man's heart and make him a Christian". When some one told her that as soon as she was able to work, she would be sent away, she changed her prayer, saying: "Lord, if you are never going to change that man's heart, kill him, Lord, and take him out of the way, so he will do no more mischief". Harriet's master finally died but she continued ill for a long time.

Even after she became stronger she still prayed at every turn. When she went to the horse-trough to wash her face and hands, she said, "Lord, wash me and make me clean". When she took the towel to wipe them, she cried, "O Lord, for Jesus' sake, wipe away all my sins". When she took up the broom to sweep, she groaned, "O Lord, whatever sin there is in my heart, sweep it out, Lord, clear and clean".

Early one morning many of the slaves in the "quarters" hurried about with a scared look on their faces, whispering something to each other as they passed. The news had leaked out that Harriet and two of her brothers were to be sold and sent the next day to the far South. As soon as the news reached Harriet, she held a hurried consultation with her brothers, telling them of the terrible things that would befall them if they did not run away to the North. As they stood for a while looking about anxiously and ready to move on, they agreed to start for the North that night.

Harriet began to scratch her head and wonder how she might tell her friends that she was going away. She thought and thought, and finally hit upon the plan of telling them in an old familiar song. As she was passing the next cabin door she sang out:

> When that old chariot comes,
> I'm going to leave you;
> I'm bound for the promised land.
> Friends, I'm going to leave you.
>
> I'm sorry, friends, to leave you,
> Farewell! Oh, farewell!
> But I'll meet you in the morning!
> Farewell! Oh, farewell!

She looked forward and backward and all around several times. No overseer was in sight. She continued to sing, casting a meaning glance at first one and then another as she passed along:

> I'll meet you in the morning,
> When you reach the promised land,
> On the other side of Jordan,
> For I'm bound for the promised land.

That night Harriet and her brothers spoke for a while in a whisper to their father and kissed him good-bye. Without disturbing their dear old mother, each started out quietly in slightly different directions, but all towards the same place. Soon the three came together. The brothers began to say to Harriet in very low tones that they were afraid that old master would send men out for them and capture them. They stood trembling with excitement. All at once, one of them and then the other broke away and ran towards home as fast as they could, falling now and then over a log or a stump. Harriet stood watching them as long as she could see their shadows in the starlight.

Fixing her eye on the North Star, she turned her face in that direction and went forward. All night long she walked until the peep of day, then she lay down in the tall grass in a swamp. She lay there all day. The next night she started out again. Night after night she traveled, occasionally stopping to beg bread. She crouched behind trees or lay concealed in a swamp during the day until she reached Philadelphia.

On her arrival in Philadelphia she stared at the people as they passed. She stood gazing at the fine houses and the streets. She looked at her hands, believing that they, too, looked new. After finding a place to stay, she walked out among the better looking houses and began to ask from door to door if any one was needed for work. Finally a woman came to the door, opened it just a little way and peeped out as though she were afraid. As Harriet was asking for work, the lady told her to wait a moment while she ran back and pushed her frying-pan further back on the stove. She appeared again at the door, questioned Harriet and then told her to come in.

Harriet walked in and stood listening to the lady's instructions about cleaning. Then she raised the windows and began to sweep. She swept and dusted and cleaned all day. She worked hard the next day and every day until pay-day, when she received her first money. She hid it away with great care and continued her work. The following pay-days she went to the same spot and hid away every penny of her money until she felt that she had enough to go back South.

She gave up her work and traveled night after night until she was again back on the plantation. She hid around among the slaves in their cabins. She whispered to them thrilling stories of the free country, until even women with babies were getting ready to follow her back to the North. After drugging their babies with paregoric and placing them in baskets which they carried on their arms, they set out with "Moses", as they called her, for the free country.

They forded rivers, climbed mountains, went through the swamps, threaded the forests with their feet sore and often bleeding. They traveled during the night and kept in hiding during the day. One of the men fell by the wayside. Harriet took out her pistol, and pointing it at his head, said, "Dead men tell no tales; you go on or die!" He arose trembling and dragged along with the party until they reached the North.

As soon as Harriet had landed this party, she began working again and making preparations to go back on her next trip. One night she went back to the plantation, secured a horse and a two-wheel cart and drove away with her aged mother and father. After placing them on the train, she traveled in the cart night after night until she made her way through Maryland to Wilmington, Delaware, where she had sent her parents.

As soon as the three of them met in Wilmington, Harriet took her parents to a well-known underground railroad station. This was simply the home of a Quaker friend. He gave them food and shelter and each a new pair of shoes. He furnished Harriet with money to take her parents on to Canada, and kept the horse and cart for sale. Harriet and her parents went on, making their way with difficulty, until they reached Canada.

Harriet remained in Canada for a short time only, then slipped back among the plantation cabins in Maryland. Again and again she went back—nineteen times—leading away in the darkness, in all, over three hundred slaves. The slave masters of that region in Maryland, whence so many were being stolen away, after trying hard to catch Harriet, offered a reward of $40,000 for her, dead or alive. They posted such a notice in all public places.

After fifteen years of such adventure, Harriet bought a little home place near Auburn, N. Y., and settled on it with her dear old parents. Frequently responding to a knock at the door, she arose and found that some one had brought to her a poor, old, homeless person. Without hesitating to ask many questions, she took in every one of them until she had twenty old people, for whom she worked and sought support.

William H. Seward, Governor of New York, once said to her when she went to him for aid, "Harriet, you have worked for others long enough. If you would ever ask anything for yourself, I would gladly give it to you but I will not help you to rob yourself for others any longer".

Many years after that, Governor Seward died, and a large number of persons gathered at his funeral. Many very beautiful flowers were received by his family on that sad occasion. On the day of the funeral, just before the coffin was closed, a woman as black as night stole quietly in and laid a wreath of field flowers at his feet and as quietly glided out again. Friends of the family whispered, "It's the Governor's friend, Harriet".

Harriet continued to work and take in homeless old people until the outbreak of the Civil War. At that time, Governor Andrew of Massachusetts sent for her. He asked if she would go South as a spy and a scout, and if need be, a hospital nurse for the Union soldiers. She stood thinking for a moment, then said that she would go. He bade her return home and be ready at a moment's notice. Harriet left his office and returned to Auburn. She went about asking friends to look out for the old people in her home while she was away.

Soon after she reached home, a messenger arrived with orders for her to report immediately. She hastily grabbed a few necessary things, kissed her parents, saying good-bye to them and to the inmates of the home, and hurried away to join the company of soldiers on its way south. They traveled several days. As soon as they arrived, Harriet was ordered to act as a scout and a spy for the soldiers. She took charge and led them through the jungle and the swamp. She approached the frightened slaves, often gaining valuable information from them. She stood in the battle-line when the shots were falling like hail and the bodies of dead and wounded men were dropping like leaves in autumn.

Being called upon to nurse the soldiers in the hospitals, she extracted from roots and herbs what she called a healing substance. As she went to a sick soldier and felt his burning forehead, she often poured out a spoonful of her medicine and placed it in his mouth. After a few days of such treatment frequently a soldier smiled at her and thanked her.

She often bathed the wounds of soldiers from early morning until late at night. She nursed many with smallpox. Occasionally, after a long day's toil, she went to her little cabin and made fifty pies, several pans of ginger-bread and two casks of root-beer. One of the men went through the camps selling these things for her. Almost as soon as she obtained the money from the sale of them she mailed it on to her old parents for the support of their home.

Once while Harriet was on this trip she went with some gunboats up the Combahee River. The frightened slaves along the way left their work and took to the woods. Some of those who fled peeped out from behind trees at the gunboats and ran away like deer when they heard the sound of the steam whistle. One old man said, "Well, Master said the Yankees had horns and tails but I never believed it till now". Eight hundred of these people were taken on board the gunboats to be carried to Beaufort, S. C. Some of them before going aboard grabbed from the fire and placed on their heads pails of smoking rice. Others had on their backs a bag with a pig in it; and some carried two pigs in their bags.

Soon after this trip Harriet returned to her little home place, which was about to be sold to pay off a mortgage. A friend, the daughter of a professor of Auburn Theological Seminary, hearing of Harriet's trouble, came to see her. Harriet greeted her friend as usual and invited her to sit down; she too sat down and began to tell about the war. Her friend listened for a long, long time but finally interrupted her to ask about the home and the mortgage. Harriet, concealing nothing from her, told her the exact conditions of the mortgage.

The friend suggested the idea of having her life story written as a means of getting money to pay off the mortgage. Harriet nodded her head in full agreement with what her friend was proposing and asked if she would write the story. The friend counted aloud the days before the mortgage had to be paid off and, realizing that they were not many, set herself at once to the task of writing the story of Harriet's life.

Harriet sat with her friend day after day, each time telling of some incident in her life which she had not told before. The story was finally finished and published, and from the proceeds of it the mortgage was paid off.

Harriet worked hard, saying all the time that she wished to free the home of debt so that she might give it to her race to be used as an Old Folks' Home. When the property was almost free of debt and there were twenty aged women in the home, she went among them with a smile dividing the little she had, until she was stricken with pneumonia and died.

Following her death, the Harriet Tubman Club

of New York City, together with the whole Empire State Federation of Negro Women's Clubs, erected to her memory a handsome monument. This monument is in the form of a shaft. One of the principal designs on this shaft is in the form of three oak logs out of which flowers are growing.

The citizens of Auburn held a memorial meeting for her at the Auditorium Theatre. Booker T. Washington, the mayor and the ex-mayor of Auburn were the speakers on that occasion. The lower floor of the theatre was filled and every box was occupied. In one box sat a group of Civil War veterans and in another sat the leading society women of Auburn. On the stage sat the Auburn Festival Chorus and Orchestra and the guests.

In the presence of this audience, Harriet Tubman's grand-niece unveiled a large bronze tablet —the gift of the citizens of Auburn to the memory of Harriet Tubman. In accepting this tablet, the mayor of the city said, "In recognition of Harriet Tubman's unselfish devotion to the cause of humanity, the city of Auburn accepts this tablet dedicated to her memory".

The tablet was placed in the county court-house with the following inscription:

IN MEMORY OF

HARRIET TUBMAN

Born a slave in Maryland about 1821

Died in Auburn, N. Y., March 10, 1913

Called the "Moses" of her people during the Civil War. With rare courage, she led over 300 Negroes up from slavery to freedom, and rendered invaluable service as nurse and spy.

With implicit trust in God, she braved every danger and overcame every obstacle; withal she possessed extraordinary foresight and judgment, so that she truthfully said, "On my underground railroad I never ran my train off the track and I never lost a passenger."

ALEXANDER SERGYEYEVICH PUSHKIN

Chapter V

ALEXANDER SERGYEYEVICH PUSHKIN

Poet and Dramatist

1799–1837

ONCE upon a time there lived in Moscow, Russia, a little boy whose name was Alexander Pushkin. Sometimes people would look at him and whisper, "Is he not homely? He is just like his great-grandfather. His great-grandfather, Abram Hannibal, an African, was captured on the shores of Africa and brought to Constantinople as a slave. Abram Hannibal's son, Hannibal, who was Pushkin's grandfather, was a distinguished Russian general during the reign of Katherine II".

Pushkin's mother often looked at him as he sat in a sort of stupor and pitied him. His father would come into the house, kiss the other children, and pay no attention to him. His grandmother and his nurse often wondered why he would not run and play like the other children. Sometimes his nurse would take him by the hand and spin around the room while she sang to him.

One day after such a spin, his grandmother called out, speaking in no uncertain tones, "Alexander, Alexander, come here!" As he approached her in a sleepy fashion, she said, "Not awake yet! Oh, if I could be a bear just for a moment, I'd make you run—Boo!" she added, as she jumped at him. He laughed and tore around the room like a little pony. She looked on in great surprise.

He ran and ran until he was all tired out, then he rushed up to her, grabbed her about the waist, saying, "Tell me about the three hundred and fifty big lobsters again, please, grandmother".

"Sit down then. If you will listen now, I may tell you about many other things which I have seen in Russia", she said.

She began, "In St. Petersburg, which is the capital of Russia, there is a large palace called the Winter Palace. This palace is the largest building in Europe. In it there are large rooms called state rooms. The walls of these rooms are covered with gold plates and dishes. There are also five hundred other rooms. The ballroom holds five thousand guests, allowing a place for the musicians and space for dancing. Sometimes great suppers are prepared for the balls.

"At one of these balls, once upon a time, the waiters brought in three hundred and fifty dishes of chicken, each dish containing three chickens with salad and jelly; three hundred and fifty large lobsters, with mayonnaise sauce; three hundred and fifty tongues; three hundred and fifty dishes of cold meats; three hundred and fifty dishes of ices; three hundred and fifty dishes of creams and jellies; several hundred gallons of soup of different kinds, and two thousand bundles of asparagus boiled for the salads. In addition to this, they brought in cakes, biscuits, fruit and wine".

"Whew! The people must have burst after eating all of that!" exclaimed Alexander.

"Listen, now", continued his grandmother. "Then there is in this palace one room with eight pairs of doors made of tortoise-shell, trimmed with gold. There is also a picture-gallery containing some of the finest works of art. There is a museum in which all sorts of relics are found—even the stuffed horse and dogs of Peter the Great. Here and there among the state rooms there are winter gardens. And in one of these gardens, there are hundreds of canary birds flitting among the palms and over the fountains of gold-fish. There are writing tables and presses which on being opened play beautiful tunes."

"Can anybody open these tables, grandmother?" Alexander asked.

"No", she said, "only by special permission can people enter the palace."

"Is all of this really true, grandmother?" Alexander asked again.

"Yes, indeed", his grandmother said.

They sat for a few moments without saying a word. Alexander nestled closer to his grandmother and kissed her on the cheek. She smiled and, shuddering a bit, said: "But oh, the poor people of Russia! They live in two-room cabins. In one of these cabins sometimes as many as eleven older people and twenty-five children live. They actually knock each other down many times in moving about the cabin. One of the rooms usually has in it a stove, a table, a wooden bench, two chairs, and a lamp, if the family is not too poor to have it. The other room often has in it no furniture at all. The father and mother and as many of the children as can be fitted on top of the stove, sleep there. The others use pillows and lie on the floor in their clothing". She stopped talking, listened for a moment, then said, "I hear the nurse coming. I must go now".

She rose. Alexander caught her by the hands. She said, "Next time, grandmother will tell you more. She will tell you about a great big bell which weighs nearly four thousand pounds. At least forty men can stand under it. Let me go".

Alexander was really awake now. He stretched

his eyes and said, "Oh—Oh, forty men under one bell, whew!"

His grandmother hurried out, found the nurse and told her how wide-awake Alexander seemed. The nurse gleefully took out a little book and wrote: "Alexander wakes up in the year 1807, when he is eight years old". She went for him and took him for a walk. Much of the time, he ran ahead of her, playing and calling back to her.

From this time on, he read books, among which was his uncle's book of poems. At the age of ten he began to write poems and little plays himself. His father, deeply interested in him now, sent him at the age of twelve to a very expensive school which only the sons of the nobility could attend.

Young Pushkin began at once to criticise the school and the teachers. He read in the library and wrote poems the greater part of each day. His first poems were published when he was fifteen years old. Soon after this, he began to edit the school paper and further neglect his studies. During his six years in this school, his reports were entirely unsatisfactory to his parents.

On leaving school, he became a clerk for the Russian Government. He mingled in the gayest society and soon offended the government by writing a poem called "Ode to Liberty". He was immediately hurried far away to Southern Russia. One day, on his way to a neighboring town in Southern Russia, he met a band of gypsies whom he joined, and with whom he traveled for a while.

Pushkin soon offended some one in Southern Russia, and had to be sent to his father's estate, in a still more remote part of the country. His father did not even permit him to associate with the other children. However, he spent his time during these two years in this far-away section writing poetry.

After returning to St. Petersburg, he went to a ball one evening, and there met a young girl fifteen years old, with whom he danced. They began to correspond, and three years later were married. Pushkin was then receiving a salary of $2,550 a year. He and his wife entertained lavishly and wore the best of clothing; therefore he had to borrow a great deal of money. His anxiety about money seemed to haunt him to the extent that all inclination to write poetry fled.

He and his brother-in-law engaged in many quarrels. Pushkin finally challenged him to a duel. His brother-in-law accepted. On the eighth of February, 1837, they met face to face, each with a sharp weapon in his hand. Each made a thrust at the other. The brother-in-law jumped aside, warding off the blow, but Pushkin fell writhing, with the blood streaming from his wound. Two days later he died in St. Petersburg.

After his death the Czar of Russia furnished $76,500 to publish his works and to pay off his debts. A great celebration was held at Moscow in 1880 in memory of him. It was said to be the greatest event in Russian literary history. During this celebration, a statue of Pushkin, the great national poet of Russia, was erected at Moscow.

His greatest poem bears the title "Eugenie Onyegin" and his greatest drama is "Boris Godunoff".

THE BIRDLET

(Translated from the Russian by IVAN PANIN)

God's birdlet knows
Nor care, nor toil;
Nor weaves it painfully
An everlasting nest.
Thro' the long night on the twig it slumbers;
When rises the red sun
Birdie listens to the voice of God
And it starts, and it sings.
When Spring, Nature's Beauty,
And the burning summer have passed,
And the fog, and the rain,
By the late fall are brought,
Men are wearied, men are grieved,
But birdie flies into distant lands,
Into warm climes, beyond the blue sea:
Flies away until the spring.

WINTER MORNING

(Translated from the Russian by Ivan Panin)

Frost and sun—the day is wondrous!
Thou still art slumbering, charming friend.
'Tis time, O Beauty, to awaken:
Ope' thine eyes, now in sweetness closed,
To meet the Northern Dawn of Morning.
Thyself a north-star do thou appear!

Last night, remember, the storm scolded,
And darkness floated in the clouded sky;
Like a yellow, clouded spot
Thro' the clouds the moon was gleaming—
And melancholy thou wert sitting—
But now . . . thro' the window cast a look:

Stretched beneath the heavens blue—
Carpet-like magnificent—
In the sun the snow is sparkling;
Dark alone is the wood transparent,
And thro' the hoar gleams green the fir,
And under the ice the rivulet sparkles.

Entire is lighted with diamond splendor
Thy chamber . . . with merry crackle
The wood is crackling in the oven.
To meditation invites the sofa.
But know you? In the sleigh not order why
The brownish mare to harness?

Over the morning snow we gliding,
Trust we shall, my friend, ourselves
To the speed of impatient steed;
Visit we shall the fields forsaken,
The woods, dense but recently,
And the banks so dear to me.

THE GYPSIES

(Translated from the Russian by Ivan Panin)

Over the wooded banks,
In the hour of evening quiet,
Under the tents are song and bustle
And the fires are scattered.

Thee I greet, O happy race!
I recognize thy blazes,
I myself at other times
These tents would have followed.

With the early rays to-morrow
Shall disappear your freedom's trace,
Go you will—but not with you
Longer go shall the bard of you.

He alas, the changing lodgings,
And the pranks of days of yore
Has forgot for rural comforts
And for the quiet of a home.

BLANCHE KELSO BRUCE

Chapter VI

BLANCHE KELSO BRUCE

SENATOR—REGISTER OF THE U. S. TREASURY

1841–1898

ON the first day of March, in the year 1841, a little slave boy started out from Farmville, Virginia, on a journey. The strange thing about it was, he did not know where he was going or how long the journey would take. However, he started out and traveled west and south and east and north for fifty-seven long years.

After his first few years of experience on the road, he reached Brunswick, Missouri. The manager of a little printing office in the town offered him a job which attracted him. He accepted it and remained in Brunswick some years, assisting on a printing-press as a "printer's devil".

At the noon hour, one day, he sat with his head buried in a newspaper. Some one said, as he slapped Bruce on the back, "Hello, Branch, what are you doing way out here?" Bruce seemed greatly surprised to hear some one call him Branch, for he had long ago changed his name to Blanche. He raised his head and looked all around but did not see any one, and so he went on with his reading. After a short time, "flap" went a sound. Something had slapped him on the back of his neck.

He jumped up and looked around but still did not see any one. Then he said in a loud voice, "Who are you, anyhow? Stop slapping me". And with that, he sat down again.

A little shrill voice answered, "Yes, you are out here working on a printing-press. I've been following you. You came all the way from Virginia. What do you know about a printing-press? In the early days no one at all could do any printing in your state, because the state did not allow it".

Blanche Bruce scowled and frowned and looked all around but did not see any one. And so he shouted out, "Oh hush! I've been reading all about printing. In the early days none of the American colonies encouraged printing. Some of the printers were even arrested for printing. For thirty years Cambridge, Massachusetts, was the only place in America where printing was done, and that was controlled by the Government. Now, you shut up!" After that, he arose and went in to begin his work.

For years, Bruce says, he heard no more of the little voice, but he could not forget that experience. In spite of it, he worked in Brunswick until he decided to move on to Lawrence, Kansas. By this time, of course, he had grown a great deal in height and size. His love for books had not waned, and his experience in the Civil War had taught him a great deal.

Seeing that the few Negro children in Lawrence were ignorant, he opened a school for them, but finding later that there were more children in Hannibal, Missouri, who needed a school, he went there and began teaching.

Bruce kept on thinking and moving until one day, in the year 1866, he found himself at Oberlin, Ohio, sawing wood. "Whew! I am so tired, I believe I'll sit down on this log and rest a while", he said to himself, as he wiped the perspiration from his forehead with his hand. No sooner had he sat down, than "flap" went something across his back. He jumped up, looked all around and said to himself, "That's strange!"

"Yes, it is strange", said a little shrill voice, "but I've been following you all the time. I hear you are out here sawing wood to keep yourself in Oberlin College. Just keep at it".

Bruce seemed really disturbed now, for this voice sounded exactly like that one in Brunswick, Missouri, years before. Said he in a gruff voice, "I don't know what you are, but get on away or

I'll saw you". He finished his sawing that day and sawed many more days before the end of the college year.

In company with other students who were going to their homes for the summer, he left Oberlin College bound for some place, he really did not know where. By some means he continued to travel, and finally found himself working on a big vessel which ran between Council Bluffs, Iowa, and St. Louis, Missouri. One day, after his vessel was anchored at St. Louis, he secured a newspaper and sat down to his old trade. He read and read and finally came across an article which told how badly Mississippi was needing educated men. Many of her men had been killed in the war, and until more food was raised there was really little left for the people to eat. Bruce read some parts of the article a second time, and while he sat there, decided to start for Mississippi as soon as he could.

The way soon opened, and after some days of travel, he found himself in Mississippi. Mississippi seemed to need him badly. Very soon, the military Governor-General of that State appointed him to take charge of the election in a whole county. The name of that county was Tallahatchie. He traveled over it from town to town, making speeches and influencing men, until after the election. Within a year, he met the Mississippi Legislature at Jackson and was elected as Sergeant-at-arms in the Senate. In this position, he assisted in many ways the one who presided over the Senate. If any one in the Senate was disorderly, he arrested him.

Bruce kept on traveling until the Governor of Mississippi noticed him and appointed him as Tax Assessor of Bolivar County. He had to determine how much taxes the people in that county should pay. He afterwards stepped into the position of Sheriff and Tax Collector, and then Superintendent of Schools of that county. Before leaving Bolivar County, he bought a plantation.

Blanche Kelso Bruce had been traveling for over thirty years now. The greatest milestone in his journey, he said to a friend one day, was now in sight. The State of Mississippi had elected him to represent her in the United States Senate at Washington, D. C. He knew little about the customs in the Senate, but one day he found himself sitting in the Senate Chamber ready to receive what was called his induction into office.

Something within him, which sounded just as plainly as the shrill voice at Oberlin had sounded, seemed to say, "You will have no one to escort you up the aisle like the other new senators have; but you have traveled all the way from Farmville, Virginia, as a slave, to Washington, D. C., as a senator, so go right ahead".

Senator Bruce straightened up and said to himself, "Ah! I guess that's the something within me that has been following me all these years. It's my turn to go up now, and I am going".

When he had gotten about half way up the aisle, a tall gentleman touched him on the arm. He stood for a moment as if he were dreaming or as if he were listening to the shrill voice again. But no, this was a real man who said to him, "Excuse me, Mr. Bruce, I did not until this moment see that you were without an escort. Permit me. My name is Conkling". He linked his arm in that of Senator Bruce and they marched up to the desk and back to their seats together.

It was this man, Senator Roscoe Conkling of New York, who assisted Senator Bruce in gaining the chairmanship of one committee in the Senate and in securing a place on other committees. A few years later, when a son was born to Senator and Mrs. Bruce, he was named Roscoe Conkling Bruce, in honor of the Senator.

Although, as he had said, the greatest milestone in his journey had been reached, and he had served in the Senate for six years, the journey was not yet completed. He went on and became Register of the United States Treasury.

One morning, as he sat in his office looking at a five-dollar bill, some one seemed to shake him. He looked up but there was nobody in the room but him. He said that he thought he had simply made a mistake, but soon something within that sounded just like the little shrill voice of bygone days seemed to say, "You've been a pretty good traveler. Here you are again. I hear that not a single paper dollar can be issued unless the name 'B. K. Bruce, Register of the Treasury', is stamped in the lower left-hand corner of it".

Mr. Bruce now leaned back and laughed outright, "Ha! ha! ha!" He seemed to realize that all these years no voice outside of his inner self had been talking to him.

He served in the position of Register of the Treasury for four years, then retired to private life as a platform lecturer. Later, he entered upon his duties as Recorder of Deeds of the District of Columbia and as a trustee of the Washington Public Schools. The end of his long fifty-seven-year journey, which came March 17, 1898, found him as Register of the United States Treasury for a second time.

SAMUEL COLERIDGE-TAYLOR

Chapter VII

SAMUEL COLERIDGE-TAYLOR

THE MUSICIAN

1875–1912

IN one of the poorer quarters of London, England, a curly-headed boy was seen one day playing marbles with one hand and holding a little violin in the other. Passers-by stopped to get a closer picture of the little marble-player with the violin until there was quite an audience surrounding him and the other boys at their play.

Many of the people in the houses in that block, attracted by the crowd, either came to their doors or looked out of their windows. Among those attracted to their windows was the conductor of a theatre orchestra, who was giving a music lesson in a nearby house. He spied the little curly-headed boy with the violin, ran out and coaxed him into the house.

After talking to the boy a few minutes, the orchestra conductor took the little violin and played a short, beautiful tune. The boy in turn agreed to play. The man set up before the child a simple violin selection and asked if he could play it. Without saying a word the little fellow looked at the sheet of music, lifted his little violin to his shoulder and began to play in perfect time and tune. The orchestra conductor stood looking on in surprise. When that selection was finished, he immediately set up another. This, too, the boy played with the same ease.

After he had played several pieces in this manner, the orchestra conductor with his arms about him asked his name.

"Samuel Coleridge-Taylor is my name", replied he. The orchestra conductor next asked the boy who his parents were and where he lived. Little Coleridge-Taylor quickly answered the question and began to pull away from his new friend. The orchestra conductor, feeling that the boy wished to get back to his fellow marble-players, patted him on the back, assured him that he would come to see him soon and let him go.

Little Coleridge-Taylor ran every step of the way until he reached the place where he had been playing marbles with the boys. He looked all around, but, seeing no one, set out for home. As soon as he reached home, he began to tell his mother about the man who played his little violin.

The orchestra conductor spoke to each of his students that day about the curly-headed boy with the violin. Even in the middle of a lesson, he stopped occasionally to speak about the boy. As soon as his day's work was done, he set out making his way to the street and the number of the house which Coleridge-Taylor had given him. He kept on looking up at the numbers on the houses until he reached the right one. He stepped up and rang the door-bell. Happily little Coleridge-Taylor came to the door; he at once recognized his new friend and invited him in. His mother, hearing a strange voice, came into the room, too.

Coleridge-Taylor said, "This is the gentleman who played my violin, mother".

The orchestra conductor bowed to her, introduced himself and offered an apology for entering her home. Little Coleridge-Taylor joined with his mother in assuring the gentleman that that was all right. The orchestra conductor thanked them both, and began to tell of the musical gifts of the child and how he should be educated.

For a long time the mother sat quietly listening. Finally she said, calling the orchestra conductor by his name, "Mr. Beckwith, you do not understand. My boy's father, Dr. Daniel Hughes Taylor, left us alone when the boy was one year old, and my present husband is just a working man". All was quiet for a few minutes.

Presently Mr. Beckwith said sympathetically, "Please tell me where the boy's father is".

The sturdy young English mother, bracing herself up in her chair, said falteringly, "My boy's father came from his native country, Sierra Leone, Africa, to London. He entered University College and was graduated as a medical student. His college career was so brilliant that he became a member of the Royal College of Surgeons. He was also connected with the Royal College of Physicians. As an assistant to another physician, he practiced for a while in London and did well.

"Unfortunately for him, his partner moved away and the patients refused to continue with my husband because he was an African. He became discouraged and returned to his native country. My boy and I lived for five years with some of my friends in their three-room apartment. It was my friend's husband who gave Samuel the little violin a few months ago on his fifth birthday."

Mr. Beckwith sat quietly listening to every word. Once or twice he took out his handkerchief and wiped his eyes. When the young mother had finished her touching story, he assured her of his deep interest and arose to go. However, before leaving, he asked if she would let the boy come to him for a violin lesson the next day. She consented and Mr. Beckwith, without further word, bade her and little Samuel good-night.

The next day at the appointed hour, little Samuel and his mother found Mr. Beckwith's studio. Seeing the sign on the door "Walk In" they walked in and took their seats. The entire surroundings—the beautiful room, the piano, the violins, the cabinet with its many pieces of music, held their attention.

In the midst of this, Mr. Beckwith entered and bowed to them. He immediately called Coleridge-Taylor forth and began to give him a lesson. The little fellow took hold of his violin, at first a bit timidly, but with encouragement and assurance from his teacher he gradually played as though he had forgotten everything but the music before him. When his lesson was over he left the studio with beaming face but returned again and again for his lessons.

When the child was six, Mr. Beckwith arranged for him to appear in a recital given by his students. Standing on a couple of boxes which raised him above the ferns on the platform, little Samuel drew forth much applause from the audience by his performance.

He continued to study and take lessons of

Beckwith. Finally, Mr. Beckwith succeeded in getting him into the Old British School, which was partly kept up by subscriptions from friends. The headmaster of the school, as the principal was called, welcomed the boy and soon began to pay attention to him and talk about his unusual ability. His schoolmates soon began to call him "Coaly". Sometimes a boy sitting behind "Coaly" would run his fingers through "Coaly's" silken mop of thick, black hair. Such attentions always made "Coaly" smile.

The headmaster and other masters, as the teachers were called, encouraged him to work hard on his music. His classmaster, fond of singing himself, created enthusiasm for the weekly singing lessons, during which Coleridge-Taylor stood on a table in front of the class and led with his violin.

At the request of this teacher, Coleridge-Taylor sat up one night, when he was only nine years old, and wrote an original tune for the hymn, "God Save the Queen". The next day, standing on a table in front of his class, he played the tune and sang it with his sweet treble voice until his classmates learned to sing it too. He often sang for visitors without seeming to think that he had done any more than the other boys.

The time of the year soon came around when the headmaster began to make his annual visit to friends for funds for the school. As usual, he called upon the choirmaster of St. George's Presbyterian Church, who was always on the lookout for boys with good voices. After greeting him heartily and chatting with him a while, the choirmaster asked if there were any good voices in the school.

The headmaster hesitated a moment and then said, "I have a little boy in my classes who takes to music as a fish takes to water, but he is a colored boy".

The choirmaster replied, saying, "Well, I am much more concerned about his voice than about his color; send him over to see me".

The next day Coleridge-Taylor went to see the choirmaster. He seemed to hesitate and to shrink away when the choirmaster called him up to sing. However, as soon as he sang, the choirmaster entered his name for the next vacancy in the choir.

Just after Coleridge-Taylor left the choirmaster's home, the thought of offering prizes to the Old British School for a singing contest suddenly dawned upon the choirmaster. He thought the matter over carefully and laid it before the headmaster of the school, who in turn presented it to the school. Twenty boys, among whom was Coleridge-Taylor, at once offered to enter the contest. A song called "Cherry Ripe" was selected. For several weeks "Cherry Ripe" was practiced and talked about as the only school topic.

The afternoon set for the contest finally came. All the boys assembled in the chapel, with the twenty boys in the contest occupying the front seats. While every one sat anxiously waiting for the singing to begin, the headmaster rose, stated the meaning of the occasion and called forth the first singer. A lad with confident air arose, walked to the platform and sang as though he thought he were a nightingale. Then another and another came forward until all had sung except one little bushy-headed, brown-skinned boy. All eyes were now fixed upon him as he made his way to the platform with his usual shyness. He found his place and began to pour forth such sweet, true, mellow tones that all began to whisper softly, "Coaly has it. Coaly has it". The song was finished in the midst of uproarious applause. The judges went out quietly and soon returned with the verdict unanimously in favor of "Coaly".

Very soon after Coleridge-Taylor had won the prize this choirmaster, Colonel Herbert A. Walters by name, took him under his care and looked after him until he became a man. Finding him quick, eager and with a wonderful ear for music, Colonel Walters, in addition to teaching him some simple theory of music, gave him voice production and solo singing. He soon placed him in St. George's choir as solo boy. Coleridge-Taylor appeared in many of St. George's concerts and later in those of another church as a singer and as a violinist.

During all these years, he had continued his violin lessons with Mr. Beckwith. When he was only twelve years old he was frequently sought out by music lovers and musicians to play for them on many important occasions. Now that he was solo boy in the choir it seemed that he had found a position for the remainder of his life, but all of a sudden, however, at the age of fifteen, his treble voice broke, making it impossible for him to continue as a solo boy.

He remained as a member of the choir for ten years longer. Since he could not continue as vocal soloist, Colonel Walters set out to secure for him a start in the larger musical world. A London firm of piano makers, wishing to help Colonel Walters and the boy, offered to apprentice him to the piano-tuning trade. Colonel Walters thanked them very graciously but went away saying that piano-tuning for such a musical genius would be even worse than using a fine razor to chop firewood.

The colonel, although he was not a wealthy man, finally offered Coleridge-Taylor a higher musical education. Both Coleridge-Taylor and his mother thanked him enthusiastically. The colonel, after visiting and comparing all the musical colleges in London, chose for his brown boy student the Royal College of Music. Coleridge-Taylor was enrolled as a student in that college and began his study at the Christmas term of 1890. He was seemingly even more shy than usual; however, he began to study the violin, the piano and harmony. Before a great while, each of his teachers in these subjects began to speak with enthusiasm about his success. Coleridge-Taylor, however, was really more interested in writing music than in anything else.

During his first year in the college, he wrote some anthems which so attracted the attention of Colonel Walters that he brought them to the notice of the professors. While Coleridge-Taylor was under the instruction of one of the greatest of the college professors in his second year, he wrote four other anthems. These anthems so interested all of the professors of the college that they began to speak freely of him as a genius and a composer.

For a long time, it had been the custom of the Royal College to offer nine scholarships to students winning in a certain musical contest. Coleridge-Taylor entered this contest during his third year in the college and won the scholarship for the best piece of music written. He composed so many pieces each year that when he was twenty years old the Royal College permitted him to give a concert at which he used practically his compositions only.

Two years later, he appeared on the program of a students' concert as a composer. At the conclusion of his number, he ran upstairs and hid in the organ room. The applause, however, was so great that his professor, who had also been intensely interested, found him and almost had to drag him down.

From this time apparently the eyes of musical critics were focused on the young musician. Sometimes he would leave public gatherings and seek his mother's kitchen. There he would sit and sing over to her this or that tune which he had composed.

During his fourth year in college, he won another prize for musical composition. Following this, there were few college concert programs in London which did not contain a musical number bearing Coleridge-Taylor's name. He took up the study of the pipe-organ and continued it for two terms but dropped it, saying, "The organ is far too mechanical and soulless for me".

II

Shortly after Coleridge-Taylor had completed his six years in the Royal College, he sat one afternoon in his humble home on a dingy street in London, composing a difficult piece of music. Near his doorway, an organ-grinder began to fill the air with his mechanical tunes. Coleridge-Taylor, greatly disturbed, threw down his pen, rushed out and bade the organ-grinder go away. A neighbor also hurried out, asking as she shook her fist at Coleridge-Taylor and ran towards the organ-grinder, "Why are you sending this man away?"

Coleridge-Taylor replied, "I am a composer of music, and I am engaged on a long composition. The grinding noise of that organ is serious for me".

"Well", said she, "my children like the organ as much as you dislike it. We have as much right to have it as you have to send the man away. As for your piano, it is a good thing that it is interrupted, for there is too much of it for us". At that juncture a policeman came upon the scene, and the organ-grinder moved on.

Coleridge-Taylor began to inquire about his neighbor's children. He was told that she had tipped the organ-grinder to come and play outside of her house for the amusement of a sick child. When the organ-grinder came the next day, Coleridge-Taylor went out and talked with him about the time of his appearance there each day so that he might plan to avoid composing music at that time. Although his evening practice had seemingly become a real part of his life, for a long time he refrained from touching his piano during the night hours because of the sick child.

Disturbed by all sorts of noises in that street, he and his mother's family moved to more quiet quarters. These new surroundings seemed to inspire him so that he was able to give evening violin lessons at the conservatory of music, conduct a small orchestral class and compose the music for "Hiawatha's Wedding Feast" during the same year.

Early in the next year, Coleridge-Taylor received from the oldest of the great English musical societies a commission, or a special invitation, to write a selection for its Annual Festival. Overjoyed because of this invitation, he set to work at once and composed a piece called "Ballade in A Minor". Soon he began his rehearsals with the orchestra and chorus which were to render it. He conducted these rehearsals until the very night of the concert, September 12, 1898.

That night people from all parts of London poured into the hall until it was crowded. The hour for the concert was at hand. The orchestra and the chorus were in their places. The orchestra conductor, Samuel Coleridge-Taylor, a light brown-skinned, quick-moving, polished young man, with bright eyes and a large head covered with rather long, thick, silken hair, entered. The audience, not knowing what he looked like, paused for a moment, then broke into a storm of applause.

He bowed, took up his baton and gave the signal. The orchestra and then the chorus began. The first strains of the music seemed to charm the people. Each part followed with increasing interest. At the close of the performance, the audience again broke forth with thunderous applause. Three times Coleridge-Taylor was compelled to come forward to acknowledge the appreciation of the audience. Many people crowded around him and congratulated him and invited him out to social affairs. The next day the London papers were all praising Coleridge-Taylor both as a composer and as an orchestra conductor.

As soon as this event was over, he again turned his attention to Longfellow's "Hiawatha". He says that he committed the whole poem to memory and lived with the words until they became a part of him. Just two months after he conducted the "Ballade in A Minor", "Hiawatha's Wedding Feast", his next composition, was sung by the choir and orchestra of his own college—The Royal College of Music.

On the evening of this concert, Royal College Hall buzzed with a crowded, expectant audience. Every seat was occupied. People were sitting on the steps of the platform and standing in the aisles. When everything was in readiness for the concert to begin, Sir Charles Stanford, a Professor in the Royal College of Music, took up the baton. The trumpets gave out the simple, charming opening subject of the "Wedding Feast". The audience sat as if in a trance. Interest grew and grew as the words of Chibiabos, the friend of Hiawatha and the sweetest of all singers, were sung:

Onaway! Awake, beloved!
Thou the wild-flower of the forest!
Thou the wild-bird of the prairie!
Thou with eyes so soft and fawn-like!
If thou only lookest at me,
I am happy, I am happy
As the lilies of the prairie,
When they feel the dew upon them!

When the last strains of the orchestra died away, the applause of the audience was loud and long. Coleridge-Taylor was called forth in the midst of the demonstration. He soon disappeared, only to be called back again and again. As the people departed from the concert, they saw Coleridge-Taylor, greatly embarrassed because of his great success, dodging into doorways to get out of their sight. The next morning, he seemed to be even more embarrassed as he glanced at the newspapers and saw in large headlines his name mentioned as a great musician.

III

One evening, long before this concert, every light in the home of the Walmisleys, a well-to-do English family, burned with unusual brightness. Vases and bowls of beautiful flowers scented the atmosphere. Mr. and Mrs. Walmisley, assisted by their attractive and accomplished daughter Jessie, stood in their large parlors receiving their guests, among whom was Coleridge-Taylor. In the midst of the festivities, it was announced that Coleridge-Taylor would play a violin selection. He came forth and began to play to the piano accompaniment of Miss Jessie Walmisley, who was also a student at the Royal College of Music. The hush of silence which always possessed audiences when Coleridge-Taylor played his violin, at once stole over this happy group of cultured people. When he had finished, his hearers called him back several times. As the guests departed from the Walmisley home that evening, they were all talking about their charming hostess and the genius of the young violinist.

Some months later, Miss Walmisley's professors required her to practice some violin and piano duets as vacation exercises. In her search for some one with whom to practice, she thought of the talented young Negro whom she had accompanied at her mother's party. She wrote to the College for his address but through mistake, the address of another player by the name of Coleridge was sent to her. She went in search of him. Although disappointed at meeting the wrong person, she continued her inquiry and search until she found the home of Coleridge-Taylor.

His mother came to the door. Upon Miss

Walmisley's request to see him about practicing with her, his mother said, "I will ask him if he can see you".

Two minutes later Coleridge-Taylor himself came to the door smiling and shaking his head, saying, "Can't do it now, can't possibly do it now. I am writing a quartet".

She replied as she started off, "I am sorry to have troubled you".

He stood looking at her and rather suddenly said, "Wait a moment".

"I could not think of bothering you now", she replied.

Coleridge-Taylor ran out and insisted that she come in. While she waited, he hurried back to his room and wrote down some notes. Soon he came forward again with a smile, saying, "I can give you an hour".

They practiced just one hour. After thanking him many times, Miss Walmisley started to go, but suddenly hesitated to ask if he could possibly help her again. He consented, and at the close of each practice he kept on promising a little more time. Perhaps before they fully realized it, two years had passed and they had become fast musical friends. She joined his orchestral class and assisted him greatly.

Their friendship, both realized, had steadily ripened. Miss Walmisley seemed puzzled to know whether she should permit herself to love Coleridge-Taylor. She ceased for a time to meet him or to have anything at all to do with his class. During this period of freedom from his company, she realized that she really loved him, and she made up her mind to stand by him. They soon became engaged.

After this, whenever it was convenient and fitting, Miss Walmisley would read through proofs of his compositions and sing his new songs for him. One day while they were attending a concert in a town near London, the usher announced to their surprise and embarrassment, their engagement.

During these days, Coleridge-Taylor was composing almost without stopping except for his meals and a long walk with Miss Walmisley each day. With invitations to write for great occasions pouring in upon him, he composed "The Death of Minnehaha", "The Song of Hiawatha" and other numbers. The theme of "The Song of Hiawatha" Coleridge-Taylor says he took from a plantation melody, "Nobody Knows the Trouble I've Seen", which he had recently heard sung by the famous Fisk Jubilee Singers. It was through these singers, says he, that he first learned to appreciate the beautiful Negro folk songs.

Now that Coleridge-Taylor, at the age of twenty-four, felt sure of his ability to support a family, he and Miss Walmisley planned a quiet wedding in a little church in Croydon. In their attempt to keep the matter a secret, they ordered an old rickety, weather-beaten carriage to wait outside of the church to take them away after the wedding. To their surprise, the news of the wedding had leaked out and when they entered the church, there sat a church full of friends waiting for the ceremony. Immediately following the ceremony Coleridge-Taylor and his bride left the town for two weeks.

During that time Coleridge-Taylor continued his work on "Hiawatha's Departure", which was afterwards given by a famous choir and orchestra of a thousand members, with the composer as the conductor.

Coleridge-Taylor soon became a professor in the University of London. He was spoken of as one of the three greatest British orchestra conductors of his time. During the thirteen years of his happy married life, he was busy composing music, teaching and conducting orchestras. It was during these years that his two children—Gwendolen and Hiawatha—were born.

He traveled England from end to end and visited America four times. On his third visit to America, he wrote the first sketches of "A Tale of Old Japan", which came next in popularity to "Hiawatha".

The greater part of 1912 was gloomy, and the sun failed to shine in England. Coleridge-Taylor seemed sad because of this, but he worked hard and so completely finished up all of his compositions that he said to his wife, "I have never felt so free of work in my life". He planned to go to the seashore but his son Hiawatha contracted influenza in a severe storm, and so he remained at home and amused himself by taking long walks.

One morning he said, "I have had a lovely dream".

"What, another lovely dream? What is it this time?" said Mrs. Coleridge-Taylor.

He answered, "Oh, I dreamt I saw Hurlstone in Heaven. [Hurlstone was a friend who had recently died.] I was just entering. We didn't speak but we embraced each other. That means I am going to die". Mrs. Coleridge-Taylor, insisting that it was only a dream, tried in vain to cheer him.

One August morning of this gloomy year, Gwendolen and he went out and bought some yellow chrysanthemums for Mrs. Coleridge-Taylor. On their return Coleridge-Taylor gave them to his wife and bade her good-bye. He left to go to a moving-picture show but became suddenly ill, and fell at the station where he bought his ticket. With difficulty he reached home. For several days, he did not seem to be dangerously ill, but acute pneumonia soon developed. He became steadily worse. On Sunday of that week, September 1st, he was propped up in bed with a pillow. He seemed to imagine an orchestra before him and an audience behind him. He conducted a performance, beat time with both arms and smiled his approval here and there. That smile never left his face. Still smiling and conducting, he sank back on his pillow and passed away.

The funeral services were held at St. Michael's Church, Croydon, England, September 5, 1912. People came from all parts of England. Many were in the church long before the services began. Mr. H. L. Balfour, organist of the Royal Choral Society, played during this period of waiting, selections from Coleridge-Taylor's works. Among them was a selection from "Hiawatha's Wedding Feast"—"Chibiabos, the sweetest of all singers, the best of all musicians". The beautiful slow movement from Coleridge-Taylor's violin Concerto in G Minor, which was not then published, was played also. The services closed with his funeral march from "The Death of Minnehaha".

The inscription on the headstone which marks his grave reads as follows:

In Memory of
SAMUEL COLERIDGE-TAYLOR
who died on
September 1, 1912
at the age of 37
Bequeathing to the World
A Heritage of an undying Beauty.
His Music Lives.
It was his own, and drawn from vital fountains.
It pulsed with his own life,
But now it is his immortality.
He lives while music lives.
Too young to die—
His great simplicity, his happy courage
In an alien world,
His gentleness made all that knew him love him.

Sleep, crowned with fame, fearless of change or time;
Sleep, like remembered music in the soul,
Silent, immortal; while our discords climb
To that great chord which shall resolve the whole.

Silent, with Mozart, on that solemn shore;
Secure, where neither waves nor hearts can break;
Sleep, till the master of the world once more
Touch the remembered strings and bid thee wake.

BENJAMIN BANNEKER

Chapter VIII

BENJAMIN BANNEKER

Astronomer and Surveyor

1732–1804

I

Childhood

ONE winter evening long ago, everything in Baltimore County, Maryland, was covered with deep snow. Icicles nearly a foot long hung from the roofs of the rough log cabins. The trees of the thick forest which extended for miles around stood like silent ghosts in the stillness, for no one in all that wooded country stirred out on such an evening.

Far away from the other cabins stood the Banneker cabin. Little Benjamin Banneker was busy before a glowing wood fire roasting big, fat chestnuts in the hot embers. His grandmother sat in the corner in a quaint split-bottom, white-oak chair, knitting and telling him about her native country, England.

She said, "When I was in England, milking the cows on a cattle farm was a part of my daily duties. One day I was accused of stealing a pail of milk which had in fact been kicked over by the cow. Instead of meting out a more severe punishment, the officers of the law sentenced me to be shipped to America. Being unable to pay for my passage, I was sold, upon my arrival in America, to a tobacco planter on the Patapsco River to serve a period of seven years to pay the cost of my passage".

Silence reigned for a few moments, then she continued, "I worked out my period of service, then bought a part of the farm on which I had worked. I also bought two African slaves from a ship in the Chesapeake Bay. One of the slaves, your grandfather, the son of an African king, had been stolen from the coast of Africa".

Little Benjamin then asked, pointing to his grandfather, who was sitting on the other side of the hearth, "Was grandfather that man, grandmother?"

"Yes", she said. She continued her story, ending with a beautiful description of the River Thames, the Tower of London, and Westminster Abbey.

All was still for a while, except for the occasional moving of Benjamin and the bursting of chestnuts. Benjamin's grandfather, who was sitting with his eyes closed, now broke the silence. Said he, "Benjamin, what are you going to be when you are a man, a *chestnut* roaster?"

"I am going to be—I am going to be—what is it, grandmother? You know you told me a story about the man who knew all the stars", said Benjamin.

"An astronomer", replied his grandmother.

"That's it, I am going to be an astronomer", answered Benjamin.

"You have changed in the last day or two, then", said his grandfather. "The day your grandmother told you about the man who could figure so well with his head, you said you would be that".

"That man was a born mathematician", suggested his grandmother.

Benjamin began to blink his eyelids rapidly and to twist and turn for an answer. Soon his mouth flew open saying, "Well, I'll be both, I'll be both!"

His grandmother interrupted by saying, "I wonder what has become of my little inventor? Benjamin, you remember what you said when I told you the story about that inventor".

Benjamin gave that look which always said, "Well, I am caught"; but soon he recovered and with this reply, "I can tell you what I am going to do. I am going to school first to learn to figure. And then while I am farming a little for my living I can stay up at night and watch the stars. And in the afternoon I can study and invent things until I am tired, and then I can go out and watch my bees".

"When are you going to sleep, my boy?" asked his grandmother.

"In the morning", said he.

"And you are going to have a farm and bees, too?" she asked.

"Yes, grandmother", said Benjamin, "we might just as well have something while we are here. Father says that he will never take mother and me to his native country—Africa—to live. Grandmother, did you and grandfather have any children besides mother?"

"Yes, there were three other children", replied his grandmother.

"When father and mother were married", said Benjamin, "mother didn't change her name at all from Mary Banneker as the ladies do now, but father changed his name to Robert Banneker.

I am glad of it, for you see you are Banneker, grandfather is Banneker, I am Banneker and all of us are Bannekers now".

"My boy", interrupted his grandfather, "I am waiting to hear how you are going to buy a farm."

"Oh, grandfather", said Benjamin as he arose, "you remember that mother and father gave Mr. Gist seven thousand pounds of tobacco and Mr. Gist gave them one hundred acres of land here in Baltimore County. Grandfather, don't you think father will give me some of this land? He cannot use it all."

"Yes, when you are older, Benjamin. But you must go to school and learn to read first", answered his grandfather.

"Yes but—ouch, that coal is hot!" cried Benjamin as he shook his hand, danced about the floor and buried his fingers in a pillow. That time he had picked up a hot coal instead of a chestnut. Some time after his fingers were "doctored" and he was apparently snug in bed for the night, he shook his hands and cried out for his grandmother.

Benjamin rose the next morning, and after breakfast, began again to roast chestnuts. Morning after morning he roasted chestnuts until the snow had all cleared away. Then he entered a pay school and soon learned to read, write and do some arithmetic. After some months had passed he began to borrow books and to study by himself.

II

Farmer and Mathematician

When Benjamin was about twenty-seven, his father died. As he had prophesied when he was a boy, his father's farm bought with the tobacco, became his. On this farm was Banneker's house —a log cabin about half a mile from the Patapsco River. In his doorway he often stood looking at the near and distant beautiful hills along the banks of this river. What he said about his bees when he was a boy came true also. These he kept in his orchard; and in the midst of this orchard a spring which never failed, babbled beneath a large golden willow tree. His beautiful garden and his well-kept grounds seemed to give him pleasure.

Banneker never married, but lived alone in retirement after the death of his mother. He cooked his own food and washed his own clothes. All who knew him, and especially those who saw that he was a genius, spoke well of him. He always greeted his visitors cheerfully, and he kept a book in which was written the name of every person by whose visit he felt greatly honored.

Some one who knew him well says that he was a brave-looking, pleasant man with something very noble in his face. He was large and somewhat stout. In his old age he wore a broad-brimmed hat which covered his thick suit of white hair. He always wore a superfine, drab broadcloth coat with a straight collar and long waistcoat. His manners, some one says, were those of a perfect gentleman—kind, generous, hospitable, dignified, pleasing, very modest and unassuming.

He worked on his farm for his living, but found time to study all the books which he could borrow. He studied the Bible, history, biography, travels, romance, and other books, but his greatest interest was in mathematics. Like many other scholars of his day, he often amused himself during his leisure by solving hard problems. Scholars from many parts of the country often sent him difficult problems. It is said that he solved every one sent to him and he often sent in return an original question in rhyme. For example, he sent the following question to Mr. George Ellicott, which was solved by a scholar of Alexandria:

A Cooper and Vintner sat down for a talk,
Both being so groggy, that neither could walk.
Says Cooper to Vintner, "I'm the first of my trade;
There's no kind of vessel but what I have made.
And of any shape, Sir—just what you will;
And of any size, Sir—from a ton to a gill!"
"Then", says the Vintner, "you're the man for me—
Make me a vessel, if we can agree.
The top and the bottom diameter define,
To bear that proportion as fifteen to nine;
Thirty-five inches are just what I crave,
No more and no less, in the depth will I have.
Just thirty-nine gallons this vessel must hold,
Then I will reward you with silver and gold.
Give me your promise, my honest old friend?"
"I'll make it to-morrow, that you may depend!"

So the next day the Cooper his work to discharge,
Soon made the new vessel, but made it too large;
He took out some staves, which made it too small,
And then cursed the vessel, the Vintner and all.
He beat on his breast, "By the Powers!" he swore
He never would work at his trade any more!
Now, my worthy friend, find out, if you can,
The vessel's dimensions and comfort the man.

III

Inventor and Astronomer

When Banneker was about thirty-eight years old he sat day after day working on a clock. Finally he finished it with his imperfect tools and with only a borrowed watch for a model. He had never seen a clock for there was not one, it is said, within fifty miles of him. An article published in

London, England, in 1864, says that Banneker's clock was probably the first clock every part of which was made in America. For many hours and days he turned and adjusted the hands of his clock until they moved smoothly and the clock struck on the hour.

Time passed, and after some years Mr. George Ellicott's family—Quakers from Pennsylvania they were—began to build flour-mills, a store and a post-office in a valley adjoining Banneker's farm. Banneker was now fifty-five years old, and had won the reputation of knowing more than any other person in that county. Mr. Ellicott opened his library to him. He gave him a book which told of the stars. He gave him tables about the moon. He urged him to work out problems for almanacs.

Early every evening Banneker wrapped himself in a big cloak, stretched out upon the ground and lay there all night looking at the stars and planets. At sunrise he rose and went to his house. He slept and rested all the morning and worked in the afternoon. His neighbors peeped through the cracks of his house one morning and saw him resting. They began at once to call him a lazy fellow who would come to no good end.

In spite of this, he compiled an almanac. His first almanac was published for the year 1792.

It so interested one of the great men of the country that he wrote to two almanac publishers of Baltimore about it. These publishers gladly published Banneker's almanac. They said that it was the work of a genius, and that it met the hearty approval of distinguished astronomers.

Banneker wrote Thomas Jefferson, then Secretary of State, on behalf of his people, and sent him one of his almanacs. Mr. Jefferson replied:

Philadelphia, August 30, 1791.

Sir—I thank you sincerely for your letter of the 19th inst. and for the almanac it contained. Nobody wishes more than I do to see such proofs as you exhibit, that nature has given to your race talents equal to those of the other races of men.

I am with great esteem, Sir,

Your most obedient servant,

THOS. JEFFERSON.

IV

SURVEYOR

This strange man, Benjamin Banneker, never went away from home any distance until he was fifty-seven years old. Then he was asked by the commissioners, appointed to run the boundary lines of the District of Columbia, to go with them. He accompanied them.

Later, *The Evening Star,* a Washington daily paper, said, "Major L'Enfant, the engineer, bossed the job while Benjamin Banneker did the work".

On Banneker's return home from Washington he told his friends that during that trip he had not touched strong drink, his one temptation. "For", said he, "I feared to trust myself even with wine, lest it should steal away the little sense I had." In those days wines and liquors were upon the tables of the best families.

Perhaps no one alive today knows the exact day of Banneker's death. In the fall, probably of 1804, on a beautiful day, he walked out on the hills apparently seeking the sunlight as a tonic. While walking, he met a neighbor to whom he told his condition. He and his neighbor walked along slowly to his house. He lay down at once upon his couch, became speechless and died.

During a previous illness he had asked that all his papers, almanacs, and the like, be given at his death to Mr. Ellicott. Just two days after his death and while he was being buried, his house burned to the ground. It burned so rapidly that the clock and all his papers were destroyed. A feather bed on which he had slept for many years was removed at his death. The sister to whom he gave it opened it some years later and in it was found a purse of money.

Benjamin Banneker was well known on two continents. An article written about him in 1864 by a member of the London Emancipation Society says, "Though no monument marks the spot where he was born and lived a true and high life and was buried, yet history must record that the most original scientific intellect which the South has yet produced was that of the African, Benjamin Banneker".

PHILLIS WHEATLEY

Chapter IX

PHILLIS WHEATLEY

First Poetess of Her Race on American Soil

1753–1784

IN 1753 a baby girl was born on the Western Coast of Africa. Her mother did not sit for hours making beautiful little dresses and doing embroidery for her, for that is not the custom in Africa. Babies do not need many clothes in that warm country. There little children, and grown people too, run around with just a piece of cloth tied about their waists.

The child was not robust, but she grew and grew until she soon became her mother's companion. Her mother, believing that a Great Spirit lives in the sun, went out of her little thatched-roof house every morning and prostrated herself to pour out water before the rising sun. The child often watched the water as it streamed down, and sometimes she jumped and clapped her little hands with glee.

One bright morning, after this religious ceremony was performed and breakfast was over, the girl ran out to play with the other children. She was shedding her front teeth, but she was not large for her age and she was none too strong. While she and her playmates were having a happy time, suddenly one of the older children exclaimed, "Hoi! hoi!" Every child looked up and took to its heels. There were strange-looking men hurrying towards them. The children ran and screamed. Our little girl stumbled and fell, and the man, pursuing her, grabbed her. She kicked and yelled but he held her fast. Her best friend ran behind a big tree, but she, too, was caught. They both kicked and yelled, but they were taken on board an American vessel. Other children who were caught were also brought to the shore kicking and crying.

When there were almost enough of them for a boat-load, the vessel sailed away. They were on the water for many days. The voyage was long and the sea was rough. The waters lashed the sides of the vessel as it rocked to and fro. Some of the children fell to the floor with spells of vomiting. Many a night everything for a time was in complete darkness and everybody was afraid. The little vessel, however, tugged away for days and nights until it sighted lights flickering in the Boston Harbor. All the voyagers, tired and hungry and lonely, rejoiced to be nearing even an unknown land. Soon the boat pulled into the harbor, and although no comforts had been provided for them for the night, weariness of body so overcame loneliness of heart that all of them soon fell asleep.

The news had gone abroad in Boston that a shipload of Africans was approaching. The next morning many Bostonians hurried to the harbor to see the Africans. Among the number of spectators there was a Mrs. John Wheatley, the wife of a tailor. She walked around and looked many of the African girls over from head to foot. Finally she handed the shipmaster money and took our girl away with her to her home.

She and her daughter were busy for a while heating kettles of water, getting out clothing and sewing on a button here and there, preparatory to giving her a good hot bath. When the child was called in she gazed at this strange-looking object which Mrs. Wheatley called a tub. She looked at the soap and felt it. She stretched her eyes as she looked upon the nice white clothes on the chair. She seemed just a little afraid and yet she did as Mrs. Wheatley told her and soon had her bath.

After she was dressed, she met another big surprise. She was taken into a dining-room, where the table was all spread with white linen. There were strange-looking things to eat. She began eating, but said that the food did not taste like the food in Africa. She picked over this and picked over that, but nothing tasted just right. Nevertheless she smiled, and it appeared that she was not very hungry. Mrs. Wheatley watched her closely as she came in touch with all of these strange new things and assured her that in a few days everything would not seem so queer. The girl adopted the customs of the family and they named her Phillis Wheatley.

Every day as Mrs. Wheatley's daughter sat reading or writing letters, Phillis stood looking at her in wonder. Miss Wheatley seemed to write with so much ease that one day Phillis went out with a piece of charcoal in her hand and began to try to write on the side of a wall. Miss Wheatley, who was seated at a window, watched her for a long time, then called her in and showed her how to make some letters. Phillis busied herself for the remainder of the day making letters and keeping Miss Wheatley busy showing her how to make new ones. That night she scarcely wished to leave her writing to go to bed, but Miss Wheatley persuaded her by promising to give her a lesson every day. They set the lesson hour and Phillis went to bed smiling and shaking with joy. Just at the right time every day she walked into Miss Wheatley's room for her lesson. When her lessons were over and she was not busy with her work, she was poring over her books. In less than a year and a half she could easily read the most difficult parts of the Bible without making a mistake. In four years people in different parts of the country began to hear of her and write to her and even furnish her with books. To the surprise of the Wheatleys, she was soon studying and reading the Latin language without any one to help her.

At the age of fourteen, Phillis began to write poetry. Often when some great person of whom she knew died, she would write a poem to commemorate his death. Sometimes she awoke during the night and composed verses but could not recall all of them the next morning. As soon as Mrs. Wheatley discovered this, she began leaving a light and writing materials on the table at Phillis's bedside every night. In cold weather, she always left a fire burning on the hearth in Phillis's room.

For six years Phillis was busy writing poetry and letters and studying and receiving visitors. Many people in England corresponded with her. The educated people of Boston were often seen making their way to the Wheatley home. They talked with Phillis and questioned her, and often asked her to read some of her poetry. When she in turn went to their homes they took great pride in showing her off as a wonder. Those who talked with her marveled at her knowing so much about English poetry, astronomy, ancient history and the Bible.

She continued to write and study. In her nineteenth year she became so thin and pale that the family doctor advised Mrs. Wheatley to give her a sea voyage. Accordingly, the following summer, Phillis set out for London with Mrs. Wheatley's son, who was going there on business. On her arrival in London, after days of travel, some of her friends with whom she had corresponded, met her and welcomed her. As she visited the different ones, she went to dinner parties and theatre parties given in her honor.

When articles about her poetry began to appear in many of the leading London papers, her friends advised her to have all of her poems published. She considered the matter and went with some of them to see a publisher. After reviewing the poems, the publisher accepted them and published them, in 1773, under the title, "Poems on Various Subjects, Religious and Moral, by Phillis Wheatley".

As soon as copies of the poems reached America

and were read, many people expressed doubt about the author being an African girl. The Governor of Massachusetts and seventeen other Bostonians, upon hearing this report, wrote a letter assuring people everywhere that these poems were written by Phillis Wheatley.

Phillis Wheatley's London friends were making plans to present her to their king, George III, who was expected in London within a few days, but word reached her that Mrs. Wheatley was quite ill and wished to see her at once. Her passage was secured for her while she packed her trunk. As fortune would have it, a vessel was sailing that day for Boston. She bade her friends good-bye and put out to sea. The vessel moved slowly, but after days of travel it landed at Boston. She was met at the dock and hurried to the Wheatley home. Mrs. Wheatley caressed her again and again, and lay looking at her for days. For two months Phillis waited upon Mrs. Wheatley and sat by her bedside night after night until she died. Four years later another shock came to the family—Mr. Wheatley died. Seven months after his death his daughter passed away, leaving Phillis alone.

Phillis lived a short while with a friend of the Wheatleys and then rented a room and lived alone. She lived in this way until she began to taste the bitterness of Revolutionary War times. At that time one goose sold for forty dollars and one-fourth of a lamb sold for fifty dollars.

One evening during these hard times she met a handsome man by the name of Peters, who wore a wig and carried a cane. He also kept a grocery store, practiced law and wrote poetry. He began at once to pay court to Phillis. Later he called on her, often took her out for a stroll or to a party until they were married several weeks later.

After the wedding day, Phillis began her daily round of sweeping and cleaning, cooking and washing and ironing. As the years came and went, three children came into their lives. Mr. Peters failed in business and then left to Phillis the support of herself and the children. She secured a job in a cheap boarding-house, where she worked every day from early morning until late at night. She became ill from overwork.

During the first summer of her illness two of her children died. The following winter, cold and snowy, some charitable organization placed in her back yard a load of wood. Although the wood lay there, Peters often went out, leaving Phillis lying on her poor bed without a spark of fire on the hearth. She lay there for weeks.

Friends and distant relatives of the Wheatleys often inquired about Phillis, but no one seemed to know where she was. Finally one December afternoon, in 1784, as a grand-niece of Mrs. Wheatley chanced to be walking up Court Street in Boston she met a funeral. Upon inquiry she learned that it was the funeral of Phillis Wheatley.

AN HYMN TO THE MORNING

Attend my lays, ye ever-honor'd nine;
Assist my labours, and my strain refine;
In smoothest numbers pour the notes along,
For bright aurora now demands my song.

Aurora hail, and all the thousand dyes,
Which deck thy progress through the vaulted skies:
The morn awakes, and wide extends her rays,
On ev'ry leaf the gentle zephyr plays;
Harmonious lays the feather'd race resume,
Part the bright eye, and shake the painted plume.

Ye shady groves, your verdant gloom display
To shield your poet from the burning day;
Calliope awake the sacred lyre,
While thy fair sisters fan the pleasing fire:
The bow'rs, the gales, the variegated skies
In all their pleasures in my bosom rise.

See in the East th' illustrious king of day!
His rising radiance drives the shades away.
But oh! I feel his fervid beams too strong,
And scarce begun, concludes th' abortive song.

—*From Poems on Various Subjects,*
Religious and Moral.

AN HYMN TO THE EVENING

Soon as the sun forsook the eastern main
The pealing thunder shook the heav'nly plain;
Majestic grandeur! From the zephyr's wing,
Exhales the incense of the blooming spring.
Soft purl the streams, the birds renew their notes,
And through the air their mingled music floats.

Through all the heav'ns what beauteous dyes are
spread!
But the west glories in the deepest red:
So may our breasts with ev'ry virtue glow,
The living temples of our God below!
Fill'd with the praise of him who gives the light,
And draws the sable curtains of the night.

Let placid slumbers sooth each weary mind,
At morn to wake more heav'nly, more refin'd;
So shall the labours of the day begin
More pure, more guarded from the snares of sin.
Night's leaden sceptre seals my drowsy eyes,
Then cease, my song, till fair Aurora rise.

Imagination! Who can sing thy force?
Or who describe the swiftness of thy course?
Soaring through air to find the bright abode,
Th' empyreal palace of the thund'ring God,
We on thy pinions can surpass the wind,
And leave the rolling universe behind:
From star to star the mental optics rove,
Measure the skies, and range the realms above.
There in one view we grasp the mighty whole,
Or with new worlds amaze th' unbounded soul.

—*Taken from "Imagination"*

Improve your privileges while they stay,
Ye pupils, and each hour redeem, that bears
Or good or bad report of you to heav'n;
Let sin, that baneful evil to the soul,
By you be shunn'd, nor once remit your guard;
Suppress the deadly serpent in its egg,
Ye blooming plants of human race divine,
An Ethiop tells you 'tis your greatest foe;
Its transient sweetness turns to endless pain,
And in immense perdition sinks the soul.

—Taken from "To the University of Cambridge, in New England"

TOUSSAINT L'OUVERTURE

"MY CHILDREN, CHOOSE YOUR DUTY."

Chapter X

TOUSSAINT L'OUVERTURE

COMMANDER-IN-CHIEF OF AN ARMY

PRESIDENT OF HAYTI

1743–1803

MANY years ago a keen-faced little boy with protruding lips, Toussaint by name, was busy, day by day, tending a great herd of cattle on the Island of Hayti in the West Indies. He started out early every morning, cracking his whip as loudly as he could and getting his cows in line. Often he ran upon one, gave her a cut and called out, "Gee, there, Sally; ha, ha, get in line there, Buck! Come on now! Get up, I say!"

That great herd of cattle marched out at his bidding and began to graze in the deep valleys or on the high mountains. Even the most unruly ones ate around and around in the high grass. All of them ate and ate, and many lay down about noon and chewed their cuds. Toussaint kept his eye on them and at the same time busied himself with other things.

One day he climbed an orange tree, sat in the fork of it and ate oranges until his stomach looked like a little stuffed pouch. Another day he sat lazily under a banana tree, reached up and pulled bananas and ate and ate, and pulled more and ate until he almost fell asleep. Still another day, he hammered away on a hard coconut shell trying to burst it with his fist. Later, he joined the natives for a few minutes as they washed gold from the sands of a stream of water.

While many of the cows were resting from the heat one day, Toussaint ran across to the two great hills of pure salt. "Oh, isn't that beautiful", he said in French. "And do we really eat that salt in our food? And is one of those salt hills two miles long? Well, there must be enough salt there to salt down everything and everybody on the island. I guess we'll be salting down the trees next", he added. The next day at noon he ran away to the blue copper mines and the sulphur mines and gathered a handful of flowers along the way.

As the time passed, he settled down to get out his reading, arithmetic, geometry and Latin. Toussaint's teacher, who was an older slave, had in some way learned quite a little of these subjects and was teaching him secretly at night.

Years passed, and Toussaint continued to tend the cattle as though nothing terrible would ever happen to him. Cattle-tending days finally ceased, and he was promoted to the position of coachman and horse doctor.

Some of the boys eyed him jealously as his carriage dashed by them. They said, "Eh, Mr. Horse Doctor! Drenching old horses, ha, ha!"

Toussaint reared back and held the lines tightly with his arms outstretched. With his horses all sleek and his carriage polished like a looking-glass, he sat back like the grandson of an African king, as he was, and drove with a steady hand.

Apparently happy now in his new position, he married an African young woman whose parents, like his own, had been brought from Africa to Hayti many years before. Many other Africans had been brought over as slaves to this island to work the land because the natives of Hayti had died out. There were also on the island Frenchmen, Spaniards and free Negroes.

Trouble arose among these people and war broke out. For days fires raged, houses were burned and thousands of people fell dead and mortally wounded by bullets. Toussaint looked on, but took no part in the war at first. When his master's home was about to be burned to the ground he broke into it, rescued very valuable articles for his master, and helped his master's family to escape from the island. Then he became a free man, joined the army of slaves and soon rose to the rank of colonel. His army joined with the Spaniards, but when the French gave freedom to all the slaves, his army joined the French and drove the Spaniards from the island.

Before the close of the war, the French made Toussaint brigadier-general. As brigadier-general he made charts of the island and studied them so closely that he knew the course of every stream and the location of every hill.

He fought the Spanish so hard that one after another of their towns fell into the hands of the French. One day a French soldier exclaimed, *"Cet homme fait ouverture partout"* (this man makes an opening everywhere). This saying was passed along by the soldiers, and ever after this Toussaint was called "Toussaint L'Ouverture" (Toussaint, the opening). 'Tis true he had been in battles and made openings, but nothing terrible had happened to him yet.

For a long time the French general seemed to have very little confidence in Toussaint, but once this general was thrown into prison on the island. Toussaint marched at the head of an army of 10,000 men, had him released and restored him to his office. For this act Toussaint was appointed lieutenant-governor of the island. Later on he became commander-in-chief of the French army in Santo Domingo. This was the most important position on the island where Toussaint had been a slave for nearly fifty years. Everywhere people gladly co-operated with him in his administration.

Now that things were going well, he sent his two sons to Paris to be educated. The French rulers publicly praised him and called him the deliverer of Santo Domingo. The French Government presented him with a richly embroidered dress and a suit of superb armor.

Finally Toussaint became president of Hayti for life. It is said that his generals were as obedient to him as children. His soldiers looked upon him as a wonder, and the people generally worshipped him as their deliverer. English officers who fought against him said that he never broke his word.

He was plain in his dress and in all his manners. His dinner often consisted of cakes, fruit and a glass of water. He often jumped on his horse and rode one hundred and fifty miles without rest. Then he would rest for two hours and start out again.

During the last two years of Toussaint's life, a terrible thing happened to him. Napoleon Bonaparte, the ruler of France, because of jealousy, it is said, sent against Toussaint twenty-six war-ships and a number of transports. On board these vessels there were twenty-five thousand French soldiers. When Toussaint looked out upon the ocean and caught a glimpse of this great fleet, he said in his native tongue, "All France is coming to Santo Domingo". The soldiers landed and began to slaughter the natives.

Toussaint's two sons, whom he had not seen for several years, were on one of the ships. When they saw their father they ran to meet him. Toussaint could not speak, but he and his sons threw themselves into each other's arms and wept bitterly. The French general, it is said, saw that he could not use these boys to play a trick on their father and thus make him yield to the French. He then said that the boys must be taken back to France. Toussaint stood before his sons with folded arms, saying in the French language, "My children, choose your duty; whatever it be, I shall always love and bless you".

One of the boys said, "I am done with France. I shall fight by your side, Father." The other boy left his father and returned to France. The cruel war continued. Toussaint and his generals with a small body of troops fortified themselves in a mountainous retreat. The French soldiers tried hard for a long time to dislodge them but they could not. Finally Toussaint sent two of his prisoners with a letter to the French General saying that he would make peace.

A few days later, when Toussaint came forth to greet the French general, guns were fired in Toussaint's honor and all heads were bowed as he passed by. Three hundred horsemen with their sabres drawn followed Toussaint to protect him. He and the French General agreed on a plan, but Napoleon Bonaparte declared that Toussaint must be sent as a prisoner to France.

It was difficult to take him as a prisoner and so a trick was played on him. At the giving of a signal, French soldiers sprang upon his guards and disarmed them. Then they bade Toussaint give up his sword. He yielded it in silence and was taken to his own home. A band of French soldiers came during the night and forced him and his wife to go aboard a French vessel.

On their way to France Toussaint's cabin door was guarded by soldiers. His wrists were chained together. He was not even permitted to talk with his wife. When his vessel landed at Brest, France, a detachment of soldiers took him to Paris and placed him in prison. Winter soon came on and he was taken to an old castle away up in the Jura Mountains. In this old castle there was a cold, wet dungeon partly under ground. He was plunged into this and there he remained for ten months, neglected, humiliated and starved. On the 27th of April, 1803, he was found dead in his dungeon.

Toussaint, the most unhappy man of men!
Whether the whistling rustic tend his plough
Within thy hearing, or thou liest now
Buried in some deep dungeon's earless den,
O miserable chieftain! where and when
Wilt thou find patience? Yet die not; do thou
Wear rather in thy bonds a cheerful brow;
Though fallen thyself, never to rise again,
Live and take comfort. Thou hast left behind
Powers that will work for thee—air, earth and skies;
There's not a breathing of the common wind
That will forget thee—thou hast great allies;
Thy friends are exultations, agonies,
And love, and man's unconquerable mind.

—*William Wordsworth.*

JOSIAH HENSON

Chapter XI

JOSIAH HENSON

The Faithful Servant

1789–1881

JOSIAH HENSON, or "Si" as he was called, tried at the age of fifteen to out-hoe, out-reap, out-husk, out-dance every other boy on his master's plantation in Charles County, Maryland. Boys would sometimes stand around and look at "Si" and talk about the wonderful things he could do and the great stories they had heard about him. One special story they liked to tell.

The story was this: As a child "Si" was such a sickly little fellow his master offered to sell him cheaply to the man who owned his mother. His mother's master hesitated to buy him, saying, "I am afraid the little devil might die. I do not wish to buy a dead brat". Nevertheless, he finally agreed to shoe some horses for Si's master and thus pay a small sum for Si.

Occasionally after some boy was through telling this stock tale, which always produced a laugh, other boys would begin to guess why Si was so great. One said one day, "I guess it's that meat

Si eats at Christmas time. He certainly doesn't get much at any other time".

"No", said another, who slept in the cabin with Si, "Si sleeps more soundly than any one of us in the cabin, and there are twelve of us who sleep in that one room, counting the women and girls. Give me a board and let me show you how Si stretches out on his plank. Now give me some straw to go under my head. How I wish there were a big fire on a hearth to toast my feet before, like Si does as he sleeps!"

"Ha, ha, ha!" laughed the boys as the young fellow stretched out on the board like Si.

A third boy then said, "Well, Si was named for two great men—his master, Dr. Josiah, and Dr. Josiah's uncle, Mr. Henson, who was an army officer". Other boys gave still other reasons for Si's greatness. However, the one thing upon which all were agreed was that Si could out-hoe, out-reap, out-husk, out-dance, out-everything every other boy on his master's plantation in Charles County, Maryland.

Si seemed to grow steadily in favor with his master and the older slaves as well as with the boys. One day he went to his master and reported that the overseer was stealing things at a certain time every day. His master sent him out to watch for the overseer. Just as the overseer came around for his booty, Si ran for his master. His master ran out and caught the overseer in the act of stealing and dismissed him at once.

Josiah, as his master called him, was then promoted to the position of superintendent of the farm, but without pay. He led the slaves. He hoed and plowed early and late. Men and women worked harder and far more cheerfully than usual. The crops were nearly doubled. Josiah often rose from his plank at midnight, hitched the mules to a loaded wagon and drove through mud and rain to the Georgetown or the Washington, D. C., market to sell the produce.

One day as he was selling at McKenny's bakery in Georgetown, he asked Mr. McKenny about a sermon which he had recently heard Mr. McKenny preach. After telling Mr. McKenny that that was the first sermon he had ever heard, he asked how men learned to preach.

Mr. McKenny told him a little about God and the Bible. He went further, saying, "My young man, you must be about nineteen or twenty years old now. You have a good mind. You must learn to preach to your people". This thought seemed to linger with Josiah as he made his way back home that evening hungry and tired.

His master, he learned, had been away at the tavern nearly all day. He ate his supper, called for his master's saddle horse, which he led to the tavern. As his master's body-servant, he alighted and went in. Just as he reached the door he saw his master cornered and a dozen men striking at him with their fists, chairs, crockery and whatever was at hand.

The moment Josiah's master saw him he shouted, "That's it, Josiah! Pitch in! Show me fair play!" Josiah pitched in. He knocked down and shoved and tripped up the fighters, sustaining many bruises on his own head and shoulders. Finally he was able to drag his master out and pack him into a wagon like a bag of corn and drive home. In the scuffle the overseer of Josiah's master's brother got a fall which he attributed to Josiah's roughness.

One week later Josiah's master sent him to a place a few miles away to mail some letters. He took a short cut through a lane which was bounded on either side by a high rail fence and shut in at each end by a large gate. As he passed through the line, he saw the overseer who had fallen that night and three slaves in an adjoining field. On his return, the overseer was seated on the fence. Just as Josiah approached, the overseer jumped from the fence. Two of the slaves sprang from the bushes in front of Josiah and the other slave leaped over the fence behind him. After listening to several commands to light at once, Josiah slipped off his horse. Orders were given him to remove his shirt, but he shook his head. Just then the men struck at him so violently that his horse broke away and ran home. Josiah, in warding off the blow, got into a corner. The overseer ordered the slaves to seize him, but they, knowing Josiah's reputation, hesitated to run upon him. The two slaves that finally ventured upon Josiah were so completely knocked out that the overseer began to fight like a madman. As he struck at Josiah with a piece of fence rail, Josiah lifted his arms to ward off the blow. The bones in Josiah's arms and shoulders cracked like pipe-stems, and he fell headlong to the ground.

When Josiah finally made his way home, his master, already anxious because of the return of the riderless horse, examined him and went in search of the overseer, whom he gave a severe flogging.

With the belief so well fixed that a slave would get well anyhow, no medical aid was provided for Josiah except what came at the hands of his master's sister, Miss Patty. Miss Patty flinched at no responsibility, from wrenching out teeth to setting bones. She splinted Josiah's arms and bound up his back as well as she could.

Five months later, Josiah began to plow, to take up his duties as superintendent, and to make his usual trips to the markets. In about a year, although he was never able after that eventful day to raise his hands to his head, he married a rather efficient, pious girl who, as the years rolled on, bore him twelve children.

Josiah kept the slaves cheerful and busy. He furnished his master with abundance of money, which his master used freely on an eighteen-year-old girl whom he soon married.

The young mistress, in her attempt to save everything, failed to provide her younger brother, then living with her, with enough to eat. The boy went to Josiah with tears in his eyes and asked for food. Josiah shared his own provisions with him. However, in spite of the young mistress's frugality, her husband's good times involved him in debt and in lawsuits with his brother-in-law and others, and finally in ruin. He went to Josiah's cabin one cold night in January. As he sat by the fire warming himself, he began to groan and wring his hands.

"Sick, master?" said Josiah. He kept on groaning. "Can't I help you any way, master?" continued Josiah.

Finally pulling himself together, he said, "Oh, Josiah! I'm ruined, ruined, ruined!"

"How, master?" asked Josiah in excitement.

The master replied, "The courts have ruled against me, and in less than two weeks every slave I have will be put up and sold. There is only one way I can save anything. You can help me. Won't you, Josiah?"

"Yes", replied Josiah.

His master then said, "I want you to run away, Josiah, to my brother in Kentucky, and take all of my slaves with you". Josiah hesitated, saying that he did not know how to get to Kentucky. His master prevailed upon him until he promised to leave the following night for Kentucky.

The next morning Josiah set about making preparations for his journey. When evening came on he counted all of the slaves—eighteen in number, besides himself, his two children and his wife, He loaded a one-horse wagon with oats, meal, bacon and children, and set out about eleven o'clock for Kentucky, nearly a thousand miles away. The men trudged all the way in the cold. Occasionally the women rested by getting a ride on the wagon. After about two months and a half of wonderful experiences on the road, Josiah and the other slaves reached Davis County, Kentucky.

In that county Josiah's master's brother owned a large plantation and about one hundred slaves. Josiah became superintendent of that plantation after several months' stay there. He made himself about as content as he could under the circumstances. He occasionally attended preaching services and camp meetings. At the end of his three years' stay in Kentucky, a Quarterly Conference of the Methodist Episcopal Church admitted him as a minister. About this time Josiah's master sent an agent to Kentucky to sell all his slaves except Josiah and his family, who were to return to Maryland.

Directed by a Methodist minister, Josiah preached his way back through Ohio to Maryland, arriving with two hundred and seventy-five dollars, a horse and his first suit of clothes. His master greeted him, commented upon his fine clothes and sent him out to feed his horse. Josiah put his horse in the stable and went to the kitchen, where he was to sleep. He could not sleep for planning how to get his master to accept money for his freedom. His master was not easily persuaded. Nevertheless, he accepted three hundred and fifty dollars in cash as part payment for Josiah's freedom. Josiah set out again for Kentucky. Days passed before he was again back in his Kentucky cabin with his family. He became angry as soon as he heard how much more he had to pay before he could be free, and yet he went about his work as usual.

A year passed. One day Josiah's master told him that his son Amos was going to New Orleans with a flat-boat load of beef cattle, pigs, poultry, corn and whiskey. He said further that Josiah was to go with his son. Josiah's countenance fell. He said he feared he would never return. When he was ready to go, his wife and children walked to the landing with him, where he bade them good-bye.

Young master Amos, Josiah and three other men were the only persons on the boat. Each one except Josiah took his turn at the helm, usually under the direction of the captain. Josiah took three turns to each of the other men's one. He managed the boat so well that when the captain was struck totally blind on the trip, all depended upon him for reaching New Orleans in safety. However, he did not know the river well enough to travel by night; therefore the boat had to lay by when night came on.

One dark, stormy night, when they were within

a few days' sail of New Orleans, Josiah sat knitting his brow and beating his breast in apparently hopeless despair. Suddenly he rose, saying, "I will kill the four men on the boat, take all the money, scuttle the boat and escape to the North". He walked alone on deck, while the other men were all asleep. Finally he went down, got an ax, and entered his young master's cabin where he lay fast asleep. Josiah raised the ax and was about to strike, but hesitated, saying, "What, commit murder, and I a Christian?" His arm dropped, the ax fell to the floor. Then he said to himself, "Ah, I am glad the thought took hold of me. Evil deeds cannot be hidden. 'Murder will out.' I must not lose all the fruits of my effort at improving myself. I must not lose my character". He shrank back and fell upon his knees.

Soon after they arrived in New Orleans, the cargo was all sold and the men were discharged. Josiah was to be sold the next day and Master Amos was to take passage back on a steamboat at six o'clock that evening.

Josiah could not sleep that night. Just a short while before daylight, Master Amos called him, saying, "My stomach is out of order". Josiah arose and went to him. His illness was so violent that Josiah saw at once that he had the river fever.

By eight o'clock that morning he was helpless. He begged Josiah to stick to him until he reached home again. Josiah sold the flat-boat, placed his young master and the trunk containing the money for the cargo on the steamer and was off for Kentucky by twelve o'clock that day. As he sat by his master, bathing his fevered head, he could not help feeling that God had opened the way for his return to his family in Kentucky.

During the days that Josiah was preaching his way through Ohio, he had heard much about fugitive slaves. He had also met several men who were engaged in assisting fugitives to escape. All of this now came back to him very vividly.

He thought and thought, and then spoke to his wife about running away to the North. Struck with fear, she attempted to show him the dangers in their way. After pleading with her for several days, he told her one night that he was going to take the children and go. She, too, then agreed to go. Josiah wondered now how he could carry his younger children—one of whom was three years and the other only two. He placed them in a tow-sack which his wife had made, lifted it gently across his shoulder and practiced carrying them on his back. This he did for several nights.

Finally the evening in September agreed upon

for their start came around. Everything was ready for the venture with one exception—Josiah had not obtained his master's permission to let little Tom, the eldest child, come home to see his mother. About sundown, he went up to the great house to report his work. After talking with his master for a time he started off as usual. Suddenly he turned carelessly back, saying, "Oh, Master Amos, I almost forgot. Tom's mother wishes to know if you will let him come down a few days; she would like to mend his clothes and fix him up a little".

"Yes, boy, yes, he can go", said Master Amos.

"Thank you, Master Amos, good night", said Josiah.

"Good night, Josiah", said he.

"The Lord bless you, Master Amos", added Josiah, as he and Tom struck a trot for home. Everybody at home was ready to start. The babies were even sitting in the sack. Soon they were all at the ferry. About nine o'clock on that moonless night, Josiah and his family were set across the river in a little skiff rowed by a fellow slave. They walked and walked until they were within two days of reaching Cincinnati, when their food gave out and they were nearly exhausted. Josiah ventured out to beg something for his children to eat. Finally a good woman filled a plate with salty venison and bread and gave it to him, saying, "God bless you".

The children ate and then cried for water. Josiah went in search of water and found a little. Seeing that his old hat leaked too badly to hold water, he pulled off both his shoes, rinsed them out and filled them with water, which he took to his thirsty children, who drank and drank until both shoes were drained.

Refreshed with food and water, they arose and continued their journey. After several weeks' travel they reached Sandusky, Ohio, where they secured passage to Buffalo, New York, with a Scotch captain. The Scotch captain, on reaching the end of his trip, paid their passage money on the ferry-boat across to Canada and gave Josiah one dollar besides. On the twenty-eighth of October, 1830, they arrived in Canada.

Josiah Henson began to work for a man with whom he remained three years. This man gave Tom, Henson's twelve-year-old son, two quarters' schooling. Tom soon learned to read well, and he read a great deal to his father from the Bible on Sunday mornings when his father was to preach.

One Sunday morning Henson asked Tom to read. Tom turned to the One-hundred-and-third Psalm and read: "Bless the Lord, O my soul: and all that is within me, bless His holy name".

When he had finished, he turned to his father and said, "Father, who was David? He writes prettily, doesn't he?" And then Tom asked again, "Father, who was David?"

Henson said he was utterly unable to answer Tom's question, for he had never before heard of David, but he tried to conceal his embarrassment by saying, "David was a man of God, my son".

"I suppose so", said Tom, "but I want to know something more about him. Where did he live? What did he do?"

Finally Henson said frankly, "I do not know, Tom".

Tom exclaimed, "Why, Father, can't you read?"

"I cannot", said Henson.

"Why not?" said Tom.

"Because I never had an opportunity to learn, nor anybody to teach me", replied Henson.

"Well, you can learn now, Father", said Tom.

"No, my son", answered Henson. "I am too old and have not time enough. I must work all day or you would not have enough to eat."

Tom said, "Then you might do it at night".

Henson thought a moment and, looking at his bright-eyed boy, said, "But still there's nobody to teach me. I can't afford to pay anybody for it, and of course, no one can do it for nothing".

Tom approached his father, saying, "Why Father, I'll teach you; and then you'll know so much more you can talk better and preach better". After wrestling with the matter a short time, Henson agreed that Tom was right. They began and continued through the winter to study together every evening by the light of a pine-knot or some hickory bark, until the coming of spring, when Henson had learned to read a little.

Now, at the age of fifty years, he was having some very new experiences. In line with his thought of establishing a school to help his people, he went to a Boston friend for aid, who in turn went to England and raised $15,000 for the school. With this money two hundred acres of land were bought at Dawn, Canada, on which, covered as it was with black walnut timber, a schoolhouse was built and opened to the public. Later a sawmill was built on this tract of land and set to running. The school and the sawmill prospered for a while, but soon both were in need of funds.

Henson had four black walnut boards so highly polished that they shone like mirrors. These he took to London, England, and exhibited at the World's Industrial Exhibition. For this exhibit he was awarded a bronze medal and a life-size picture of the Queen and royal family.

This was neither Henson's first nor his last trip to that country. After some years of trouble and sorrow and loss, he returned to England, just after the news had gone abroad that he was the original "Uncle Tom" of Harriet Beecher Stowe's "Uncle Tom's Cabin". This time many honors were heaped upon him. He even visited Windsor Castle and was presented to Queen Victoria, who presented him with a photograh of herself on an easel frame of gold.

On his return to the United States in 1878, he was received at the White House in Washington, D. C., by President Hayes. Before returning to Canada to spend the last three years of his life, he visited the old home place in Charles County, Maryland, where his former mistress, for whom he had worked fifty years before, and who was now poor and decrepit, wept for joy at the sight of him.

SOJOURNER TRUTH

Chapter XII

SOJOURNER TRUTH

The Suffragist

1800–1883

AMONG Isabella's earliest recollections was a picture of her father and mother sitting night after night in their damp cellar, lighted by a blazing pine-knot, talking over their experiences of bygone days. Occasionally they would refer to one snowy morning when an old-fashioned sleigh drove up to their door and took away their unsuspecting little boy, Michael, and their little girl, Nancy, locked in the sleigh-box.

Whenever this story was mentioned, Isabella seemed to fall into a deep study. However, she was left to remain in Ulster County, New York, her birthplace, until her mother and father died. She was then sold to a man whose wife scolded and frowned at her creeping gait, her dull understanding and slovenly ways. In spite of his wife's impatience, the man insisted that Isabella could do as much work as half a dozen common people and do it well.

Isabella, therefore, fond of trying to please her

new master, often worked several nights in succession, taking only short naps as she sat in her chair. Some nights, fearing that if she sat down she would sleep too long, she took only cat-naps while she rested against the kitchen wall.

One morning the potatoes which Isabella had cooked for breakfast seemed unusually dingy and dirty. "Look!" said Isabella's mistress to her husband, "a fine specimen of Bell's work! It is the way all her work is done!" Isabella's master scolded her and bade her be more careful in the future. The two white servant-girls in the family also abused Isabella for preparing such food.

Isabella moped around apparently wondering why the potatoes looked so dingy and dirty. As she stood wondering how to avoid this the next time, Gertrude, her mistress's little daughter, stole quietly up behind her. Said she, catching Isabella by the arm, "Bell, if you will wake me early tomorrow morning, I will get up and attend to your potatoes while you go out to milk the cows. Then Father and Mother and all of them will not be scolding you". Isabella bowed, thanked her and promised to wake her early; then off Gertrude ran.

The next morning, just as the potatoes began

to boil and milking time came, little Gertrude walked into the kitchen and seated herself in the corner by the fire. She opened her little sewing basket and busied herself with making something for her doll. As she sat there, one of the maids came in with the broom in her hand and ordered her out, but Gertrude refused to go. The maid began to sweep hurriedly. When she reached the fireplace, she pretended to be in such a hurry, she caught up a handful of ashes and quickly dashed them into the potatoes. Gertrude ran out of the kitchen, saying, "Oh, Poppee! oh, Poppee! the girl has been putting ashes into Bell's potatoes! I saw her do it! Look at those that fell on the outside of the kettle!" She ran about the house and yard telling her story to every one. Her father listened to her story, called the maid in and, brandishing his fist at her, gave her orders to let Bell alone.

For many years, Isabella tried harder each year to please her master. Even after she had married and become the mother of five children, she obeyed him to such an extent that she would not steal even a crust of bread for her hungry children. When her household duties were done, she went to the field to work. After placing her baby child in a basket, she tied a rope to each handle and suspended the basket to the branches of a tree.

She then set one of the larger children to swing the basket "in order to make the baby happy and keep the snakes away", she said.

Isabella's master promised that if she would continue to be faithful he would set her free one year before all the slaves in New York State were to be free. As the time drew near, her master claimed that because of her sore hand that year, she had been of less value and would therefore have to remain longer. However, Isabella decided to remain only until she had spun all his wool.

One fine morning, a little before daybreak, she stepped away from the rear of her master's house with her baby boy on one arm and her clothes and provisions tied in a cotton handkerchief on the other. Fortunately, she landed in the home of a man who made no practice of buying and selling people. Nevertheless, he gave Isabella's master, who came in search of her, twenty-five dollars for her freedom.

Just before Isabella left her master, he had sold her five-year-old boy to a man who was on his way to England. The man, finding the boy too small for his services, sent him back to his brother, who in turn sold the boy to his brother-in-law in another state. When Isabella heard that her boy had been sold and sent away, she started out to find the guilty party and, if possible, to make him return her boy.

She went to her former mistress and others concerned in the sale, saying, "I'll have my child again". Finally she went to her former master, who told her to go to the Quakers and they would assist her. Straightway she went to the home of a Quaker family. They welcomed her and placed her in a room where there was a high, clean, white bed. In all of her twenty-seven years she had never slept in a bed. She sat for a long time looking at the bed and getting ready to crawl under it. However, she finally crawled gently up into the bed and soon fell asleep. The next morning, her Quaker friends took her nearly to town and gave her directions for reaching the court-house, where she made complaint to the grand jury.

On reaching the court-house, she entered. Thinking that the first fine-looking man she saw was the grand jury, she began to complain to him about her boy. He listened for a few moments and then told her that there was no grand jury there; she must go upstairs. When she had made her way upstairs through the crowd, she again went to the grandest-looking man she saw. Immediately she began to tell him that she came to make her complaint to the grand jury. Greatly amused, he asked what her complaint was. As soon as she began in her impressive way to tell her story, he said, pointing to a certain door, "This is no place to enter a complaint—go in there".

She went in, and finding the grand jurors sitting, began to tell her story. One of the jurors asked if she could swear that was her boy.

"Yes", she answered, "I swear it's my son."

"Stop, stop!" said the lawyer, "you must swear by this Bible." Taking the Bible, she placed it to her lips and began to swear it was her child. The clerks in the office burst into an uproar of laughter. None of this seemed to disturb Isabella. After understanding that she was simply to make a pledge of her truthfulness with her hand upon the Bible, she did so and hurried away. With a piece of paper, called a writ, in her hand for the arrest of the man who had sent her boy away, she trotted to the constable eight miles off. Although the constable by mistake served the writ on the wrong brother, it had its effect. The brother who had sold the boy went in hiding until he could slip away to get the boy.

The distance was great and travel in those days was slow. Autumn days came and went and then winter, and finally spring came before the man arrived with the boy. During all these months

Isabella kept going about seeing this friend and that one, until she said she was afraid that she had worried all of her friends, even God himself, nearly to death.

The news finally reached her that her boy had come, but that he denied having any mother. When she reached the place where her boy Peter was, he cried aloud against this tall, dark, bony woman with a white turban on her head. He knelt down and begged with tears not to be taken from his kind master. When some one asked him about the bad scar on his forehead, he said, "Master's horse hove me there". And then some one else asked about the scar on his cheek. He said, "That was done by running against Master's carriage". As he answered both of these questions, he looked wistfully at his master, as much as to say, "If they are falsehoods, you bade me say them; may they be satisfactory to you, at least".

Kind words and candies at last quieted Peter and he said, looking at his mother, "Well, you do look like my mother used to look". They embraced each other and went their way.

After Isabella and Peter had been free one year they went to New York City to live. Peter was growing tall and rather nice-looking, in spite of his hard life. He often attracted attention by his winsome way; but tempted by the gay life of New York City, he was soon drawn into a circle of boys whose sole object was to have a good time. He began to conceal from his mother those things of which he thought she would not approve. For example, for two years he was known among his worthless companions as Peter Williams, without his mother's knowledge of his new name. However, a friend of Isabella's, much pleased with Peter's appearance and bright mind, said that Peter should have an education if any one else should. Believing this, she paid ten dollars as tuition for him to enter a navigation school. Instead of attending school, Peter went irregularly, making some reasonable excuse each time to his teacher for not being able to attend school that day. Isabella and her friend, believing that Peter was doing well in school, secured for him a part-time job as coachman. Peter soon sold the livery and other things belonging to his employer.

He became involved in one difficulty after another, but each time Isabella managed to get him out. Each time she tried to reason with Peter. He would always confess, saying that he never intended to do wrong, but had been led along little by little until before he knew it, he was in serious trouble. At last, seeing no improvement in her son, Isabella made up her mind to let him go unassisted in his difficulties. Finally, he fell into the hands of the police, who sent for Mr. Peter Williams, a barber. Mr. Williams's interest was so aroused by the boy's having his name, that he paid the fine on Peter's promise to leave New York City on a vessel sailing within a week.

Mr. Williams seemed surprised to find that the boy had such a mother as Isabella. Isabella said that she was afraid lest her son would deceive Mr. Williams and be missing when the vessel sailed. However, Peter sailed; though for over a month Isabella lived in fear of seeing him emerge from some by-street in New York City. More than a year had passed when Isabella received the following letter:

My dear and beloved Mother:

I take this opportunity to write to you and inform you that I am well, and in hopes of finding you the same. I got on board the same unlucky ship "Done of Nantucket". I am sorry to say that I have been punished once severely by shoving my head in the fire for other folks. We have had bad luck, but in hopes of having better. We have about 230 on board, but in hopes, if we do have good luck, that my parents will receive me with thanks.

I would like to know how my sisters are. Do my cousins live in New York yet? Have you received my letter? If not, inquire of Mr. Peirce Whitings. I wish you would write me an answer as soon as possible. I am your only son, that is so far from home, in the wide, briny ocean. I have seen more of the world than I ever expected, and if I ever return home safe, I will tell you all my troubles and hardships. Mother, I hope you do not forget me, your dear and only son. I should like to know how Sophia and Betsy and Hannah are. I hope you all will forgive me for all that I have done.

Your son,

PETER VAN WAGNER.

Isabella's last annual letter from Peter said that if he did not do well, she need not expect him home in five years. During the five years of expectant waiting, Isabella joined Zion's Church, in Church Street, New York City, where she worshiped for some time. One Sunday morning, after services, a tall, well-dressed woman came up and made herself known to Isabella as her sister Sophia who had just moved to New York City. She also brought to meet Isabella her brother Michael, whom Isabella had never seen. The brother Michael told Isabella that her sister Nancy, who had been for many years a member of Zion Church, had just passed away. As he described his sister Nancy's features, her manner, her dress, and named her class leader, Isabella stood shaking as though she would fall to the floor. She caught hold of the back of a bench, exclaiming, "I knelt at the altar with her. I took the Lord's Supper with her. I shook hands with her! Was that my sister who was taken away one snowy morning in the sleigh? Are you my brother Michael who was taken away in the sleigh-box?" The three of them stood there mingling their tears each with the other.

While Isabella was a member of Zion Church she often visited the pavement meetings of a band of religious fanatics. These fanatics were in the habit of fasting every Friday and sometimes as long as two nights and three days, refusing even a cup of cold water. Isabella asked one of the leaders why he fasted. He said that fasting gave him great light on the things of God. "Well", said Isabella, "if fasting will give light inwardly and spiritually, I need it as much as anybody, and I'll fast too". She further said, "If such a good man as that needs to fast two nights and three days, then I certainly ought to fast more. I will fast three nights and three days".

She fasted three nights and three days, not drinking even so much as a drop of water. The fourth morning when she arose and tried to stand, she fell to the floor. Feeling very empty and light, she crawled to the pantry, but fearing, as she says, that she might now offend God by eating too much, she compelled herself to eat dry bread and drink water. Before she felt strong enough to walk she had eaten a six-penny loaf of bread. She says that she did get light, but it was all in her body and none in her mind.

During Isabella's first years in New York City, she was always trying to place a little money from time to time in the savings bank for the rainy day. Influenced by her fanatic friends, she drew her money from the savings bank and placed it in their common treasury, or kingdom, as they called it, not even asking about interest or taking account of what she had put in. In later years Isabella often said in her witty way, "The only thing I recovered from the wreck of that common kingdom was a few pieces of old furniture".

With all of her savings gone, she started anew, working early and late, to lay aside enough to buy a home for herself in her advanced age. If the people in the home where she worked gave her fifty cents to hire a poor man to clean away the snow, she arose early, performed the task herself and pocketed the money. She began to feel that she, too, was robbing the poor in her selfish grasping.

She talked much about this. It seemed to prey on her mind. Finally she decided to leave New York City and travel east and lecture. With the secret locked in her own bosom, she made ready for leaving by placing a few articles of clothing in a pillow-case. About an hour before starting out, she went to the woman at whose house she was staying and said, "My name is no longer Isabella, but 'Sojourner'. I am going east. The spirit calls me there, and I must go".

On the morning of June 1, 1843, Sojourner, now forty-three years old, set out from New York City with her pillow-case in one hand, a little basket of provisions in the other and two York shillings in her purse. As she crossed over to Brooklyn, she says she thought of Lot's wife, and, wishing to avoid her fate, was determined not to look back until New York City was far in the distance. When night came on she sought for a lodging place wherever she could find one.

It was her plan, as she explained, when she became weary of travel and needed rest, to stop at some home for a few days. The very first time she felt the need of rest badly, as she walked along the road, a man addressed her, asking if she were looking for work. "Sir", she said in her queenly way, "that's not the object of my travels, but if you need me I can help you out for a few days". She went in and worked so faithfully that the man offered her at the time of her departure what seemed to her a large sum of money. Refusing all except two or three York shillings which she considered sufficient to take her on her mission, she went her way.

After she had traveled far out on Long Island, one evening, in her search for a night's lodging, she met two Indians who took her for an acquaintance. They asked if she were alone. Not knowing anything at all about them, she replied, "No, not exactly", and kept going.

In her search for lodging places, Sojourner Truth occasionally went into dance-halls and hovels of the lowest kind. Nevertheless, she traveled on foot lecturing in many New York and Connecticut towns. Then led, as she claimed, by the spirit, she continued her journey to Northampton, Massachusetts.

One night, while she was living at Northampton, she attended a camp-meeting which was being held in the open air. Those attending the meeting slept in tents. A company of boys present said they were going to set fire to all the tents. Those in charge of the meeting sent for the sheriff to arrest the ring-leaders. Sojourner Truth rushed to hide in one corner of a tent. She said, "Shall I run away and hide from the devil? Me a servant of the Living God? Have I not faith enough to go out and quell that mob when I know it is written one shall chase a thousand and two put ten thousand to flight?" She walked out from her hiding-place, under the moonlight, to the top of a small rise of ground and began to sing:

It was early in the morning—it was early in the morning,
Just at the break of day—
When He rose—when He rose—when He rose—
And went to heaven on a cloud.

The boys with their sticks and clubs made a rush towards her and crowded around her. She stopped singing and after a few minutes asked in a gentle but firm tone, "Why do you come about me with clubs and sticks? I am not doing harm to any one".

Many of them said, "We are not going to hurt you, old woman. We came to hear you sing".

"Sing to us", another cried.

"Tell us your experience", said another.

"You stand and smoke so near me, I can't sing or talk", she answered. They immediately removed their cigarettes and cigars. At their suggestion and with their help, she climbed upon a wagon nearby and spoke and sang for nearly an hour. Upon asking the third time if they would go away and act like men, all yelled out, "Yes, yes!"

She traveled a great deal, holding many meetings for the sake of the freedom of her people.

Imagine this big, bony, black woman, six feet tall, walking along the highway or riding along with a small clay pipe in her mouth from which rolled columns of smoke. One evening she was riding in the State of Iowa on a railroad train. A man sitting in a seat just behind her saw her smoking and said to her, "Do you believe in the Bible?"

"I do", she replied.

"Well, then", said he, "what can be more filthy than the breath of a smoker? Doesn't the Bible say no unclean thing shall enter the kingdom of heaven?"

"Yes, child", she answered, "but when I go to heaven I expect to leave my breath behind me".

Even before the Civil War, she held meetings in many states. At the close of a meeting in Ohio one evening, a man came up to her and said, "Old woman, do you think that your talk about slavery does any good? Do you suppose people care what you say? I don't care any more for your talk than I do for the bite of a flea".

"Perhaps not", she answered, "but the Lord willing, I'll keep you a-scratching."

Once when she was out on a speaking tour she met a man who asked, "What business are you following now?"

She quickly replied, "Years ago when I lived in New York City my occupation was scouring brass door-knobs, but now I go about scouring copper-heads".

She could neither read nor write. She seemed to know, however, something about many of the big subjects of the day, such as "Suffrage", "Temperance" and "Abolition". She even attended the first big woman's suffrage convention, held in Ohio. This convention was held in a church. Sojourner Truth marched in like a queen and sat on the pulpit steps. In those days men thought women should not vote. The men and even the boys were laughing at the women and teasing them for holding such a meeting.

Old "Sojourner Truth" rose and walked out in front of the speakers' table. She took off her sunbonnet and laid it at her feet. Many of the women said, "Don't let that old woman speak. She will do us harm".

But the presiding officer rapped on the table for order and "Sojourner Truth" began by saying, "Well, children, where there is so much racket there must be something out of kilter". She had something sharp to say in reply to every minister who had spoken. One minister had said that women should not vote because Eve had acted so badly. To him she said, "If the first woman God ever made was strong enough to turn the world upside down, all alone, these together [glancing around over all the women] ought to be able to turn it right side up again".

She took her seat in the midst of great applause. Many women rushed to her, shook her hand and said, "You have saved the day".

One day while Lincoln was President of the United States, Sojourner, old and bent, walked into the marble room of the Senate Chamber. It was an hour not soon to be forgotten. Senators rose and shook her hand. They asked her to speak. As she spoke, some sat with tears in their eyes. When she had finished they shook her hand again, gave her a purse and bade her good-bye. A Washington Sunday paper had a long article about Sojourner Truth's speaking to the United States Senators. This article said: "Sojourner Truth has had a marvelously strange life. The leaven of love must be working in the hearts of all people".

In her old age and suffering, Sojourner Truth was supported by a friend. The end came at Battle Creek, Michigan, November 26, 1883.

CRISPUS ATTUCKS

CRISPUS ATTUCKS SPOKE AGAINST THE BRITISH SOLDIERS.

Chapter XIII

CRISPUS ATTUCKS

1723–1770

CRISPUS ATTUCKS was born many years ago, at some place, but nobody in the world seems to know just where. And no one seems to know anything at all about him, or about his people, except that he was a sailor. He received public notice just twice in his lifetime. The first time it was through an advertisement in a Boston newspaper, which came out on the second of October, 1750. The advertisement read:

> Ran away from his master, William Brown of Framingham, on the 30th of September, last, a Molatto-Fellow, about twenty-seven years of age, named Crispus, 6 feet 2 inches high, short curl'd hair, his knees nearer together than common; had on a light color'd Bearskin Coat, plain brown Fustain Jacket, or brown all-wool one, new Buckskin Breeches, blue yarn stockings, and a checked woolen shirt.
>
> Whoever shall take up said Runaway, and convey him to his above said Master, shall have ten pounds, Old Tenor Reward, and all necessary charges paid.
>
> Boston, Oct. 2, 1750.

The name of Crispus Attucks appeared in the Boston papers just once more, and that was twenty years later, at the time of the Boston Massacre. In those days Crispus Attucks knew nothing about the United States, and nobody else did, for there were no United States. There were only the American colonies of Great Britain.

Because Great Britain knew that these colonies were angry with her, she sent several regiments of soldiers over to Boston, Massachusetts. These soldiers were to make the colonies obey England. Every one in Boston seemed to be speaking against these British soldiers.

Finally a group of men led by Crispus Attucks began to pelt them with missiles and chunks of ice, and to dare them to fire their guns, but the British soldiers fired. Shells from their guns struck Crispus Attucks and three other men. Crispus Attucks and one of the men, by the name of Caldwell, fell dead. The other two were mortally wounded.

The whole city of Boston was in an uproar. Bells were ringing everywhere, and people were running here and there as if they were crazy. In the midst of all of this excitement, the bodies of Crispus Attucks and Caldwell were taken into Faneuil Hall. It is said that their faces were looked upon by the largest gathering of people ever assembled there. One of the men who fell was buried from his mother's home. Another was buried from his brother's home, but Attucks and Caldwell, being strangers in the city, were buried from Faneuil Hall.

The four hearses bearing the bodies of the dead men met in King Street. From there the funeral procession moved in columns six deep. There was an extended line of carriages containing the first citizens of Boston. The four bodies were buried in one grave, and over the grave was placed a stone with this inscription:

> Long as in Freedom's cause the wise contend,
> Dear to your Country shall your fame extend;
> While to the world the lettered stone shall tell
> Where Caldwell, Attucks, Gray and Maverick fell.

Crispus Attucks is sometimes called a madcap, because he led the Boston Massacre charge, which was the beginning of the Revolutionary War. He had apparently been around Boston for some years and had listened to the fiery speeches of some of the orators of that day.

A memorial shaft was later erected on Boston Common to the memory of these men, and a memorial tablet was placed on State Street in Boston.

CRISPUS ATTUCKS

Read at the Dedication of the Crispus Attucks Monument in Boston, November 14, 1888

Where shall we seek for a hero, and where shall we find a
story?
Our laurels are wreathed for conquest, our songs for completed glory.
But we honor a shrine unfinished, a column uncapped with
pride,
If we sing the deed that was sown like seed when Crispus
Attucks died.

Shall we take for a sign this Negro-slave with unfamiliar
name—
With his poor companions, nameless too, till their lives
leaped forth in flame?
Yea, surely, the verdict is not for us to render or deny;
We can only interpret the symbol; God chose these men
to die—
As teachers and types, that to humble lives may chief
award be made;
That from lowly ones, and rejected stones, the temple's
base is laid!

When the bullets leaped from the British guns, no chance
decreed their aim:
Men see what the royal hirelings saw—a multitude and a
flame;
But beyond the flame, a mystery; five dying men in the
street,
While the streams of several races in the well of a nation
meet!

O, blood of the people! changeless tide, through century, creed and race!
Still one as the sweet salt sea is one, though tempered by sun and place;
The same in the ocean currents, and the same in the sheltered seas;
Forever the fountain of common hopes and kindly sympathies;
Indian and Negro, Saxon and Celt, Teuton and Latin and Gaul—
Mere surface shadow and sunshine; while the sounding unifies all!
One love, one hope, one duty theirs! No matter the time or ken,
There never was separate heart-beat in all the races of men!

But alien is one—of class, not race—he has drawn the line for himself;
His roots drink life from inhuman soil, from garbage of pomp and pelf;
His heart beats not with the common beat, he has changed his life-stream's hue;
He deems his flesh to be finer flesh, he boasts that his blood is blue:
Patrician, aristocrat, tory—whatever his age or name,
To the people's rights and liberties, a traitor ever the same.
The natural crowd is a mob to him, their prayer a vulgar rhyme;
The freeman's speech is sedition, and the patriot's deed a crime.
Wherever the race, the law, the land—whatever the time, or throne,
The tory is always a traitor to every class but his own.

Thank God for a land where pride is clipped, where arrogance stalks apart;
Where law and song and loathing of wrong are words of the common heart;
Where the masses honor straightforward strength, and know, when veins are bled,
That the bluest blood is putrid blood—that the people's blood is red!

And honor to Crispus Attucks, who was leader and voice that day;
The first to defy, and the first to die, with Maverick, Carr, and Gray.
Call it riot or revolution, his hand first clenched at the crown;
His feet were the first in perilous place to pull the king's flag down;
His breast was the first one rent apart that liberty's stream might flow;
For our freedom now and forever, his head was the first laid low.

—*John Boyle O'Reilly.*

ALEXANDRE DUMAS

Chapter XIV

ALEXANDRE DUMAS

Playwright and Novelist

1802–1870

ALEXANDRE DUMAS was the son of a French general. Once Alexandre went to Paris with his father to see a friend, and while talking with this friend, the general said, pointing to Alexandre, "After I am dead, I want you to help my boy".

His friend replied, "Oh, you will outlive me".

The general, however, did not live long after this. He died when Alexandre was only four years old. Then this rosy-cheeked, curly-headed boy had no one to help him but his poor mother, whom he kept busy. One moment he was pointing to letters here and there and asking about them; the next moment, he was begging for a story; and the next moment, he was into something else. It was not long before this busy boy was putting words together and beginning to read, but his mother was so poor that he could not go to school until he was ten years old.

The first day he went to school, he wore a suit of clothes which his mother had made out of a riding coat once worn by his father. His schoolmates hustled him around and even squirted water on him until his new suit was all wet. He sat down and cried bitterly. Suddenly, the teacher appeared on the scene. All the pupils gathered around the weeping boy in seeming real surprise, saying, "Why is he crying; what is the matter with him?"

The teacher made his way to the boy, bent down over him, and asked, "What is the trouble, Alexandre?" Alexandre looked up and was about to open his mouth, when he saw all the children behind the teacher shaking their fists and their heads at him.

The teacher suddenly turned around. All the pupils were smiling. "Tell me what it is all about", said the teacher.

"We can't make out", said the pupils, "he has been crying that way ever since he came." Alexandre then blurted out the whole story and showed the teacher his wet clothes.

"Very well", said the teacher, "I shall whip every one of you, and you shall have no recess today. March into the room."

In the meantime the pupils cast fierce glances at Alexandre and called him a spy. Time passed rapidly, and soon school was dismissed. All left hurriedly, as it seemed, for their homes, but just around the corner, the fighting gang waited for Alexandre. The ringleader laid off his coat and walked up to him with his fists clenched. Alexandre drew back and gave him a staggering blow which knocked him flat to the ground. The others in the gang rolled up their sleeves and strutted about, saying in French what they would do.

This happened in France more than one hundred years ago, for Alexandre Dumas was born on the 24th of July, 1802. His native town was Cotterets, forty miles from Paris, and twenty-one miles from Château-Thierry.

After his father died, he often went hungry and shabbily clad, until he was old enough to work. One day he walked and walked, looking for a job, but nothing seemed to turn up. Now that it was about time for offices to close, he started home, but decided to try one more place. He walked into a nice-looking office and asked for work. The head man said, "Do you know how to fold letters?"

Dumas hesitated a moment and replied, "I can learn, sir, pretty quickly".

The man then asked, "Do you know how to get to your work on time?"

"Yes, sir!" said Dumas.

"Then you may come in tomorrow morning", said the man.

Dumas hurried home. He rushed into the house and called his mother. His cheeks and his lips were flushed like a red rose. He said, "Mother, I am so happy. I have an office job. Now I can help you, Mother". The evening passed joyously, and the next morning he walked briskly to his work.

All day long he was busy at the office, dusting the furniture, folding letters, sealing and mailing them, running errands and taking care of visitors who came to the office. When evening came, he was very tired, but not too tired to read and study a little.

Some of the boys in the office tried to tease him about studying so much, nevertheless he kept on working and studying. In a few months, he began to tease them because he had been promoted to a better job as clerk and they remained in their same positions. He seemed very happy and kept on reading and studying at night.

One afternoon while he was reading, he saw the following advertisement, "Shakespeare's Hamlet"! At once he was interested, for he had read about the writer Shakespeare and had read the play called "Hamlet".

"I must see this play; but it is given out of town", he said as he read further. However, he repeated, "I must see this play". He hurriedly put on the best clothes he had, reached the station, boarded the train, and in forty minutes was in the little town where the play was being given. He made his way to the theatre at once and followed every movement of the actors.

He said at the close of the performance, "I must see a play now in a larger theatre in Paris".

This determination to go to a Paris theatre continued, until one afternoon he dressed in his long coat, which touched his heels, brushed his hair, which was ridiculously long, and set out for Paris. Just as he entered the theatre, some one cried out, "Oh, what a head!"

People began to laugh at him. Soon an usher came up. "Tickets", said he. Alexandre handed him his ticket. He took it, looked at it and looked at Alexandre; then he shook his head. Alexandre stood there, in spite of the fact that the usher kept saying, "Your ticket is no good. Your ticket is no good". Angry because he had been deceived in buying his ticket, Alexandre Dumas stood there until the ushers came and put him out.

In spite of his first night at a Paris theatre, Alexandre Dumas seemed enthusiastic about the theatre. He spent all of his spare time in writing plays, which no publisher would publish. One publisher said to him, "Get yourself a name and then I'll publish your books".

Nevertheless, he often visited the theatre and kept on studying and writing. Finally, he finished a play which he named "Christine". One day, although he was just a boy clerk in an office, he had the boldness to say, " 'Christine' will be played in the finest theatre in Paris".

Soon after "Christine" was finished, the great theatre of Paris accepted it. On the evening that the first performance of it was given, Alexandre Dumas sat in this fine Paris theatre with a cheap suit of clothes on, while all around him sat the great actors of France in their finery and splendor. The curtain rose on the beautiful scenery. The actors came forward, talking, making gestures and performing. The audience seemed pleased with every act and applauded loudly.

When the performance was all over and the curtain had fallen, Dumas ran home to tell his mother of this wonderful evening. He ran so fast that he lost the only copy of his play. However, the play was all in his head and so he sat up that night and wrote it out again.

He set to work, and in two months, wrote another play, which he called "Henri III". Just as he was about finishing this play, the head man in his office said to him one day, "Dumas, you must either give all of your time to your office work or lose your job. I can't have any theatre man around".

He held his job, however, and finished the play. "Henri III" was very popular. On the evening when a performance of it was given, the gallery of the theatre was filled with princes and nobles. The boxes were filled with ladies glittering with diamonds. All the writers of Paris were out. Every seat in the theatre was taken a week before the play was given.

While the play was being presented, Dumas hurried away between the acts to see his mother, who was very ill. The next day, every one in Paris was talking about this brilliant young writer. The rich people of Paris sent so many beautiful flowers to his sick mother that they almost filled the little room where she lay. By two o'clock that afternoon, the first copy of this play, called the manuscript, had been sold for $1,164. Each performance of the play brought him $1,212.50. In later years, he even had a grand theatre of his own built for his plays.

In addition to his plays, Dumas wrote stories. One day he sat down and wrote a story very quickly. "Ah," he said, "I am going to keep at this." He kept at it until he wrote the two great stories called "The Count of Monte Cristo" and "The Three Musketeers". He also wrote many stories about his grandmother, who was a native African woman. In one year, it is said he published about forty books.

Once he promised to write so many books for a certain company that the company began to look into the matter, and discovered that Dumas was hiring young writers to write stories, which he edited and changed to suit his own style. Dumas was arrested and tried. The judge said, "Alexandre Dumas is paying these writers for their works and is thus helping them. He is so changing their writings that they sound like his own. He is not guilty of any offense". Many young writers, apparently fond of him, spoke in his defense. His door was hardly free for a moment from strangers, who were coming and going, asking his opinion on their writings.

It is said that he was just about as extravagant as he was famous. He wore handsome and even gaudy clothes, kept fine horses, and gave many dinner parties. After some years all this was changed. He lost control of his great theatre and was sunk in debt.

Years passed and little was heard of his plays; but later they were revived. On the same night, three years before his death, four of his plays were being given in four of the largest theatres in Paris. Again people in the theatres were crying out, "Long live Dumas!"

Even in his old age, he worked almost without stopping. While he was in the home of his son in Puys, France, his brain and his limbs became so paralyzed that he died on the fifth of December, 1870. Two years after his death, the name of the street in Paris on which his house stood was changed to "Rue Alexandre Dumas", or Alexander Dumas Street, in memory of him.

Thirteen years after his death, the French people erected in Paris a monument to his memory. He is represented sitting with a book in his left hand and a pen in his right; in front of the pedestal there are three figures—a young woman represented as reading, and two men, one of them in workman's garb; the idea being to show how popular he was among all classes. At the back of the pedestal, there is a fine figure of one dressed as a musketeer or soldier.

The citizens of his native town—Cotterets—also erected to his memory a monument on Alexander Dumas Street.

PAUL CUFFÉ

PAUL CUFFÉ'S BRIG.

Chapter XV

PAUL CUFFÉ

THE SAILOR

1759–1817

THE Cuffé home at Westport, Massachusetts, was always ringing with laughter and merriment. Somebody in that family of four sturdy boys, six girls, mother and father, was ever ready with a snappy joke, or a ghostly yarn which sometimes made even the old folks afraid to go to bed.

One night the family was seated around the hearth. Father Cuffé began to tell what he called a true story about his native country. He rose and pictured a great boa-constrictor gliding into his African home and swallowing a little boy. As he represented the great open mouth of that huge snake with the boy slipping down its throat, one of the girls jumped and looked behind her. The boys laughed very heartily and pointed their fingers at her, saying, "You thought that boa-constrictor had you!" Mrs. Cuffé, who was of Indian descent, attracted the family's attention just at that point by springing forth suddenly with a war-whoop and dance.

As soon as this came to an end, Paul Cuffé, the youngest of the boys, began telling one of his whale stories. He, too, arose and described his boat as it rocked to and fro on a stormy sea. He pictured his men tugging at a great whale, which suddenly pulled one of them overboard. Just then one of Paul's brothers gave a quick jerk on Paul's coat-tail. Paul leaped forward, looked back and landed flat on the floor. His sisters and brothers laughed and laughed until some of them said their sides ached.

Such evenings in the Cuffé farmhouse at Westport were common until Father Cuffé died. Paul was then fourteen years old. For two years, he and his brothers worked their poor farm of one hundred acres and thus supported their mother and sisters as best they could.

Every day spent in the field seemed harder and harder to Paul. He had made up his mind, he said, to try his fortune on the sea, but dreaded to tell his mother. One morning he lingered around until there was no one in the house but him and his mother. "Mother", he said, "I am big for my age, and if I can get a job on a schooner, I can earn a man's wages. I can make it on the sea better than on the land."

His mother held up both hands, saying, "Paul, my dear boy, can't you find something else to do? Sailors are such rough men. They drink, they swear, they are reckless".

"Mother", said he, "I have always longed to be a sailor. Give me your consent." For several days there was no laughter in the Cuffé home. Paul's mother said she feared he would be swallowed up by the angry waves or by a whale.

During these days, Paul was as busy as he could be trying to get a job on a schooner. Finally, he succeeded in hiring out as a common hand on a vessel leaving on a whaling expedition for the Bay of Mexico. His mother was sure now that Paul would never return alive, so she gave him a small Bible and her blessing. He kissed her goodbye, pressed her hand and assured her that he would remain a good boy.

By nine o'clock the next morning, everything was in readiness for the start. The wind was favorable. The skipper was on board. Every sailor was busy making sail or getting up the heavy anchor. At length the schooner glided away from the shore.

For a time, Paul and the rest of the hands

were busy coiling lines, stowing away odds and ends and making the vessel comfortable. As soon as Paul had a few spare moments he filled a small keg with fresh water and put several dozen ship-biscuits into a box, around which he wrapped an old oilskin jacket. One of the boys on board laughed at him and said in loud tones, "Are you afraid of being lost in a fog? Boy, your mamma's apron strings are many miles away. You should have been tied to them instead of being on a boat."

One of Paul's friends started to answer back, but Paul said, "Let him alone. It will make him feel worse not to be noticed at all".

The schooner tugged away until the end of the journey was finally reached. The trip was exciting to say the least; and their return trip was equally exciting. They had been gone for some weeks. In those days vessels traveled only about seven knots an hour. Paul had just a few hours at home with his mother before setting out on a trip to the West Indies. At the end of this trip, he seemed to feel that he was a full-fledged sailor. It had taken him only two weeks to get sufficient experience in navigation to command a vessel. He went out on a third voyage, but the Revolutionary War broke out. His ship was run down and captured by a British ship, and he was held as a prisoner for three months.

After his release, Cuffé had to give up the sea for two years. He visited the Island of Cuttyhunk, near New Bedford, where he was born. Then he returned to his home at Westport, worked on the farm and gave much of his time to the betterment of his people. He was not yet twenty years old, but he and his brother drew up a petition and presented it to the Massachusetts Legislature. This petition asked that all free people of Massachusetts be given the full rights of citizens. The Massachusetts Legislature carefully considered this respectful petition. Soon afterward it passed an act granting to all free people, irrespective of color, the full privileges of citizens.

Cuffé was busy these two years and yet his old longing for business and for the sea, he said, kept stealing over him. He laid before his brother, David, a plan for trading with the people of Connecticut. His brother agreed to the plan. They built an open boat and put out to sea, but his brother's fears so increased that he resolved to turn back. Paul finally submitted and returned home.

He worked a while for more materials and

again put out to sea, but soon lost all he had. He went home and set himself to the task of making a boat from keel to gunwale. It was without a deck, but Paul had been on whaling expeditions and was thereby skilled in its management. He launched his boat into the ocean. As he was steering for Cuttyhunk, one of the Elizabeth Islands, to consult his brother about future plans, he was discovered by pirates, who chased his vessel, ran it down and captured both it and him.

He went home again and applied to his brother David for materials to build another boat. When the boat was finished, through his credit (on his respectability), he purchased a cargo and set out for Nantucket. On this voyage, he was again chased by pirates, but he escaped them as night came on. However, his boat struck upon a rock and was so injured that he had to return home for repairs. As soon as the repairs were made, he set out again for Nantucket and arrived in safety. On his return trip, however, he fell into the hands of pirates and was robbed of all he had except his boat. He made his way home, secured a small cargo and again directed his course towards Nantucket, where he sold his cargo to advantage.

On his return to his home this time, he secured a small covered boat of about twelve tons, hired some one to assist him, and made advantageous voyages to different parts of Connecticut.

He now became attached to a young woman—a descendant of his mother's tribe—whom he married. After his marriage he worked on a farm for a short while, then removed his family to a small house on the Westport River. He procured a boat of eighteen tons in which he sailed to the banks of St. George, obtained a valuable cargo of codfish and landed at home safely.

Cuffé soon entered partnership with his brother-in-law and built a vessel of twenty-five tons, in which they made voyages to Newfoundland and Belle Isle, securing profits enough to build a vessel of forty-two tons.

After the death of Cuffé's father he learned to read, write and do some arithmetic and yet he often said, "I would have made fewer mistakes and a great deal more money had I been an educated man." He called the people of his neighborhood together and spoke to them on the need of a schoolhouse and a teacher for their children. No two of the parents seemed to agree on anything. They talked and discussed and separated, each going to his own home. Paul Cuffé took the matter into his own hands, erected a schoolhouse on his own land and opened it to the public.

With this task completed, he set out to the Straits of Belle Isle on a whaling expedition, with two boats and ten men. Although he was ill prepared for the business, he and his crew killed six whales; two of which died at Paul's own hands. In due season he returned home heavily laden with bone and oil.

After selling his cargo, he bought iron and other materials, built a schooner of sixty-nine tons and launched it, in 1795, under the name of "The Ranger". He sold his two boats and placed on board "The Ranger", which was manned by a black crew, a cargo valued at two thousand dollars, and sailed for Norfolk, Virginia. This trip and similar ones brought him handsome returns.

With some of this money he bought a farm and placed it under the management of his brother-in-law. He also took one-half share in building and fitting out a large vessel, and three-fourths' share in building and fitting out still a larger one. One of these vessels, of one hundred and sixty-two tons burden, was commanded by Paul Cuffé's nephew. The other one, "The Alpha" by name, of two hundred and sixty-eight tons, was commanded by Paul Cuffé himself, with seven other Negroes making up the crew.

In 1811, Paul Cuffé and his crew, in command

of "The Alpha" sailed for Sierra Leone, Africa. After many days of travel and stormy sea, they arrived in Sierra Leone. Cuffé, attended by several natives, made his way to the governor's office, where he remained for a long conversation and visit with the Governor.

Following this, he entered into many of the natives' experiences. He put on armor and went elephant-hunting with them. Once he joined a party on a leopard hunt. One of the party said in his native tongue, "These leopards go about in pairs, and sometimes raid farms and carry off young children and chickens after dark. They step rather softly, steal upon one and attack him in the back". When the party reached a certain spot, every one stopped. Some of them proceeded to drive down two posts. Others loaded a long-range gun heavily and fastened it to these posts with the butt end resting on the posts and the muzzle about two feet from them. Then they placed a big piece of meat around the muzzle of the gun and drew a strong string round one of the posts connecting the meat to the trigger. All was in readiness now for Mr. Leopard; and so the party left the spot. After a long wait a leopard came walking softly by and sniffing around. He walked up to the meat to take a bite. "Pow", went the rifle. The leopard fell dead. Paul Cuffé and his party came out from their hiding place, and stood around looking at the beast.

Cuffé seemed very busy, even on such trips, studying the needs of natives and planning how the people in London might help them. One morning a monkey party came to take him along. He could not resist the invitation. Every one in the party had a sword or a stick. Several monkeys were caught that day and brought in tied hand and foot and hung on poles. The suckling ones were carried clinging underneath their mothers' bodies. Cuffé continued to study the natives and finally recommended to the Governor that they form "The Friendly Society of Sierra Leone" as a help to the people.

After this was done, he went to England on two trips. Then he returned to the United States in order to get teachers to take back with him, but the War of 1812 broke out, and his plans were delayed. For several years he had to remain in the United States. All this time, however, he was arranging to take teachers to Sierra Leone.

Toward the end of the year 1815, he sailed with thirty-eight teachers for Sierra Leone. For fifty-five days they were tossed and driven on the ocean. Even African soil, they said, was a welcome sight to them. They finally reached their destination safely. Cuffé bore the entire expense of the trip.

He remained in Sierra Leone two months, during which time he wrote a very touching letter to the natives. It is said that his departure from them was like that of a father taking leave of his children.

Cuffé returned to his own country, where he became ill early in 1817. From then until the day of his death, on the seventh of the following September, he was busy writing letters and making friends for the natives of Sierra Leone. Some one has said that he devoted even the thoughts of his dying pillow to the interests of the African people.

ALEXANDER CRUMMELL

Chapter XVI

ALEXANDER CRUMMELL

Minister and Missionary

1819–1898

ONE moonlight night about eighty-four years ago, a stage-coach rattled along from Hanover, New Hampshire, towards Albany, New York. Away up on the top of this stage-coach, sat two fast friends, Alexander Crummell and Henry Highland Garnet, and twelve other Negro boys. Apparently not even the rattle of the stage-coach wheels, or the jingle of the traces, or the hoot of an owl far off in the woods, disturbed their thoughts. It is true, they had been riding all day and had been under excitement for two days before they left the little town of Canaan near Hanover, but they neither slept nor stirred.

A thoughtless gang of Canaan boys had yoked about one hundred and ninety oxen together and driven them up to the little schoolhouse. Here and there, one ox tried to go one way while his mate tried to go the other way, but several yoke of them did team-work. They later bowed their necks and chased off through the woods, with the boys swinging to the lines and bumping against stumps and logs and trees. Finally, with the assistance of big boys, these unruly animals were brought back to the schoolhouse, to which the oxen were hitched.

At the crack of many long whips and the sound of loud calls, "Get up there, now! Pull steady", the oxen gave a mighty pull, and the sides of the little schoolhouse began to crack.

After two days of being pulled and pushed about, the little schoolhouse tottered into the swamp. The village boys, who had declared they would not let the Negro boys remain there and go to school, gave a cheer and a whoop. Still more excitement followed until Crummell and his friends took the stage-coach en route for their homes.

This bitter experience seemed only to sharpen Crummell's desire for an education. In a few months, he was off again to a school some distance from New York City—his birthplace and home. After his graduation from that school, a ceremony was performed and he became a priest in the Episcopal Church.

He worked at home a while, and then crossed the Atlantic Ocean and preached throughout England. While he was there, he entered a great university known as Cambridge University, from which he was graduated at the age of thirty-four.

Crummell often spoke of wishing to return to the United States to see his family and friends, but because of poor health, he went to Africa to do missionary work and, as he said, to die. Strange to say, the hot climate and the African fever seemed to disturb him not at all; in fact, his health improved.

For twenty years, he remained there and preached to the people, and taught in the Liberian College. The natives often asked why he kept at his writing so closely. Later they discovered that he was writing a book called "The Future of Africa".

During his twenty years in Africa, he made only two visits to the United States. In 1873 he returned for good and took charge of an Episcopal Mission in Washington, D. C. He presided over this Mission, which developed into what is now St. Luke's Church, for twenty-two years. Often during these years, he went by invitation to the leading cities of the country, either to preach or to give lectures. In 1896, he founded "The American Negro Academy" at Washington, D. C., and gave some lectures before this organization.

He was a striking character, tall, erect and of noble carriage. He was dignified and fearless in manner, yet easy to approach.

During the last year of his life, he worked at his desk from six to seven hours every day, when he was able to write. Finally, for a little change, he went to Point Pleasant, New Jersey, and while there, passed away on the tenth of September, 1898. Just a few hours before his death, he dictated a letter to Paul Laurence Dunbar on the philosophy of poetry.

JOHN MERCER LANGSTON

Chapter XVII

JOHN MERCER LANGSTON

Scholar and Congressman

1829–1897

JOHN MERCER LANGSTON was a frail child, only four years old, when his father and mother died. According to the will of his father, Captain Quarrels, he and his two brothers were to have all of their father's land, lying on Hickory Creek in Louisa County, Virginia. They were to have all of his stock of horses, cattle, sheep and bees, together with household and kitchen furniture and plantation utensils. They were also to have all of his money, in cash or in the form of debts due or bank stocks. Provision was made in Captain Quarrels's will for selling his property and dividing the money among John Mercer and his other boys, should they leave Louisa County.

The time came when this provision in the will was to be carried out. John Mercer and his brothers, with their attendants, remained in Louisa County two months after their father's death, getting ready to start for Ohio.

During this period of preparation, they secured

the proper papers to take on such a journey. They and their attendants obtained a carry-all—a light wagon with horses and harness—and set out early one October morning, in 1834, to what was then known as a far-away state—Ohio. The road over which they traveled was mountainous and frequently broken by small swollen streams which they had to ford, and rivers which they had to cross by means of crude ferries. However, there seemed to be no cause for anxiety except for little, frail John Mercer.

They continued their journey for one week, traveling by day and pitching their tents at night. One evening while some one was unhitching the horses, and two of them were pitching the tent, and John Mercer and the rest of them were bringing water from a nearby stream, a man on horseback with saddle bags came down the highway. The older Langston boys, recognizing him as their half-brother, whom their father had sent to Ohio long before his death, ran to meet him. Little John Mercer, whom he had never seen before, he took up in his arms, caressed him and looked at him, saying, "My! but you are like my dear mother, Lucy Langston! You have in a marked degree her Indian family likeness!" All of the boys made their way to the tent. The night passed.

The next day as the party proceeded on its journey, the half-brother shortened the stirrup leathers of his saddle to fit John Mercer's legs, and put him in his saddle. John Mercer took hold of the bridle reins timidly, but soon began to knock his little legs against the sides of the horse, saying, "Get up, sir". At length, he seemed weary and was again taken into the battered carry-all. They traveled on for two weeks longer, until they reached Chillicothe, Ohio.

John Mercer was taken to the home of Colonel Gooch, who once on a visit to Captain Quarrels, had promised that when John Mercer came to Ohio he would care for him and educate him. John Mercer was given a hot bath, his clothing was changed, and a chair was placed at the table for him by the side of Mrs. Gooch. He ate heartily, romped and played, and grew rapidly under the kind treatment of the Gooch family. Soon he was known to the neighbors as "Johnnie Gooch".

Four years for him in the Gooch home passed. One beautiful Monday morning, in 1837, he, with his little new dinner-pail in one hand, and his book in the other, accompanied by Mr. Gooch, started out to school. Clad in his neat dress of roundabout and pants of Kentucky blue jeans, he and

Mr. Gooch trudged along until they reached the schoolhouse.

John Mercer was soon assigned to his class and his seat. As he sat upon the high seat without a back, he almost toppled over backwards. Then, apparently afraid of falling backwards, he leaned so far forward that he fell over on his nose. He twisted and turned on the tiresome seat for several days, then told his teacher that he was needed at home at two o'clock every day to drive up the cows. For one week he went home every day at two o'clock. Mr. Gooch asked the reason for John Mercer's early arrival home every day, and informed the teacher that John Mercer's whole business was to attend school.

Many agents were in Chillicothe at this time telling of the rich farm land in Missouri that could be bought very cheaply. The Gooch family was among the old residents who were selling out and preparing to leave for Missouri. They chartered a canal-boat and a steamboat for moving their things, and planned for a wagon and team to take the family across the country. Mr. Gooch called John Mercer in and asked if he wished to go with them. John Mercer replied, "I do, Colonel Gooch".

"Then you shall go", said the colonel.

When everything was in readiness, the family set out one night on their journey. The next morning, John Mercer spied two objects in the distance coming towards them. As they approached, he saw that they were two men, and one of them was his half-brother. The other gentleman made himself known at once as the sheriff, who had come to arrest Colonel Gooch for kidnapping John Mercer. Colonel Gooch, obeying orders, saddled his horse, took John Mercer up behind him and rode with the men back to Chillicothe. The court ruled that John Mercer should be left there.

Upon the advice of some one, he returned to the old Gooch home and farm, which were now in the hands of another. The first question the man asked was, "What, sir, can you do?"

John Mercer promptly answered, "I can't do anything".

The farmer then asked, "How do you expect to live? Get the horse and cart out and haul those bricks up from the distant field". John Mercer started forth to try to hitch the horse to the cart and to haul the bricks.

The third day, the farmer said, "You are doing well, and if you continue, you will make a good driver". The boy not only hauled bricks, but he plowed and hoed and became strong and healthy.

On leaving the farmer, he went to Cincinnati, Ohio, and secured work for afternoons and Saturdays, in a barber shop. Thus was he soon able to enter school in that city. One day as he sat with his class, studying his lesson, a man appeared at the door and asked for him. His teacher said, "John Mercer may go to the door. Some one wishes to see him". He arose and walked forth. At the sight of Colonel Gooch, who had sought him in Chillicothe and had come on to Cincinnati, he leaped out of the door and grasped his hand. They talked for a long, long time. Mr. Gooch kissed him good-bye, and John Mercer promised to join him in Missouri later on.

John Mercer's two years' stay in Cincinnati was interrupted by a call to Chillicothe, on business connected with his father's estate. While he was on this trip, he met an Oberlin College student who was teaching in Chillicothe, and who agreed to give him lessons. He studied under this teacher until his brothers agreed to send him to Oberlin College.

On Thursday morning, March 1, 1844, he and his teacher left Chillicothe for Oberlin. When they arrived the following Sunday morning, they saw hundreds of college students making their way through the muddy streets to early prayer service and Sunday School. Lodging for the night was secured in the only hotel then in Oberlin. The next day John Mercer registered and was taken to the home in which he was to live.

Seeing how busy every one about the college was, he secured his books and settled down to hard study. Before many weeks had passed, he was invited to join two college clubs—"The Young Men's Lyceum" and "The Union Society". Because of having friends in "the Union Society", he joined it, and was immediately called upon to take part in a debate.

On the evening of the debate, a very capable young man came forward as the first speaker. When he had finished, another young man was called forth. He, too, presented his side of the question in a convincing manner. John Mercer Langston was called upon as the third speaker. He came forward, took his place on the platform and said, "Mr. President—Mr. President". He stood there unable to say another word. Finally he rushed to his seat and began to cry. He wiped away the copious tears until his handkerchief, his cap and his coat sleeve were soaking wet. Then he hurried to his room, threw himself on the bed and cried until his pillow was wet through. The next morning, he arose with his face and eyes all swollen. As he stood before his little mirror, he held up his hands to God, with the vow that he would never fail again in making a speech. When friends sympathized with him, he said, "I thank you, but never mind".

After leaving breakfast, as John Mercer walked up the street, he met a friend who said he was called home. Immediately he asked John Mercer to take his place in the Society debate the next Thursday evening. He agreed at once and began to get ready for the debate. Thursday evening came; the hall was full of young men. When John Mercer was called forth, he took his place, addressed the presiding officer and spoke his ten minutes amid applause. Some young man called out, "Mr. President, I move by common consent that Langston be given ten minutes more". The motion was carried and Langston spoke ten minutes more, interrupted by frequent applause.

He remained in college to the end of the fall term, and returned to Chillicothe. No sooner had he arrived, than a committee called upon him to get him to teach school. Hicks Settlement, eight miles in the country, needed a teacher. The committee offered him ten dollars a month—and "board around". He accepted the position, although he was not quite sixteen years old. When he reached the schoolhouse the first morning, he says that he was more greatly surprised perhaps than any one else, because he was smaller than any of the pupils except one.

"Boarding around" had its surprises, too. Every week he stayed with a different family, and each family tried to outdo the preceding ones in furnishing him good things to eat. Sometimes he just had to eat and eat until he felt like a stuffed goose. Finally he made arrangements with a man to give him and his son lessons and thereby obtain from them board and lodging for himself and his horse. At the end of every month, the school committee waited upon him and counted out to him his ten dollars in five and ten-cent pieces.

When Langston's three months at Hicks Settlement were up, he sat down with his bag of five- and ten-cent pieces and counted out the thirty dollars. Before many days had passed, he was on his way back to Oberlin College.

He entered and worked hard for four years, graduating at the age of twenty as a Bachelor of Arts—"B.A." He continued his studies at Oberlin and received his Master's degree—"M.A."

Three years later, he was graduated from the Oberlin Theological Seminary as a Bachelor of Divinity—"B.D." He remained in Oberlin and studied law under a prominent judge. When he had finished this course, he passed his examinations and under great odds was admitted to the bar in Ohio, where he practiced for a time and won notable cases.

He often said, in later years, that around Oberlin College centered many happy memories. He courted and married an Oberlin College girl by the name of Miss Wall. He settled in Oberlin and practiced law there until the bloody Civil War.

At that time, the United States was calling to her aid the ablest men she could find. John Mercer Langston was among those called. He responded immediately and began to travel over the West and the North getting men for the army. He secured them for three regiments—the Fifty-fourth and Fifty-fifth Massachusetts and the Fifth United States of Ohio. After the war he continued to travel for the Government for two years and a half, helping the people organize schools for their children.

When that work was finished, Howard University called him to organize her Law Department.

For seven years he taught in that Department, and served for a time as Acting President of the University. He was admitted to practice law before the Supreme Court of the United States. And the President of the United States appointed him a member of the Board of Health of the District of Columbia.

Later on, another President appointed him Minister to Hayti, at a salary of $7,500 a year. After serving on that island for seven years, he returned to the United States and soon afterward was elected President of the Virginia State College at Petersburg. The state of Virginia claimed him as her own son. She honored him as a scholarly man. She elected him to the United States House of Representatives, in which he took his seat in 1890.

His last years were spent with his family at his home on College Street, Washington, District of Columbia. Before his death, November 15, 1897, he published a book of addresses called "Freedom and Citizenship".

THE BLACK BOY OF ATLANTA

MAJOR RICHARD ROBERT WRIGHT

THE BLACK BOY OF ATLANTA

By

ELIZABETH ROSS HAYNES

THE HOUSE OF EDINBORO, PUBLISHERS
BOSTON, MASSACHUSETTS

PRINTED IN THE UNITED STATES OF AMERICA

CONTENTS

ILLUSTRATIONS

FOREWORD

Some years ago, in a quiet search for an unsung American Negro whose life and solid achievements would be an inspiration to folks irrespective of race, my thoughts turned to Major Richard Robert Wright of Philadelphia. So obsessed was I with my decision, a letter was dispatched to him asking his permission and help in writing his life story. He replied cordially; and finally affirmatively.

Upon his and Mrs. Wright's invitation, I visited them in their home; was given access to his important documents, papers, correspondence stretching over the years, pictures, writings — everything. Subsequently, he came to New York and spent the night in our home. Over a period of years, I made many such visits to Philadelphia; and occasionally, he came to New York City. Whenever there was an important occasion in his honor or in which he participated, he either wrote or telephoned me to come over. As a supplement, he mailed regular consignments of his life, work, and cherished hopes; and always sent them on time. One of the latter — mentioned here because of its major importance to him, and we hope to you — was his fond desire to establish Business Scholarships for young people without regard to race or creed.

His work as president of the Citizens and Southern Bank and Trust Company and of National Freedom Day still goes on. In accordance with his plans, the U. S. Congress has passed a bill proclaiming February 1st National Freedom Day; and more than thirty States have sent delegates to its annual Celebration. His political faith as portrayed in the context was his own — expressed freely and left as a trust.

His life story, it is hoped, will return some of the actual cash spent on it, inspire younger folks at least, and help to establish Business Scholarships in his honor and through his bank.

For assistance in bringing this book to fruition, I'm deeply indebted to the following: the Wright family for intimate data, for welcoming me into their homes, and for loyal cooperation in general; the Reverend Mr. Clifford L. Miller of Boston, a devoted student and writer himself, for his frank, searching, constructive criticism of the manuscript, able suggestions, and everlasting encouragement; Miss Lura Beam, Associate in the Arts and staff member of the American Association of University Women for her constructive criticism of the manuscript, fine appreciation of the subject matter — the labor spent on it and its folk language flavor; President Rufus F. Clement for his criticism of the manuscript, acceding to Major Wright's and my wish for him to write the Introduction, and for his never failing help; a Manhattan Professional Writers group for its fine evaluation of the manuscript; stenographic help — Miss Olyve L. Jeter, for years Office Executive of the Race Relations Division, Federal Council of Churches — now National Council of Churches; Miss Alice Thomas, stenotypist U. S. Government; Miss Bernice Glanville, bookkeeper Trade School of Harlem Branch Y.W.C.A.; Mrs. Dorothy Money Robinson, R. W. Justice Business Academy, Harlem, N. Y. C.; Mr. George Glanville, now Patrolman, Police Department, N. Y. C.; 42nd Street Library and the Schomburg Collection of The Countee Cullen Branch for rare research material; and not by any means least, my publisher — House of Edinboro Publishers — for a quick understanding of the broad possibilities of the book.

E. R. H.

PREFACE

There is no story more interesting than the full account of the life of a human being. The detailed story of almost any life is thrilling.

A man may see his neighbor day after day for many years. He may feel that he knows him very well indeed. For he can tell you where his neighbor works, what he does and when. Or he may tell you what his neighbor likes and why. He may know his neighbor's hobbies, friends, pet peeves and weaknesses. But with all of this knowledge, he may actually never know his neighbor.

Few, if any of us, live just one life. Most of us live many lives between the dates of birth and death. Most of us have been several people over a span of years. During our different periods we have come into contact with different groups of people and in most cases we have different groups of friends or acquaintances. We live through years of infancy and childhood, school days and young manhood, work and play, then other work at other places. In each of these areas we may really live a different life.

This volume illustrates this point to a remarkable degree. Herein we find the story of a life — several lives. Here is a man who has been slave and is now free, who has been soldier and advocate of peace, who has been student and teacher, who has been both a borrower and a lender and has profited in each role. Here is the story of a man who from his earliest days has had supreme confidence in himself and his race. As a child we find him telling in ringing tones of the progress of his people; as a man we see him making definite contributions to that progress.

In the pages which follow, the author has in simple languages given us an opportunity to watch the growth of an eminent man and, at the same time, the evolution of a race. This is not the story of a single life. Much of the story of America can be gleaned from these pages. America, from the days of dirty slave vessels dumping their human cargoes upon the eastern coasts, down to the days of a United Nations Organization attempting to care for the basic needs of all the people.

Here is also something of the growth of a minority group family in a land struggling to be the sort of fine democracy its founders and their descendants desired that it should be. And the story includes the sacrifices and the contributions which this family made towards the realization of the democratic goal.

This is also the story of a Black Pioneer! Of a little Negro boy who dared to go to college and an elderly Negro man who decided that the pleasures and advantages of flying high above the clouds in a modern airplane outweighed the risks which age and gravity and capricious winds imposed — one and the same person. He left a successful career as a college president to begin another life which was to make him a successful chief executive of a bank.

Here is the modern version of a little black Alladin who was something of a Horatio Alger and a Tiny Tim combined in one flaming spirit.

Rufus F. Clement

President, Atlanta University

The Black Boy Of Atlanta

CHAPTER I

THE BLACK BOY OF ATLANTA

On a cold morning in 1866, a brown barefoot boy edged his way into the Box Car School on Walton Street in Atlanta, Georgia. With his slate in one hand, numb with cold, and his little tin bucket in the other, he pushed through that dusky crowd of one thousand eager learners from six to sixty years old.

When he was near enough to the front to see and hear the Yankee teacher, Mrs. Frederic Ayer, call the roll, his fingers and toes began to thaw and ache. His attempt, though, to see the smaller children rise from their puncheon seats and respond to their names caused him to forget his aches and pain. Soon he was rising on his tip toes, bending and peeping in response to the answer "present" as it came from some tall boy or girl, gray haired man or woman standing in another part of the Box Car.

He watched white-headed men and women, more accustomed to a plow or a hoe than to a book, adjust their brass-rimmed spectacles, turn their little Blue Back Spellers this way and that way in an effort to see their ABC's. He saw others point to each syllable of a word and laboriously spell it out in a monotone.

He was absorbed. Nevertheless, he was the first to reach Mrs. Ayer's table when she called the new scholars forward to enroll.

"Your name?"

"Richard Robert Wright from Cuthbert, Georgia." He answered in such a high-pitched tone of voice everybody in the Box Car smiled and tried to get a peep at him.

"How long have you been in Atlanta?" ....

"Jest a week. Me and my mamma got here Christmas Day."

"How did you come?"

"We walked."

"Walked all the way, Richard?"

"Yes, mam!"

"Then I know you are eager to learn to read and write!"

"I can read; and write my name, too. Want 'o see me?"

At her nod he laid his slate on the table, gathered up the string to which his slate pencil was tied and wrote: "Richard Robert Wright."

He looked up into her face and at her suggestion lifted his slate to the view of all the students. He squirmed at the grunts of astonishment, "En! En!" and the waving of old red bandannas. Unaccustomed to so much attention and unable to look in any direction except upward, his eyes traveled the length and breadth of the 32x80 feet Box Car.

"This old car — a former Confederate Commissary," he mused. "It's come a long way — all the way from Chattanooga, Tennessee. The Yankees who brought it here without tearing it up were smart people."

In his search for more information about that car and the Yankees who brought it there he discovered that the latter were workers of The American Missionary Association. At the direction of its District Secretary, the Reverend Erastus Milo Cravath, the Box Car had been brought to Atlanta; and some months earlier Mr. and Mrs. Frederic Ayer had come and opened school in the Negro Methodist Episcopal Church. When that was crowded out and there was no other schoolhouse for Negro children, and no public schools in the city for any children, the box car was brought as a temporary schoolhouse.

Its name and fame had traveled so rapidly, Richard's mother had heard about it and brought him on the two-hundred-mile hike to Atlanta to enter him. One of the first pieces of news he picked up was, the Box Car was already overcrowded and if he should go out there he probably would be turned away. This was disturbing news. Nevertheless, he and his mother agreed that he should go out the following Monday morning early and try. He went with a feeling of apprehension, arrived, and wormed his way into the crowded Box Car.

As one of its thousand pupils he was a preoccupied, happy boy until he began to see boys and girls, men and women just as hopeful and as hungry as he was for learning turned away. This distressed him so he ran all the way home to tell his mother about it. Suppose he hadn't gotten there just when he did. He would have been in the same fix. He kept on worrying. Finally, his teacher announced that the American Missionary Association and the Freedmen's Bureau were engaged in securing funds to purchase a site and erect a new building. Very soon he was assured that a monthly concert collection of eight hundred twenty dollars had come from Dr. Storr's Church, the First Congregational Church of Cincinnati, Ohio.

In Richard's estimation that was a lot of money. He imagined such a fine building going up when the ring of hammers actually sounded on Houston Street, he was among the first group of students to go around to take a look. He watched the progress of that building, and none too soon was called back to its dedication and christening as Storr's Schoolhouse.

He was among the four hundred day scholars admitted to that school December 8, 1866. As one of the "four hundred" for the first time in his life he was proud, polite and studious. From nine o'clock in the morning until two in the afternoon every day except Friday he was as busy as he could be. Friday afternoons for him were different in that he took part in the school prayer meeting. Another distinct occasion for him was the Sunday School in Storr's Schoolhouse every Sunday morning.

At one of these Sunday School sessions in the fall of 1868 he heard that General O. O. Howard, Commissioner of the Freedman's Bureau, would speak from that platform the following Sunday morning. He knew of General Howard, the forty acres of land and the mule which the Freedman's Bureau was supposed to give every freedman. Therefore, he and his fellow freedmen moved about that week in high gear. He listened to their wonderings and discussions. He saw their hopes soar and their expectations mount.

The next Sunday morning he was in the vanguard of that variegated crowd assembled at Storr's Schoolhouse. As he took part in repeating the Twenty-third Psalm he saw the new principal of the school, Miss Jennie E. Twitchell, ascend the platform accompanied by a tall, commanding young man with one arm. He heard a rustle behind him and looked back into dim eyes filled with tears. He too was stirred by Miss Twitchell's introduction of General Howard as a distinguished graduate of West Point, Major General in the U. S. Army, and now Commissioner of the Freedmen's Bureau. As Commissioner of the Freedmen's Bureau he would see that Negro boys and girls had food, clothing, fuel and schooling besides.

Feeling the pinch himself of all these things, Richard bent forward to catch every word General Howard would say. He watched him stretch his one arm over their dusky heads and begin:

"You have come up out of narrow cabins and cellars dowered with new freedom. Who hears can never fear for or doubt you. What shall I tell the children up North about you?"

In the stillness he — a dark brown barefoot boy, four and a half feet high, spare of build and wearing a clean white jacket, stood with his right hand uplifted.

"What is it, my boy?"

In a thin high-pitched voice he replied: "Tell 'em we're rising."

"What's your name, Sonny?"

"Richard R. Wright."

Richard was commended for his answer, and as the General moved about Atlanta the story of little Richard R. Wright, "the black boy of Atlanta," was passed on to others. In Atlanta that night over the black folks' dimly lighted supper tables his reply was the major topic of discussion.

"I reckon you heard what the little cullud boy said at the new Storr's School, ain't you?"

"I sho is, Sister Harriet Wright's boy."

"Yes, the chillun says he's smart as a whip, studies so hard he ain't no bigger'n a bar of soap."

As "the Black Boy of Atlanta," too poor to continue in school, he went to work in the home of Mr. Hannibal I. Kimbal, builder of Kimbal House, the finest hotel then in Atlanta. In the meantime he was brought to the attention of Mrs. Edmund Asa Ware, wife of the President of Atlanta University. At her request he went to see her one evening. He answered her questions relative to his family, and gladly accepted her offer to give him lessons at night. Then he hurried home to tell his mother the good news. He had little time for study, she agreed, but God would help him find a way or make one. He believed so firmly in her and what she said he lay awake that night until a solution popped into his mind. Oh, yes, he had it: He would write out his Latin declensions, stick them up before him and commit them to memory while he worked in the day.

Frequently as he worked and glanced up at his paper Mr. Kimbal would say, "Dick, I never studied any Latin. Throw that book away, come and go with me to Europe."

This invitation was such a temptation, had it not been for his mother he might have given up school, gone to Europe and into business. On the contrary, he stuck to his Latin, worked hard on his other subjects, and prayed to get back into day school.

One night as he knelt down it seemed that Jesus came so close to him he felt His hands and heard Him say: "Richard Wright, you are going back to school."

In order that he might get back in school he brought his monthly pay of five dollars to his mother every month. He presented it to her and often wondered why she always said, "I'm going to save my money and live off the interest."

This expression took such hold upon him he began to think of having money in the bank some day. One afternoon as he passed along the street and saw a sign of the opening of a savings bank, he stopped in front of the doorway. He watched men walk into that bank like gods, reach back into their hip pockets and pull out rolls of money. His eyes bulged as he repeated the saying, "I'm going to save my money and live off the interest." As he stood outside reading again the sign on the front of the bank building a man paused and asked him if he had any money in that bank.

"No, sir, but I mean to have."

The man straightened up and asked his name.

"Richard R. Wright, sir; and may I ask yours, too?"

"J. W. Alvord."

Later Richard learned that J. W. Alvord, then General Superintendent of Education, and formerly Secretary of

THE LOG CABIN near Dalton, Georgia, in which Major R. R. Wright was born, May 16, 1853

AN OLD BOX CAR

the Freedmen's Bureau, wrote a letter that day to General Howard as follows:

> "The lad who in this school gave you the message immortalized by Whittier is a promising scholar. I am sorry to say he is not at present in school. His mother aids him in all her power, but the step-father has taken him from school, insisting that he help support himself and the family. I don't hesitate to sanction measures to have him returned. His name is Richard R. Wright."

While other folks also worked for Richard's return to day school, he continued his night school studies with Mrs. Ware. His progress pleased her so much she gave him a brand new suit of clothes — the first suit he had ever owned. Many times he had stumped his toe looking back at white boys in their nice suits. To have one of his very own was almost too good to be true. He hurried home and showed it to his mother. He tried it on; turned front, then all around for her to admire it. With his head up and shoulders back he walked out upon the floor and showed her how he would step in it on Sundays. It was a grand experience. It thrilled him so, he set out to earn enough money to buy a pair of Sunday shoes to correspond with it. To do this he made himeslf a shoe shine box. He threw it over his shoulder at his lunch hour and often ran out munching a sandwich, watching folks' feet as well as their faces and bidding for a shine.

With each successful bid he tried first to do a better job than any other bootblack. Secondly, he used his best manners and behavior which his mother had taught him would carry him places where money couldn't. Accordingly, after several months of persistent effort, study and politeness, he had not only made enough money to buy a pair of Sunday shoes, but friends who assisted him in his effort to return to day school.

As he hurried back to Storr's School on a rainy Monday morning, his eagerness to catch up with his classmates and graduate with them left no time or thought of his Sunday shoes, his struggle to get back, the distance he had come, or his achievements as the Black Boy of Atlanta.

CHATER II

CHILDHOOD

Those childhood traits — the pursuit of learning and forging ahead against great odds — in a world where ancestry is not expected of the American Negro, so dominated Richard's whole life, he had little inclination for looking backward or dwelling on the past. To him as a busy American, the history of his illustrious forbears who influenced Egyptian religion and civilization and inspired the traditions of our own civilization was fantastic and mythological.

In tracing his ancestry he always began with his Grandma Lucy, a Mandingo princess who was brought to this country on a slave ship the latter part of the eighteenth century. From her own lips he had so often heard the story of her landing at Havre de Grace, Maryland, being sold and taken to Abbeville, South Carolina, where his mother, Harriet, was born — he could repeat it verbatim.

He also learned that while his mother Harriet was still a young girl, hers and Grandma Lucy's master bought a plantation in northwest Georgia and moved them there. On that plantation his Grandma Lucy was married to a fellow slave, became the mother of a son whom she named Richard, and in later years became the plantation mother of her little grandson Richard, and ninety-nine other slave children.

Before her Grandson Richard was born, however, his mother Harriet obtained the enviable position of maid to her young mistress at the Big House. As such she came in contact with the coachman, a half breed Cherokee Indian named Robert Waddell. They fell in love, and, as favorite servants were given a fine slave wedding in the Big House. Despite their favored positions, though, they soon began to deplore the possibility of a child coming to them as slaves. He might have to come up as a hewer of wood and drawer of water.

Notwithstanding their lament, their son whom they named Richard Robert Waddell, was born in the month of May, 1855, in a log cabin on that plantation. He was a tiny baby; and homely, too, according to the old slave women's comments. His mouth was too small, his color was too dark to suit anybody; his hair grew too far back on his little head and was nothing like that Indian glory on his father's head. His bright eyes, his only redeeming feature, could see through a person and not flinch. He would never be afraid of an overseer or anybody else, his Grandma Lucy predicted.

The name, Richard Robert Waddell, given him before his birth, pleased everybody. He was an unusual child. Unlike many of the other slave children he had a name, a wedded mother and grandmother, too. Yet, he was a sickly, puny child who neither walked nor talked until he was more than two years old. This disturbed his father so he took him up whenever there was opportunity and taught him to thumb the brass buttons on his livery and to try to say "Dad." Finally, he began to recognize the carriage which his father drove as its wheels sank in the sand and threw back clouds of dust.

One day he saw the carriage pass with its sleek bay horses in a trot, but the coachman neither waved his hand nor looked in his direction. He ran to Grandma Lucy with disappointment written on his face. As he stared at her she sighed and petted him nervously. When he began to cry she took him up, hugged him close to her bosom, rocked him in her arms and crooned plaintively.

"Dad's gone bye-bye, Dad's gone . . ."

Under the spell he cried and even yelled as if he knew his father had suddenly run away and the bloohounds were on his track. His increasing awareness of his father's absence touched his mother Harriet, too. He didn't know what had happened, but she knew his father's mistress had spoiled him by allowing him to be fed at the Big House instead of given slaves' food. Neither did he know at that tender age that one day when his father refused to eat what was placed before him his mistress insisted and finally broke down in tears. Her husband came home and ordered Bob to be strung up for a "cat hauling" instead of a plain thrashing. Bob's Cherokee spirit revolted and fought back. He fought his master to a standstill, and in some mysterious way escaped.

Little Richard's continued attempt to say "Dad," to feel for his father's brass buttons, and to gaze for the carraige, disturbed his mother more every day. However, as he began to run and play with the older children these associations crowded out thoughts of his father. When he was three years old he carried his own tin bucket to the spring and refused to let any one dip up water for him. Yet, he was so small more than once he barely escaped being catapulted into the spring head foremost. Often in cold weather his fingers ached and he spilled all the water along the pathway up the hill. His descent to the spring was so difficult he slipped and frequently fell. In tears but undaunted he wiped his running nose on his osnaburg shirt sleeve, picked his way down and refilled his bucket.

In the evenings at feed time he climbed upon the rail fence which separated the barnyard from his mother's yard. With his thin bare legs and shirt tail astride it he watched the chickens, the ducks, the goslings, the guineas and the turkeys pick up corn. When a big handful was thrown out in the direction opposite his gaze his little bright eyes dazzled and he bobbed up in excitement as the fowl ran thither.

One evening as he rode that topmost rail, he fell off on the hard ground and hurt his right arm. He looked around, rebounded, and with his face in wrinkles attempted to climb back with his left arm but couldn't make it. The pain was too excruciating.

"You won't listen to nobody," scolded Grandma Lucy. "A hard head always makes a soft behind."

His fractured right arm was bound up, put into a sling and blessed with her command to be careful. In spite of her injunctions he bumped into something about every day. The fracture knit so slowly his arm remained in the sling for weeks. During its bondage he began using his left and discovered it was just as amenable and efficient as his right had been. After the bandage was removed he used both interchangeably and gave demonstrations to the other children of his ability to throw stones as well with one hand as with the other.

During one of these demonstrations he threw back and knocked a boy down. For this carelessness his mistress decided to punish him. She broke a small limb from a peach tree and ordered him to come to her. He stood still, looked up at her, bit his finger nails and tried to decide what to do.

"When I get through with you, sir, —" she threatened.

While she waited impatiently, shed the unctious leaves from the switch and ordered him to make haste and come, he entreated her: He didn't mean to do it; he wasn't going to do it anymore. If she would let him off this time he would never do it again. Still pleading he walked slowly towards her. Finally, seeing his entreaties were of no avail he broke away and ran until he came to a hollow log. Into it he crawled on his hands and his stomach while his shirt-tail rolled up about his waist and left his behind and legs scratched and bleeding. There he lay panting and listening for footsteps. Instead, he saw a lizard and thought it was a snake.

"Gee!" He bumped his head against the top of the hollow log. He kicked and scrambled and scuffled and backfired. As soon as his legs and naked back parts were out in the open he expected every minute his mistress would grab him. He couldn't go back in and he trembled as he pushed outward. He bumped his head again, but soon landed on his feet and started off.

He hadn't run far before he paused, turned his head and listened. Yes, that was his mistress calling:

"Richard — — Rich — ard!"

He scratched his head. If he went back he would get a whipping. If stayed away he would get two whippings when he did return. He didn't know which alternative to try, until he heard that voice come over the air again:

"Ri—c h a r d —— hot biscuits for you, R i c h a rd !" Hot biscuits!"

He still hesitated — but the continued call to hot biscuits so excited his taste, he licked his lips in memory of the last biscuits he had eaten, and struck a trot. As he entered the gate his mistress came from behind the house with her switch in hand and dared him to run. He pleaded, but she took hold of his thin arm and his shirt-tail, too. He screamed with the first lick. However, she thrashed his back and bottom until they tingled. As soon as he was turned loose, his mother Harriet grabbed him and whipped him with a similar switch, for his disobedience to his mistress.

His associations with that plantation — its hollow log and its peach tree switches — were severed when he was five years old. His master moved to the little town of Dalton — five miles away — and took him, his mother, his grandmother and the other slaves. There among the foothills of the beautiful Blue Ridge Mountains trying war experiences awaited them.

Soon he and his mother were given to old master's son-in-law, John B. Griffin, as a wedding present. Consequently, he and she were taken away to his home while Grandma Lucy remained with their former master. Richard missed his grandmother very much. The separation was grievous, but before many months had passed, under fear and pressure of shot and shell and brigandage, both families — the Kirkseys and the Griffins — had fled southward. Richard and his mother along with other Griffin slaves found refuge at Cuthbert, Georgia, while Grandma Lucy and the Kirkseys refugeed on to Dawson, Georgia.

At Cuthbert, Richard's old job as water carrier was not quite the same. Instead of dipping water from the spring he now used a tin bucket tied to the end of a plow line which he let down into the well. Against the wooden rounds and curbing he banged and battered the bucket. Once in a great while he let the line slip out of his hands and stir up mud in the bottom of the well, in spite of the field hands' thirsty calls. Small of stature, barefooted and clad in an osnaburg shirt he stepped lively with the water bucket on his head and the muscles of his neck and little skinny arms twitching. He apologized.

"The water got muddy 'cause the draw-bucket jumped out of my hands."

"Yes," replied the overseer in his white uniform, "next time this lash will jump out of my hands. Can't draw water, and talking about plowing."

Everybody else, it seemed to Richard, also contended he was too small to handle a plow. His determination, it was agreed, was strong but it took more than that to break up new ground and bar off cotton. He might let the plow lines slip out of his hands and the mule run away and cut himself with the sweep. Or he might cut up the cotton in his attempt to bar it off. His undersize and all the consequent preditions did not deter him very much. As soon as he reached the age of seven years, his work was changed to that of plow and hoe hand. He knew how to hitch up his mule and plow too; still, handling a plow from early morning until noon was a large order. However, his master told the overseer to let him alone. He was Harriet's child. He would get broken in pretty soon. With that encouragement Richard held his plow more steadily and feared much less the whipping post which stood behind his mother's house as a silent reminder.

Another situation, though, began to disturb him. He saw a man of unusual intelligence and force, Alexander Wright from Charleston, South Carolina, come into their cabin home and life. He noticed that the man's visits were frequent and his and Harriet's attentions to one another were progressing rapidly. This excited the boy's jealousy and rendered him quite unhappy. When he first realized that his mother and Alexander Wright were to be married he was sad indeed. Contrarily, when he learned that their wedding was causing a great deal of talk among the slaves because it was to be held in the Big House, he was as proud as his pet turkey gobbler.

Every slave who could come to the wedding was there. Richard had never witnessed the like before. His well combed coarse hair which grew far back on his forehead, appeared to stand on end. His sparkling black eyes were agog, his small mouth hung open. He was amazed to see so many slaves in the Big House; and proud to detect his master and his mistress over in the corner enjoying the fiddling. When he saw his mother come forward in her "trail" (train) and veil, he blurted out in a lisping voice:

"That's my mamma."

Before the words were out of his mouth one of the old slave women slapped her hand over it. Neverless, with his well scrubbed dark face glistening against the white background of his clean osnaburg shirt as his only garment, he followed his mother into the main dining room. After the simple ceremony he drank so much sweetened water his little stomach was distended and he suffered with the bellyache.

He often wondered why his step-father, Alexander Wright, was such a quiet man. During the several years in which two other children were born into the family Richard could never fathom his thoughtful demeanor. He couldn't understand him at all until he learned that his step-father's transcendent thought was the emancipation of his people. Having gotten that much, he was not surprised to see him kiss his two children, caress Harriet, kiss him and steal away one morning early to join the Yankee Army.

Richard was so afraid something might take his mother away to join her husband he would scarcely let her get out of his sight. One night he followed her to the parlor door upon hearing her master call her. He listened intently to her master address her.

"Hattie, I have something to say to you. — If you are fool enough to go out of here and starve to death, you may go."

"What do you mean, Mos Griff?"

"I don't want to drive you out. You have little children. I don't want them to go out and starve."

"Do you mean I'm free to go, Mos Griff?"

"Yes, if you are fool enough to go, you may."

"Well, Moster, if I'm free to go tomorrow mornin' and take my chillun, I'll go."

Richard scampered away from the door in great glee. As he and his mother walked to their cabin he whispered to her and tried to find out where they were going. To his repeated question she shook her head, "Don't know, Son."

Finally he realized she was in too much distress to talk, so he gave up.

The next morning he rose with the chickens and helped his little sister and brother to get dressed. He ran out in the yard while his mother gathered up her few bedclothes in her arms, got the old axe and put it under his coat. Soon he and the other members of the family were on their way; not one of them knew where. When they reached a small clump of woods on the outskirts of the city he proposed that they stop there. His mother hesitated. If she had an axe to cut some poles to build a shelter, such a place might do. To her surprise, he pulled the old axe from under his coat, went out and began to chop. He and she cut poles, gathered moss and grass and dirt and built a shelter. With a shelter of some kind over their heads he settled down with a feeling of relief and security, and even tried alone to bring for his mother the bundle of wash from the Yankees near by.

His contentment was soon upset. His erstwhile master came out and demanded that his mother give up him and his little brother. His erstwhile master's father-in-law had shown him the error of his way in freeing them. Richard clung to his mother until his master overpowered her and forcibly took him away. He cried and grieved thereafter, but she began a five months' struggle for his recovery. She went to the Yankees and obtained an order for his delivery. Then she hired a wagon and set out for her former master's plantation.

When her wagon rolled up to the Big House about noon one day, Richard heard whisperings of her arrival. He ran out, peeped and got a glimpse of her climbing down on the hub of the wagon. He waved frantically when the mad rush of barking dogs stopped her, but was afraid to venture further. As soon, however, as he saw his master come to the door, stamp his foot and yell to one of his men servants to keep the dogs off of Harriet, he rushed back and brought his little brother out by the hand. He vied with him, old master and everybody else in welcoming his mother.

With surprise and acute pleasure he heard his mistress invite her into the dining room for a bite to eat. That was such an unheard of thing, he ran around the house in an attempt to peep in at the back door. Foiled in that endeavor, he climbed up on the picket fence enclosing the yard outside the dining room window. In his endeavor to stand on top of two of those sharp pickets he fell over head foremost into the yard and just missed a trough of water for the chickens. He bounced up, shook his right arm and kept running from the scene, with his brother in close pursuit. His arm hurt so badly he cried for his mother and made for the dining room door. As he entered, his mother was handing his master some papers and explaining that they acknowledged the freedom of her children and gave her the right to take them away with her.

On hearing that, Richard stopped crying, watched his master's hands shake, and heard his voice tremble.

"Hattie, they are your children."

He pulled at his little brother, skipped out and made a bee-line for the wagon. He climbed up part way, then reached for his little brother's hand. After quite a tug he pulled his brother up and sat down on an old quilt spread on the floor of the wagon body. Soon after they had adjusted their osnaburg shirt-tails, Richard answered his mother as she stepped off the porch, bade her master and mistress good-bye, and called him: "Richard!"

"Here we is, Ma." His face was aglow. He rose and tried to help his mother climb up on the wagon hub. He giggled and bumped up and down as she slapped the mules with the lines and the wagon gave him a jolt. He was excited. Nevertheless, he listened and understood every word his mother said. He was free now and as soon as he reached home he would enter the Chip School taught by a Yankee teacher. If he behaved himself and studied hard he would learn to read and write and figure like the teacher.

He was young and still undersized for his years. He was free but couldn't understand all the possibilities of his new freedom. However, his mother's words aroused something within him. He awoke at daylight the next morning thinking about the Chip School and the smart Yankee teacher. He hopped out of bed, got the wash-pan, washed his face, and at his mother's command washed his ears too and combed his tight, unruly hair. With his osnaburg shirt as a fine background for his narrow dark face, black sparkling eyes and bare feet he ran nearly every step of the way to the Chip School.

His great ambition was to write and to figure. He had often admired his former master's ability to sign his name and stick the pencil up behind his ear. He was determined to do likewise. The first week of his attendance at the Chip School he learned to say his alphabet forward and backward and to write his name. Proud of his achievement, he stood out in the middle of the floor and recited them every night to his mother. He slipped to his neighbors' cabins, showed them how he could write "Richard Robert Wright" and then stick the pencil up behind his ear. Partly through his quiet exhibition he caused the Chip School teacher's fame to circulate. One day one of the county authorities stopped by and asked what so many little Negro children were doing there.

"Nothing but picking up chips," replied the teacher.

Among Richard's eager competitors there was a little girl who was learning to play the piano. As he noticed his schoolmates stand around her and comment about her learning to play the piano he wondered if she were smarter than he. Finally, one afternoon he was lifted up when he heard her mother compare her ability to learn to play the piano with his to learn to read and write. Richard Wright, her mother told her, had learned to read and write in a week's time and it had cost his mother twenty-five cents. There she was paying her former mistress one dollar per lesson with the use of the piano for practice. She had been taking lessons two whole weeks and couldn't play a hymn. She would give her one more week's trial. If she hadn't learned to play by then she would stop throwing her money away on her. If Richard could learn that much in one week, she should learn something in three weeks.

Richard was proud because his achievement was attracting the attention of the neighbors. In fact, he was so inspired he never missed a week-day night reciting to his mother what he had learned that day. He knew she couldn't read or write, but she could understand and work for his advancement. He had heard her pray on bended knees for wisdom and understanding and a way for her children to get to Atlanta and enter the Yankee school.

He became deeply concerned with her early morning prayers for him and the other children. One morning early a distressed, low voice called her name. He noticed she didn't answer until the call was repeated. He was so afraid he jumped out of bed and ran to his mother. He shuddered as someone broke the news of an uprising on the Kirksey plantation led by his Uncle Richard, now an overseer. He pleaded with his mother to leave there for fear the aftermath might cause her former master to pursue them.

Accordingly, Richard and the other two children were bundled up and left shut up in the house while their mother went away to make arrangements for leaving. On her return the two younger ones were helped into a covered wagon with a white family. Behind that and two other wagons with families in them, Richard, his mother, another woman and her husband started out on their two-hundred-mile journey for Atlanta.

CHAPTER III

COLLEGE DAYS

Richard's graduation day at Storr's School was a memorable occasion. He and ten of his classmates were selected to enter the greatly publicized Atlanta University. He was all the more thrilled because he had heard of the sixty-acre site out on Diamond Hill purchased for the University by the American Missionary Association. He was also familiar with some of the achievements of Dr. Edmund Asa Ware who had been elected President of the University.

As a boy fanning the flies from his mother's boarding-house table, he had listened to Senator Alperio Bradley and Senator William Henry Harrison discuss these aspects of the University as well as its legislative outlook. Consequently, he, too, knew of Dr. Ware's interest, as a teacher in the South, in the litigation on the status of the freedmen. He, too, knew the story underlying Dr. Ware's decision to devote his life to the betterment of the Negro people. In Dr. Ware's class at Yale University, the year prior to Lincoln's issuance of the Emancipation Proclamation, a vote was taken on whether the Negro should be free. Every member in his class voted "no" except himself. He felt so badly about this he decided to devote his life to the betterment of the Negro people.

Richard was so moved by this account he was eager to see President Ware. He was also interested in the sixty-acre site out on Diamond Hill which none of his folks seemed to think much of. Therefore, he welcomed the opportunity to lead his ten classmates out on a hot day in

June to attend the cornerstone laying of the University's first building. Impressed by what he saw and heard, especially with Mr. John Mercer Langston — noted Negro lawyer and graduate of Oberlin College — orator of the day, he wrote an essay of a few lines and deposited it in the cornerstone.

In September of that same year, 1869, he went back to see that four-story brick building, North Hall, completed. The experience was almost too wonderful to be real. He went into every room and nook — the parlor, the dining room, the kitchen, the classrooms on the second floor, the dormitory space on the third floor for sixteen gentlemen. He was a gentleman, yes, but he didn't have the one dollar monthly tuition and the ten dollars per month for board including furnished room, light, fuel and washing, required for tenancy.

However, in one month's time he returned and enrolled as one of the thirty-three day scholars. He passed the qualification tests of good moral character, fixed purpose to improve his time, and earnest desire to fit himself for usefulness. His approval was gratifying because he had read in the catalogue that those who had not these attributes were advised not to seek admission, as their presence would not be tolerated.

His registration brought the total enrollment of the two departments — preparatory and normal — up to eighty-nine students. He was enrolled in the former department. His new teachers as well as the new building impressed him very much. Familiar as he was with the story of his President's Yale classmates, he was shocked to learn that the President had brought down one of these classmates, the Reverend Cyrus W. Francis, as a teacher. When he discovered, however, that the Reverend Cyrus Francis had his Master's Degree and knew the Greek language, he introduced himself to him and told him of his burning desire to conjugate a Greek verb. He was de-

BOARD OF DIRECTORS — 1947

R. R. WRIGHT, SR.
Founder

President EMANUEL C. WRIGHT
Secretary, WALTER C. BECKETT
Treasurer, HARRIET W. LEMON

WILLIAM NEWMAN	R. R. WRIGHT, JR.
JAMES H. IRVIN	NATHANIEL S. DUFF
W. C. WILLIAMSON	EARL S. DALES
RANDOLPH WINSTON	SAMUEL E. ROBERTSON

termined to change the concensus of opinion that a Negro would never learn to conjugate a Greek verb. From the Reverend Cyrus Francis and his other teachers he says he not only learned to conjugate a Greek verb, to translate Virgil, to do higher arithmetic and algebra, but to understand the meaning of opportunity and incentive.

He appreciated these virtues, worked hard, and was well spoken of by all of his teachers. He avoided playing in class, talking loudly and being discourteous to his teachers and schoolmates — practices for which the President was known to deal severe rebuke. Politeness and order, cardinal requirements of all the students, Richard observed.

He was all the time hoping that by his good behavior and excellent marks he would get into the boys' new dormitory, South Hall, then under construction. He went so far as to select the room he liked best in the accommodations there for sixty "gentlemen." He thought perhaps his mother's boarding house receipts would improve since there was great rejoicing in the Negro section of Atlanta over the ratification of the 13th, 14th and 15th Amendments to the Federal Constitution. Although he heard repeatedly that better times were in the offing and that every Negro should rejoice in the Act which made him not only a free man but a citizen, he couldn't rejoice for thinking and wondering how he would get into the boys' new dormitory.

He knew not how it was managed; but in the fall of 1870 he entered the boys' new dormitory as one of the one hundred and seventy gentlemen. He worked one hour every day to supplement what his mother paid plus the fifty dollar scholarship given him by the Ladies' Benevolent Association of a northern church. In addition, he was given shoes and clothes from barrels of clothing which came from the north. His small stature and normal size feet as compared with the size and the large feet of many others were in his favor. He received enough of these articles on the quiet (just as though he were the only student dressing out of the barrel) to dress up every day in the week and Sundays, too.

As a work student, one of his first assignments along with other boys was to rake and clean up the unsightly campus. The location of the University on the grounds where the Confederate forces in the Civil War threw up their entrenchments to resist Sherman on his famous March to the Sea, and the surrounding area were considered so unpromising, the owner of the latter began to sell off lots on the edge of the campus to Negroes. In cases of default the University bought in the interest of purchasers.

Unimpressed with his work assignment and seeing what he thought was an opportunity to earn an extra dollar, Richard participated with a friend in selling off several of these lots. He did his work assignment on the campus too, but did it grudgingly because he thought he had come to college to get a quick education and not have to work with his hands.

Finally one day he and his fellow workers stared in ominous silence at President Ware, a tall, fine-looking gentleman, as he came out on the campus with a rake in his hands. Despite their gaze, he took off his coat and led them in cleaning up the unsightliness. Richard was struck with awe. He watched to see if President Ware hadn't lost some of his dignity and learning. When he could detect nothing missing he was surprised. He was equally pleased, because the courageous president never scolded them for their slothfulness in doing the work. Instead, he shook their impression that work with the hands was beneath a college man. After years of dealing with him, Richard felt that he was the only white man in the world without any race prejudice whatever.

Richard's progress with his studies pleased his mother

so much she bought him a linen handkerchief to stick up in his coat pocket, like President Ware. One of his classmates, William Finch from Augusta, made fun of it and talked about it in class until Richard was quite peeved. He said nothing to Finch, but as soon as they went out for recess he pounced upon Finch with both fists. "Because your daddy's the richest colored man in Augusta, you needn't think you're better'n anybody else." As he pummeled Finch, Finch ducked and ran, with him in hot pursuit.

They ran into the building and almost into the arms of Professor Thomas N. Chase, better known to the boys as "Old Man Tommy." Old Man Tommy, a powerful man, grabbed Richard by the nape of the neck and shook out the prediction that somebody would kill old "biggity" Finch yet. His manner of handling Richard amused the other boys very much. "Old Man Tommy," they said, "had Richard on his shoulder, holding him up."

Another amusing incident in Richard's early college life was an experience with Miss Gordon who was hostess of the table at which he took his meals. He knew she was very economical, and never allowed a student at her table to throw away any food whatsoever. Each one was required to eat everything he took on his plate.

One cold day as he entered the dining room, the savor of the good hot soup increased his appetite. After he had drunk one bowl of it he asked for just a little more. Instead of serving a little the mischievous student who acted as host dipped up the bowl full. Richard couldn't say a word. The sight of that bowl full heated his temper and took away his appetite. He looked at the bowl and shook his head. Miss Gordon insisted that he drink every drop of that soup.

"I can't, Miss Gordon."

She insisted, and finally gave the command.

"Leave the table then, and go to your room."

He went to his room, undressed and got in bed. In a few minutes he heard footsteps coming down the hall. He covered up his head. There was a vigorous knock on the door — another — and another.

"Richard!"

"Yes'm, Miss Gordon."

"Open this door."

"I'm asleep, Miss Gordon."

"Open this door, I say."

"I'm in bed, Miss Gordon."

"Get up and open this door."

He rose slowly, turned the key in the lock and cracked the door. By him stepped Miss Gordon with the bowl of soup. She pointed to a chair on the far side of a little table.

"Sit down in that chair."

He dropped down in the chair.

"Are you trying to knock the bottom out of it?" She rolled her pretty gray eyes and took a seat in the chair across from him. She set the bowl of soup in the middle of the table.

"Now, you are to drink every drop of that soup."

He pleaded; he was full up to his neck and couldn't take another drop to save his life. She looked him through, rose and knelt down by the little chair. She closed her eyes and said, "Let us pray."

He told her he couldn't pray; he was too full. She prayed, nevertheless, to her Heavenly Father to help him drink that soup. Her prayer was so fervent he rose and drank two spoonsful of soup. She patted him on the back and said he might return to his class.

As he returned to his class, he kept his eye on his closest competitor, James B. Lucky, and decided that Lucky was slyly giggling at him. Before he and some of the other boys — Henry O. Flipper, Samuel Benjamin Morse, Jim Lucy, London Waters, George White (who became the father of the distinguished Walter White), Edward J. Penny, and William Crogman — could settle down, all of them burst out with laughter. Richard, they said, was chock-full of soup and couldn't study.

Richard looked the girls of his class over and selected the most brilliant one of all, Lucy Craft Laney, as his sweetheart. To him she was the loveliest, most energetic and attractive brown skin girl he had ever met. Even their intellectual tilts over algebra and geometry were sweet to him. Her unwillingness to give up intrigued him. One day there was a problem in geometry which she was unable to solve. Since he had solved it, the teacher requested him to put it on the board and demonstrate it. Before he had finished, Lucy raised her hand.

"I do not understand that problem and I don't think Richard is working it correctly."

In a very polite manner the teacher corrected her: "You must not say 'Richard,' you must say 'Master Wright.' "

"Well," replied she, "he's no 'master' of mine."

Richard not only laughed heartily along with the other members of the class but conceded she was correct. He was not her master in mathematics or anything else, despite the fact that he often disturbed her conclusions as much as she upset his. On another occasion there were uproars and snickers over the pronunciation of the "t" in "but." The teacher had admonished the class to enunciate the final "t's" and "d's" of words. Richard, apt in correcting these small mistakes, fixed his eyes on the "t" in "but" in the next line as Lucy Laney read. The minute she called the word "but," he raised his hand.

"Mrs. Chase, I understood the reader to leave out the "t" in "b-u-t." In mockery of his correction there were turns and twists of heads and eyes. He was worsted in that combat but his embarrassment was soon transposed into wishful thinking.

He made it possible to happen to meet Lucy and drop alongside of her as she passed from that class to the next. He wrote her, declaring he disliked the common saying, "Roses are red and violets are blue; sugar is sweet and so are you," but nothing else fitted the situation so well. He even went so far as to seek her hand. To his chagrin she told him books and boys wouldn't mix. She was too busy with her books and her preparation for life to be bothered.

His love for her soon cooled through other attractions and interests. His new position as Sunday School Superintendent was heralded abroad. He was so smart, the gossip was, he had been chosen not only as the "black boy of Atlanta," but as the youngest Negro Sunday School Superintendent in the world. When it came to reciting the Catechism, the Twenty-third Psalm and the Books of the Bible, he had no competitor. Naturally, with his winsome personality he became a favorite among the girls of the Church and the Sunday School.

His success with the Sunday School led his mother to think he might get a country day school to teach for the summer. Now that he had studied in college it was about time for him to quit hard work. Then, too, she thought school-teaching would be a lucrative profession. He might thereby earn enough to put him through Atlanta University the coming session.

With the approach of spring and sunshine and new life, the idea took shape in letters which he wrote to several Georgia communities. To them he awaited what he thought would be immediate replies and open arms begging him to come out to teach. In the meantime President Ware sent for him and asked if he would like to go to Ellaville, Schley County, Georgia, to teach for the summer. A request for a teacher had come in from Professor Floyd D. Snelson, a prominent teacher out there. Professor Snelson said he was writing for Mr. William Styles, one of the leading Negroes of the County, who had requested him to secure a teacher. The latter, Professor Snelson's letter stated, was a very responsible man and well thought of by the white people of the community. He would be responsible for the teacher's coming.

Richard's usual ready reply failed him. He hesitated —. He looked up at President Ware.

"President Ware, that's the place where the Yankees were imprisoned, isn't it?"

"Yes," the president agreed.

He called Richard's attention, though, to the fact that he needed money to get back to school in the fall, and his mother had two other children to support and educate. There was the additional fact that the folks near Ellaville were calling for a teacher. They were offering too small a salary, it was true, but President Ware thought with a little pressure from Professor Snelson they might pay more. Richard acceded the possibility and consented to talk it over with his mother. If nothing better presented itself in the next few days he would accept that position.

As he talked it over with his mother she too was terribly disappointed with what she termed "mighty po weges" for a schoolteacher. To her who was sweating in the kitchen for her son to be a schoolteacher, the Schley County salary of three dollars per month and board around was a great disappointment. He could earn more than that working at Kimball House, she argued.

However, after he waited a few days and nothing better came in, she advised him to accept that. He was young and didn't have the mother wit to bolster up his education like an older person. Yet, he might go out there, "learn" the children so fast, have such nice manners and behaviour with white and black folks alike and maybe teach some of the older folks at night to read the Bible, they would sell chickens and eggs and pay him more than they thought they could.

Encouraged by her advice he got in touch with Professor Snelson. In about a week he received a letter from Mr. Styles inviting him to board at his house altogether. He was also informed that Professor Snelson would be in Atlanta on a certain date and he could come back with him if he liked.

Richard washed his clothes, and had his old shoes half-soled. He bought a watch and chain and a new neck-tie. On the date for Professor Snelson to come to town he rose at sun-up, dressed and waited out on his mother's little front porch. He watched the sun rise higher and the time pass. He pulled out his biscuit watch again. He couldn't understand. He looked up and down the street. He watched every wagon pass. He went back into the house and pulled his little tin trunk farther from the doorway that he might not create the impression of having been disappointed. Finally, when he saw a stranger stop opposite their house and gaze up with an air of uncertainty, he rushed out with a broad smile.

"Is this Professor Snelson?"

"Yes. Is this the place where Professor R. R. Wright lives?"

"Yes, sir, I'm Professor Wright." He extended his hand and they greeted each other, but Professor Snelson looked at him as if he didn't believe him. He held his own, however, and assured Professor Snelson that he was the man for whom he was looking. He was small of stature but he was superintendent of one of the largest colored Sunday Schools in Atlanta. He could hold down a small school near Ellaville. Professor Snelson scratched his head and informed him that the school was near Americus, but a wagon would be waiting at Ellaville to meet him.

He and Professor Snelson left Atlanta but missed connections at some little junction, therefore did not reach Ellaville until the next day. The sun was very hot and the wagon which had waited for Richard had just gone when he arrived. If he would hurry, though, someone told him, he could overtake it down the road. It had just gotten out of sight. With no time to lose he raised his cheap umbrella and struck a trot. He ran with all his might and without looking to the right or the left. However, he never caught sight of the wagon and he was afraid lest somebody meddle him in those early years of freedom.

After he had gotten far out in the country he saw a man who demanded to know where he was going. He stopped, answered in as broken English as he could and started on.

"Take down that umbrella!" the man ordered. He closed his umbrella, sauntered away and began to run so fast the man was left far in the distance.

He ran nearly every step of the twelve miles to Americus. Then he was so nearly dead he dropped down on the Courthouse steps, unable for quite a while to do anything but sit there. As soon as he gathered sufficient strength he went over to a man and inquired of Mr. Styles' whereabouts. Yes, he had run the whole twelve miles, he told Mr. Styles as they drove out to Mr. Styles' house, and he had little left except a good appetite.

When the wagon rolled up to the gate and stopped he jumped out and stretched his limbs. As he did so two big country fellows passing by called to Mr. Styles, "New teacher didn't come, did he, Mr. Styles?"

"Yes, that's him."

They looked at each other and snickered.

"That little chap; he can't teach nobody."

"Look here!" reprimanded Mr. Styles. "Looks are mighty deceiving sometimes." Then he informed them that the President of Atlanta University said Professor Wright's size was no index of his ability. He was one of the brainiest scholars in the whole University.

Despite his ability the country folks began to speak with pity of the child teacher. He was too young and too small to teach those big country boys and girls. They even pleaded with Mr. Styles to send him back. "No," Mr.

Styles said, "we'll give him a trial and if he won't do I'll take him back."

The following Sunday he made a fine impression on the Sunday School. "He ain't much bigger than a minute," the folks who heard him explain the Sunday School lesson said, "but he's a Bible scholar as 'sho as you're born." They were still talking and making predictions when he opened the day school the next morning with twenty-five scholars. To his regret some of these scholars were older and much bigger than he. Yet he endeavored to keep his poise and courage. He looked them over carefully and picked out from among the larger ones a muscular fellow about twenty-five years of age whose name was Hicks. Hicks spent so much time courting a girl about twenty years old that neither of them could learn to spell. Yet, in the spelling matches when he was turned down he refused to move. No amount of persuasion or abuse had any effect upon him. He simply stood in his tracks and would not move. He also threw out the threat that if that little chap of a teacher said anything to him he would take him down and 'stomp' him.

Richard, aware of his own disadvantage in size as compared with Hicks' great bulk figured out the situation. There was nothing to do but outwit him or lose his position as teacher. He decided to organize a Board of Trustees similar to that of Atlanta University, and elect Mr. Styles as its president. No sooner than that was done he called together the members of the board and presented to them the Hicks matter. Everyone of them agreed to cooperate with him and meet him at the schoolhouse on a certain morning at a specified hour.

In the meantime he and Mr. Styles talked the matter over. He had spent a few nights at Professor Snelson's home and noticed he had a pistol. He borrowed it and took it to school one morning. He arrived one hour before regular school time, stood his large switch up in the corner of the room near his table and tried to put the long black revolver in his table drawer, but it was too long. Instead, he laid it out on the table.

The day before he had told his pupils if anyone missed three words of the spelling lesson he would get a whipping. Hicks missed the first word and refused to move down when the next person spelled it. Professor grabbed his pistol.

"If you don't move down, sir, —" Hicks moved down. He missed the second word, and when he couldn't spell the third one Professor Wright struck him with the switch. He lunged forth but Professor grabbed his pistol which was not even loaded, "If you don't move down, sir, I'll —"

Hicks stepped down and Professor Wright went on with his spelling bee. The news of Professor Wright's triumph went through the hamlet "like a house afire." On his way home that afternoon he was hailed from the cotton patches and cornfields. He had put "Biggerty Hicks" in his place. Any colored man who could make Hicks take orders was a Godsend to the community. He looked small but his looks were deceiving. He had used his head learning and proved himself a match for the bully. To seal his prowess he went around that evening and arranged with each of his board members to visit the school the next day at a specified hour. Naturally he was at his best — greeting everyone and introducing them in a body to the school. Afterwards he made a few remarks and presented Mr. Styles, President of the Board, who had something in his heart to say.

Mr. Styles, a stout, dark man, aimed straight at Hicks on the rear seat. Said he: "Professor Wright has made up his mind to rule this school. If you are as big as a house or as old as Methuselah you've got to behave or get out."

He took his seat. Instead of applause there was a deathly silence.

These were dramatic days for Professor Wright and black Americus, Georgia, as well. He was unaccustomed to anything like it. For black Americus — unaccustomed to anything more exciting than the cotton patch, the cornfield, the washtub, a log-rolling, a protracted meeting or an occasional murder — the Hicks incident fed their instinct for gossip and dramatic action. Professor Wright rejoiced too because it furnished something different from post mortems over an occasional death or gossip about the slip of some young girl on thin moral ice.

"Hear about Sis Mandy's gal? She done broke her leg."

The Hicks incident, he realized, had turned on all the human loud-speakers of the community. He felt the vibrations, and instead of teaching and disciplining Hicks in his sleep, retired with the chickens and rose at their call with a refreshed body and mind.

He began preparation for his Commencement exercises just a month before Commencement time. His recess periods, his noon hours and after school hours were used for drilling students. He had every student committing something to memory — a recitation, a declamation, a dialogue, a song, a pantomime, or something. During that month he caused the schoolhouse, the roadsides, the homes, the chimneycorners and the front yards to be converted into a stage. In preparation for his closing mothers traded eggs and chickens to the one store in the community in exchange for a few yards of goods for a dress, a shirt or a pair of pants. He, as well as his closing day, was so well thought of parents brought out baskets of fried chicken, barbecued pig, biscuits, cakes, custards and pies. Such a summer's experience, Professor Wright told everybody was worth its weight in gold.

Upon his return to Atlanta he related his summer's experience to many of his mother's friends, to the Sunday School and to his classmates. He said nothing of his three-dollars-a-month-salary, but explained that he "boarded around" and, therefore, had no board to pay. His boarding around meant he spent one night, or, in some instances one week, with one family and the next night or next week with another family. With a salary of three dollars per month, the only remuneration he had left to bring home was a couple of juicy hams from some old-fashioned smokehouse, as many chickens as he could manage to tie together by their feet with homespun strings, a dozen or so fresh eggs tied up in someone's white headcloth, and several pounds of soft, country butter in a bright tin pail.

Nevertheless, in spite of the fact that Atlanta University had increased its tuition and board to twelve dollars a month, he entered on the opening day. He encountered another change: it was that every person entering that year must sign a pledge to abstain from the use of intoxicating drinks and tobacco in every form while a member of the University.

What concerned him more were the hard studies listed for his class. He wrestled valiantly with four of Cicero's Orations, four books of Virgil's Aeneid, three books of the Anabasis, three books of Geometry, Ancient History and Algebra. He missed the discussions in which he had previously engaged, but every one of his subjects required from one to three hours study a day.

He and his classmates were frequently reminded of the necessity of thorough preparation in each subject. No one could tell what day the Board of Visitors from the University of Georgia might be out to pay them a call. The State Legislature had almost unanimously passed a recent Act for an annual appropriation of $8,000 to Atlanta University on three conditions. First, a Board of Visitors from the University of Georgia must visit Atlanta University. Secondly, three commissioners of this University must approve the plan of the Trustees of Atlanta University for the expenditure of money. Thirdly, Atlanta University must give free tuition to one pupil nominated by every member of the House of Representatives.

After the fall term examinations were over, Richard began to think of spending one or two of the Christmas holidays with his mother. Further back in his mind was an idea for the next summer which he wished to talk over with her. He would need more books and more of everything to enter college the next fall. If he taught school he thought he should be paid enough to help him with his school expenses. He had talked the matter over with President Ware.

Through the latter's intervention he was sent to Floyd County to teach. Since there was neither a schoolhouse nor a church building in the community he started his school under a brush harbor fitted out with puncheon seats. If it rained he couldn't have school. If the sun was very hot it was difficult for him and his students to protect themselves from its rays.

After two weeks of such a makeshift he hit upon an idea. He invited the people of the neighborhood to come out, cut logs, saw boards and put up a building. The log-rolling and throwing up the body of the building was a great social event. The men sawed, sang and told tales of slavery and the bygone, while the women brought pails of greens, corn bread, fried chicken and biscuits. At the end of the first day Richard was surprised to see the body of the building up and the rafters on. He was equally pleased to hear everyone call it "Wright's Academy."

That evening he went around to as many homes as he could and pictured the possibilities of Wright's Academy. The grown-ups as well as the children could learn to read and write and figure too. To his astonishment some of the workers came back the next day, rived boards for the covering, put on the laths and covered the building.

Money was found for the flooring and a few planks for seats. In a few weeks he opened school in Wright's Academy. His reputation not only as a great teacher but as a business man was promulgated. In the estimation of the parents of his school he was a stirring little man. Put that building up "in a hurry." His name was Wright and he was the right man for them.

During the succeeding winter months he had occasion to go back for a weekend engagement to a town in Floyd County. He arrived at the small station house at night, but Negroes were not allowed to tarry there. He kept on walking and soon met an old man who told him to go down the railroad track about half a mile. On the right-hand side of the road he would see a new log house in which a colored man lived. There he might be allowed to spend the night. He thanked the man and trudged on. The night was dark and cold and the roadway was still and lonely. With trepidation he followed instructions and came within fifty feet of the house. He hailed, "Housekeepers, housekeepers!"

There was no response. He heard a child's voice. She was pleading with a man who said.

"No, we got smallpox here. Can't 'commodate nobody."

Despite his gruff manner of speaking Richard called again. This time louder than before. He heard the little girl say, "Oh Papa, oh Papa, that's Professor Wright the schoolteacher; I know his voice."

By that time Professor Wright had recognized her voice. It was that of little Katherine, one of his pupils at Wright's Academy. He was invited in. There was one bed in the house and one fireplace. As was the custom, he was prevailed upon to take the bed.

Familiar with such situations, when bed-time came he insisted that the women sleep in the bed and let him and the father sleep on the pallet. They were so non-commital he thought he had persuaded them to do as he suggested. However, when he went out-of-doors to give the women privacy to undress and get in bed the family covered the fire with ashes to keep until morning, took the pallet on the floor and left him the feather bed.

Feathers were not bad on a night like that when cold air whistled through the boarded cracks in the walls, through the roof, through the wide plank floor, through the cat-hole by the hearth, under the door and through the dirt chimney. However, he took no cold, and was able to establish contacts through which he gained a better school the next summer. In the fall following that summer he returned to Atlanta University with enough money to enter the college department.

He had passed all the requirements, was a full-fledged freshman with his Xenophon's Memorabilia, Homer's Odyssey, Horace's DeSenectute et Amacitia, Greek and Latin Prose Composition, Grecian and Roman History, Loomis' Algebra, Loomis' Geometry, Composition and Declamation.

His classmates, now eleven in number, were all boys. He and they rather entertained the notion that Xenophon, Homer, Horace and Livy were too difficult for girls to master. Even Lucy Laney, they joked, had chosen the Normal Course despite the fact that she had never allowed boys to enter her head. Not even Richard Wright could make an impression on her. Richard smarted under the jest but attempted to exhibit his independence of spirit. Still he had great regard and a little lingering affection for her. The old saying, though, "There's just as pretty a bird in the air as there is on the bush" buoyed him up while he looked around for another girl.

At a picnic one day given by Atlanta University's students on the croquet grounds, he met Miss Lydia Elizabeth Howard of Columbus, Georgia. She, too, a bright student of Atlanta University captured him absolutely

BOARD OF DIRECTORS
Citizens & Southern Bank and Trust Company, 1933

with her charming manner and lovely, refined voice. He went so far as to visit some of her classes. He discovered that she was a great favorite with her teachers. He began to linger in her pathway, carry her books, send her notes, call on her in her parlor on the two calling afternoons a week, and escort her to exercises in the chapel on Friday nights. One of the students from Columbus informed him that her people were among the "big niggers" of Columbus. Her father was proud of the fact that he worked and bought his own freedom and ran hacks in slavery time. He wouldn't be so keen about her going with the son of a slave. He threw out the fact, occasionally, that he was a free Negro in slavery time. He might permit her to keep company with a fellow like Richard, but serious doubts were expressed.

Such information Richard kept to himself. His love for Lydia Elizabeth Howard and her warmth of response were not to be chilled by any such foolishness. In fact, he had already accepted a job for the summer which would allow him to travel over the state and incidentally visit her. He began to crack jokes and practice book-sales talk on some of his classmates who in turn practiced on him. Instead of visiting his girl in Columbus, they teased, and selling a lot of books in the St. John's African Methodist Episcopal Church, he would have doors slammed in his face. He took it good-naturedly and related the joke to Lydia.

He spent the latter part of June peddling his books through the streets of Atlanta. At first he was florid with enthusiasm. He thought many people would be almost standing on their doorsteps waiting to buy a book from him because he was a poor boy working his way through college. Instead of that, many doors were slammed in his face and many insults were hurled all over him. However, he departed always with a tip of his hat and a polite, "Good-day."

Reports of his good manners and behavior came in to the man for whom he was salesman. Pretty good returns also came in for the first month or more, but apparently the good spots had been covered. The sales dropped off. Therefore, when he apprised his employer of his possibilities in Columbus — a great big church run by his girl's people — his employer agreed for him to go there. As a further aid to him his employer wrote Lydia's mother, urging her to take Richard and board him.

With a small tin trunk, mostly full of books, and a satchel full of books on his shoulder, Richard left Atlanta on an early morning train for Columbus. On his arrival he rushed up to a drayman to find out what he would haul his trunk and satchel for.

"Twenty-five cents for the trunk and fifteen cents for the satchel," replied the drayman.

Richard hesitated. Forty cents was a lot of money for two small pieces of baggage. He shook his head. Finally he decided to leave his trunk until later and carry his satchel. About five feet high and small of stature he took up the satchel by its strap and threw it across his shoulder. He stopped at nearly every corner, mopped the perspiration from his face and inquired if he were on the right track. When he reached the Howard residence Lydia and her mother greeted him so cordially he felt at home immediately.

This homey atmosphere continued until the whistles began to blow for twelve o'clock. Lydia's expression changed to one of uneasiness. Her father came in from his blacksmith's shop for dinner.

"Whew." He mopped his face as though the heat had him. When he was introduced to Richard he looked at him somewhat critically and bobbed his head.

"En hen! you're a book peddler Lydia tells me."

Richard made an effort to explain that he had taught school but was trying salesmanship for the summer and was doing very well at it, etc. The old man made no reply. Yet he had said plenty for Richard to understand he had little respect for a peddler as a prospective son-in-law, and none at all for a book peddler. Richard shrugged his shoulders. He held one of his books in his hand but made no attempt, as he had planned, to show it to Mr. Howard. He hesitated a little when Mrs. Howard invited him into dinner. He told her he had just eaten a little snack before he came out. The "butter" beans, though, new Irish potatoes and the stewed chicken smelled so good, he reluctantly accepted.

As he took his seat at the table, Mrs. Howard remarked about the hot weather and handed him a palmetto fan. He accepted it and fanned a stroke or two, but the atmosphere around that table with Mr. Howard at its head was so cool he laid it aside and attended to his eating. As soon as the dinner was over he thanked gracious Mrs. Howard and left the house in a hurry, as if by appointment.

He had to impress the old man. He had gotten a few leads from Lydia, so he started out to sell, if possible, and, if not, to lend someone a book that afternoon. If he could induce someone to take a book to look over he thought he might get a chance to sell it to him. On that theory he talked his way into the borrowing graces of a man who took one of his books which told how shiftless Jack Spratt was.

The next day he returned full of hope and expectation that the book would be purchased. He lifted the latch of the gate to the front yard and pushed it open. It squeaked. The lady of the house peeped out, drew her head back and said in a muffled tone to her husband, "Here comes that fellow — the book peddler."

Richard's hopes fell, but this was no time to turn back. Before he could get up on the little front porch, however, the man came to the door with the book in his hand. He threw it at Richard's head with a vengeance, stuttering, "Some old — old — white man tel — tel — telling all these lies on us. I — I don't want your old book."

The rebuff was so fierce and such a surprise to Richard he started to run not knowing what might come next — brick-bats or what. He hesitated, picked up his book, knocked off the dirt and continued on his way mumbling his disapproval of such ignorant old Negroes.

Despite these trying experiences, he sold many books in Columbus and completed his stay there by asking Lydia to marry him. She would not promise him, yet he did not lose hope. He felt she loved him. He was only eager to make his position with her more secure because he knew of two other younger men who were in love with her. One of them, Jake by name, lived in Atlanta.

Jake, not knowing that Richard was in love with her too, had sent a message to her by Richard. When the latter returned to Atlanta University he told Jake he had delivered his message. Since Jake received no letter from Lydia he came back to Richard and asked what he had told her. Richard assured him he had given her his message; but also confessed he too liked Lydia, had told her so, and thought she felt as he did about the matter.

Jake was furious. He challenged Richard to a duel. They called in one of Richard's classmates, George Smith, to arbitrate the matter. George Smith said, "Jake must be the loser. You must not fight about that girl; there are others."

Jake refused to relent. George Smith was equally inexorable. Therefore, they had to stack their arms and plan no more war over Lydia.

Richard entered the sophomore class the following fall. In his class there were the same eleven other boys. His studies consisted of Greek, select Orations of Demosthenes, the Prometheus of Aeschylus, Latin Odes of Horace, Tacitus, English, Literature, Solid and Spherical Geometry, Trigonometry and Surveying.

He and his classmates recited Demosthenes' orations with so much feeling and dexterity and did so well in their other classes, when the Board of Visitors from the University of Georgia came out they were astounded. They wrote President Ware a letter and in their report to Atlanta University which was signed by the chairman of the Board and one other member, they stated that "The recitations before the Board of Visitors were most flattering to the teachers and pupils. The results exhibited extraordinary skill and patience in the former and remarkable docility on the part of the latter."

This report amused Richard and his classmates very much. They were young and always ready to reap a little fun out of almost any ludicrous situation. They mimicked each other's docility. They also took special delight in buffooning Richard's experience as a book peddler and as a teacher in the Hicks' pistol drama. When a mischievous boy would occasionally throw a book at Richard in repetition of the Jack Spratt incident, or pull out a toy pistol and a big switch on him, he would make the others roar with laughter by retaliating as the real actor.

He was a courting man that year, and sometimes told facetiously of his experience in meeting Lydia's father. His pride was so pricked, however, he forsook book peddling and went back to teaching. His future father-in-law's traditional ideas about the type of man his daughter should become engaged to could not be tossed aside.

The next summer he went to Wilkes County, the home of Bob Toombs. Judge Reese who represented that county in the State Legislature sent to Atlanta University for a teacher. Their former teacher had been killed because of his political activities. As a warning to Professor Wright this information was passed on to him the day of his examination in the Hall of Representatives at the Capitol.

On that day the Hall was packed with white and black folks to witness the spectacle of examining a Negro for the first time. Representatives gathered around to hear him read from the third reader and work arithmetic. Disturbed by such a crowd he made some mistakes. However, he was pronounced a wonder.

The crowd was so interested one of the representatives suggested that he be examined in Latin also. He had studied it in Atlanta University. That aroused the ire of General Toombs who was bitterly opposed to the teaching of Latin in Atlanta University. However, a copy of Virgil's Aeneid was brought out and Richard was asked to read a passage at the beginning of the First Book. He took hold of the text with trembling hands. He had been so well drilled in those lines he read them first and then translated them to the utter amazement of even General Toombs who rose after the reading and presented him with a fifty-cent piece for industrial education. He thanked the General, and even as poor as he was, kept that piece of money as a souvenir and finally gave it to President Ware for higher education. In later years President Ware told that story in his presence to Atlanta University and concluded it by stating that the General Toombs' fifty-cent piece had netted Atlanta University Fifty Thousand Dollars.

In the capacity of a teacher Richard visited Columbus that summer and was graciously received by all the members of the Howard family. He was invited out to Mr. Howard's blacksmith shop where horses were being shod, sweeps sharpened, wagon-wheels leaned against the weather boarding. The anvil rang, the forge and the bellows emitted hot flames, and a smell of burning embers filled the shop.

In order that Richard might continue in Mr. Howard's good graces he decided early in the following college year to make application for a summer school at Lumpkin,

Georgia. Upon the acceptance of his application for the Lumpkin position, he went again that summer to the State Capital to take the examination. Quite an eager crowd of spectators came out as before to see him read, spell and write. The correcting Commissioner in charge of the examination crossed out one of his words as misspelled. He scratched his head and asked with a puzzled expression for the correct spelling of it, if his was wrong. The face of the Commissioner flushed and Richard was threatened with discharge from the examination because of his impudence. One of the white spectators spoke out, however, and said he thought that Nigger was right. Then more fuel was added to the fire when Mr. Tiff Harrison, Executive Secretary at the Capitol, looked in the dictionary and declared that the Negro's spelling was correct. So much heated argument followed it frightened Richard nearly to death.

After the battle of words and emotions had subdued, he was given his certificate of authorization to teach in Georgia. He opened his summer school at Bluff Springs, just nine country miles from Lumpkin. One of his best students in that school, Emma F. Hudson, was unable to continue her own education; nevertheless, she followed Professor Wright's career and twenty years later sent her son to be educated under him.

At the close of his summer school he called at Mr. Howard's blacksmith shop again and related his experiences in his examination and in his summer school. Fondly in love with Lydia and realizing that her father's attitude towards him as a teacher had completely changed, he made frequent visits to Columbus and to Mr. Howard's blacksmith shop. One night he screwed up courage and asked him for her. Mr. Howard did all of the talking. His daughter had always had a good home, plenty to eat, and had never been abused, he assured Richard. There was one other important factor in the situation, namely: if Richard ever got tired of her he was to bring her back and leave her where he found her.

With that ordeal successfully met, Richard left Columbus that night feeling as fit as a fiddle. He wound up his summer school with less display and more money than usual. He entered Atlanta University as a proud junior with the profound secret of his engagement to Lydia Howard well guarded. He didn't even tell his mother about it. There would be plenty of time, he thought.

Then, too, everytime he saw his mother she was saying she wished he would visit her old master and mistress, the Kirkseys. They would be glad to see him, and they might help him some with his tuition. He might not have time the next year to visit them. He would leave College and perhaps never see them alive.

After the close of Atlanta University that spring, he made a trip to the old Kirksey homestead on horseback. They squinted their eyes and did not recognize him at first; but when he told them who he was they exclaimed, "My, my, Harriet's boy!"

As he alighted from his saddle — well-groomed on a week-day for a poor black boy — shoes shined, trousers creased, collar and necktie in place — they looked at him with great pride. Yes, old master said, he brought Harriet up "respectable and smart." Therefore, he wasn't at all surprised to see her boy come up with good manners and behavior and get a good learning. They asked if his mother still kept a boarding house. How much she made a week. Was his grandmother still alive and as determined as ever. Where his brother and sister and step-father were — and other questions — "ad infinitum."

The most wonderful news to them was the fact that he had been through, as they expressed it, six courses in Atlanta University and was about to enter his seventh course and graduate. Another astounding piece of news was that he was studying law and after his graduation from Atlanta University planned to take a regular course in law in the office of Judge Freeman of Atlanta.

A feeling of kinship and ownership different from that of former years pervaded the atmosphere. They were proud of him. He too, was moved by the changes which time had wrought in them and their surroundings. Some of them were getting along "mighty well" and others of them were working in the field. Everything, even the atmosphere and the people, had changed. As they took him into the dining room in which his mother was married as a slave, he could almost see the ghost of his uncle fiddling for dancers to swing their partners.

His mother, upon whom hard work, major responsibilities, five deaths in the family in the past fifteen years (including her mother's), and Father Time had begun to lay their hands — listened with eagerness to his portrayal of that visit. She rejoiced to hear how proud they were of him and how well they received him.

Richard realized that his senior year would be an expensive one. He had heard of college caps and gowns but there was no traditional standard of dress for a black boy graduating in the first college class of Atlanta University. The cost of tuition had to be met. His books — Greek and Latin, Mathematics, Natural Science, Ethics and Christian Evidences, Gardening and Farming, and English — had to be purchased.

As he and his classmates neared their coveted goal they often expressed to one another their appreciation of the friendship which had developed among themselves during their college years. It had meant so much to them; they divulged a desire that their children in after years would become like friends and would even intermarry.

Richard's senior year was one of his happiest. His girl had promised to marry him the following October. Plans for going to Howard University Law School was apparently assured. Tentative arrangements for a summer school at Cuthbert, Georgia, were in progress, and his class standing was excellent.

At his Class Day exercises one of the members of the class gave the class prophecy. His prophecy for Richard was that after graduation from the Howard University Law School, he would aspire to a seat in the United States Congress. As soon as the class prophet took his seat one of the other boys provoked laughter by pointing his finger at Richard and declaring:

"Dick Wright, the day you aspire to become President of the United States, that day you die."

He had aspired to be Valedictorian of his class and had lived to attain that goal. There was a lesser one which was giving him and his mother concern and which he was determined to arrive at before the Commencement season was over, namely, that of an understanding with one of his girl associates, Hilda Holland. The night of the Baccalaureate Sermon he dressed in his Commencement black broadcloth suit and went down early to call on Hilda. Her people were so much better off, economically, than his, her mother had said she didn't see why her daughter wanted to have anything to do with that little black nigger. Her remark reached Richard's mother and she expressed her dislike of it.

To straighten out the situation, Richard, spare of build, dressed in his new black broadcloth suit and feeling proud as the first Negro Valedictorian of a college class in Georgia, called at Hilda's home. Shortly after he was admitted another fellow called to see Hilda; but her mother quietly told the latter that Hilda wasn't very well. Richard was so surprised to catch that false excuse he made up his mind to confess the truth to Hilda that night. Accordingly, as soon as an opportunity presented itself, he confided that he had something to tell her but couldn't tell it to her there.

"Let's go to church — to the Baccalaureate," he whispered.

To him, screwing up his courage on a warm evening, the Baccalaureate exercises appeared tedious, but none too long. Finally, he and Hilda slowly made their way back towards her home. Several times he opened his mouth to tell her but he simply couldn't do it. However, as they turned the corner nearest her house, he realized this was his last chance. It was difficult, but he straightened up and confessed that somehow he didn't love her. He was sorry, but he loved a girl in Columbus and was engaged to her.

As hard as this confession was to make, its relief to him was equaled only by its shock to Hilda. He had lived up to the letter of his Commencement oration, the subject of which was "The Decision of Character." As he further rehearsed it for delivery on Commencement Night of that week, he could more forcibly throw himself into the spirit of it. His illustration of the Biblical character, Joseph, appeared to take on new reality.

The exercises held in Friendship Baptist Church were largely attended. There was not standing room for all who tried to get in. Richard as Valedictorian of the class was the last one of his classmates to be called upon to speak. As he walked upon the platform in his black broadcloth suit, white shirt, black bow-tie, black shoes well shined, and looked down at his mother in tears on the front seat, his speech left him. He couldn't get started. He looked the audience straight in the face, however, and wouldn't give up. He stood there until the first words broke in upon him. Then with all the decisiveness he could command he pictured Joseph and his people. He held him up to the light of possible temptation and ruin, and finally left him fully clothed with uprightness born of the decision of character.

CHAPTER IV

EDUCATOR AND ORGANIZER

PART I

With Atlanta University closed for the summer, students and teachers all gone, Richard's stay at his mother's gun-barrel house for a call to teach at Cuthbert was long and anxious. Every morning he dressed in his Sunday suit, brushed his Sunday shoes, walked the piazza as he had seen the Congressmen do, and met the mail-man on the steps.

"My, no letter for me yet?" He shook his head. They were taking a mighty long time to answer. If he should miss getting the principalship of that school it would be the disappointment of his life. If he did get it, he would be near Lydia's home and wouldn't have to peddle books in the hot sun or go to some lonely country place to teach. Throughout each day he kept on the move — walking, wondering, hoping.

At night he met his mother at the door with a pan of food from her boarding-house table. No, nothing had come yet; but he was still hoping, he confessed. Even if some of the folks who were there in his day had gone elsewhere or passed away he doubted that his reputation for learning to read and write in a week's time had completely faded out. Secondly, he was sure reports of him as the Black Boy of Atlanta and as Valedictorian of the first college class of Atlanta University, had reached Cuthbert. Therefore, down deep in his heart he expected a favorable reply and even said that no authority would come around to his school and ask "What's all these little Nigger children doing here?" Another thing: Negroes through the use of their own ballot had helped to close the Chip Schools and to institute public schools. Those changes didn't come overnight. He consoled himself and waited as patiently as the circumstances permitted until news of his appointment came.

Now that he had completed his college course and would soon become the principal of a school at Cuthbert, his old home, brought joy to his mother's heart and tears to her eyes. He had come a long way in a few short years, so far he wouldn't have to return to his former home as he had left it. Instead of as a refugee in his shirt tail, he would return as a college graduate — among the first few of his race — with the torch of learning in his hand. The thought of it all so exhilarated him morning didn't come fast enough.

Before daylight he rose, dressed and set his little tin trunk near the doorway again. At his mother's call he hastened into the kitchen and ate his fried chicken and hot biscuits. While he ate she advised him to eat enough to last him until he got to Cuthbert, and when he got there to give everybody — white and black alike — his manners and behavior.

He kissed her goodbye, grabbed his little bag and kept answering her motherly injunction, "Be good. Take kere yo'self, Son. Don't git into no trouble now. Write, you hear?"

"I will, Ma, I will —" he waved his hand and departed.

The Monday morning after his arrival in Cuthbert, he opened his little school. The old landmarks about which he and his mother had conjectured had suffered little change. Many of his Chip schoolmates and their forbears had gone elsewhere or passed, and new faces were there instead. He looked over his schoolroom with an air of disappointment.

The people hadn't taken the interest in sending their children he had expected. The situation worried him so, he decided to talk it over with Aunt Dinah in spite of the fact that she had challenged him to teach her to read the Bible. All of the other teachers who had been there had promised to teach her.

"Didn't any of them teach you, Aunt Dinah?"

"Hadn't teached me this morning."

He, as the other teachers had done, was boarding at her house — a low, ramshackle structure with two rooms. He liked it theer because she cooked opossum, sweet potatoes, rabbit and other wild meats. She couldn't read the Bible, but as soon as he began to tell her about his problem she saw the advantage her learning to read could be to him. If he would teach her she would get out and show the people how much he had taught her. She would boost him as the most wonderful teacher they had ever had.

Knowing her influence in the community he accepted her proposition and made an engagement with her. At first he attempted to teach her the alphabet at sight, but soon desisted because she would begin and wind up about halfway, in a nervous dither. Finally he decided to try to teach her a few verses of the twenty-fifth chapter of St. Matthew, by rote. His mother had taught him that chapter when he was a child. The verses were short and easy to learn.

His calculation was not far wrong. She did learn about ten verses by rote. He noticed whenever she read her Bible she invariably turned to the red string which marked the 25th chapter of St. Matthew. He said nothing to her since she couldn't learn anyway, besides, she was a great booster for him and his school. With all of her approbation the situation didn't improve. He was just as worried about the small attendance as he was before she started.

To get away from his problems and see his fiancé at the same time, he hitched old Dolly, a neighbor's gray mare, to the buggy one Sunday morning and drove over to Columbus. It was thirty miles distant and over none too smooth roads. He was welcomed by Lydia and made very happy. After dinner they took a long buggy ride and returned before sundown. He mentioned starting for home but they sat on the piazza as late that night as her folks allowed. He looked at his biscuit watch. My, how swiftly the time had passed! He kissed her fondly, stepped into the rattling buggy and grabbed the lines. He held on to them as old Dolly trotted down one hill and up another and into the big road which led to Cuthbert. As she crossed a long bridge in the darkness he heard planks rumble and crack and break under her well-shod hoofs. He trembled, too, but old Dolly was homeward bound.

Back in Cuthbert his small school attendance loomed large and even plagued him. He never once thought that his love affair, with most of his week-ends spent in Columbus, had anything to do with it. He worked diligently on the scholars he had. With their advancement in reading, writing, arithmetic, and enthusiasm, and Aunt Dinah's constant boosts and declarations about how she had "learnt" to read the Bible, he brought out a great crowd for his remarkable school-closing. The parents cooperated, too, by bringing baskets of fried chicken, fresh meat, cakes, custards and pies which were served in individual helpings on long bed sheets and tablecloths spread on the school grounds.

On Monday morning subsequent to a delightful week-end in Columbus, he received a letter. As he read it his countenance fell and his usual brisk step slowed down. The gentleman, Mr. E. D. Whipple of the American Missionary Association, who had promised to finance his law course at Howard University, had suddenly died. He wrote Lydia the sad news. He was doubly worried because on that promise hinged his plans for getting married to her the following October. He was so disturbed and lonesome he could scarcely sleep for several nights. In the meantime, he decided to feel out some of the leading citizens on how they liked his school work. To his surprise, everyone was pleased and wanted him to continue as principal for the next session.

He wrote Lydia again immediately and proclaimed the good news which he had gotten from the citizens, both white and black. He told her he could not do without her any longer, and proposed that they get married right away.

Since this would necessitate quick action, he made a trip to Columbus and secured her and her parents consent to the plan. As a further guarantee he received from her father a sockful of big silver dollars for the wedding invitations. After these were printed he, now Professor Wright, and Lydia and three of their friends got into a carriage and delivered them to their friends.

He went back to Cuthbert and on the seventh of June returned to Columbus with a minister to whom he paid Ten Dollars and expenses for officiating at the wedding ceremony. This was held in the midst of presents and a profusion of flowers in the home of Lydia's parents. Professor Wright — spare of build and weighing about one hundred and twenty pounds — held himself erect and his face at attention. Dressed in his graduation suit and a white vest, he marched in slowly to the strains of sweet music. He waited for Lydia — somewhat petite, plump, Indian brown and charming in a gray Nunsveiling dress made by a first-class dressmaker. The officiating minister, Reverend Holmes, was assisted by Bishop Campbell and Bishop W. J. Gaines, both of the A. M. E. Church.

The next morning he took his bride on the boat down the Chattahoochie River to the landing nearest Cuthbert.

STORR'S SCHOOL, ATLANTA, GA.

On their arrival he had fifty cents left in his pocket. Inasmuch, though, as practically all of the Negroes of Cuthbert were at the dock to meet them he didn't have to spend that to reach the minister's house in which he had engaged two rooms. In fact, the folks with brand new buggies and two-wheel carts vied with each other for the opportunity of taking them out.

Many thoughts had run through his mind since he had received the letter about the passing of his would-be benefactor. He had complied with the one he considered to be of major importance — the possession of the girl of his choice. With her as his wife, he was now committed to the job of teaching.

He was not satisfied with the progress of his school. In his effort to find out what the trouble was, he turned his mental searchlight upon himself. He was so disturbed, one moonlight night he went to the spring, got a cool drink of water and fell out flat on the ground. He heard a voice. He looked up and around to see who was there. He saw nothing but the moon. To him it had never shown so brightly. He stretched out again. "Pshaw!" nothing but his fool imagination, he concluded. He closed his eyes. "Gee!" that same voice, as clear as the moonlight. "Get up from there! Go around to all the folks in the community!" He jumped up and ran to the nearest house.

The next day he started out and went around "like a house afire," he said. He visited every home. He talked with parents and students. He told them of his plan to have an assistant teacher, to enlarge the school, and to have a boarding department. He acquainted them with the possibilities of a Farmers' Institute through which farmers could sell their own produce. He also interested them in having a County Fair.

Immediately the community began to take new interest. The children came to school in such large numbers he made his wife, Lydia Howard Wright, his assistant teacher without salary, and named the school "The Howard Normal School."

He went out among the farmers and organized farmers' institutes. Through these he demonstrated how the farmers could cooperate and market their own produce instead of selling it to peddlers for a song. He attempted to convince them that they could even build a factory.

While he got around and stirred up the community, his wife's charm of manner and thoughtfulness of everybody won the hearts of the people. In addition to her regular classroom work, she began to teach the girls to darn stockings, mend their clothes and do plain sewing. As an incentive to them and to please her husband, she looked up all of his old socks — about a peck of them — darned every hole and mended every sock so beautifully the girls were amazed.

In her eagerness to do something else to please him and to offer a demonstration to the girls, she made him a couple of fine tucked bosom linen shirts and two "narr'd" homespun undershirts. She purchased drilling and made him two pairs of heavy long drawers. She said he was so proud of his new things and made such a "to do" over them, she called them his trousseau. She sought other avenues of assistance and pleasure to him. For example, when she washed his "Sunday shirts" she always put a little perfume in the rinse water.

That spring, with her assistance, he organized a County Fair, the first of its kind in the State. Negro farmers brought bushels of great, long ears of corn, peas, peaches, peanuts, potatoes; horses and cattle. The women came, too, with turkeys, chickens, eggs, butter, lye-hominy, and beautiful log cabin quilts. In response to invitations which had been verbally broadcast and inserted in the papers as well, leading white citizens and white farmers came from every corner of the county and even from adjoining counties. Some of them made speeches and were fulsome in their praise of Professor Wright, the school, and the County Fair.

Through the medium of this Fair, Professor Wright's name and influence as an organizer began to cross county borders. It's success and the possibilities of organized farmers attracted his attention to similar probabilities in the teaching profession. He knew that Negro teachers from Atlanta University, Augusta Institute — now Atlanta Baptist College — Clark University, Fisk University and other colleges, were entering the public school system of Georgia. He made a brief canvass of some of the teachers in 1878 and advertised a State Teachers Convention — the first of its kind of Negro teachers to assemble in Georgia.

About forty teachers attended. He organized them into what was later called "The Georgia State Teachers' Association." In turn they elected him as their first president. Through his leadership and planning ahead for the meeting, it was said to be a wonderful success. The teachers went away full of enthusiasm and better informed about their work and their relationship to the Georgia State Teachers' Association and to each other.

Professor Wright had the minutes of that meeting published in a weekly paper and a copy of the paper sent to every Negro teacher in the State. He also encouraged the organization of County Teachers' Associations and assisted with that work as often as his school duties permitted.

One afternoon just at the close of his school, an outstanding minister from Augusta, Dr. William J. White, editor of "The Georgia Baptist," also a weekly newspaper, came in to see him. He greeted Dr. White and accepted the latter's felicitations on his winning the election as a delegate to the National Republican Convention. Then he apologized for not giving him a definite answer about coming to Augusta to organize a Negro high school. He didn't quite see how he could pull up and leave Cuthbert. He had been successful there and the future was brighter than ever for his work there.

Notwithstanding, he was urged to come to Augusta. Now that he had been a delegate to a National Republican Convention, he was just the man to organize the first public high school in Georgia for Negro youth. When he intimated his interest in a possible business venture, but in no wise divulged his secret ambition to establish a Tuskegee Institute in Georgia, the minister painted in warm colors the possibilities in Augusta. He might have a business adjunct to his school, or he might establish a larger business among the many Negroes in Augusta.

He also received urgent communications from other prominent citizens of Augusta who made the inducements attractive and urgent. At their insistence he took a trip to see them and to look into the matter. To make a favorable decision was not easy, but he finally concluded his arrangements with the Cuthbert School authorities by having Mr. Fletcher H. Henderson of the Atlanta University Class of 1879 succeed him. He placed a man in charge of his newspaper there, pulled up and moved to Augusta.

He organized the high school and named it Ware High School in honor of President Ware of Atlanta University. Since a law had been passed permitting no child under six or over eighteeen years of age to enter the public school system, the former wide wariations in the ages of his pupils were obviated. His instructions from the Board of Education were that the Colored High School be conducted on the same basis as the Tubman High School for white young ladies, with one exception. The exception was that the Negro students should pay a fee of five dollars a term in advance, or ten dollars for a school year. This amount would also cover the janitor's wages.

In his new position he was determined to make the best possible beginning. Believing that order is Heaven's first law, and since corporal punishment could be inflicted on boys only, he started out with strict regulations for the girls as well. He remembered his experience at Cuthbert; went around and visited as many of his prespective pupils as time permitted. He also attended their churches — Thankful Baptist Church and Springfield Baptist Church, both formerly designed for the use of the slave population; Bethel, St. Marks, Mount Zion or Trinity, and Holsey Chapel.

Because of his community activities as well as his principalship of the only Negro public high school in the State, he was well thought of, and Ware High School's enrollment increased to seventy-one students.

During his ten years of principalship of this high school, seventy of his students passed creditable examinations and were graduated. As his students they were considered to be so well qualified, their diplomas were sufficient evidence of their ability to teach.

After Ware High School had made a place for itself in the community and in the state, Professor Wright opened a bookstore. His family was on the increase. His salary was stationary. His pupils all had to buy book of someone, and pupils in other Negro schools had to do likewise.

He fraternized with the principals and visited the parents of the grammar school children. He opened his bookstore with a full line of school text books: Swinton's Word Primer; Butler's Speller; Independent Readers, Numbers 1, 2, 3, 4 and 5; Brown's First Lines in Grammar; Maury's Manual of Geography; Parker's Exercises in Composition; Stephen's History of the United States; Mason's Primary and Intermediate Music Books, Latin,

Algebra, etc. His success in this business was immediate; and so marked, he introduced also toys for children.

He went in person to see Lucy Laney, his former classmate, who had come to Augusta by stagecoach from a Methodist conference in Saint Paul, Minnesota. He not only sold her school children books, but advised her in the establishment of her school — Haines Institute, named in honor of Mrs. Haines whom she had met at the conference and who donated a large sum of money to her work.

Another educational venture for Negroes in which he took deep interest with the founding of Paine College in Augusta. He was more or less enthusiastic about it because it was to be a college located there in Augusta and would afford opportunities for many of his students to secure college training. Therefore, whatever scepticism he possessed at that time because Southern white people were its founders, he was careful not to divulge. As principal of the Negro Public High School and as a newspaperman too, he familiarized himself with Paine College, named in honor of Mr. Moses U. Paine, who made an initial gift of Twenty-five Thousand Dollars to it. He attended the cornerstone laying of its first building — Haygood Memorial Hall.

On that occasion he met its first president, Dr. George William Walker. Acquainted with the attitude of Dr. Walker's friends, and having heard of Dr. Walker's fiancé — a beautiful Southern girl who put it up to him to choose either the Negroes or her — he was eager to meet the man who had chosen the presidency of Paine College. His esteem for that man and his interest in Paine College continued through the years. As time passed, he worked more closely with Atlanta University, and on important occasions went North many times with President Ware in the interest of his Alma Mater. This work and further active services as an alumnus caused the board of trustees of Atlanta University to elect him to its membership in 1887.

Through these connections, his educational work in the state, and his newspaper, he was brought to the attention of the Georgia State Legislature.

PART II

In 1890, when this body appropriated money for the Georgia Industrial College for Colored Youth, he was elected as its first president. His salary of one hundred dollars per month, considered to be large at that time, created as much discussion as the location of the new school at Thunderbold, Savannah's fashionable resort. At Thunderbolt, renowned for its healthful sea breeze, its grand old oak trees with abundance of shade, and its delicious fish and oysters, he was within calling distance of the Cream of the South.

Prior to the establishment of the Georgia Industrial School for Colored Youth, he was acquainted with the work of the Haven's Industrial School for Colored Girls, located in Savannah. Realizing the importance of this work he continued to watch the progress of this school after it was moved to the country in a new brick building, erected by the Northern Methodist Episcopal Church.

With the education of the Negro girls of the state thus provided for, the Georgia Industrial School for Colored Youth was meant for boys only. Its opening exercises were held on the first Wednesday in October, 1890. President Wright had given the occasion wide publicity. As he predicted, many from Savannah, Augusta, Cuthbert and the rural districts of the state came in all types of conveyance — double horse wagons, single buggies and carts, ox carts, double horse buggies, riding on horseback double and single, and afoot with their Sunday shoes thrown across their shoulders or in their hands.

He as President of the institution welcomed the guests and marched into the chapel at the head of the procession of Board members and distinguished visitors.

In his remarks he referred to his four teachers — the professor of mathematics, the professor of science, the professor of English, and himself as President and professor of Latin and Greek. However, he omitted mention of the Latin and Greek. Instead of apologizing for the eight students who matriculated, he pictured poor boys who would soon pour from homes in the city and on the farms to work their way through the Georgia Industrial College. He mentioned the three college buildings on the thirty-acre plot. One of them, erected by slaves who came on the last shipload of slaves to Georgia, was furnishing dormitory space for the grandsons of some of those slaves. He introduced the members of his Board of Commissioners: General Peter Meldrim, chairman; Mr. Otto Ashmore, and others — all Southern men. He called attention to the fact that Sherman marched across that campus en route to Savannah, took a fort near by, and ordered his men to tear down the chimes of a then nearby Catholic church. In President Wright's house on that campus, Sherman lived while stationed there. Because of those associations, President Wright felt that the foundation of The Georgia Industrial College for Colored Youth was being laid on holy ground.

After the exercises were over and the visitors had all departed, he walked briskly towards his home with an air of satisfaction and confidence. He caught up his baby girl as she toddled behind several other small children who ran out to meet him. He entered the house, kissed Mrs. Wright, as was his custom, and began to tell her of his future plans. He ate meagerly the white meat of the chicken, vegetables, fruit, buttermilk, and continued to lay his proposition before her.

In the late afternoon, about sundown, when the water in the creek began to look chilly and the fall breeze began to sigh, he and Mrs. Wright strolled like lovers, arm in arm, along the bank of the creek and picked up acorns here and there.

The next morning when he rose, she had his bath water on the stove hot and ready to be poured into the tin wash tub. While he took his bath she got out his clean clothes and prepared breakfast for him as though she loved to wait on him. After breakfast he read the Bible and offered prayer in his home. Into his school he carried this habit of daily worship. Every morning he called the professors and students together for chapel exercises; and on Sunday he conducted Sunday School.

His reputation, too, as a disciplinarian followed him into the Georgia State College from his home, as well as from his former teaching positions. In time every one of his students knew he whipped his eldest daughter and a nephew openly in his office every day at 12 o'clock for a month. The nephew, another nephew and his eldest son — R. R. Wright, Jr. — occupied a room together in President Wright's home. He noticed their distaste for cleaning their room, and called them to task about it. The next morning he saw his eldest daughter cleaning it for them, but did not question her. She, however, proffered the information that the three boys had agreed to pay her a specified sum to do it for them. After several weeks had passed and her cousin's part of the debt had accumulated to the amount of twenty cents, she went after him for it and performed in great style. Her father heard her and stepped into the picture. He told both of them he was going to break up their foolishness. He whipped both of them with a little whip openly in his office every day at twelve o'clock for a month.

His favorite method of punishment, however, was to make a boy work one hundred hours on the farm. To anyone who came before him for breaking some rule he would ask: "What are you here for?"

"I don't know, Mr. President, you sent for me."

"You take one hundred hours on the farm!"

Whenever he rose in chapel with his head lowered, his keen eyes peering above his glasses, and repeated Proverbs X:1 — "A wise son maketh a glad father but a foolish son is the heaviness of his mother," — every boy began to shiver and wonder, "It it I?"

President Wright's own sons were no exception. He disciplined and expelled them just as quickly as he did other boys. "He played no favorites," says Dr. Perry W. Cheney, one of his graduates and a prominent physician of New York City.

One night the leader of the band, Tom Brown, left the campus without permission. The next morning President Wright had him come to his office.

"Good morning, Mr. President."

"Who are you?"

"I'm Tom Brown, Mr. President."

"What do you want?"

"I just came in to see how you're getting along, Mr. President."

"You take one hundred hours on the farm."

Another night his own son, Whittier, now Dr. Whittier Howard Wright, one of Philadelphia's leading physicians, and several friends remained out later than was permitted. As punishment for that infraction of the rule, he expelled all of them from the College. He didn't allow his students or teachers to smoke, play cards or dance. He never found time to indulge in these pastimes himself, he said.

He arranged the classes of the College alphabetically, with the work of Class A conforming about to that of the eighth grade. He opened at eight o'clock in the morning and closed at four in the afternoon. He opened at eight p. m. and closed at ten p. m. He arranged the schedule so that students studied half the day and worked the other half. By so doing he furnished them board, lodging and laundry for five dollars per month. He had them repair the old building, clean up the campus, lay out walks and flower beds, milk the cows, wash dishes and wait on tables.

To furnish these green country boys away from their homes for the first time, some amusement, he and Mrs. Wright instituted an old-fashioned Hallowe'en Candy-Pull. Each of the boys had a clean white bed sheet thrown over his head. In the early days when only boys were in attendance, President Wright suggested that some of the boys retain their own names and identity and others take the names of girls. Each girl drew from a hat her supposed beau, the person with whom she was to pull candy. When the molasses was done enough to pull, it was poured into platters to cool. Each girl took one end of a batch, her fellow took the other end of it, and pulled until it was creamy white.

A couple of months later, each of the boys received a written invitation from President and Mrs. Wright for a Watch Meeting at their home. It read, "Come after tea and spend the rest of the year with us."

President Wright played games with them, socialized and had refreshments with them. Just before twelve o'clock he got out his Bible and invited everyone to be seated. He read from what had been in early days his Mother's favorite chapter. Following the reading he rose from his chair and got down on his knees. Everybody in the room did likewise. He prayed not only for those at the school, for their steadfastness of purpose and future success, but for their parents who had toiled in the heat of the day that their sons might not have to come up as they had come — as hewers of wood and drawers of water. He rose, shook hands with the person next to him, bade him "A prosperous New Year," and then greeted each one around the room in similiar fashion. Everybody as soon as his hand was shaken joined the others in the march and the hand-shaking around the room. "A prosperous New Year."

After such a party was over one night and members of his immediate family had retired, President Wright sat alone thinking. Negroes had come a long way from serfdom to positions of responsibility. As his thoughts turned backward he decided to write his former master and mistress a letter and tell them of his new position as President of the Georgia State Industrial College. He wrote them also about his large family of small children, his good wife and himself. In a short time he received a reply in which they congratulated him and assured him his success was no surprise to them. They had "raised" him all right and he couldn't go wrong.

Another New Year's pledge of his was to renew his efforts in the field of research. He was aware of difficulties especially since he was unable to work in the public library. As he leaned backward in his chair, his eyes stared right into that ever-present motto, "I'll find a way or make one."

He made up his mind to seek admission to the Georgia Historical Association's collection in the Savannah Public Library, on the ground of getting information about the Negro schools in Georgia before the war. In search of the person to whom he would go for this privilege, he made contact and succeeded in getting in, but was screened off from the other readers.

Nevertheless, he unearthed some very valuable material. For example, he discovered that the first donation given to the University of Georgia was contributed by a Negro man who had been in the Revolutionary War and received a bounty. He also discovered that a Scotchman by the name of Mr. McLauren who had once lived in Savannah had manumitted his slaves forty years before the Emancipation in the United States. He had also placed in the bank in Scotland a sum of money for the education of slaves.

This data President Wright called to the attention of his Superintendent of Education who in turn took it up with the President of the United States. The sum of money was obtained from Scotland as the McLauren Fund and given to the Georgia State Industrial College for the erection of a library. As a consequence of such an achievement on behalf of the College, he secured the consent of his Board of Directors for a leave of absence to make a comparative study of some of the leading industrial schools and colleges of the country.

He went first to Girard College in Philadelphia. After intensive study there he spent a while at Hirsch School in New York City which had been opened by Jews to teach boys and girls who had recently come from Russia. Then he went to Hampton Institute and Tuskegee. He had already met Dr. Booker T. Washington and had correspondence with him, but had never visited Tuskegee Institute. In fact, as a graduate of Atlanta University, he felt that the Negro needed higher education at least as badly as he needed industrial education. He studied both institutions with the thought that he might find suggestions and adaptations which he could make for his own work.

On his return to the Georgia State Industrial College he didn't change his conclusions as to the relative importance of these two educational systems. He had already organized his own plan to divide the day in half — one part for literary work and the other part for industrial and agricultural courses. He had also decided to establish three departments — Industrial, Normal and Collegiate.

He introduced blacksmithing, brick masonry, carpentry and painting. He asked his Board of Directors if his school might compete in the State Fair for raising the highest number of bushels of corn to the acre. The Board's reply challenged him to organize a colored State Fair. The fact that he had already conducted a successful County Fair heightened its expectations and gave him confidence.

His plans, too, for establishing a monthly school paper which could be used to reach every Negro farmer in the state coincided with the challenge of his Board of Commissioners. With their approval, he went ahead and organzed the College Journal Publishing Association. He had R. R. Mobley (one of his students) elected president; William H. A. Howard (another student) secretary; and Lewis B. Thompson (one of the professors) editor. The name of the paper selected by the Association through his suggestion was "The College Journal." Subscription rates were twenty-five cents a year, and five cents a copy. In its final form it consisted of four sheets 12 x 18 inches, published at first monthly then semi-monthly during the school year.

The first issue President Wright pushed to its completion and sent over the state as a trial balloon. The response to a colored State Fair was so encouraging he initiated plans immediately for sending students out to work up enthusiasm and give instructions.

He linked it up with his school which had grown in personnel to one hundred and ninety students from fifty counties; and to eleven professors and instructors. He sent a personal letter to all the boys who had applied for work, saying five cents an hour was paid for extra work on the farm, all of which was done by the boys; and the same amount was paid for extra work on the campus. So many more boys came than there was work for, if one signed the payroll at the end of the month and received one dollar and fifty cents, he thought he had a "lot of money."

President Wright taught them to raise vegetables and corn for the school and to sell the excess in the city. He had certain boys milk the dairy cows twice a day. One of these boys, now Dr. Perry Cheney, whose mother, Mrs. Emma F. Hudson, had been a country student of President Wright — earned six dollars per month and a twenty-five cent tip on Saturdays. He rose at four o'clock every morning during his first year at the college, milked a professor's cow and delivered the milk for the college in Thunderbolt.

President Wright also introduced a chicken farm and took time to watch the baby chicks and the fine breeds furnish employment for the boys as well as fowl and eggs for the school.

For the promotion of the State Fair, he organized the boys into groups of three and sent them out in different directions as advance agents to canvass nearby counties and some counties in adjacent states. He sent them on foot without money and with just enough food for one meal. He told each boy upon leaving, if he couldn't make the trip better than anybody else, he had better quit. He cautioned each group about walking the five-mile trestle across the Savannah River. If a train should come along, each boy was to act with neatness and dispatch, catch hold of the cross ties and hang down underneath. He instructed each group to notify in person the farmers on its beat and so interest them that they would attend the State Fair at the Court House in Macon that fall. He had each group on its return write a report and read it at one of the chapel exercises.

He sent out postcards with the inscription: "You must see the Georgia State Fair at the State House in Macon!" There was also the picture of a Negro boy on an American Flag saying, "Tell 'em we are rising." He gave the

Fair such wide publicity it attracted the attention of Ray Stannard Baker who was then writing a series of articles entitled "Following the Color Line," for the American Magazine.

In the one which portrayed the Georgia State Fair, Mr. Baker presented President Wright with his hat on, as "Organizer of the Negro State Fair in Georgia," and as being "of full-blooded African descent." He continued, "I was at Macon while the first State Fair ever held by Negroes in Georgia was in progress. In spite of the fact that racial relationships, owing to the recent riot at Atlanta, were acute, the Fair was largely attended and not only by Negroes but by many white visitors. The brunt of the work of the organization fell upon R. R. Wright, President of the Georgia State Industrial College (coloured) of Savannah. At the Negro Fair, crowning the charts which had been prepared to show the progress of the Negroes of Georgia, I saw this motto, 'We are Rising.'

"The attendance at the Fair was between 25,000 and 30,000. Negroes raised $7,000. In this enterprise they had the sympathy and approval of the best white people."

Another vivid glimpse of what the Fair meant was given by the *Daily News* of Macon, a white newspaper:

"The Fair shows what progress can be accomplished by the industrious, thrifty Negro, who casts aside the belief that he is a dependent and sails right in to make a living and a home for himself. Some of the agricultural exhibits of black farmers have never been surpassed in Macon. On the whole the exposition just simply astounded folks who did not know what the Negro is doing for himself."

In addition to these achievements, President Wright furnished every visiting farmer free board and lodging for the three days of the Fair. To those who had exhibits he rented concessions at a nominal fee. He invited there experts and farmers as well who presented criticisms. He

A luncheon in honor of Major Wright, by prominent bankers and citizens of San Francisco, California

had some of the ablest experts in the country to lecture and give demonstrations on scientific farming, on soil fertility, on the business side of farming, on cooperative buying and selling, on poultry raising, on improvement of livestock and tick eradication, on disease: tuberculosis, hookworm, pellagra; on health and preventive medicine, and on the best method of reaching the people.

At one of the evening sessions addresses were delivered, and a discussion of the moral and religious condition of the Negro people was held. President Wright also conducted a women's meeting in which a household economics discussion was led by some expert in that field.

He gave out free government seeds and literature, and thousands of dollars in cash prizes for the winning products.

He sponsored an aeroplane flight over those same fairgrounds where an aviator had recently been killed in his feats for the White State Fair. He accomplished it, and with great success, despite that accident and other odds. In the first place, an advertised Negro aviator in Pennsylvania with whom he was in correspondence, finally could not come to Georgia because he had not paid for his plane. Then, with little time left before the Fair was to open, President Wright engaged a white aviator of New York State. The latter brought his plane down to Georgia by train; signed up; got his five hundred dollars and skipped town the night before his scheduled demonstration was to take place.

Sorely disappointed but undaunted, President Wright entered suit against him; established contact with another aviator who was flying in Georgia, and before the Fair adjourned the latter flew over the Fair Grounds without any mishap and to the amazement of black and white alike.

Finally, in connection with the Fair, he had a sociological study made of some occupation or industry. One year, for example, he had two studies made. One of these — made by the late Professor Monroe N. Work — was of the Georgia State Industrial College student body. It ascertained how many local communities were represented in the school, what the people of these communities engaged in, their needs — educational, religious and material — kinds of homes, kind of houses owned or rented, home training. The other study was of the Negro in the oyster industry in Georgia. It concerned itself with the number in this industry, their wages, what improvements could be made in the three hundred oyster Negroes studied, etc.

Results of the state conferences were published. Accurate record of all the farmers, their property and how they were progressing, was kept. Inasmuch as the boys of the school erected the buildings on the campus under supervision, tended the vegetable farm, the chicken farm, the dairying, President Wright had practical demonstrations for them in certain phases of building and repair, vegetable and chicken-raising and dairying.

During the ten years duration of these State Fairs, he organized the Good Cheer Club. Its Certificate of Membership, which read as follows, was mailed out to prospective attendants to the State Fair:

"United States of America

Capital Stock

CERTIFICATE OF MEMBERSHIP

All Fun No. 152

GOOD CHEER CLUB

Know All Men by These Presents:

That the bearer is hereby appointed a member of the Good Cheer Club, and agrees to spread sunshine and happiness everywhere.

Meetings daily at the Georgia State Colored Fair, Macon, Georgia, November 18-21, 1914. The biggest event in years, and every member obligates himself to attend daily and bring his family and friends.

IN WITNESS WHEREOF, We have hereunto subscribed our names and seal, effective only upon the member's attendance,

Georgia State Colored Fair.

R. R. Wright, President
L. B. Thompson, Secretary"

The Georgia State Colored Fair was so well publicized and conducted its President was invited to appear before a commission in Washington, D. C. which was investigating labor conditions in the South. As a consequence he wrote an article on "The Negro as a Farmer," which appeared in the Congressional Record under Mr. Blair. Another result of his appearance before this Commission was, more money was appropriated by the United States Government for the Georgia State College.

Realizing that the boys were now in need of play and sports, he organized more effectively a baseball team, a basketball team, a track team and a football team. He had become so interested in sports himself that in 1910 he attended the Jack Johnson-Jeffries fight in Reno, Nevada.

When the question of uniforms was threatened with cancellation because of the poverty of the boys, he worked out a special method by which he furnished them uniforms at nine dollars a suit. He was so interested in seeing his students do their best and have the best, after nine years of his Presidency he prevailed upon the State Legislature to appropriate funds for new buildings, for water works to replace the old pump, for machinery for the shops and equipment for the laboratories.

In thinking further of what his college needed most, he said to himself, "Look here, these boys must have wives." And as he cogitated upon the assumption that their wives should be educated women, he decided to admit girls to the college and give them one-half the day, as the boys had, for academic study and the other half for courses in housekeeping and cooking. For recreation he encouraged them to learn to swim in the creek on the border of the campus. With his help they not only learned to swim but conducted swimming parties.

In order that they, as well as the boys, might get the best out of their studies and from their contacts in the classrooms and on the campus, he surrounded himself with such teachers as the late Nathan B. Young, L. B. Thompson, Henry Pearson, Monroe N. Work, and D. C. Suggs.

As vice-president of the Board of Trustees of Atlanta University, he presided over the deliberations of that body the day Dr. William E. Burghardt DuBois was elected professor of Social Service Research of Atlanta University. His support was given to the election of Dr. DuBois in the face of great opposition on account of DuBois' so-called radical tendencies. He gave it, he said, because he was interested in having the most competent man possible for the position. He knew of Dr. DuBois' training and work, and at the request of Dr. DuBois, he himself had already been doing some research in the field of the Business Urban Problems of Atlanta University Graduates.

For his own teachers he often applied to the leading colleges of the country. Once Yale University sent him an English teacher whose father and grandmother he knew well. This young teacher's old grandmother had struggled and sent him through college. When he came to the Georgia State College in which there were 800 students at that time, President Wright assigned him a Sunday School class in addition to his week-day classes. He informed the President in a somewhat stiff manner, "I cannot teach something I don't believe in. No, I don't believe in this rot about God. All of this old fogyism should be done away with." The next day in chapel the President read the Scripture lesson, "The fool hath said in his heart there is no God."

The young teacher, greatly riled, rose and asked if the President meant him. The President replied, "I'll see you on the outside after these exercises."

When the President walked out the young teacher accosted him. As a result the Board of Education ordered the young man to leave the campus in twenty-four hours.

President Wright, eager for his students to have also that type of education which comes through outside contact, was always on the alert for some of the leaders of the country to visit his college. Among those he was fortunate enough to obtain was Mr. William H. Baldwin of New York who as a trustee of Tuskegee Institute spoke on "The Necessity for Industrial Education." On many occasions Professor George W. Carver came, lectured and gave scientific demonstrations to the students.

In President Wright's attempt to have the Hon. William Jennings Bryan attend one of his State Fairs, he appealed to Dr. Booker T. Washington, who wrote the following letter to Mr. Bryan:

"July 12, 1907

Honorable William Jennings Bryan
Lincoln, Nebraska
Dear Mr. Bryan:
I am taking the liberty of introducing to you Professor R. R. Wright, President of the State Normal and Industrial College, Savannah, Georgia. I have known Professor Wright for a number of years and do not hesitate to say that he is a conservative and sensible man and is doing a fine work for our race. I had the pleasure of speaking at the State Fair under his auspices last fall and was more than pleased at the evi-

dence of progress which I saw at this Fair. Not only was this Fair the means of bringing the best white and colored people of the state together but it was the means of increasing good feeling between the races.

If you can accede to Professor Wright's request, I feel quite sure you will be interested in your reception at Macon. Professor Wright has the hearty cooperation of the best white people in Georgia in his efforts.

Signed)

BOOKER T. WASHINGTON"

In a lecture course which President Wright planned out in his early days as President of the Georgia State Industrial College, he invited Mr. T. Thomas Fortune, Editor then of *The New York Age,* to come down as the first speaker. As a newspaperman himself he made Mr. Fortune's visit and lecture on Abraham Lincoln, a great occasion. It was on a Friday evening in the late fall of the year. He thrilled his students with his introduction of Mr. Fortune, the incomparable Negro editor from far away New York — the city of competition, thrills and possibilities for the Negro in the field of journalism.

In his endeavor to bring to them information on Negro inventors — since nearly every scientifically-minded Negro appeared to be inventing something — he went to Washington, D. C. to see the Honorable B. K. Bruce, then Registrar of the United States Treasury and father of Mr. Roscoe C. Bruce, later Assistant Superintendent of the Washington D. C. Public Schools. Mr. Bruce got Mr. Henry E. Baker, Assistant Examiner in the United States Patent Office, to look up the material. When Mr. Baker appeared before his Chief, the Hon. Hoke Smith of Georgia, then Secretary of the Department of Commerce under which the Patent Office belonged, he asked, "Have you ever heard of R. R. Wright? He's from Georgia. He's President of our State College." Then he advised Mr. Baker to get together all the available material on

Negro inventors and whip it into shape for publication. President Wright needed it for the Georgia State Colelge.

The result of President Wright's inquiry was a twelve-page phamphlet, "The Colored Inventor," by Henry E. Baker, published by The Crisis Publishing Company.

Another means whereby he brought home a lesson to his students was through his own activities and connections for the betterment of the community and the state at large. He organized The Negro Civic Improvement League in Savannah, and as its first President gave the land for the erection of a home for the aged. At Christmastime and on the 4th of July a wagonload of produce was taken to the Home for the Aged Poor.

For the benefit of poor children he established a Christmas Fund which netted annually around $350.00. He appointed a committee of ladies on which Mrs. Wright served, who investigated the needs of children in all parts of the city and distributed three hundred or more baskets of food, dolls and toys.

He organized in Savannah a home for wayward girls. The immediate occasion for this was the plight of a fourteen-year-old girl from a neighboring island who had been despoiled in Savannah and left stranded. Other similar cases had so often been brought to his attention, he was now thoroughly aroused. He went to a prominent woman in Savannah, Mrs. George S. Williams, and said to her, "You and I must start a home for girls." To her question of where they would get the money he replied, "I will put in ten cents. You put in ten cents. And both of us will get our friends to put in ten cents." She agreed.

President Wright wrote and went to see five hundred of his friends. He presented the case and the need in such a manner that with the aid of Mrs. Williams he was able to purchase six acres of land on which there was a house. He solicited furniture and furnishings for it and opened it for wayward girls. When he proposed plowing up the land so as to plant corn, vegetables and even a little cotton, the people thought he was a fool. Despite their attitude, he went there himself, supervised the work and even learned again to plow.

In similar fashion he was rebuked for introducing in Savannah the first Negro Probation Officer, Mrs. Rebecca Styles Taylor. He felt so strongly the need of her services, he paid her salary; and had to do so because of the opposition to her work. Even his President of the Board of Commissioners of the Georgia State Industrial College for Negroes came to him and told him he was starting a cripple. He couldn't continue to pay the salary of a Negro Probation Officer and the city couldn't afford to pay it.

Instead of giving up this undertaking, President Wright decided to attract public attention away from this project to another eye-sore: the uninhabitable shacks in which Negroes lived in Savannah. To accomplish his ends he fixed up an alarming story and gained the ear of two city councilmen. They were so worked up over it that they arranged for him to appear before the whole body.

Said he, "Councilmen, do you know that Mrs. 'X' sends her wash to a shack right over measles and typhoid fever?" The councilmen turned pale with fright. They voted in that meeting to send to Philadelphia and have a housing expert come down to advise with them. In a few weeks the housing expert came out to the college to talk with President Wright. The latter took him to some of the worst shacks in Savannah. He in turn was so alarmed he recommended immediate sanitary improvements, several of which for the time being were put into effect.

With some realization of his own influence as President of a college such as his, he organized The National Association of Presidents of the Colored A. & M. Colleges in the U. S. — and served as its president for five years. His successful administration of the affairs of this office coupled with his services in establishing The National Association of Teachers in Colored Schools, influenced the latter organization to elect him as its president.

He worked night and day. During the first thirteen years of his Presidency of the College he enrolled over 3,000 students, and sent out one hundred and thirteen graduates. One of them secured a position as head of the Department of Masonry and Plaster of his Alma Mater. One became an inspector in Carpentry and Mathematics in the North Carolina State College for Negroes. One became instructor in the Industrial Department of the Florida State College. Two of them entered the ministry. Two of them became physicians. Three of them secured positions as constables. Four of them entered business. Four of them entered the United States Mail Service. Twenty of them worked at their trades and continued their studies in their Alma Mater and in other schools. Fifty of them passed the Public School examinations and secured positions in the Public School systems. The Georgia State Industrial College under President Wright's leadership was unique among colored state schools in the South in that it was the only one in the strictly Southern states that had a Collegiate Department. It was also unique in that it held annually a farmers, mechanics and laborers conference.

It furnished a forum for the students through is literary societies such as The Phi Kappa Literary Society and the Philosophian and Phyllis Wheatley Societies. There were also societies composed of students of what was known as the Subnormal Department. On one occasion in 1890 one of these societies held a debate the subject of which was RESOLVED, That the United States should sympathize with Japan in its present conflict with Russia. President Wright sat in, not as one of the judges but as one ready to congratulate them on their decision in favor of the negative.

One of his graduates says of President Wright: "The old man preached higher education and it didn't suit anybody."

One day one of the Commissioners of the school, Mr. Ashmore, came out and entered President Wright's class in Virgil. He listened awhile, and as he left the room said: "Wright, I want you to cut this Latin out and teach these boys to farm."

In an ingratiating manner President Wright told Mr. Ashmore they were learning to farm and he didn't see why they could not learn a little Virgil, too. Mr. Ashmore flew into a rage and threatened to have him relieved of his position. Other members of the Board of Trustees, he reminded President Wright, felt just as he did about the matter. President Wright didn't answer him further, but lost no time in arranging an interview with General Peter W. Meldrim, president of the Board of Trustees.

General Meldrim had supported him, for the most part, in all his plans for the school. This time, the General told him he was in complete agreement with Booker T. Washington. A college education was not best for the Negro. He would have to cut out that Latin and Greek and teach the students to work and make a living. President Wright went home almost discouraged. He thought the matter through and decided to "find" a way or make one.

In his next interview with General Meldrim he was as pleasant as a basket of chips. He agreed with the General in everything except one. They saw eye to eye, he told him; but he would have to apologize for saying one thing. He couldn't understand how he, a white man and a leading citizen of Georgia, had to let a Negro from Alabama in the person of Booker T. Washington, tell him how to run the Georgia State Industrial School. He said as

General Meldrim winced under this comparison he didn't try to press his point; just sat there disappointed and dejected. General Meldrim looked at him with a half smile and replied, "Wright, you're doing all right. Go ahead the way you're going."

Many of President Wright's students also said he was a great President and teacher. Dr. Perry Cheney who worked with him and knew him about as well as any other one of his graduates, says of him:

"As a teacher he had no equal. He was well informed on all the issues of the day. He knew finance and he understood men. He could pick out a boy or a girl who would amount to something. Do that better than anybody else. Sometimes he would say to a student, 'You had better quit.' He entered every student's life — low or high. He followed each to the bedroom, to the dining room, through school and out into life. No man who has headed a school has put more of himself into it than he. No other school would have taken so much time to guide me. Major took the job. Boys from the rural districts with no hope entered the first grade of his college and became professional men, business men. If it hadn't been for him many of us boys would still be down South hoeing and plowing and picking cotton for fifty cents a day. He disliked to see anything half done, or to have a student fail to keep his word. One of his pet sayings was, 'Cheney, don't promise to day anything and not do it. If you can't do it, say so.' He was remarkable in that many times he looked men of opposing views between the eyes, told them what he thought and yet retained his position; and not as a handkerchief-head, either. He fought against the tide."

For years his equal emphasis on higher education for Negroes was not understood by some of his own people. He felt that even the late Dr. Booker T. Washington misunderstood for a time. Yet he acknowledged that

Dr. Washington was the greatest business man the Negro race had produced up to the time of his death.

One of President Wright's elections to a political position was not understood by some of his own people, either. They complained that he was a Republican getting Democratic money and using it to teach the young Negro Latin and Greek in an Industrial College. They even attempted to get publicity on it through the *Atlanta Constitution*. Because of this he was sent for by the editor and the owner of that paper, Mr. Clark Howell and Mr. Henry Grady. When he appeared Mr. Howell said,

"You have a good job; and now I don't see why you run with the Republicans."

"Look here, Mr. Howell," he replied, "you think well of me, don't you? How useful do you think the people would think I am if I were just looking out for a job?" The matter was of such moment Mr. Howell sent for Dr. Brooker T. Washington and talked it over with him. The latter stated that President Wright was wasting state money teaching Latin and Greek. He could send the Board of Commissioners the right man for the presidency of the Georgia State Industrial College.

President Wright was informed that letters from both Dr. Washington and Dr. Frissell, president of Hampton Institute, to the chairman and other Commissioners of the Georgia State Industrial College advised that the matter of a president be turned over to Dr. Washington. He had just the man for the position. The Commissioners held a meeting at which both letters were read. One of the Commissioners said, "Turn this school over to Booker Washington in Alabama to ruin? I'll be damned if I'll do it."

President Wright got busy, sold his home and what little he had in Augusta. Had nothing, he says, but some books — about 5,000 of those. He came back, however, and was re-elected. Everybody greeted him with a smile. Some of the folks behind his back accused him of being a Republican politician. In one of his blue moments he said to Mrs. Wright, "Mama, they are going to put us out."

"Don't worry," she replied.

He did worry, nevertheless. He also awoke to the fact that he had taught in a noble profession nearly fifty years and had nothing but a large family — eight living children: three boys and five girls — and some books.

He knew two men who were as greatly worried as he was. One of them, Mr. Black, said to him:

"Wright, I have a house I want to sell. I'll sell it to you for $1,400."

He didn't have that kind of money, he told Mr. Black. Then Mr. Black offered to let him have it for Fifty Dollars "down payment." Another man, a white friend of his, said, "You take Black's offer. I'll lend you the Fifty Dollars."

He bought the house and sold it later for twice the amount. Through this transaction he awoke as never before to the possibilities in business — the profession he had earlier intended to pursue.

He said it took him five years to get out of the Georgia State Industrial College. Some folks said he was getting too old for the presidency of that institution. He laughed quietly and his eyes sparkled as if he were both amused and insured: "Some may think I'm getting too old to run a bank."

Just before his retirement from the college, the faculty, alunmni and undergraduates sent out invitations to his friends over the country inviting them to his Golden Anniversary — 50 years in the noble profession of teaching; thirty of them as president of the Georgia State Industrial College. This celebration was held on the 25th of November, 1920, in St. Phillips A.M.E. Church, Savannah, Georgia. President Wright, still small in stature, erect, and with his head up and his best blue suit on, stood in line and received like a Major in the army.

When his friends heard he was leaving for the North to open a bank some thought he was crazy, losing his mind, and said so. Others simply couldn't believe it. Savannah business men advised against it. He was giving up a lifetime job to get into something he knew nothing about, they cautioned. He would be back there in less than two year's time begging for a job, others predicted.

In spite of their admonitions and prophecies, he made ready to leave. However, his services as a teacher and as an educator were attested by the fact that one of his graduates of the Georgia State Industrial College in the person of Mr. C. G. Wyley succeeded him as President. He was proud of this fact and of Mr. Wyley as well.

Among his other graduates of distinction he listed: Bishop David H. Sims, A.M.E. Church; Dr. Julian W. Ross, Howard University Medical College; Dr. W. C. Cuthbert, physician, Pittsburgh, Pa.; Rev. W. O. P. Sherman, presiding elder, A.M.E. Church; Mr. Maceo W. Hubbard, Attorney-at-Law, Philadelphia; Mr. LeRoy Humbert, Attorney-at-Law, Philadelphia; Mr. Benjamin A. Judkins, Department of Agriculture, Washington, D. C.; Dr. William A. Harris, physician, Savannah, Ga.; Dr. Henry M. Collier, physician, Savannah; Dr. Edward W. Verner, physician, Savannah; Dr. Whittier C. Atkinson, physician, Coatesville, Pa.; Mr. Luther Ison, principal, high school, Waycross, Georgia; Mr. Foster R. Lampkin, principal, high school, Columbus, Georgia; Mr. Allan Dingle, Attorney-at-Law, New York City; Mrs. Essie L. Monroe Edwards, Undertaker, Savannah; Dr. N. B. Hester, dentist, Palatka, Florida; Professor J. S. Frazier, Georgia State Industrial College; Mr. Samuel A. Grant, Real Estate, Chicago; Mr. Peter A. Cosey, tailor, Chicago; Mr. Carleton W. Gaines, Real Estate, Detroit; Dr. C. C. Strickland, physician, Detroit, Dr. H. M. Scarlett, physician, Greensboro, N. C.; Mr. Frank A. Callen, Probation Officer, Savannah; Mr. Samuel Anderson, undertaker, New York City; and the late Henry Lincoln Johnson, a graduate of Ware High School under President Wright, as well as a student of the Georgia State College.

President Wright loaned Mr. Johnson money to move to Washington when the latter became Recorder of Deeds. He also visited Mr. Johnson and not only persuaded him to buy a house for his family but went with him and his two sons and assisted him in the selection of a house. He was proud of the fact that Mrs. Georgia Douglas Johnson, poetess and widow of Henry Lincoln Johnson, still lives in that house. In that house, he said, she wrote a book of poems, "Bronze." Taking out his copy he called attention to the section on the services of John Brown, Abraham Lincoln, William E. Burghardt DuBois, Stanley Braithwaite and Richard R. Wright. Of the latter she sings:

To Richard Wright, Instructor,
Son of a race . . .
Erect, unbending, note his sable brow,
The rugged furrows where deep feelings plow,
The step of vigor and the noble air,
The subtle halo of his wintry hair,
Up from the furnace of the Earth's red sea
A man is fashioned for the years to be!

In the year 1926, fifty years after President Wright's graduation from Atlanta University, and the Thirty-Ninth Anniversary of his services as a Trustee of that University, he was called back as its Commencement Day Orator. On that occasion he was introduced by the President of

Atlanta University as the "black boy of Atlanta," invaluable citizen, great teacher, editor, college president, politician, banker and senior member of the Atlanta University Board of Trustees — outranking by 15 years the next member of that Board in point of service.

As speaker of the Day the black banker from the City of Brotherly Love could not lay aside his old axe, his 200-mile walk into Atlanta, his entry into the Box Car School — now Atlanta University — his Black Boy of Atlanta message, his Bob Tooms fifty-cent piece, and his half century as an educator and organizer.

During succeeding years his genius as an organizer expressed itself in the development of The Citizens and Southern Bank & Trust Company; the Haitian Coffee and Products Trading Company; and in the birth of a Philadelphia Negro Chamber of Commerce. The inauguration of this Chamber of Commerce was marked by President Wright's flight at the age of 84 in his own aeroplane — a Wake four-passenger cabin type of the latest design and improvement — from Philadelphia to Richmond, Virginia, and back.

CHAPTER V

JOURNALIST AND POLITICIAN

President Wright's fifty years of service as an educator and organizer were interspersed with Journalism and Politics.

In 1879, shortly after his organization of the Georgia State Colored Teachers Association, he entered a Cuthbert newspaper office to have the minutes of that Association's first meeting printed. He saw a weekly newspaper which met the requirements of the organ of expression which he had in mind for his growing work. Upon inquiry, the owner who was also a banker, offered to sell it to him for four hundred dollars. Surprised and pleased, he agreed to the price and bought it almost on the spot. He named it, "The Weekly Journal of Progress" and gave it the motto of President Ware's Yale class and subsequently that of his own Atlanta University class. "I'll find a way or make one."

The Weekly Journal of Progress was the only newspaper in Cuthbert with one exception. That exception's editor began and continued to roast Professor Wright in every one of it's issues, but Professor Wright made no reply.

He was now the owner and manager of "The Weekly Journal of Progress," but he didn't know how to set type. There was no one else in town he could hire except the typesetter who had formerly worked on what was now Professor Wright's own paper. When he went to see that typesetter, the latter refused to work for less than $75 a week. Despite Professor Wright's argument about his new venture, his people's inability to support two Negro newspapers in the State, the overhead, etc., he had to hire that typesetter at the latter's own price. When the typesetter came on the job, to Professor Wright's keen displeasure, he refused to allow a Negro to come into the office to work. Instead of hiring a Negro to help him, he hired a drunkard whose favorite sport was cursing Negroes.

After four issues had come off the press, Professor Wright aware that the two salaries were eating up all the profit, decided to make a change. He took one of his students — Theodore Seward — and entered the newspaper office one Sunday morning. All day and into the night, he and Seward studied type setting and the general run of getting out the paper. When he reached the point where he thought he could get it out in some sort of fashion, he locked the door behind him and went home.

The next morning the typesetter's helper — a bit groggy from his weekend's spree — came to Professor Wright for a key. He had misplaced his, he apologized. "I haven't got your key," replied Professor Wright with a frigid air. The helper raved, cursed and swore. Professor Wright complained to the typesetter about his helper's conduct, and offered the typesetter two weeks pay and leave to go about his business. To Professor Wright's great relief, he took the money and left.

Relieved on the one hand, but on the other, Professor Wright and his student had a time getting out the paper. It was full of defects and scarcely looked like itself; but it came out on time.

One day as Professor Wright was at work in the editorial room, he looked out the window and saw an old whipping post which he thought he recognized. He went out and inspected it. Yes, that was it. He viewed the surroundings but found no trace of his mother's cabin. He turned and walked back over the yard. He located the spot where the cabin once was. He went back into his editorial room, looked at the old mantle piece and the room as a whole. He brought his mother who was living with him over to confirm his discovery. "Yes, the dining table set "this er way," she told him. "Old Moster sat there." "Miss Bettie sat here." He, a little black boy in his shirt tail, stood on the side near the middle, fanning the flies from the table in the hot summer time.

He shook his head. A train of thought ran over him like a Twentieth Century Limited he said and almost stunned him. Upon recovery, he was so morose for a while, he couldn't do his work. He came to the conclusion, if he spent too much time looking backward he would soon be turned into a reminiscing old man. He braced up and said to himself, "What of the next fifteen years?"

He set himself to the task before him. He had to find or make a way to get out the next issue of "The Weekly Journal of Progress" — a four page paper about 12x16 inches. In the first column on the front page, he discussed the Sunday School lesson, "The Power of Christ", Matthew 8:18-31. In another front page article he presented the facts concerning a colony of 109 emigrants who had prepared to leave Arkansas for Liberia but had been disappointed in getting a vessel.

In spite of all handicaps and difficulties, the editor and owner of "The Weekly Journal of Progress" — learned rapidly and gained headway in the field of Journalism. His paper brought his capabilities to the attention of the Republican Party, as well as to such historians of Georgia as I. W. Avery. In the latter's "History of Georgia" 1850-1881, the following statement about Professor Wright's paper appears: "It has been an extraordinary mark of progress that the colored people have two well established weekly newspapers; one the "Journal of Progress" at Cuthbert, edited by an intelligent man named Wright, and the other, "The Blade," at Atlanta edited by W. P. Pledger, Chairman of the Republican State Executive

Committee and a very well educated and smart person, a good writer and excellent speaker."

When Professor Wright was about to leave Cuthbert to organize the high school in Augusta, he placed a man in charge of "The Weekly Journal of Progress" and his newspaper office in Cuthbert. Under the new manager, the paper did not succeed. Therefore, Professor Wright moved it to Augusta, and instead of inserting a headliner Ad "Under New Management," changed its name to "The Weekly Sentinel." He gave it a new motto, "With malice toward none. With charity for all. We Watch and defend." He placed in charge of it as president, the Reverend Charles T. Walker, D.D., and able Baptist minister whom he and others often referred to as the Black Surgeon. On securing Dr. Walker's services he told him he wanted someone who could shove out from the shore and not be taken for a little fish.

His reference was to one of Dr. Walker's sermons in which as the latter waxed eloquent, an unlettered churchman in the audience yelled out, "Preach it! you black sturgeon you: I know you can do it!" Editor Wright in his recital of this story told how deliberately Dr. Walker stopped in the middle of his peroration and replied as he wiped the perspiration from his face. "Thank you brother, I'm mighty glad you didn't mix me up with any of the little fish."

The other officers whom Professor Wright placed as associates on "The Weekly Sentinel" were: T. Seremus Seward, Business Manager; E. K. Love, D.D., Editor in Chief, and Silas X. Floyd, A.B., Managing Editor.

Of this weekly paper, another historian — Charles C. Jones, Jr. LLD, in his "Memorial History of Augusta," writes, "Two papers are published in Augusta in the interest of the colored population. One is "The Sentinel," a political journal edited by Professor Wright; the other a religious paper, "The Georgia Baptist," edited by Reverend W. J. White." As the former weekly espoused the cause of the people of the State it was sometimes referred to as the States Rights Sentinel.

The fact that his paper was also called the States Rights Sentinel was no surprise to Professor Wright. He had elected as its President — a man who was not only Pastor of Augusta Tabernacle but able to speak the white man's language in the Negro's way. As Editor in Chief, he had elected an aggressive race fighter and pastor of the oldest and largest Negro Baptist Church in the world at that time. In so doing, he had not only benefitted his paper but had formed a Wright - Walker - Love political offensive and defensive, similar to the one he had read of in Mississippi.

His group was a combination of black men, and the other group was composed of light skinned Negroes.

It was said his black offensive was often able to steal a convention where the white Negroes had planned to freeze them out, and make it home and go to bed with E. K. Love elected chairman of the State Committee and Professor Wright elected as delegate to a National Convention.

Professor Wright was aware of the popularity and influence of his paper at this time of two important campaigns. One of these campaigns was for the election of a governor of the State. This election savored of such a contest, the Editor of "The Weekly Sentinel" received a communication from the famous Henry W. Grady, editor of the Atlanta Constitution. The latter favored a certain candidate and desired the influence of "The Weekly Sentinel" for his candidate. Professor Wright went to see Editor Grady. As a consequence, the following weeks "The Weekly Sentinel" took up the cudgel for Editor Grady's candidate in such States Rights Sentinel fashion that it became one of the leading newspapers of that section.

The other campaign was for the election of delegates to the Republican National Convention to be held in Chicago. Professor Wright was a candidate for election. Naturally, his paper boosted him to the highest. At that time too the cry went up, "Young men to the front! Georgia needs new blood in politics." With this call for young men, he, just twenty years old, was unanimously elected alternate delegate-at-large among the twenty-four successful candidates. Upon their arrival in Chicago, they stopped at the Palmer House, the leading hotel in that city. Professor Wright was elected Secretary of the delegation.

The daily newspapers, including the Atlanta Constitution, in speaking of Professor Wright described him as "a slim, reticent young colored man who, when he did rise and speak at the convention showed that he was one of the most cultured and eloquent in the convention." Such flattery and fullsome praise coming from the leading daily in Atlanta sent his stock up to a high degree.

He and the other members of his party were excited over the news that the Edison electric lights would be turned on in their hotel for the first time in history. Accordingly, he was on hand the night they actually came on.

He said people shouted, men, women and children fainted. A disastrous stampede was just averted. He stood in the midst of a throng on the portico of that hotel and like most of the others was compelled to cover his eyes. The lights were so bright they blinded him. As they were displayed on State Street, he followed the throng who blocked the street. He felt if there had been nothing else of importance, that display would have been worth his trip to the convention.

There were issues though in that convention which were new and interesting to him. The foremost one which produced the famous fight of the Convention was a "third term." In this he and the other Negroes present found themselves terribly mixed up. With the notable exception of Representative Robert Brown Elliott of South Carolina, he and most of the others stood by President U. S. Grant who had already served two terms. To President Grant for a third term they were so ardently devoted, they voted for him on thirty odd ballots without a break.

Although Professor Wright was for Grant, and no one else, he was so thrilled by Robert Brown Elliott's speech on behalf of Senator John Sherman, his paper, "The Weekly Sentinel," in keeping with the Chicago dailies conceded it to be the greatest speech ever heard in a National Republican Convention. In addition to Elliott, he listened to Benjamin Harrison, James A. Garfield, Robert G. Ingersoll and Frederick Douglass. At one of the gatherings outside of Convention Hall, he met William McKinley who subsequently became Congressman, Governor and President of the United States.

He had read of Senator Blanche K. Bruce and of the Bruce-Hill-Lynch Offensive and Defensive. Therefore, he was eager to meet these men. In his opinion, Hill was one of the most spectacular delegates of the Convention. He admired the way the latter and Bruce supported Secretary Sherman and controlled the Mississippi delegation, while Major John R. Lynch favored Grant. Knowing Lynch was a candidate for the congressional nomination in the 6th or Shoe-String District, he watched his every intrepid move. Another one of the able Negro delegates who impressed Professor Wright was Wright Cuney of far away Texas. The young Editor admired Mr. Cuney's western manners and impressive personality.

After the Convention adjourned, he returned to Augusta with enthusiasm and ideas for his educational work as well as for his Political Arena. As an editor, a politician, and President of the Georgia State Teachers Association, he seized the opportunity to use "The Weekly Sentinel" in publicizing the several colleges about to be launched in the State.

His paper carried an article on the A.M.E. ministers of his own connection who were raising money to establish Morris Brown College in Atlanta. In it there was mention of two northern white ladies, Miss Packard and Miss Giles, who had opened the Atlanta Baptist Seminary in the basement of the colored friendship Baptist Church with eleven pupils — all full grown women. Later it carried a report of the change of name from Atlanta Baptist Seminary to Spelman Baptist Seminary; and emphasized the fact that Mr. Spelman in honor of whom the change of name was made, was the father-in-law of Mr. John D. Rockefeller who had given large sums of money on the payment of the property.

Through Professor Wright's direction and interest, one of his reporters visited representatives of the Freedmen's Aid Society and obtained information on the purchase of four hundred and fifty acres of land just outside the city limits of Atlanta, for the fabulous sum of twenty-five thousand dollars. One third of this amount the editor was informed had been donated by the Reverend Gammon of Batavia, Illinois. Therefore, one of the colleges established thereon was named Gammon Theological Seminary in his honor. The other college, Clark University was named in honor of Bishop D. W. Clark, who had visited the South after the war as a great organizer. Professor Wright was especially interested in the latter institution because his younger sister and brother attended it when it was only a primary school in Clark Chapel on Frazer Street.

With the assistance of his newspaper, he as principal of Ware High School interested in the civic and governmental welfare of the people, moved up from the chairmanship of the Congressional District Convention to that of chairman of the County Convention and member of the State Central Committee. In addition, he was nominated more than once for the office of representative in the State Legislature, representative in the Senate and Secretary of State.

After four years of intensive work for his party, his paper was again employed as a weapon for the National Republican Convention of 1884, and he was again elected as a delegate. For the second time too there were three presidential candidates.

As before, the Convention was held in Chicago. Early in its deliberations, he met two unusually aggressive brilliant young men in the person of Theodore Roosevelt and Henry Cabot Lodge. He was present at a conference with these two men, together with Senator Hoar, Mark Hana, George William Curtis and others. It was held to select a southern man as temporary Chairman of the Convention. He was amazed when Mark Hanna — more friendly to colored people than any other leading Republican has been since his day, Professor Wright thought, suggested the name of John R. Lynch. Theodore Roosevelt seconded it and Senator Hoar insisted that Lynch was the best man for the post. Lynch mas unanimously selected.

Accordingly, a committee of which Professor Wright was a member was appointed with Ex-Governor Pinchback of Louisiana as Chairman, to wait on Mr. Lynch and insist upon his acceptance. The committee urged him, but he didn't decide until the day the Convention was to be organized. That morning after Professor Wright's Committee pressed him again, Mr. Lynch conferred with Major William McKinley and Hon. Mark A. Hanna and raised some questions which they brushed aside. His candidacy was announced and Theodore Roosevelt and George William Curtis spoke in support of it. Professor Wright was among those who voted for his election, heard him make a brief speech of acceptance, and sat under him as presiding officer of the Convention for the greater part of two days.

When the time came to select some one to second the nomination of one of the candidates for the presidency, Professor Wright as a brilliant young newspaper man from Georgia was chosen. The fellows, he said, among whom was Senator Henry W. Blair of New Hampshire, famous author of the widely known educational bill — got around him and helped him prepare his nomination speech; but his nominee failed to obtain the party's nomination.

Following the Convention; with his activities in the State Central Committee, with a newspaper at his disposal, and his finger tips on the pulse of the Large Negro population of his section, he received the nomination for Congress from his district. A great gesture, that was, but of course he was not elected to the office.

In 1885, though, he received an appointment and served for a while as special agent for the Land Department in the U. S. Interior Department. In this position, his work consisted of investigation of timber in the state of Alabama from Birmingham northward to the border line. There had been many depredations and much stealing of timber in that section. In fact, there had been clandestine saw mills in the woods; and so much timber had been shipped out that Professor Wright's predecessor had been paid, it was said, ten thousand dollars a year to keep his mouth shut. When all of this came to light, the government arrested the latter and sent him to the penitentiary.

Under these circumstances, when the young Negro officer disembarked at Gadsen, Alabama, he was afraid to let the people know he was a government officer. He went to the home of an old white gentleman and gave him the sign of the Master Mason. The old gentleman recognized it! took Professor Wright in and gave him dinner. He then hired the old gentleman to take him into Cherokee County, presumably to look up his brother. As they passed the home of the Justice of Peace, the latter asked, "Where are you taking that Nigger?"

"Taking him up in Cherokee to see his brother," the old man replied.

"Been no Niggers up in this section for twenty-five years," answered the Justice.

Nevertheless, they continued their journey into the quiet depths of the big woods of Cherokee County. They met no one. They heard nothing but the chirp of birds and the sigh of the wind in the tall pine trees. After a while, Professor Wright persuaded the old gentleman to take him further into the woods by way of some of the numbered posts of which the old gentleman began to tell him. At length, they came to a post and then a double log house, with a cow lot, a pig pen, a chicken house, and a little garden which stretched out on the back of the upper side. They asked of a woman who sat on the "entry" patching an old pair of jeans trousers.

"Madame, can you tell us where John Wright lives up in here?" she stopped her sewing and looked out at them as though she was afraid.

"He's about my color; and small of stature," explained Professor Wright.

She shook her head. "Ain't up in here."

They continued their journey until they came to another post. Professor Wright asked as many questions of the old man as he dared and got the number of that post. They started on in supposed search of his brother; but the tell tale shadows of their horses and themselves and the ever sinking sun like a far off blaze reminded them of the vanishing day. Finally, with both eyes and ears full of the timber depredations and the posts, Professor Wright agreed with the old gentleman that perhaps his brother had long since left those parts and gone elsewhere. They fed their horses the six "years (ears) o'corn apiece which they brought along. They ate the cold biscuits and fried chicken from the old gentleman's saddle bags and turned back towards home.

Since the Justice of the Peace had said there were no Negroes around Gadsden, Professor Wright was somewhat apprehensive about a place to spend the night. The old gentleman was also thinking about the matter since they had failed to locate the presumptive brother. Their minds worked together on it; and the old gentleman's wife put him up for the night. He hadn't gotten all the information available, therefore, he had to in some way justify his position for making a longer stay.

The next morning, he awoke with this thought in mind. He decided to ingratiate himself first into the protracted good graces of the old lady. He had noticed the wood pile just beyond the front yard and the axe lying under the side of the house. He dressed, shouldered the axe and went out to the wood pile. It had been a long time since he had cut any wood. However, he hadn't forgotten the stroke. He started in; cut a big log into five lengths and split up some of the lengths. He split several big knots of fat kindling. "Whew!" He decided to get a cold drink of water from the well. Afterwards, he filled up the trough with water for the horses and cattle. By the time he was called in to breakfast, he felt like a man who had done a hard days work. In the estimation of the the two old people, he was just "plum alright." They didn't care how long he staid.

When Sunday came, he went to the old man's church — a hard shell Baptist Church — and got himself a seat on the back row. He recognized the Judge, a hard Shell, footwashing Baptist; and the Judge in turn paid him his compliments as a good nigger. By means of such make believe, he made many excursions into the woods, investigated a number of posts and obtained sufficient data to make a full report to the Interior Department.

With the completion of this special assignment for the Interior Department, he returned to his principalship in Augusta and his political activities in the State of Georgia. Since his party was out of power nationally, he welcomed the time when he was elected again as a delegate to a National Republican Convention for a third time.

This convention also met in Chicago. It opened on a hot day in June. The tempo of the weather and that of the balloting for the six nominees in the race were in keen competition. Finally, he cast his vote for Benjamin Harrison who was nominated. Knowing that his party leaders were determined to win the election, he and the other delegates on their return home began to organize clubs, work up mass meetings, 'caroll' the voters with money until his candidate was overwhelmingly elected.

After his party came into power, he was appointed to important government positions, some of which he accepted and served as long as his School Board would permit, and others he had to decline. He was appointed as Deputy U. S. Revenue Agent. Following this declination, his friend General James Longstreet who fought at Gettysburg on the confederate side and had turned Republican, recommended him to the President of the United States for appointment as U. S. Deputy Marshall for the southern district of Georgia.

He accepted the post and entered upon his duties which were similar to those of a sheriff. But inasmuch as he had been recently elected to the presidency of the Georgia State Industrial College, he had to give up his position as U. S. Deputy Marshall. Nevertheless, through his newspaper—"The Weekly Sentinel"—he attempted to appease the farmers and the unemployed. He warned the Negro people against such labor disturbances as were perpetrated at the time in the vinicity of Pittsburgh, Pennsylvania.

For all of his good offices, he was elected for the fourth time as a delegate to a National Republican Convention which met this time in Minneapolis, Minnesota. He managed to attend this Convention and there again met Frederick Douglass. As a young man, he sought Mr. Douglass' counsel and advice on the political future for the Negro. Frederick Douglass revealed to him his fear that the day of the Negro in politics was rapidly coming to a conclusion; that after 1892 Negroes would hold few political offices. For Mr. Douglass and his opinion he had great regard; but as a younger man he told Mr. Douglass if his party lost in the coming election, he would double his efforts for the election of his friend William McKinley in '96.

With that sort of reasoning and determination, on his return from the convention, he was interviewed by a representative of "The Weekly Sentinel." The interviewer's article headed the "The President's Trip" with a sub-heading "R. R. Wright Returns from The National Convention And Is Interviewed By A Sentinel Representative" was as follows:

"Professor R. R. Wright — President of the Georgia State Industrial College and Delegate-at-Large to the recent National Republican Convention held at Minneapolis, reached Augusta last Saturday night. With a keen scent for news, a Sentinel man hunted him down and proceeded to quiz him for the benefit of the people." "Well Mr. Wright, the people of Georgia are anxious to have you give an account of your stewardship. They want to know what you did; why you supported Harrison, etc. President Wright, continued the reporter, "was looking his best and was as happy as a big sunflower. It is not necessary to tell the people of Georgia that he is one of the most brilliant conversationalists and readiest talkers and thinkers in the State. His suavity and affability are simply charming. When he talks attention watches his lips and conviction closes his periods. He replied, "In the first place, I was a member of the committee on resolutions and put in a few planks in the platform as I desired. I favored the nomination of Mr. Harrison because I felt his high administration entitled him to renomination, and in addition to the worthy and acceptable manner in which he had conducted the affairs of the country for the past four years, there was a universal endorsement of his administration by Republican State Conventions throughout the country. That of itself entitled him to renomination and I think foreshadows his election."

"Did you ever at any time favor Mr. Blaine?" queried The Sentinel reporter.

"No sir, I never was a Blaine man."

"How about '96?"

"In '96 I would like to see Major McKinley or Senator Sherman somewhere in the lead. Before leaving for the Convention, I received letters from both of them. They both supported Mr. Harrison. Personally, I am very much inclined to support Governor McKinley. I have known him for some years, and know him to be an outspoken unflagging friend of the colored man. His support of Harrison was hearty and unwavering."

"How about you, and General Clarkson who has always been your friend?"

"I regretted very much to have been in opposition to my friend, the general, and I told him so. I regard Mr. Clarkson as one of the most substantial friends the Negro has ever had in politics. It was pleasing to notice that Mr. Clarkson seconded the motion of Major McKinley to nominate President Harrison by acclamation. This will show that General Clarkson will be in the forefront for Harrison's election."

"How were you generally treated?"

"I was accorded every courtesy I could have desired and more than I could have reasonably expected, both by the delegation and the leader of the Harrison movement." The Weekly Sentinel's representative concluded his story with the assertion that President Wright was the ablest colored man in the South.

Despite his and "The Weekly Sentinel's" able defense of his party's candidate, the latter was defeated. During the ensuing four years, unsatisfactory conditions in all walks of the country's life finally developed into a panic. President Wright who was now President of the Georgia State Industrial College, and his party leaders, therefore, were jubilant in their preparations for the next National Convention which met in St. Louis. It was less spectacular than former ones, yet the campaign which followed, he thought, was one of the most momentous, except that of 1860, in the history of our country.

He in his endeavor to use every opportunity to elect McKinley President named the two football teams of the Georgia State Industrial College, McKinley and Bryan. He arranged a big football game between these two teams, for election day — November third. He had them meet on the gridiron and play a hard, close game which resulted in the score of 8-0 in favor of McKinley. His friend — William McKinley — whom he had met the first time he attended a National Republican Convention was elected President. Shortly after his election, he said to President Wright he intended to give colored people more offices than General Grant had given them, and more than they would ever receive again during the life of the Republican Party.

As a reward for his services to the Republican Party, President Wright was next appointed as Postmaster of College Station, Georgia, an office which his daughter Julia in reality filled. Under his next appointment as supervisor of the census in Georgia, half of the enumerators were to be Negroes. This appointment created such a furore among cowardly Negroes, as well as whites, he said, he gave it up. He received all sorts of warnings in the mail. Even such men as Judson Lyons and Henry A.

SECURITY CONFERENCE, San Francisco, Calif., May. 1945 Major R. R. Wright with Haitian Delegate. (Dr. Whittier H. Wright, former Army surgeon standing at extreme right directly behind Major Wright.)

Rucker asked him not to jeopardize their lives by continuing in the position.

He was almost immediately appointed to another position as Minister Plenipotentiary to Liberia. At first he thought with his son — R. R. Wright Jr. — who was then attending Chicago University, as his secretary, he might accept the appointment. But it soon became evident to him that his young family of Afro-Americans here needed him quite as badly as did the natives and the Americo-Liberians there. Therefore, he declined it.

His declination was a great disappointment to President McKinley, but the President assured him of an early appointment to something else. Shortly after-wards, he received a communication offering him the position of Paymaster in the U. S. Voluntary Service with the rank of Major. Again he declined. This time he stated as the bases for his declination: "In the first place, Mr. President, I'm President of a college. Secondly, I'm not a soldier." President McKinley replied, "Wright, the government has taught the colored people how to pray. It has given them chaplains. I want to teach the country that the colored man can pay as well as pray." At the conclusion of the interview, he promised President McKinley he would put the offer up to the chairman of his college board of Commissioners.

By arrangements, he met Commissioner Meldrim alone. After a few complimentary remarks, he said, "Mr. Chairman, President McKinley wishes me to accept the position of Paymaster with the rank of Major. Shall I accept it?"

Commissioner Meldrim asked him several questions and then said, "Well, I guess you had better accept."

"What about my school pay, Mr. Chairman?"

"You will get your pay just the same."

He accepted the position with the realization that such a rank in the United States Army would do him honor and give him influence and power. He was also conversant with certain situations in the Spanish American War which would make such a position difficult for him to handle. However, with the confidence and backing of the President of the United States, he knew he could succeed. He accepted the appointment and when he learned that John R. Lynch of Mississippi had been made a similar offer, he urged him to accept. Subsequent to Major Wright's acceptance, he and Major Lynch on several occasions posed together for their photographs.

He entered upon his new duties as Major as soon as he could make arrangements with his school Commissioners to carry on his college work. In the meantime, he received many callers, and a raft of letters of congratulation among which was the following:

Augusta, Georgia
August 26, 1898

Dear Major:

Your friends in Augusta were delighted to learn of your recent appointment in the high position in the United States Volunteers, which you now hold. In testimony of this appreciation, they cordially unite in asking you to visit them on Monday, the 29th inst, so that they might have the honor of entertaining you at a public reception to be tendered you on the evening of that day. Earnestly hoping that your duties will allow you to comply with this request, we beg to remain,

Yours Respectfully,
H. M. Porter
C. T. Walker, D.D.
W. H. Clark
A. N. Gordon, M.D.
N. A. Nixon, Treas.
Silas X. Floyd, Sec.
Committee

Not long after he assumed his duties as Paymaster, he received orders to go to St. Simonds Island in Georgia to pay off a South Carolina regiment. The amount to be paid out, about $100,000, Major Wright had shipped to Brunswick, Georgia. In the meantime, the regiment which had made up its mind not to receive money from a Negro officer took up the matter with President McKinley. Major Wright threatened with being lynched, hid in the loft next door to the college. When nothing happened, he arranged with a Negro hack driver to come to College Station at three o'clock in the morning and take him to the train. The driver disappointed him. Therefore, he thought it best to wait until three o'clock the next morning.

Since he didn't arrive at the camp at the time designated, a report came out in the Brunswick newspaper tha he had absconded with the money and the soldiers had ridden him out of the camp on a barrel. Major played a trick on them. He and his aide started out for the camp. When they embarked on the boat to go out to the Island to pay off, some of the men decided to kill Major Wright. Knowing their feeling, he had established himself on the lower deck. Despite that, one man brandished a revolver and sang, "all niggers look alike to me." As soon as they disembarked at the camp, a guard marched Major Wright and his aide up to the General. Major saluted the flag and informed the General he didn't intend to pay off. At that moment, a courier rushed in with a telegram from President McKinley. The General read it, turned to Major Wright and asked, "Major what is the trouble?"

"General, as an officer of the United States Army, I have not been accorded the treatment which my office demands. Please give me an escort out of your camp." Captain Lapousky from Galveston, Texas spoke up and offered the General his tent for Major Wright's use. Major Wright accepted the courtesy, took over the tent and won the respect and friendship of the officers and soldiers to the extent he had his picture taken with them. The old General proclaimed him the best paymaster in the U. S. Army; and the soldiers saluted him so much his hand became tired returning their salute. On a similar trip to Huntsville, Alabama when part of a regiment fired on the 10th Calvary, he succeeded in quieting the soldiers and quelling the disturbance.

Sometimes he was compelled to use great strategy to hold his own as Major and Paymaster. Once on his return from Atlanta to Industrial College Station at Thunderbolt, a mob awaited his arrival. The last street car ran into Thunderbolt from Savannah at one o'clock in the morning. The mob rushed upon that car as if to drag Major Wright off of it, but Major Wright was not on it. Some of the angry disappointed crowd began to leave; but others of them waited until two o'clock before they straggled off. Just after the last one had disappeared, Major Wright came driving up leisurely in a buggy.

The next day he called up Mr. Bryan, a Major in the Army who lived at Thunderbolt, and invited him out to Georgia State College. Major Bryan readily accepted the invitation and came out. It was not long before he and Major Wright were such staunch friends, all of Thunderbolt warmed up to Georgia State College and its president.

He was also successful in having the President of the United States in the person of William McKinley visit the Georgia State Industrial College. On the memorable day of that visit, he like a statesman and a soldier introduced President McKinley as the President who had given more good jobs to the Negro people than any other president had done before, or would do in a long time. In turn, President McKinley said to the faculty and the student body, "It gives me peculiar pleasure to meet you, and to meet you in this institution of learning presided over by one whom I have known for more than twenty years and whom I have come to admire and respect as, one of the splendid leaders of his race. I congratulate you and your people on the acquisition of property and the support of the government. I congratulate you on learning. Keep on, is the word I would leave with you. Keep on in your effort upward. Another thing, do not forget the home. I leave with you this word, Keep on, and you will solve your own problems." President Wright's face beamed with joy as he extolled this speech and President McKinley.

His school paper — "The College Journal" carried a glowing account of the visit of the President of the United States to the college. In addition, to this and all the other school news 'Fit to print' this issue carried his usual article, on business. This time it was "What to Know in Business." Other times it was, "A College Education for Business," "Negroes Savings," "Negroes' Investments in Insurance and Savings Banks." In 1904 his business article declared, what we need are good farmers, good school teachers, good mechanics and good business men.

Another subject on which Professor or now Major Wright usually wrote was health. For example, —

In 1890, "Life's Secrets" appeared in "The College Journal." They were:

"Don't worry

Don't hurry

Too swift arrives
As tardy as too slow

Simplify, simplify, simplify

Don't overeat

Don't starve

Let your moderation
Be shown to all men

Court the fresh air, day and night

Don't carry the whole world on your shoulder

Trust the Eternal."

He was inclined to poke fun at his own verse making. He was such a lover of good poetry, when Paul Lawrence Dunbar's "The Haunted Oak" came out in the "Century Magazine" he appreciated it so much he had it copied in his school Journal. He also published reviews of leading articles of the day.

In 1908 just before the conflict between his educational work and political activities began to assert itself, he wrote the Commissioner of Pensions in Washington, D. C. in quest of a pension. He told him, as additional Paymaster while paying off in Huntsville, Alabama and in Jacksonville, Florida, he was forced to stand on the damp ground for quite a while in the discharge of his duty. In so doing, he contracted a cold which had affected his heart. Therefore, he had been under the care of physicians "off and on" nearly ever since. At the same time he was in correspondence with an influential friend in New York City to whom he wrote that he had been under the care of eminent physicians for neurotic trouble for sometime and was not relieved. He would like to retire, he explained, but was unable because of a large family including four single daughters. He likewise took up the matter of his pension with Dr. C. C. Barrow, Chancellor of the University of Georgia of which his college was a branch; and finally received his pension.

In 1913, he secured the passage of an act by the United States Senate for the appropriation of $250,000 for the promotion of a Semi-Centennial Emancipation Exhibition. During the first World War, he was appointed by Governor Dorsey of Georgia through the good offices of President Wilson to a position first, as Chairman of the Colored Associated Council of Food Production and Conservation in Georgia. A little later, he was appointed by Governor Dorsey as Negro Historian of enlisted colored troops in France. In this latter position, he went to England, France and Belgium to collect Historical data for the archives of Georgia and for a book on the Negro in the Great War.

After he moved to Philadelphia, his absorption in business and his absence from Georgia failed to blot out his deep interest in Politics and Journalism. In fact, he was at one time a candidate for the Philadelphia City Council. Likewise, he was so ambitious for his former students and Georgia political co-workers, in November, nineteen hundred twenty-four, he sent the "Savannah Journal," Savannah, Georgia, the following letter:

Mr. Editor:

I have just read with a great deal of interest mingled with pleasure and amusement the distribution of the spoils of victory which may fall to the colored brethren after the magnificent victory which we have helped President Calvin Coolidge and H. M. Dawes to win. The list of those who will get the jobs given out by G. O. P. is certainly portentous.

I imagine that the triumvirate of the political group consists of my good friends, Mr. Clarence Mathews, Mr. Emmet Scott and Hon. Roscoe Simmons. All of these are my most interesting friends. If the list is inspired by this triumvirate this would be important, but it is rather amusing to me to see in selecting "the black cabinet" etc., the Black Triumvirate has so deftly shelved the Hon. Henry Lincoln Johnson and The Hon. Perry W. Howard together with the committee women — Mrs. George S. Williams and Mrs. E. P. Booze. Having been so signally honored by their States, it is suggested that they will be satisfied with their present honors and leave the appointive positions to the workers in the ranks. Now this is truly amusing. The aforesaid Hon. Henry Lincoln Johnson and Hon. Perry W. Howard and Mrs. George S. Williams and Mrs. E. P. Booze, having toiled incessantly to obtain a name and a place for the Republican Party.

Sincerely yours,
R. R. Wright

Major Wright remained Henry Lincoln Johnson's bosom friend despite the fact "Linc," as Johnson was called tied up with the light skin Negro block and thus became his political enemy.

He also remained faithful through the years to the Republican Party despite his understanding of its shortcomings. In turn, the Party in its acknowledgement of his loyalty and his influence in his community, for many years sent him a ticket to each of its National Conventions.

In 1900, 1908 and 1916, he was elected to the National Republican Convention but failed to attend. He said, "I lost all interest in politics during the last few years. Our men became so self-centered and so bent upon office seeking, I felt they had lost all interest in the real welfare of the people.

"You will recall," continued Major Wright, "in 1892 the Republicans did lose out and Cleveland was elected President, but I am glad to say, in 1896 my friend William McKinley was elected President. Mr. McKinley said to me, he intended to give colored people more offices than they would ever receive again during the life of the Republican Party. This turned out to be a fact," emphasized Major Wright, "I believe a larger number of Republicans received offices under McKinley than perhaps under any other Republican during the entire history of the Republican Party. Since the days of McKinley, the Republican office-holders have been few and far between. Then, we had Register of the Treasury, Recorder of Deeds, Collector of Internal Revenue of Georgia, Collector of Customs in Georgia, Collector of Revenue in New York, Postmaster in a number of States and numerous offices all over the country. Most of these are now but memories. Colored men do not aspire to these places. They have lost practically all hope of ever again occupying many of the places which they occupied during the days of McKinley."

Major Wright crossed his legs and yawned a conclusion. His interviewer asked what he thought of the Negro Politicians of today. He continued, "As I look back to that period and compare it with the period of today and the men of today as representative of our race in politics, I cannot help wincing. It reminds me of the story of an old colored man who went fishing. Perhaps I might introduce this fish story right here. The story is this: A colored man and a white man went fishing. The colored man caught a very large, fine trout. In fact, it was an unusually large trout. The white man was very unsuccessful and got only a small croaker. After fishing for quite a while, they decided to retire to a place and have a fish dinner. They had brought along some whiskey. The white man calculated the 'colored' man was much fonder of whiskey than he should have been; and decided to make the 'colored' man drunk and invite some friends to help him take care of the fine trout.

He succeeded. They cooked the trout and the croaker. After a short while, the whiskey in the 'colored' man took effect and he went to sleep. The white man and his friend ate the trout, and rubbed the colored man's mouth with some of the grease from the fish. Then they cut the croaker in two and left it lying there. After a while, the 'colored' man awoke at the instance of prodding. The white man said, "You have eaten up all the fish while I was gone." The 'colored' man rubbed his eyes and then his mouth and then his stomach and said, "Boss, my mouth seems to have eaten that fish but my stomach doesn't feel it has." The white man said, "Of course, you ate the fish." He rubbed his mouth and his stomach again and said, "How this fish of mine am swunk."

If I were to apply this, laughed Major Wright, to the situation today, I would say, how the political capacity of the colored man in the days of B. K. Bruce, John R. Lynch and others compared with that of the men of today has "swunk." How these great Negro politicians have "swunk."

"It is a sad story to see how we have lost out, it seems to me, not only in positions, but in the ability of the men of our day to cope with the white men of today," concluded Major Wright.

CHAPTER VI

WRITER AND LECTURER

President Wright recalling his experience in Chicago when the electric lights were turned on for the first time, said that was the beginning of a period of inventions which changed our mode of living existent for three hundred years. Not only was arc lighting introduced, but the telephone as a business and as a piece of machinery of communication, the hot air furnace, the cook stove, the sewing machine and many other business and domestic conveniences were brought into existence.

This was the period, as President Wright saw it, when nearly every scientifically minded Negro, appeared to be trying to invent something. Therefore, he again called upon the Honorable Blanche Kelso Bruce — Register of the U. S. Treasury for his assistance in securing data on Negro inventors. Mr. Bruce again took up the matter with Mr. Henry E. Baker — Assistant Examiner in the U. S. Patent Office. The latter showed Professor Wright such data as was recorded in that office.

With these facts in hand, and inspired by what he saw at the New Orleans Exposition, President Wright wrote an article for the A. M. E. Church Review on "The Negro As An Inventor." This dissertation written April 1886 was in the form of a crisp answer to charges against the Negroe's inventive ability made by such writers as the Cables, the Dudleys, the Gilliams, the Gradys and the Ralls.

In his introduction, he stated two incontrovertible facts. The first was that a few years prior to his writing, any serious discussion of the Negro's inventive genius would have been considered perhaps a wild and profitless speculation. The second was that few persons had up to that time inquired into the fitness of the Negro for any special intellectual feat. The majority of the public, he contended, was so tickled by Negro minstrels and "some peculiar Negro musical geniuses" that they had failed to consider these as a possible basis for Negro achievement in art, science, literature and politics.

In the discussion of the Negro question by such writers as those mentioned above, he claimed they have approached it from the angle of "How Much Should Be Given" the Negro rather than "How Much The Negro Has Won." This latter angle he stressed in order to substantiate two of his conclusions. One of them was there is no apriori reason why the world should not find in the Negro, under favorable circumstances, rich mental vigor and inventive genius, despite his nine generations of enforced ignorance and unintelligent toil. The other one was that the Negro has already made sufficient achievement in mechanical arts to make it morally certain he possesses inventive genius in large degree.

As an adverse opinion to these conclusions, he first discussed a pamphlet "The Industrial, Political and Moral Aspects of the Negro Race in the South" written by a Mr. Ralls in 1877. The latter claimed that the Negro exhibits little or no originality in his mental organization. That the Negro's faculty for invention and contrivance, where a principle is to be studied and applied, is rarely drawn upon or improved, and whatever proficiency he may attain in any branch of art or science is due rather to the process of memory and his skill at imitation than to any proper understanding of the rules of art or principles of science. "We have never," continued Mr. Ralls, "heard of a colored person, even at the North, in contact with the ingenuous Yankee, applying for a patent right to any implement or other useful article of his own invention. This defect in the mental constitution of the Negro is not confined to mechanical operations merely, but operate against him in every field of enterprise that he may enter upon."

When Mr. Ralls' statement was discussed anew by the Southern press in 1883 and indorsed as true, President Wright was riled and stirred to the point of making research to disprove it. In his first effort of refutation, he wrote letters to the Negro educators, ministers and leaders of the country whose replies convinced him of what he called their discouraging ignorance and indifference to the subject. In an epoch of study to harness and make air, water and electricity serve the needs of mankind, he asked if a nation of six million native American citizens could not assist in that useful and important task.

In his attempt to discuss the question thoroughly and stimulate inquiry, he reached back into the Negro's previous condition of lack of opportunity and forward to his present condition of enforced inferiority and incapability view point. Because of the psychological effect of the latter on the Negro, he discussed his intellectual constitution and the mystery of invention.

It still remains to be proved, he held, that there is anything in the Negro's intellectual constitution different from that of the Greeks to whom Aristotle taught that every kind of menial labor and mechanical work was to be avoided. Therefore, instead of a Watt, a Stephenson or an Edison, Greece gave to the world a Homer, a Socrates, an Aristotle. It still remains to be demonstrated, he further said, that the Negro's inventive ability up to 1860 was different from that of his white Southern brother who up to that time had not produced a single great native inventor. It still remains to be made clear he concluded, that the Egyptian Pyramids were not made by black people with woolly hair.

For a prevalence of inventions among any race, he mentioned three prerequisites. The diffusion of general information among the laboring classes; a prevailing spirit of universal freedom; and time. According to his deductions the history of the great inventors proves that the educated laborer advances furthest in the line of inventions. Then he asked should not every useful invention made by American Negroes so recently deprived of both freedom and education, be considered an evidence of their inventive genius?

To further substantiate his contention, he gave citations from Professor J. F. Blumenbach — well-known scientist and eminent ethnologist. After speaking of the great musical talent of Negroes, Professor Blumenbach gives as examples of their capacity for mathematics and physical science, Haumbal, the Colonel of Artillery, and M. Lislet, of the Isle of France, who on account of his superior meteorological observations, and trigonometrical measurements was appointed its correspondent by the Paris Academy of Science. After mentioning Anthony Amo, who was created Doctor of Philosophy of the University of Wittenberg, Germany, the learned scientist says: "Finally, I am of the opinion that, after all the numerous instances I have brought together of the Negroes of capacity, it would not be difficult to mention entire well-known provinces of Europe out of which you would not expect to obtain off-hand such good authors, poets, philosophers, and correspondents of the Paris Academy. On the other hand, there is no other so-called savage nation known under the sun which has so much distinguished itself by such examples of perfectibility and original capacity for scientific culture and thereby attached itself so closely to the most civilized nation of the earth as the Negroes."

Following these arguments and citations, President Wright jotted down what he called a few evidences of the Negro's inventive genius, seen by him at the New Orleans Exposition and in the Patent Office Record at Washington, D. C.

There were, he argued, over one hundred oil paintings and crayon drawings; several pieces of statuary among which was Edmonia Lewis' "Hiawatha." There were dental tools, wagons, carriages, plows, black smiths' anvils, a pulpit made of two hundred pieces of wood; cigars of forty manufacturers of cigars; handicraft, and over fifty patents taken out by and in the name of Negroes during that past ten years, in addition to others taken out jointly with white inventors. There was a corn-stalk harvester, a Shield for Infantry and Artillerymen, fire extinguisher, Cotton Cultivator, Joiners Clamp, Smoke Stack for locomotives, cook stove, Printing Press, window ventilator for Railroad Cars, etc.

In conclusion, President Wright asserted that, therefore, the Negro's genius for invention did not die with the early Negro inventor — Benjamin Banneker — inventor of the first clock all the parts of which were made in this country.

So interested was President Wright in this subject of Negro inventors, ten years later he called upon the Honorable Hoke Smith of Georgia — Secretary of the U. S. Interior — for further data on it. In response to his request Secretary Smith sent for Mr. Henry E. Baker. As the latter entered the office, Secretary Smith asked, "Have you heard of R. R. Wright? He's from Georgia — President of our State College." Then he advised Mr. Baker to get together all the available material on Negro inventors and whip it into shape for publication. President Wright, he said, needs it for the Georgia State College. The result of that inquiry was a twelve page pamphlet "The Colored Inventor" by Henry E. Baker.

President Wright's pursuit of facts relative to the Negro inventor, in no way closed his eyes to the needs of the Negro farmers all about him. During this period he also appeared in Washington, D. C. to testify before a Commission investigating labor conditions in the South, relative to the farmers. As a result of his special preparation for this occasion, he wrote an article on "The Negro Farmer" which appeared in an 1888 issue of the Congressional Record and also in a United States Labor Department report.

In the meantime, he began his research in the field of Negro history and went North to speak on special occasions for Atlanta University. On his first trip North, he went to Worcester, Massachusetts with President Ware and appeared on the program with John B. Gough, General Samuel Chapman Armstrong and General O. O. Howard. Young and full of zeal he was introduced as The Black Boy of Atlanta, who would speak on the subject — "The Needs of The Colored People." He surprised everybody in the audience. Some of those present who had never heard a Negro speak before, wanted to know if there were many other Negroes well educated and able to speak like him.

On his trip to Oberlin College, similar questions aroused President Ware's thinking on the wisdom of having him speak at a subsequent meeting in Boston. Therefore, at that meeting held in the celebrated Trinity Church of Boston, he sat on the platform as an exhibit of the poor, ignorant Negro while President Eliot of Harvard University spoke for Atlanta University.

Ready and eager to loose his pent up emotions in defense of his people, he was of course disappointed at not being able to speak. Nevertheless, he was neither dismayed nor discouraged. His keenness in sizing up the situation, and his unshaken confidence in President Ware tided him over until such a time when he could speak again from his own experience as well as from a background of research which he was making between times.

The opportunity soon came for him to speak for the

Pres. Harry S. Truman signing the National Freedom Day Bill. Witnessing are: Mrs. Harriet Wright Lemon, J. E. Mitchell, Dr. Mary McCleod Bethune, Mr. Emanuel C. Wright, Dr. W. H. Jernagin, Elder Solomon Lightfoot Michaux

annual meeting of the American Missionary Association, held in Plymouth Church, Worcester, Massachusetts, November first, second and third, 1881. As a listener, he attended all of the first day's sessions beginning with the prayer meeting at 8:30 on Tuesday morning. Wednesday morning — the date he was scheduled to speak on "The Strength, the Weakness and the Needs of the Colored People" — he rose early, dressed, stationed himself in front of the chest of drawers in his room and proclaimed quietly in preparation for his address.

He attended the 8:30 Prayer meeting; and was present when the Association was called to order and the minutes of the previous day were read. As the first speaker, preceding President E. H. Fairchild of Berea College whose subject was "God's Designs for and Through the Negro Race," Secretary Streiby of the American Missionary Association on the "Duty of America in the Conversion of the World and especially in the Conversion of Africa," President E. A. Ware, General O. O. Howard and General Samuel Chapman Armstrong, he pleaded as one who had risen from the ranks of a poor ignorant race.

He was also touched that day by reports from the various A. M. A. colleges on their Revivals and Religious Interests. He laughed but not then, he said, as he recalled the report of his own college — Atlanta University. "With us, a very gracious revival prevailed for the last five months of the school year; and further, "It is refreshing to one's soul to get into a live prayer meeting like ours." One who is spending his first year at the South writes, "When I listen in the prayer meetings to remarks and prayers, especially the latter, I cannot help wishing that the churches of the North could be present to be edified."

President Wright not only responded to subsequent invitations of the A. M. A. to speak at its annual meeting, but complied with requests of organizations in other parts of the country for a speaker.

For example, at the close of the National Republican Convention in Minneapolis, Minnesota, he and former Congressman — John M. Langston — father of Professor Langston of St. Louis and Mr. Tobe Langston, business man of Chicago, addressed the Afro-American League of that city. They not only referred to the corner stone laying of the first building of Atlanta University, but President Wright dwelt upon what had been accomplished by Negroes in the past thirty years.

None of them he declared, were very rich or very learned, but many had gone beyond the rudiments; and seventy-three of them in the State of Georgia had received the degree of Bachelor of Arts. Nobody, he contended, however skeptical, could predict the limit of the Negro's intellectual ability. The Negro according to President Wright was as eager for education as he was at the close of the War. To substantiate his claim, he cited the fact that seventy-three out of every hundred colored children in Georgia could read and write. They were also learning to be more reliable and business like; more intelligent producers and developers of the resources at hand; and more sensitive to discourtesies and insults. The fact that they were not being over-educated, he buttressed by the citation of the seventy-three Negroes with college degrees as proof that in thirty years the so-called Negro colleges and universities of Georgia were not making Latin and Greek scholars out of all their students at a rapid rate.

One of his observations made on that trip was that while schools in the Northwest were all open to Negroes, there were few of them in the higher branches of high school and college. To him, they appeared to be indifferent to their advantages while Negroes in the South were more progressive and likelier to advance the best interest of the race.

The following Sunday morning in company with Frederick Douglass, President Wright spoke to quite a large audience at Bethesda Baptist Church — the largest church in Minneapolis and one of the largest in the Northwest. That night he was the main speaker for the largest white Congregational church in Minneapolis, whose pastor — Dr. Wells — was regarded as a true friend of the Negro race.

In addition to his lectures which were largely based upon as much of nine years of research as he could squeeze in between his other responsibilities, he continued to record the results of his research and thinking.

His next study he developed into a fifty page monograph. It was published under the title of "A Brief Historical Sketch of Negro Education in Georgia." In it he traced the educational history of the Negro people of Georgia from 1863 to 1893. At the beginning of the former year, he declared not even one-tenth of one per cent of the Negroes of Georgia had ever looked inside of a book or saved a dollar. Their ignorance was equaled only by their poverty and their friendliness.

Nevertheless, he further contended, they were sent forth to develop character, to get education and money and thus prove themselves worthy of the freedom which was thrust upon them. They were to maintain themselves as free men and citizens in the midst of their old masters who had enjoyed the fruits of their labor and centuries of civilization. Therefore, according to President Wright, to understand the difficulties which Negroes had overcome in Georgia in thirty years — and to estimate their progress one must keep in mind their condition when emancipated.

As an aid in this direction, the author discussed the first colored schools in Georgia. These schools had their beginning in a conference of white and Negro men held in an old Southern mansion one night about Christmas time, 1864.

This, the first joint conference of white men and free Negro men in Georgia, was attended by Secretary of War Edwin M. Stanton, General William T. Sherman and several of his generals and aides and eight or ten of the leading Negro ministers of Savannah. Among the Negro ministers in attendance were Reverends Garrison Frasier, Alexander Harris, Charles Bradwell, John Cox and William J. Campbell — all notable men. Their wisdom, tact and untrained eloquence so astonished Secretary Stanton, he said they understood and could state the principles discussed as well as any member of the United States Cabinet.

That was a great night in Georgia, President Wright recalled. Other Negroes were also aware of the fact that in that same city — Savannah — almost exactly one hundred years before, laws had been enacted making it a penal offense to teach Negroes to read or write.

At this first joint conference it was agreed to open schools at once for all colored people who would apply; and to examine all who felt competent to teach. A few of the latter class who had come from South Carolina had attended the colored school there taught by an educated Negro from England. The majority, however, of those who could read and write and therefore felt competent to teach in the first schools had received instruction in the Clandestine Schools of Savannah and Augusta taught by Negroes or by poor whites who eked out a miserable existence by clandestinely teaching Negroes in the "Chip Schools."

The first of these Clandestine Schools, President Wright pointed out, was opened in Savannah about the year 1818 and taught by a Negro Frenchman from Santo Domingo named Julian Froumontaine. Out of this and similar schools came the first colored teachers after the war. However, their number thought President Wright, must have been small in as much as outside of Savannah, Augusta and Columbus not a dozen Negroes in Georgia were able to read and write.

To attenuate this dense ignorance as President Wright stated in his monograph, the American Missionary Association came in and took over the "old Bryan Slave Mart" used by the Negro teachers in Savannah, and besides opened more schools for Negroes. Among the other far reaching agencies for the education of the freedmen were the Military Educational Bureau promoted largely by General Grant and General Sherman; the Freedmen's Bureau which expended for education in the South under the supervision of General O. O. Howard, five million dollars from March 1865 to August 1871; Churches such as the Congregational, the Catholic, the Baptist, the Meth-dist, the Presbyterian and the Episcopal; and Philanthropic agencies such as the Peabody Fund, the Slater Fund, the Rockefeller Foundation and others.

Shortly after most of the above organizations began to function, and during President Wright's early years as an Atlanta University student, he cited the fact that the first public schools of Georgia were opened for a period of three summer months. At that time the total enrollment of Negro school children was 6,674 and the estimated number of Negro teachers employed was about 150. In twenty years, that enrollment had increased to 140,625 and the percentage of Negro illiteracy had been reduced to 27.

After discussing the larger city school system, the Georgia State Industrial College and the denominational and missionary schools and colleges of the State to whom Negroes of the State are largely indebted for all of their higher education, Professor Wright made reference to the Negro's moral education. Said he, "In 1862 there was scarcely a Negro Home in all Georgia. Today the Georgia Negroes taxable property of some $16,000,000 is a guarantee of thousands of comfortable homes in city and rural districts. No people in the world have made in thirty years greater advancement in moral and Christian character than the Negro people."

As a student not only of the recent past but of the future; as a dreamer as well as a man of facts, figures and action, he continued, "I cannot conclude this paper without expressing the great hope which I cherish for our race in this country. There are many and almost ancient ties that bind the Negro to the United States. There are numerous reasons why he should feel as much at home on the American soil as any man of any nation that treads our shores. The oldest American city was named for one of the most eloquent sons of Africa. Among America's earliest explorers and discovers some of the boldest, bravest, and most successful of her pioneers as early as 1529 were woolly haired Negroes. From then until now, whether as a pioneer laborer making our own State — Georgia — habitable and prosperous, or fighting the battles of the nation, the Negro has by blood and sweat identified himself with every phase and fiber of American history and life. The hopeful and thoughtful readers who peruse these pages will see that though the pathway of the race was not strewn with flowers, it has steadily led toward the light. Today thank God, the Negro stands upon higher ground where the light of liberty shines upon him steadily. Standing upon this vantage ground he has new duties, new responsibilities. In this brighter day the demand is for men of thought, men of action."

So desirous was he of arousing men to accept their new duties and responsibilities, he transformed his desire into a demand as follows:

Men of thought, be up and stirring,
Night and day;
Men of action, aid, and cheer them
As ye may

There's a fount about to stream;
There's a light about to beam;
There's a warmth about to glow;
There's a flower about to blow;
There's a midnight blackness changing
        Into gray
Men of thought and men of action,
        Clear the way,
Once the welcome light has broken,
        Who shall say
What the unimagined glories
        of the day?
What the evils that shall perish
        in its ray?
Aid the dawning, tongue and pen;
Aid it, hopes of honest men;
Aid it, paper; aid it, type
Aid it, for the hour is ripe,
And our earnest must not slacken
        In to play.
Men of thought and men of action
Lo, a cloud about to banish,
        From the day
And a brazen wrong to crumble
        Into clay!
Lo, the right's about to conquer
        Clear the way
With the right shall many more
Enter, smiling at the door;
With the giant wrong shall fail
Many others, great and small,
That for ages long have held us
        For their prey
Men of thought and men of action
        Clear the way."

President Wright's prolific pen bore evidence of the fact that he was up and stirring night and day. The following year when associates of the late Abraham Lincoln in the person of Mayor Seward, George William Curtis, General O. O. Howard, Murat Halsted, Frank B. Carpenter who spent six months in the White House painting the picture of the signing of the Emancipation Proclamation, Governor Rice of Massachusetts, Henry Knight who was Lincoln's body guard in his walks at midnight from the War Department to the White House, Mr. Herndon and Judge Weldon — his associates at the bar before he became President of the United States — Secretary Hugh McCulloch of the Treasury, Senators Dawes and Morgan and ExPostmaster-General James and other distinguished friends — more than 40 in all — answered "The Independents" call to write their appreciation of the Emancipator, President R. R. Wright's response on behalf of the Negro people was "A Negro's Tribute to Lincoln" as follows:

"As the American Missionary Association has selected the birthday of Abraham Lincoln as the day on which to commemorate the art of liberating four million American slaves, Major Wright thought perhaps the accompanying letter from the late George W. Curtis, on Lincoln would prove interesting. In a sense Lincoln and that Association are intimately connected in work for the American Negro. The one secured, the other has done much to preserve his liberty for him. Neither could perhaps have been of true service to the Negro without the other.

Mr. Lincoln was, in truth a great and good man, the man not only for his time, but for the colored people. It has occurred to a distinguished correspondent of mine, Senator Hoar, that Mr. Lincoln had many traits for which colored people are noted. Among the traits were a sweetness of disposition, great patience of the wrong; he had no memory for injustice; was forgiving; was ready to wait for the slow processes by which God accomplished great and permanent blessings for mankind.

Like the Negro, Mr. Lincoln was born in a hovel. He had to labor incessantly for his daily bread. His educational advantages were the poorest. He had scarcely a year's schooling. He was deprived of books. The Bible, "Pilgrim's Progress," "Life of Washington," "Robinson Crusoe," and "Aesop's Fables" were the books to which he owed most. His early narrow escapes showed that he was a providential man. With all this, Mr. Lincoln's religious sense was deep and pervading. The biography of Mr. Lincoln's struggles for bread, for clothes, for money and for "a little learning" reads much like the story of some Negro battling against adversity. Had Mr. Lincoln been a member of the Negro race it is doubtful if he would have outstripped Frederick Douglass in the race of life. May it not be stated that the two typical Americans were Abraham Lincoln and Frederick Douglass?

Mr. Lincoln was noted for his great common sense and for his political sagacity. Mr. Lincoln was a born politician and was even a perpetual wire puller. It was by his great shrewdness that he secured the adoption of the Thirteenth Amendment; kept the border states from going out of the Union, and held back the anti-slavery sentiment of the North until the time was ripe to strike the blow for his Emancipation Proclamation. There is no doubt of the fact that Mr. Lincoln had great political sagacity and an abundance of common sense. He knew what to do next and when to do it. Some people believe or effect to believe that Mr. Lincoln was not ardently earnest and sincere in the desire to free the slaves. Indeed, they seem to believe that he was indifferent to this; that his only desire was to save the Union. I cannot think so, says Major Wright. As a great statesman and "Student of the slow processes of the great mills of God," he abided God's time with the profoundest and most reverent faith. As he had expressed his belief that this nation could no longer exist half slave and half free, he undoubtedly felt that in the course of events the great Ruler in the Affairs of nations would accomplish the freedom of the American slaves.

Major Wright's tribute to Lincoln was written at a time when he was engrossed in research on the black man. He made great sacrifice to study this subject at the Library of Congress; Brown University and Harvard University Libraries; and Philadelphia and New York City Libraries. He studied Spanish records at the British Museum. He studied at a Library in Paris, and at the Bodleian Library of Oxford University.

With-al, he found time to lecture. In the Spring of that year he accepted the invitation of his alma mater — Atlanta University — to deliver its commencement address. Having accepted this invitation as the first Alumnus to be so honored, he attempted to make his speech no less outstanding than those of former commencement orators. He took as his subject, "The Negro in Our History." In his brief, he presented the claim of the Negro to recognition in the discoveries and in the development of our country. To substantiate this claim, he produced the thesis that a Negro, Estevanicao or Estenvanillo, came from Spain with Navarrez in 1527 and discovered New Mexico and the Zuni Indians.

This new historical declaration coupled with his ability as an orator was reported by the Atlanta University Press, the Sentinel and other Negro papers of the country. It provoked quite a little discussion and loaded him with correspondence, but with all the other interests that crowded his life, he found time to reply to every paper.

Because of his civic activities and his presidency of the Georgia State Industrial College — he was asked that year to have an educator come to Atlanta to speak for the Cotton Exposition. In answer to this request, his friend and classmate — Professor Crogman insisted that he himself make the speech; but he dissented. He gave the name of President Booker T. Washington instead, despite the fact that President Washington was not so well known at that time. However, the following June he did deliver the Emancipation address in Atlanta on the topic "The Value of Historical Research." To use one of his own expressions, "All of this fetched up to the same point," namely, his brochure entitled "Negro Companions of the Spanish Explorers."

This study as well as some jottings on his ancestors — the Mandingoes — was one of the major results of his research in many of the libraries of this country and abroad. It was first published in the American Anthropologist — April-June 1902 — on the recommendation of Dr. Franz Boas of Columbia University who was then a member of the Editorial Board of that journal. In it, President Wright claimed that Negroes were introduced into the New World with the first discoverers and explorers perhaps even before Columbus made his discovery.

To substantiate his contention, he cited Peter Martyr — a learned historian and an acquaintance of Columbus — who mentions "a region, not two days journey from Juarcquas' territory, in the Darien district of South America where Balboa found a race of black men, who, it was conjectured, had come from Africa and had been shipwrecked on this coast. In further support of this theory, he quoted the late Justin Winsor of Harvard University who in a letter to him expressed the possibility that at some early time the ocean currents may have swept across from the Canaries and the African Coasts, canoes with Gaunches and other African tribes from which some considerable strains of Negro blood may have mixed with the pre-Columbian people of tropical America.

After establishing the fact that hundreds of Negro slaves accompanied Spanish explorers and that some of them took part with the Spaniards in their early expeditions and discoveries on this continent, he presented the most conspicuous one of them all — Estevanico or Estevanillo. Estevanico — one of the four survivors of Navarraz's ill fated expeditions from Spain in 1527 to this country — according to President Wright's thesis, was the true discoverer of New Mexico and the Zuni Indians.

In the twenty years subsequent to this publication, its author's duties as President of a college, as organizer and President of the National Association of Presidents of A. and M. Colleges for Negroes, as President of the Georgia State Agricultural and Industrial Association, as President of the National Association of Teachers in Colored Schools etc., so absorbed him, although he collected historical data for the archives of Georgia and for a book on the Negro in the Great War, he never had time to write the book.

In his twenty-six years as a banker and business man, his outlet for literary expression was the Negro press, and the platform, except in very rare instances. As a tiny example of the exception, when he was campaigning in Florida for money to organize a Trust Company, he wrote with lead pencil in a tablet among his business notes the following verse:

"I'm here where gay
Poinsettias bloom.
Where grows the stately palm
Where sunshine drives away the
Gloom, and nature brings her balm
To those who come and linger here;
And fills their hearts with joy and cheer."

Shortly after the establishment of his Trust Company, he returned to Atlanta University for a second time as the Commencement Day orator. On this significant occasion of the Fiftieth Anniversary of the granting of college degrees to Negroes in Georgia, he not only pictured again his walk from Cuthbert into Atlanta and the old box car school, but presented his fifty year diploma. In addition, he stressed the fact that rights and privileges are not given to a man simply because he's educated. By severe judgment, severe toil, severe sacrifice, he should win the place to which his education entitles him. By diplomacy, organization, coralling his votes and his money and making jobs for himself he can make the world understand he is a "man for a' that." If he can control his economic resources, he can control his labor; and with his labor he can do something. President Wright further said he went into banking as an example of what he expects generations to come to improve upon.

As a banker, catering to every class of depositor, he often spoke in the Philadelphia churches and encouraged deposits of scarcely more than ten cents, according to the Philadelphia Tribune — owned and edited by Mr. and Mrs. Eugene Washington Rhodes. During the depression, at the first meeting of the White Rock Baptist Church in its new church home, 52nd and Arch Streets, Philadelphia, he mounted the rostrum that Sunday morning dressed in his navy blue suit with the points of a white kerchief sticking out of his pocket as of Atlanta University days. He shook hands with the minister and took his seat in an unassuming yet soldierly manner. As one of the speakers of the occasion, he quoted the Scripture lesson, "Seek ye first the kingdom of God and its Righteousness, and all other things will be added unto you."

"The latter part of this quotation," he said "is an important part of the scripture which the church must also seek to develop. "This is a new day," he continued, "the hitherto dominant civilization is cracking. Who knows but that God is holding the darker races to step into the place of those who withdraw or fail? Let us prepare then for the new opportunities and obligations. Let us take an inventory of our means for meeting this new day and be ready to use every available organization or other means to measure up to the demands."

In December of 1938 he was called back to Georgia State Industrial College to deliver one of the addresses at the dedication of their four new buildings.

CHAPTER VII

TRAVELER

Richard Robert Wright's irrepressible impulse for action found expression in getting from one place to another at an early age. When he was five years old, he was moved from a slave plantation five miles in the country, to the one horse town of Dalton. From that little town in Whitfield County, North West Georgia, slavery and the Civil War forced him to travel to Randolph County in the South West. In about two years he was on the go again. This time, with what few rags of clothing and bedding he had, on his back and the old ax under his coat. Even in the skirt of woods outside of Cuthbert where he went, he was only a sojourner, a pilgrim destined to tarry but a night.

On his next trip over the two hundred country miles stretch to Atlanta he was not so much in pursuit of life as of learning. As a college student in search of money to pay his expenses, he spent his summers in several of the backwoods sections of Georgia. One summer he went back to Whitfield County; taught school and visited his erstwhile master's family.

After he had graduated from Atlanta University and gone out as a full fledged teacher, organizer, newspaper man and politician, one of his early trips out of the State of Georgia was as a delegate to a Republican Convention in Nashville, Tennessee, in 1877. It was there that he first met William McKinley, John W. Cromwell, John R. Lynch and P. B. S. Pinchback. It was these men who more firmly fixed his attention on Politics, and helped to send him forth into the political arena, and to the four succeeding National Republican Conventions out of which came political offices and more travel. When he was stationed as paymaster with his regiment at Columbia, South Carolina, misapprehending citizens wanted to lynch him. On the contrary, Negroes of that city were so proud of him they gathered in the street to see him march. One old Negro woman in the crowd stood akimbo and said one day as he passed, "Look lack he done melted and poured in dat 'nuniform.' Look at 'im! Look how he tips!" She tipped off in imitation of him with his chest out and chin up.

Before he obtained this position, he had visited many of the larger cities of the United States, and had done research in the British Museum, the Bodleian Library of Oxford University, and in one of the libraries of Paris. On his first trip to Europe he went first class on a White Star Liner.

At the pier in New York City he got in line for his ticket. As he had been advised to tip the waiter heavily before he started, if he wanted a good trip on the vessel, he watched for this opportunity, and gave a waiter two dollars. That waiter looked after him so well and to the neglect of the other passengers, the second day out a passenger across from him expressed his disgust with English boats and their poor service. He complained and finally looked across at President Wright and addressed him, "Friend!" President Wright didn't look up. He called again, "Partner!" When President Wright raised his head, the passenger said to him, "I think you could wait on us better than these English waiters."

"Yes," answered President Wright politely, "can you pay the price? I'll charge you $100.00 a day."

That reply attracted so much attention, President Wright was invited to make a speech to the passengers on the boat. It also gained for him an invitation to the home

Major R. R. Wright receiving the annual Merit Award (1946) presented at the Merrell Dobbins Vocational School

of Edward A. Freeman of Oxford University. It afterwards served as a money raising story for Atlanta University.

One Sunday afternoon in later years, while President Wright and his Vice President, Professor D. C. Suggs, were sitting in a room at the Georgia State College talking, that former passenger on the White Star Line who had addressed him as 'partner' rang the doorbell and asked for him. The passenger greeted him humbly and confessed, "I have come all the way here to apologize to you for what I said on that White Star Liner years ago."

To continue that first trip on the White Star Liner, as President Wright disembarked at Liverpool, he mailed a card back home to Mrs. Wright. On it he wrote he was near the place where Gladstone lived; and he would go to Dublin, Ireland, thence to Scotland and back to England. Just as he was mailing the card, an Irishman came up and offered to take him and his baggage to a hotel. When they entered the hotel, the proprietor scolded the Irishman, "You get out of here and don't let me see you here again." He hustled the Irishman out. On the contrary, President Wright was welcomed and treated royally. Yet, the experience in some way deterred him from his plan to visit Ireland. Later he wished he had gone. That opportunity never came to him again.

He went to London and to the British Museum for study and research. He visited Spurgeon's church at the invitation of his son who had taken charge upon the recent death of his father. On that trip he didn't see Gladstone's home, but on a later one, he heard that Gladstone's son was going to preach at one of the churches on a specified Sunday, and Gladstone, himself would be present. He made note of it. On that morning he started out early more with the hope that he might get to see the father than to hear the son preach. He took his seat, and shortly on hearing a little rustle behind him, turned his head and recognized Gladstone himself. It was he, President Wright was sure; but the thing that astonished the latter was Gladstone's size. He was a small man. "No bigger than I," interpolated President Wright. His wife was tall though. His son — a remarkable speaker — took as his text: "The Summer is ended. The harvest is past and we are not yet saved." President Wright met Gladstone after the service, and later went to his castle.

Before he left England, he also went out to Stratford-on-Avon. In that little town on a street near Shakespeare's birthplace, a small boy ran up to him and offered to show him around. When he questioned the little fellow's ability, on account of his size and age, the boy screwed up his courage and asked "Did you ever hear that Shakespeare stole a deer?" He admired the pluck and business acumen of the lad, but went alone into the old schoolhouse and searched for a place to write his name among the millions perhaps of those already written in every tongue and from every clime.

He continued his journey to Rome and to the prison where Paul was incarcerated. He visited Paul's hired house. He sat on top of the Coliseum and gathered up some of the stones. He looked down into that amphitheatre about which he had read so much, and didn't wonder that Byron wrote "I see before me the gladiator lies. He leans upon his hands — his manly brow consents to death, but conquers agony —" President Wright went on to the Roman Forum where he said he could almost see Cicero and hear him say to Catiline, "Quo usque tandem abutere, Catilina, patientia nostra?" "Why will you continue to abuse our patience, O Catiline?"

He quoted the Latin with zest and with his right arm uplifted, as if he actually saw Catiline. When he had finished, his inquirer who had also studied quite a little Latin, marveled at his great memory. "How do you do it?" she asked.

Well, he said, at one time he knew all o'that 'stuff" but making a living these late years had caused him to forget a great deal of it. However, his hold upon it and his apparent visualization of Cicero in the Roman Forum were such that his son who was present asked facetiously if he saw old Demosthenes, too? He in an equally jovial vein replied that Demothenes was out of commission, therefore, he didn't even go to Greece.

He visited Naples though. "See Naples and die," he quoted as one of the common expressions. He also saw the Bay of Naples, and went on one of the trams which took him up an incline to an amusement park. On the ascent, he attempted to speak Italian to the conductor so as to gain some informationn about the park. He couldn't make the conductor understand. In his dilemma, a passenger marched right up to him and said in English, "Friend, I heard you speak to the conductor, I'm going right there. I will show you." President Wright looked at his informer and was so surprised, he was almost frightened. He asked the man where he had learned his English; if he had been to the United States? "No,", answered the passenger. He had learned his English right there in Naples. Up they went for 200 or more feet until they reached the Amusement Park; but President Wright was so afraid of his English speaking informer, he turned and joined the ranks of those on the descent.

The next morning he started out to Pompeii. He watched men excavate a plain little almond shaped button with no letters on it. He examined it and learned that it was on that same little button that some enterprising individual had placed the letters CSA and made a fortune thereby. He was eager not to fall a victim to his imprudent curiosity and advance within the range of the thickly falling ashes of Vesuvius as the elder Pliny did. Therefore, he attempted in his broken Italian to gain all the information possible.

As he hired a donkey to ride out to Vesuvius he was aware his naudic onlookers were standing around watching every move he made. However, inasmuch as he was the only man of color around this didn't disturb him. He paid for his donkey and thought he was ready to ride. As soon as that transaction was completed, the owner of the donkey told him, "You can't ride this donkey. You must have a man to hold him down." No, he didn't need any man to do that, he thought. He had ridden mules at home. He contended and finally mounted the donkey. The donkey reared up on his hind feet. Despite President Wright's attempt to hold on with his hands and his feet, he slid off backwards, to the great amusement of the boys and other onlookers. He wasn't to be outdone. He mounted his donkey and gripped what little scrubby mane he could catch hold of. The donkey reared up on his fore feet. To President Wright's chagrin there was nothing in the world for him to do but slide off over the donkey's head. The spectators roared with laughter. To their further amusement, he had to pay for a man to hold down the donkey's tail. When he arrived at Vesuvius, he discovered two men had been holding down the donkey's tail.

Four men took him up on a stretcher to the top of the Volcano. He looked down into the crater and saw lava shoot up. He inquired in his Italian about the Elder Pliny's death, and about his own danger. He moved back somewhat thoughtfully, then one of the men told him he had seen all there was to be seen. They were going to take him back to the station. They carried him a circuitous route by way of a cavern. In it there was a saloon. He was terribly afraid. He studied each of the men's faces as well as the situation. "Komen zie herein," they beckoned him. Afraid, tired, hungry, and thirsty he went to the edge and peeped in.

"Gentlemen," he said to them, "Just help yourselves. Take everything you want and all you want." After they had taken $5 worth, he told them he would have to pay them back as soon as he got down to the station. He had nothing but checks. When they arrived at the station, the whole town apparently was out to see the Negro who had ridden the donkey. The fellow whom he had paid to hold down the donkey wanted more money and couldn't understand a word of explanation to the contrary. In President Wright's bewilderment, he went into the station and had the station master lock him up until he could send for the United States Consul. In a short while the Consul came, straightened out the whole affair and had him turned loose.

In Rome, he visited the Catacombs in company with a dark skin man who spoke French, and was Secretary to the Vatican at St. Peters. He paid the guide as the other travelers did who wanted the guide to explain in French. When he asked explanation in English, the others said in French, "This Negro doesn't understand French." In reply, the dark skin man came back at them with his crisp French until the guide turned to President Wright and apologized, "I beg your pardon, I'm going to explain to you in English."

From Rome, he went to Venice. His hotel, he says, was right on the ocean. To and from it he rode in a gondola. Quite a novel experience it was to ride in gondolas from island to island — about one hundred and twenty of them on which Venice is situated. He went to the home of Byron. He didn't stand as Byron did "in Venice on the Bridge of Sighs, a palace and a prison on each hand," but he realized Tassos echoes were no more; and all silent rowed the songless gondolier. He recognized the Doges like those in Haiti all around except in the one spot left vacant for the Doge who betrayed Venice.

In his journey up the Rhine to Germany he took note of Mainz, the home town of Gutenberg and the place where printing with movable type was first begun. He laughed about the business shrewdness of two brothers in Cologne. Each sold first class cologne in his shop across from the other's shop. President Wright not knowing they were brothers, went from one to the other to get a reduction in the price of the cologne. He said to one, "Pretty high isn't it?"

"Yes. Go across the street, and that fellow will charge you the same thing."

He also recalled with pleasure the friendship of an Ohio banker whom he met in that city. He was urged to go to some place of entertainment with him. He needed diversion from the ordinary routine of sightseeing. The banker pleaded until President Wright finally confessed he had just enough money to get back to England.

"Money! If it's money you can have —! He pulled out a thousand dollars and begged President Wright to take it.

"No, I don't want it."

He besought him, saying he had left home with four thousand dollars to make the trip. No. President Wright refused to take any money. The banker also refused to accept his excuse for not accompanying him. His action surprised the banker so, he recommended him and made life long Ohio friends for him politically.

One day he went into a barber shop in Cologne to get a haircut and a shave. Both the man and the woman barber felt his hair fore and aft and were puzzled to know what to do with it. They felt his face and were equally perplexed. The woman exhorted the man in German to be careful. Some of that black might rub off. They spoke to each other in German and acted so much like they were at a funeral, President Wright became amused. His only difficulty was the fact that they took so long — nearly two hours — to give him the haircut and the shave, he didn't know what to offer them as remuneration. When he asked what the charge was, they shook their heads and shrugged their shoulders — "Gar Nichts!" Nothing.

President Wright, commonly called Major Wright, told the amusing experiences of his first World War trip abroad with so much zest and reality, one hearing them was made to share them in large measure. After his appointment by the Governor of Georgia during the first World War, as Negro Historian of enlisted colored troops in France, he applied to Dr. Emmet Scott — Assistant to the Secretary of War for a passport. Dr. Scott replied saying it was impossible to obtain a passport at that time. The matter had been taken up with the Secretary of War, and he had declared it couldn't be done. Upon receipt of that letter, Major wrote Dr. R. R. Moton who was close to the President of the United States. Dr. Moton replied saying he was very sorry but he was unable to do anything about it. Upon the receipt of that letter, Major Wright made up his mind to go to Washington. He took with him a letter which President Wilson had written him as Chairman of The Colored Association of Food Production and Conservation in Georgia. He also took along one of his own photographs, having had a little previous experience in obtaining passports. First, he approached Secretary Newton D. Baker and found him in fine spirit. The secretary gave him this assurance, "I can get you over there, but I can't promise to get you back."

Disturbed but undaunted, Major Wright went to the State Department and sent his card and President Wilson's letter to Mr. Tumulty. Mr. Tumulty wrote on the card, "Dr. Wright is a friend of the President. Give him a pass." Major Wright took the card and the President's letter to the proper office of the State Department. "Have you a picture°" asked Mr. Phillips who was in charge at the time. "Yes, sir." He pulled out his picture, and in fifteen minutes had his passport and was gone.

He sailed from New York City for France. On his arrival in London, he secured a room in a hotel and went over to the State Department. There he met Hugh Wallace and was given every assistance on his trip through England, France and Belgium. In addition, he went on General Pershing's invitation to his home and met his young son Warren — "who was married the other day" added Major Wright. As he told of that visit to the General's home, he suddenly recalled his writing a recent congratulatory letter to General Pershing on the occasion of his son — Warren's marriage. "Nothing but a boy when I met him," asserted Major with an evident recall of the march of time.

At Oxford, England, he spoke in Eaton Hall for the Young Men's Christian Association; and for the first time, took out his membership in that organization.

When he reached Paris, he hired a French secretary. By appointment he met Marshal Foche, Georges Clemenceau, General Dodds — Negro General in the Boxer War and a native of Senegal; Honorable Henry White—member of President Wilson's Peace Conference; General Goybet — Commander General of the French black troops and Senegal Deputy. In the latter's report to Major Wright was the statement that there were 249, 558 African-French troops in the World War. Among the other distinguished officers who came to Major Wright's hotel to see him was Commander Mortenol, a black man, assigned to command the air craft guns, and the first Negro in France to command as Admiral. Major Wright upon the invitation of the Conde attended an entertainment at Conde.

He sat in the Chamber of Deputies in Paris and was introduced to that body. He also met the fourteen colored representatives in that official body and heard Boise introduce his resolution on "No Discrimination."

In Belgium, he said he visited one of the most wonderful museums in the world. Its Congo exhibit, he thought is a marvel. The Belgian library was also a wonder to him. "Strange," he commented, "Leopold was supposed to have exploited the Congo." The strangeness of it came out of his description of two statues at opposite doors of the library. As he was about to enter one door, he became highly incensed — angry — when he saw the statue of a Negro down and being lashed. He was too indignant to enjoy the great exhibits as he might have; but he went on through and had to acknowledge they were extraordinary. As he came out the opposite door, he was amazed to see a statue of that same Negro with a dagger in his hand reaching for a man whom he had on the run. "Well!" Major Wright came away impressed and a bit confused over what he saw and what he had read and heard.

He, in his narration of his Belgian and his World War experiences, like Childe Harold in his pilgrmage was about to say, "Farewell! A single recollection not in vain." Already he had stayed up long beyond his eight o'clock bed time, and the early May air was "getting cooler and cooler." But his innate qualities of a gentleman of culture responded to his inquiring pursuer's remark about Waterloo. "Oh, yes, Waterloo is right out of Belgium, you know." He paused to say also that he went there too, in 1895. He was in the room where Napoleon is said to have been and where Wellington was, after the battle was won. As a parting word, he not only recalled that Byron's poem was written that night when Napoleon came up from the Battle of Waterloo, but on the spur of the moment recited the lines:

There was a sound of revelry by night,
And Belgium's capital had gather'd there
Her Beauty and her Chivalry, and bright
The lamps shone o'er fair women and brave men;
A thousand hearts beat happily; and when
Music arose with its voluptuous swell,
Soft eyes look'd love to eyes which spoke again,
And all went merry as a marriage - bell;
But hush! Hark! a deep sound strikes like a rising knell!"

As he concluded, his weary eyes and face lighted up with a faint smile. He bowed his hoary head and slight body; and with a "Good Night Madame," departed a bit jaded and fatigued, but climbed the stairs to his bedroom.

The next morning he was up and dressed and ready at 8:30 to start out for the New York World's Fair. As the sun shone brightly and the warm air stirred little, he descended his steps somewhat stiffly and leaning on his cane but unaided otherwise, and got into his car. Yes, he told his accompanying inquirer and two members of his family, he had been to every World's Fair since the Paris Exposition, except the present one in California, and he would probably see it before it closed. As his car sped along on the outskirts of the city, he said to his chauffeur, "Gums, turn on "WCAU, Philadelphia." He listened to the greeting, "Good morning ladies and gentlemen — Reverend George A. Buttrick," and had an enjoyable time while the inquiring friend became so car sick, she had to ask the chauffeur to stop for a few minutes.

He was in the midst of a somewhat similar situation in 1933, he said, when he and his youngest daughter, Harriet, were on a trip to Haiti. He had experienced such a shock and was so nearly ill, his family and friends tried to dissuade him from taking that long trip. He wasn't sick a minute on the voyage, he emphasized crisply, and he didn't miss a meal, but his youngest daughter was ill two whole days.

As the oldest passenger on the vessel en route to Haiti he continued, the officers were beautiful to him. They showed him every inch of that boat. And after he landed in Haiti, he was on the go nearly every minute. He met three ex-presidents of that island, one of whom, ex-president Legitime, a most distinguished gentleman, was eighty years old. His first night there he spent in what was President Borneo's Executive Mansion, now a hotel; and slept in the Executive bedroom. The housekeeper of the hostelry sent his daughter up on the fourth floor to see which room up there was preferable. When his daughter explained the situation as to her father's age, etc., a gentleman guest in the Executive bedroom insisted that Major Wright have that room.

The deference paid him throughout the trip, the way the Haitians run their own affairs, the change, and his new interest in the importation, and sale of Haitian coffee in this country gave him renewed vigor, fire and driving power which kept him on the go.

With such a quenchless thirst for productive adventure, soon after his return home, he made a five thousand mile tour of the United States in the interest of the promotion and sale of Haitian coffee. On that tour, he visited the scenes of his birthplace and that of some of his forebears. He took pictures of the remains of the old house where he was born and the old spring out of which he is supposed to have had his first drink of water. He gazed upon the old cemetery of his masterclass.

On his way to Pickens, South Carolina, he stopped over in Greenville, not far away. He went to the home of a Negro teacher, a professor as he was called, and engaged the professor to drive over to Pickens with him. When he informed the professor of his interest in Pickens because his grandfather and great grandfather were born there, the professor took great pride in accompanying him. When he told him as they drove along that he also wanted to look up the daughter of his former master, the professor shook his head.

"Professor Wright, you can't go up to those folks house to see them. Not in Pickens." He continued to shake his head. "No." But Major Wright pleaded with the professor to go along and show him where they lived. When they drove up to the house and got out of the car, the professor shook his head again. They would simply have to go around to the back door to see those folks. When Major Wright started up the front steps, the professor got behind him. While Major rang the doorbell, the professor stood on the top step. A girl came to the door with a surprised expression on her face, "What is it?" she inquired.

"My name is Richard R. Wright. I came to see Miss X."

"What is it you want?"

"We were children together. I —".

The girl went back and brought out Miss X.

"Is that you Dick? Come right in. I'm so glad to see you. The last word papa said to us was, get in touch with Dick and have him come to see you." She told him of her marriage, of her husband's death and of her children. Then she called those that were there by name and had them come in so he could see them. After she had heard about his great loss, Mrs. Wright's death, and about his children her next question was, "Dick how old do you call yourself?" with that settled to the best of their ability; but with her thinking they were the same age; and with him not sure but what she was two years older; she assured him that her father and they thought him a remarkable man. She also told him of the schoolhouse they had given the colored people, despite the fact that they were land poor. He enjoyed seeing her and hers at such a time of very deep sorrow in his life, and wound up back at home feeling fine and encouraged over the prospects of the future sale of Haitian coffee.

After that tour, he went on two other foreign trips: one as a member of a commission to Haiti and the other to Europe for change and the kind of rest that soothed and satisfied him. He attended the Reunion of the Veterans of Foreign Wars at Gettsburg, the Century of Progress in Chicago, and the New York World's Fair, 1939. He also looked in upon the Father Divine-Spencer Mission at Hyde Park, New York, and incidentlly viewed the estate of the late President Franklin Delano Roosevelt and the future home of a government Library of Records.

Like the distinguished suffragist who said in her late years her heart was as young as it ever was, his youthful, aspiring ambitions drove him to the controls of his own Wako four-passenger aeroplane, four thousand feet in the air, traveling at a speed of one hundred thirty-five miles an hour.

He left the Mayor Davis Wilson Airport, Philadelphia, at 2:15 P. M. on a Sunday, February 19, 1939, in his Wako four passenger plane piloted by Charles Alfred Anderson, one of the four Negroes who then held a commercial pilot license in this country. Accompanying him on this the first leg of his Good Will Flight was the President, Raleigh H. Merritt, of his newly organized Chamber of Commerce. Along with him, he also took one hundred pounds of Haitian Coffee to E. C. Burke, President of the Consolidated Bank and Turst Company of Richmond, Virginia.

Enroute, after they had reached an altitude of 4000 feet, and a speed of 135 miles per hour, he said to the pilot by whose side he sat, "Anderson, its hot here. I think I'll sit on the back seat." He stood up. As he did so, Mr.

Merritt, about half his age, leaned forward with consternation in his eyes.

"Sit down, Major! This is no place to be walking around." On the contrary, just before they approached the Byrd Air Port in Richmond, and as the Wako nosed down from her high altitude and picked up speed, Major Wright said, "Let her go Anderson!"

On his arrival in Richmond with a broad smile, he stood by his plane while snapshots of it and him were made for postcards. He mailed one of these cards bearing the inscription — "To encourage Aviation and Commerce," — to his son, Dr. Whittier Wright at the Gettysburg, Pennsylvania C. C. Camp. On that card he wrote in his own splendid penmanship the announcement, "Here I am, Whit."

On his return trip, between Washington and Philadelphia, and about 200 miles from Richmond, he said, "Anderson let me try this thing out." He took the controls and flew along five minutes just like he had been flying all of his life, said the pilot, while Mr. Merritt pleaded, "Don't tempt him, Anderson!"

The day after his flight, a prominent Negro citizen called at his bank to see him. As the citizen said with a broad smile and a confident air, "Major, I heard you were going up in an airplane; but I know you had too much sense to go up in a Negro airplane, and with a Negro aviator."

"Yes, I've been up in an airplane," replied Major calmly.

"You have? My! My! I didn't believe it!"

In less than one month's time Major Wright's son, Mr. Emanuel C. Wright, two other prominent citizens of Philadelphia and Washington, D. C., and the same pilot, Mr. C. Alfred Anderson, had signed up with the Aeronautics Authorities and the State Department for the second leg of Major Wright's Good Will Flight. This time it was to be in the Major's same Wako four-passenger plane, but he was not to go. It was to take the Good Will Spirit of the American Negro to the Haitians in Haiti.

As his moral assistants in sponsoring this flight, Major Wright had the cooperation of Mr. R. H. Merritt, Bishop David H. Sims, Attorney Raymond Pace Alexander, Mr. Joseph H. Fason, Mr. J. B. Deans, Judge Edward W. Henry, Mr. Herbert T. Miller and Dr. W. C. Williamson. He had his Wako plane gone over thoroughly; and he was fortunate enough to have the Standard Oil Company donate 6,000 gallons of Esso gasoline, provided his plane could pick up that quanitity at the Standard Oil Stations en route. In addition, the plane was christened by three charming little girls on Wednesday, April fourth — the day before the take off — and provision was made for bon voyage speeches by representatives of the Governor, the Mayor, the Clergy, the professions and business.

Everything appeared to be in readiness for the farewell and the take off, as Major Wright had planned.

To his great surprise, about ten minutes before he was to start for the airport on April fifth, he received a letter from one of the men who had signed up to make the trip. The gentleman's letter stated he was confined to bed with a temperature of 110 degrees; and his doctor had advised him to stay in bed. He was sorry to disappoint him. Disappointed, Major Wright was, but he went out to the airport with an apparent courageous front. He listened to the farewell words of the speakers who stressed the importance of improving commercial relations and strengthening good will between this country and Haiti.

He kept his eye on the Washington citizen who had signed for the trip. When Elder Solomon Lightfoot Michaux declared that flight was under the three "H's"— Haiti, Heaven or Hell. The Washington citizen turned pale and attracted the attention of Major Wright and others by his unusual lamb-like demeanor. The Major was fearful of its effect on his son and the pilot. However, after other messages of greeting and bon voyage were brought by Mr. L. A. Jackson, Dr. Harry Barnes, and Bishop David H. Sims, Major Wright was called upon for the final word.

He stated he was trying to start and aid something to give encouragement to our young people. "Really it is pathetic," he asserted, "to see so many of our young Negro men and women so hopeless." It had been his misfortune in the past six or eight years he further said, to see many of our well educated young people who saw no way out — hopeless. "I see opportunities to make opportunities. Takes vision to see the opportunities," declared Major Wright. His subject was to encourage young people to hunt for and make opportunities for themselves.

At the conclusion of his remarks, the second prominent citizen came up to him and told him he hadn't been feeling so well, and he had an engagement in Washington. However, he got into the plane. Major Wright fearing the effect of all this on the pilot and his own son, suddenly got into the plane himself, and the public was none the wiser. The take off was perfect; but when the plane made a landing at Patco — about ten miles away — to pick up a battery, the uneasy citizen got out in a hurry. He had to take a train to Washington to meet his important engagements.

During Major Wright's and the flier's lay over in Washington on account of weather conditions, a meeting was held in one of the churches to greet them. Again to the Major's surprise the signed up Washington citizen appeared and spoke at the meeting. He told the audience the white people all come to the White House in Washington. "Now," declared he, "I'm going down to Haiti to the Black House."

On the day of the take off from Washington for Norfolk, Major Wright in the presence of Dr. and Mrs. W. J.

A group of high school pupils visiting Major Wright in response to his efforts to secure scholarships for a business career.

Thompkins, Dr. Emmett J. Scott, Bishop C. C. Alleyne and other distinguished citizens saw the signed up Washington passenger drive up to the airport in his car without bag or baggage. The latter parked his car and went over to the pilot. "Anderson," he declared, "I've got to discuss this training program with the Secretary of War who has just landed at Bolden Field. Very important to see President Roosevelt, too. I'd better see these folks and meet you by train in Jacksonville, Florida." To that urgent detention, Major Wright didn't reply except to assure the pilot that he himself would go on to Norfolk with his son and him.

At Norfolk they were met by Mayor John A. Gurkin Mr. P. B. Young, of the Norfolk Journal and Guide and other distinguished citizens. Major Wright's ease and pleasure in flying so aroused Bishop C. Manuel Grace, founder and leader of the House of Prayer, that he too entered the cockpit for his first time and was shown elementary operations of the plane. After a special flight to Hampton Institute and a pledge that Norfolk would take 250 pounds of Haitian Coffee, Major Wright took a train back to Philadelphia. Nevertheless, inasmuch as he knew nearly every Negro of note in the Urban Centers on the route, and he himself had made two trips by boat to Haiti, and he was in close telegraphic connections with the fliers, he followed them with his mind's eye throughout the journey.

He was particularly interested in the fliers reception at Durham, North Carolina, and in Mr. C. C. Spaulding, President of the North Carolina Mutual Insurance Company at the controls. He took note of the old Negro man in Columbia, South Carolina, who let the fliers ride four miles in his conveyance to meet Dr. Miles and Dr. Manse who brought out 20C people in forty minutes to see the take off for the Georgia State College in Savannah. He followed them with a keen sense of their enthusiastic reception by citizens, faculty and students. At Jacksonville, Daytona Beach and Miami, there was no diminution in their reception and no let up in Major Wright's joy.

His enthusiasm was heightened, nevertheless, when word came that they had completed their over-water hop to Havannah, Cuba. There Colonel Batista's special representative together with 1,200 citizens met them at the airport. As their guests and the special guests of Mr. J. H. Defoe, they were entertained at a banquet and reception. This good news was only equaled in Major's estimation by their report of an experience with a doctor in Havannah. In view of the fact that neither Pilot Anderson nor Major's son, Mr. E. C. Wright, could speak Spanish, the doctor whose home was in Santiago thought he had better go down there with them as their interpreter. On the way down the shadows lengthened, the clouds thickened and a storm was brewing. Night and thick clouds they ran into when they were half way to Santiago. They couldn't get through them. They turned back and flew as far as Canagwi. The plane circled over a sugar cane field on which the cane had been cut. Night, clouds, storm, a railroad tressle! They couldn't see. However, the pilot decided it was best to land there. He brought that plane down with such speed, folks in the neighborhood came running to witness what they thought was a disaster. A door was heard to open and slam. As the Spanish people began to jabber, the fliers looked around for the Doctor to interpret for them, but he had disappeared. The next day he came around with his own English interpreter to whom he said in Spanish, "That son of a gun brought that plane down so fast, he scared all the English out of me I ever knew."

Major Wright laughed over the Cuban Doctor's story as much as he did over many others in his repertoire. He likewise took pride in the fact that his fliers were so royally received in Cuba and in Haiti. He was conversant with all the situations which they met — their entertainment at the Marguerita the night they were in Santiago; their over water flight to Port-au-Prince, Haiti; his friend President Stenio Vincent's reception; and their three-day visit to that island whose possible resorts might equal Ostend in Belgium, and whose other marvelous undeveloped resources he viewed on a visit two years prior.

On his Good Will Flier's return trip through the southland, he was hailed by the thoughtful Nego College youth as the ex-slave who was opening new doors and helping to make possible employment opportunities, undreamed of a few years ago. At Tuskegee Institute for example, students together with President Frederick M. Patterson and the late Professor George W. Carver were elated over the success of his Good Will Flight and the possibilities it would teach. At the Tennessee State College, the late President W. J. Hale and his students were so enthusiastic that Major was immediately invited to deliver their Commencement Day address June, the fifth of the next year.

In May 1945, he made a trip to San Francisco, California, to attend the United Nations Organization Meetings. He went as an observer, appointed by the State Department. While there he was the guest of the Ethiopian Delegation; and the guest of honor at a beautiful luncheon given by prominent bankers and citizens of San Francisco.

Two years later, up until the thirtieth of May 1947, he was busy planning what might be called the third leg of his Good Will Flight.

This time it was to be over one of the Commercial Air line routes to his Grandma Lucy's native Africa. There on the West Coast he was to attend the Liberian Centennial Celebration not only as an observer but as an invited guest.

CHAPTER VIII

GREAT ASSOCIATE

In addition to Major Wright's superior qualties of mind he possessed other natural endowments which made for fine human relationships. Among these human traits, were a certain goodness of heart and appreciation of real worth, irrespective; a sense of justice and fair play; a moderate portion of diplomatic tolerance; a spark of humor; and a spirit of loyalty that was not blind. These coupled with his other attributes enabled him to see and talk on the Negro question with every President of the United States except one, from President Garfield down to President Franklin Delano Roosevelt. He discussed educational questions with such college presidents and authors as Charles E. Eliot, William DeWitt Hyde, Lew Wallace and William Dean Howells.

Yet, when asked to name some of his great associates, he thought a moment and mentioned first an old colored Baptist preacher at whose home in the country he boarded in 1871. "From him I got my first inspiration," said Major Wright. The old minister's cabin was in a vale, but prayers were said in that home night and morning; and naught was there but kindness and fairness and peace. The old man had learned to read his Bible only indifferently, but he lived long and learned out of the book of experience how to meet the conditions of life. He was so energetic in helping to build Wright's Academy which was used as a church home, as well as a schoolhouse instead of the bush harbor; he was such a good man, Major Wright as a lad in his teens desired to be like him.

Major Wright's next mention was of an old Negro

charwoman of Savannah, Georgia. Just before his election to the presidency of the Georgia State College, a few envious Negroes spread the rumor that he was opposed to white people. They went so far as to report he said the whites were robbing Negroes of educational money. They even brought one of his speeches to a mass meeting, misinterpreted it and declared a man who would speak like that against good white people was too dangerous to be President of the State College. After all of their verbal fervor was spent, the Chancellor of the University of Georgia rose in that meeting and made this declaration. "We have already decided to have Professor Wright as President of the Georgia State College. If the appointment doesn't turn out satisfactorily, we'll get somebody else." In reply to that announcement, nobody utttered a mumbling word. The meeting was peacefully adjourned.

When Major Wright subsequently made his first visit to Savannah, he was a sick man. "Five feet five," weighed only 121 pounds. Sickly then," he interposed with a twist of his hoary head. Therefore, as soon as he got off the train he fainted and fell out. No one around knew who he was or apparently cared except an old black charwoman. She looked on him and felt his pulse. "None o'y'all know 'im?" she asked the men who had crowded around him. "Well, I'm gwi take 'im to my house," she replied, "Cause he's a sick man." She got two of the men to help her take him through a dark, dirty alley, into an old crowded, dilapidated shack. She threw cold water into his face; she held a glass bottle of salts up to his nostrils, and nursed him back to life. When he became conscious, he asked if she knew Dr. E. K. Love. She didn't "zactly" know him but she went out, found Dr. Love and brought him there. Major Wright straightened up from that alley recollection and said emphatically, "That was at the bottom of my workbaskets, etc., given to the needy." After another second's retrospection; and in almost a stirred from the depths whisper, he confessed, "I said to myself when Dr. Love got me out of that alley, and I've said it many times since. That class has helped me, and if I have a chance —!" He adjusted himself in his chair and thoughtfully toyed with bringing the ends of his forefingers and little fingers together across the back of his hands.

Like his appreciation of real worth in a vale or in an alley, his sense of justice many times met the test on the educational frontiers as well as in the army ranks as Major. Perhaps all the more successful it was because of his quick perception and ability to couple with it a fair portion of diplomatic tolerance. The operation of these traits was never more evident than in his early association with the Commissioners of the Georgia State College. Even at that time his immature attitudes and actions spoke so much more loudly than anything that might now be said, his letters of that period together with his abundance of telling correspondence should be published as a sequel to this volume. Not only should they appear as a conclusion to this volume, but rather as a wonderful revalation of the mind and character of the man.

His thoughtful rather than instinctive tolerance was also noted twenty-five years later, June 1, 1917, by one of the reporters, James Calloway of the Macon Telegraph who wrote, "All of us applaud the sentiments of Professor Wright when he says, "Let us prove what has never been proved before — that two races of different color and of different social station can live together in harmony and peace and mutual helpfulness."

Major Wright held the view that where even two individuals are closely associated, a difference in age or point of view or something else may make not only tolerance but a spark of humor a great asset. His spark of humor was attested in the following story as told by the Aviator, C. Alfred Anderson, a man of 32. Once they were riding together in Major's automobile, and Aviator Anderson attempted to locate a station on the radio. He turned the dials and played around with them, and yet the music didn't come in full. After a while, Major Wright said to him in the spirit of another young fellow, "Anderson have you thought what might happen were you to push that aerial up a little?" Laughing at what he termed his own stupidity, Anderson called Major Wright a great sport.

Once when he was President of the Georgia State College, he was planning for a visit of President Grover Cleveland and other distinguished guests. Realizing the importance of having something striking and different from what might be found at the other colleges, Major Wright advised his Professor of Biology to catch several big snakes from a nearby marsh and preserve them in alcohol. The Professor preserved so many big snakes when President Cleveland visited that department and looked at the jars of snakes, he asked in great seriousness, "Do you raise anything else?" Major Wright laughed heartily as he thought of the expression on President Cleveland's face.

Major Wright was also able to claim the friendship and association of another President, the Honorable William McKinley. When the latter was a member of Congress and served on the tariff issue, he invited Major Wright to his office and made him welcome to use it as his stopping place.

As president of several educational organizations as well as of the Georgia State College, Major Wright often opened doors to Negro talent in search of a stage and an audience. Among the musicians who came to Georgia State College in search of such an opportunity was Blind Tom and Marian Anderson. Blind Tom whom he had heard play the piano in white residences when he was a slave boy, was born, he recalled, in Columbus, Georgia, the home town of his mother-in-law. In later years, he invited Marian Anderson to sing at the Georgia State College on her first trip south.

Whether he was giving encouragement to a struggling musician or writing on Negro inventors, or traveling in France in the interest of Negro soldiers in the World War, he was always seeking facts to prove the equality of at least a few Negroes with whites under similar circumstances.

Among the many signatures of distinguished French officials and generals in his album are those of Georges Clemenceau, P. Singuart, Commissioner General Diagne, General Dodd, A. Dodeh, Gourand and Gal Goybet. Clemenceau wrote with his own pen:

"Il n'est pas un de nous qui ne puisse a toute heure, ou quil soit place et sous quelque forme que sa personnalite se revele, apporter un concours passager ov durable aux grandes realisations d'humanite. G. Clemenceau." (There is not a single one of us wherever he may find himself and under whatever circumstances, who cannot make some passing or lasting contribution to great human events.")

To Major Wright from Gal Goybet (157 DI) came the words: "En sourvenir des deux beaux regiments Americans Noirs (371 o et 372°) que jai en l'honneur de Commander dans la Bataille Victorieuse de Champagne.
(Sept. - Oct. - 1918) Gal Goybet Cnt la 157 e DI)"

Translation

In remembrance of the two fine colored American regiments (371st and 372nd) which I had the honour to command in the victorious battle of Champagne.

J. Sinquart wrote in his individual penmanship:
"Traveler World War
A la memoire de mes vaillant soldats noirs, Fo in bis pour la civilization et La France; pour L'honneur de la race des braves, e gaire a leurs camarades les poilus de la grand guerre - Le 19 Aont 1919."

Commander J. Singuart.

Translation

"In memory of my brave colored soldiers who died for civilization and France; for the honore of the race of the brave ones, the equals of their comrades, the French soldiers of the Great War." August 19, 1919.

The Commissioner General of the Colonial—

In combination, the qualities which singly enabled Major Wright to be a soldier or a great associate made him a superb friend.

Of all the Negroes of his acquaintance, he does not hesitate to give first place to Frederick Douglass. Many times he visited the home of Frederick Douglass and always found Mrs. Douglass deeply interested in all the problems her husband encountered. When Mr. Douglass was to visit Savannah and the discussion over the Negro home in which he would stay became heated, Major Wright saw to it that the question was decided on its merits. Douglass stopped in the finest Negro home there, and that was owned by a black not a light skin Negro. Another home which Major Wright and his family visited was that of his friend, Captain and Congressman Robert Small's in Beaufort. Major Wright heard from this Captain of the Steamer Planter the story of his taking by strategy his steamer over to the Union forces when South Carolina seceded from the Union. Thereby, both the Captain and his steamer won a unique place in the history of the Civil War.

Major Wright's friendship and admiration transcended sex and marital boundaries. His appreciation of the poetry and the worth of Frances E. W. Harper caused him to name one of his charitable Savannah Clubs "The Frances E. W. Harper Club." On Frances Harper's visit to his home, she wrote while there some of the poems in "The Sparrow's Fall and Other Poems." With the years their friendship ripened to the extent that in her declining days, her poems were published by Major Wright's son, Bishop R. R. Wright. Another woman whose friendship Major Wright held dear was Flora Batson, the black Patti, admired and praised by Schumann Heinck.

Some of the people whom Major Wright knew "in days gone by" appeared to him to be or to have been among the most worthwhile men and women of any race. Their number is so great he could by no means mention half of them here. However, in passing his mind reverted to Dr. Scarborough, Greek Professor and writer of the first Greek book by a Negro; the late Dr. Joseph C. Price, a truly wonderful orator and President of Livingstone College; the late Dr. Kelly Miller — scholar, journalist, and for many years Professor of Howard University; the late Dr. R. R. Moton — interracial Expert and for years President of Tuskegee Institute; the eminent Scientist — the late Dr. George W. Carver of Tuskegee Institute; the unequaled educator and Negro leader — the late Dr. Booker T. Washington; the late Maggie Walker of Virginia — banker and business woman; the distinguished banker and business man, C. C. Spaulding of North Carolina; the remarkable trio of educators Mary Macloud Bethune, Charlotte Hawkins Brown, and Nannie Burroughs.

An interview which took place between Senator Mark Hanna, Dr. Booker T. Washington and Major Wright in the Senate Chamber at Washington is another example of the country's great men seeking Major Wright as an associate. Major Wright was there in response to a telegram from Dr. Washington who desired him to come to talk over a situation which affected T. Thomas Fortune. On the left of the great Senator, Mark Hanna, sat Major Wright, while Dr. Washington sat on the right. In their discussion of the political situation, Senator Hanna mentioned Theodore Roosevelt who was being considered a running mate for Vice President, with William McKinley as President of the United States. Major Wright's recollection was that Senator Hanna not at all enamored with Theodore Roosevelt, warned them saying, "This fellow will walk into the Convention with his Rough Rider hat on and stampede the Convention. We might have trouble. Therefore, we have decided to accept him as Vice President."

Major Wright's comment on this thirty-nine year old interview was that it was probably the first one held with Negro men in regard to Theodore Roosevelt who on the assassination of President McKinley became President of the United States. Secondly, that Theodore Roosevelt ranked perhaps as one of the three or four great Presidents of the United States. As concrete evidence of this interview and arrangements thereto, Major Wright in his methodical way had preserved the thirty-nine year old letters of T. Thomas Fortune, publisher of The New York Age, Number 4 Cedar Street, Manhattan.

By no means least in the long list of associates now already mentioned was the late Dr. John Hope, President of Atlanta University. Major Wright wished to pay special tribute to Dr. Hope who gave unsparingly of his best for the larger establishment of Atlanta University.

In the sphere of religion, Major Wright's friendships and associations were such that at one time he was a trustee of Central City College, a Baptist institution at Macon, Georgia, a trustee of Morris Brown College, a Methodist institution in Atlanta; and a trustee of Atlanta University, for many years a Congregational institution.

His friendship not only soared beyond social cultures, race, geographical barriers and religious division, but lasted through the years. Such folks as John Greenleaf Whittier — for whom one of his sons, Dr. Whittier Wright, is named; President Edmund Asa Ware; Governor Dorsey of Georgia; and his own erstwhile master's family were his life long friends.

In verification of these transcendent qualities of friendship in Major Wright; in 1935, after the March of seventy-five years, he received the following letter from his young mistress:

"Easley
South Carolina
February 6, 1935

Well, Dick, I hardly know how to write you. Sallie Griffin has sent me your address and I am sure its welcome. Sallie came to see me after you had gone back home and told me about you coming to Pickens. I would of liked to have seen you when you were in Easley, you were not very far from me, we live about three miles from the incorporation. I guess you have changed a lot since I have seen you. We have plaied together many times when we were children. I waunt to know if you have a family. I haven't seen Sallie to be with hur. She came by and only staid a few mints. She had visited Morrie at Anderson, that is my Sister do you remember her? She was the youngest one of us.

My father got a letter some years ago from you and we have never known your whereabouts untill you come to Pickens. How old are you? It seems you and myself were Born in the same year. I will be eighty-three next August. I was Born 1851.

My Mother and Father was so glad to hear from you they did think a lot of you I have herd my Father say you was so smart and Mother would say Dick is the smartest little boy I can send him down Town and tell him what to get and I never have to send a note he brings me the change back and everything that I sent for tell me if you have a Brother or a Sister. I have fore childred living and three dead my eldes child died last February 13 I lived with him after Mr. — Died he has only one child a Boy I am still with them my children all live in sight can see all their dwiling from our Poach I have a Boy living in Kansas he is my only Boy he was in the World War and when he came out of the war married a Kansas girle he sold his propertis hear and bought in Kansas he has a government job I have three girls all married have nice homes. I have tin Grandchildren and Eight Great Grand Children Dick I never got mutch of and education there was no schools near my Father taught School and I learned very little only going to a country school. My father was a good scholar and a fine Scribe I learned all I know from him and my mother. Well guess you will answer this badly writen letter my adress is Easley, S. C."

CHAPTER IX

BUSINESS MAN AND BANKER

PART I

Major Wright in answer to a question as to why he entered business, said the business idea with him was an evolution. The thing that first put it into his head was the jocular remark he heard his mother make when he was a boy; namely, "I'm going to save my money and live on the interest."

Since she never had any money to spare from their daily needs, he thought it was said as a joke. He surmised, if she were still alive she couldn't believe she had planted that seed thought in his little mind by a casual remark. As the son of such a mother and as a father himself of experience, his observation was that one doesn't always know what he may do for his children, through a casual word or a thoughtful deed. He may plant an idea which he little thinks will bear good or evil fruit.

When Major Wright was Paymaster in the United States Army, one of his children attempted to sell his iceman a picture of him in his Army attire. The iceman shook his head. He didn't want to buy any picture. Mrs. Wright also shook her head. She didn't want to buy any ice.

Another observation of Major Wright was "One can't get blood out of turnip." His Mandigo ancestors as well as the Cherokees on his father's side were traders. He inherited the instinct from them. This business seed thought inherent in his nature, had germinated into more than an idea the day he stood reading the sign on the front of the savings bank in Atlanta. If this hadn't been true when the depositor asked, "Have you any money in here?", he knew he could never have replied with such resolve, "No, sir, but I mean to have."

There was little opportunity for him as a lad in grammar school to translate this determination into business and money in the bank. He recalled however, when he was about eleven years old, he had a contract to haul bricks at three dollars a day. Also, in the early days when the adjoining property to Atlanta University appeared to be so undesirable, and the owner of it was selling off lots to colored people, he and a friend attempted to act as agents for some of the lots.

His enforced experience as a book peddler; his Cuthbert perception of organizing the farmers of Randolph County, Georgia, so they might have a business of their own instead of giving their profits to itinerant buyers; his book store in Augusta; his State Fair; his Georgia State College Boys Thrift Club; and even his newspaper organization all "fetched" up, he acknowledged to the same point — business.

He was strongly inclined towards business when he was in Cuthbert, but as he put it, he was pulled away to organize a high school in Augusta.

"Worst mistake I ever made," he broke off his words at the age of eighty-three and fidgeted regretfully in his chair as if he had lost everything he had, and his life had been a complete failure. Yes, he might have established a Tuskegee in Georgia, if he hadn't left Cuthbert. This regret, like a rebellious child, slipped out one day as he conversed with a friend.

Nevertheless, during the eleven years in Augusta he purchased a home there and a piece of property which he rented out. Both of these pieces of real estate he retained as rental property for a long time as he put it, after they "broke me up again. Sent me to Savannah this time." In fact he kept them for about twenty-five years. Then rather suddenly, he sold the home place and everything he had in Augusta. "Had nothing" was his humorous, sarcastic way of putting it.

He sold them during the summer the Board of Commissioners of the Georgia State Industrial College refused to reappoint him as President — a situation which grew out of one of his acts of displeasure to a member of this Board.

He presided over a meeting of Negroes which Judge Hammond, an Aristocratic, powerful and well liked member of his Board of Commissioners, addressed. In his speech Judge Hammond praised Negroes but called the 13th, 14th and 15th Amendments to the Federal Constitution a grave mistake. They should be repealed he said, so as to give Negroes a chance to work up to them.

At the close of this address, there was a furore of discussion. As if to quell the opposition to the repeal of these Amendments and ingratiate himself into favor with such a big man as Judge Hammond, a Negro minister, Reverend J. A. Lindsey — rose, indorsed the speech and moved its acceptance with thanks. Major Wright — about five feet, five inches tall, slender, erect and fiery eyed that night — rose and told his hearers he as presiding officer would absolutely refuse to put the motion. Of course no one else attempted to supercede him, and the meeting just "broke up." As a consequence the Board of Commissioners of the Georgia State Industrial College took a whole summer to reappoint him as President.

While he was greatly worried over the retention of his position as President, he knew two white men who were similarly worried about their positions. One of them, Mr. Black, said to him, "Wright, I have a house I want to sell. I'll sell it to you for $1400."

"I haven't that kind of money, Mr. Black," he answered. Another white friend — and army officer — who heard Mr. Black's offer to sell it to him with the initial payment of fifty dollars, said "Wright you take Black's offer, I'll lend you the fifty dollars." He accepted the loan against the expressed wishes of his wife. It worried him because it was the first and only time in their married life she had opposed his contemplated action on account of its having him go into debt or anything else.

However, he took the offer and accepted the loan. Shortly thereafter, he sold the house for $2800 and received $1300 of the amount in cash. From that cash he took $90C and bought another piece of property on which he erected an apartment house which he rented to people who could pay better rental. This he later sold for $9,000.

In another business venture he purchased a small unimproved city square in Savannah and built on it twenty, one-story, six-room houses which he painted green with yellow trimmings. These he also rented out for a while and then sold at a profit. His next investment was in farm lands on which there was valuable timber.

In planning ahead for his retirement from the Presidency of the Georgia State Industrial College, he thought he would go to California and spend the balance of his days in writing. He made a forecast; went out to Los Angeles and liked it so well he bought a house, two lots and a little store. The house he conceived would make a lovely residence for Mrs. Wright.

After his return home, his daughter Julia who had a small bank account in a Savannah bank went down one day to the bank to transact some business. The official with whom she dealt, despite the fact she always signed her name "J. O. Wright," called her Julia and refused to say "Miss." In an altercation over this, he struck her. She grabbed a chair and struck him back. President Wright went into town and to the bank immediately. He walked in, trying with difficulty to keep back the fire in his eyes and the Indian in his blood. He listened as long as he could, then broke loose.

"If I were a white man, I would have come down with my gun on my shoulder. The very idea! I'm going to organize a bank where anybody may come and be treated like a lady or a gentleman. I'm going to bring suit against this bank." Driven out of the bank by bank officials, he went to see a lawyer and filed both civil and criminal suit against the bank. He went home in feverish haste; dictated his resignation to the Board of Commissioners of the Georgia State Industrial College and waited to hear the verdict of the people of Savannah.

Among the dignitarial conclusions which came to his attention was the statement of a Bishop of a high class denomination which declared it would be a disgrace to call a Negro woman, "Miss or Mrs." In his confirmation of many of them said the Bishop, he had never called one of them "Miss or Mrs." Another significant comment came from a member of his Board of Commissioners as follows, "Professor, I didn't think you wanted social equality."

Major Wright terribly aroused over this as well as the fact other Negroes were seeking his position, went back to see his lawyer. His lawyer told him he couldn't win. The judges wouldn't render a decision in his favor. He might as well let the matter drop. He was tactful, but didn't let it drop until there was so much comment pro and con, the bank dismissed the employee who had started the trouble.

With the heart and the nerve of a true soldier, Major Wright resisted all persuasion to remain in Savannah. He tossed off many predictions of his failure to organize a bank in a section of the country with which he was not more familiar. He told his friends he had been teaching and telling folks what to do so long he thought he might as well take some of his own medicine. He had studied men and business and taught men and business and he couldn't see how he could fail in business.

He smiled in a dry fashion; placed the tip ends of the middle fingers and of the ring fingers on both hands against each other, as he often did in talking and continued. He went to California and all around seeking a place to 'light'. His eldest son — Bishop R. R. Wright, Jr. was then with the African Methodist Episcopal Book Concern and 'Christian Recorder' in Philadelphia. That was an attraction, he admitted, Greater than that though was his own conclusion that Philadelphia was slow enough for an old man.

Accordingly, he decided to locate there. As he confided his decision to some friends, they kindly told him he was going to a dead town. He wouldn't have to lay it out; for it was as nearly dead and buried as any town they had visited. He took no offense, but jocularly replied that Philadelphia according to their description, was just the place for him. Upon their thinking too, fifty percent of the Negroes, who were anybody, would be his friends. His keen eyes twinkled on his eighty-third birthday and a mischievous, boyish smile broke through as he remarked that he couldn't have held one percent of the Negroes in some of the fast towns like New York City.

With enthusiasm, he was welcomed to Philadelphia by his eldest son, R. R. Wright, Jr., to open a bank. His son arranged to have him meet a dozen of the leading citizens of Philadelphia to plan the new financial institution Such a meeting was held, and every man present pledged from $1,000 to $5,000 toward the capital of the bank.

When the day arrived for these subscribers to put up the pledged capital that would enable the incorporators to get their State Charter, capitalized at $5C,000, a meeting was called. Not one subscriber was present. Major Wright and Dr. Wright called on each of them at his home and found each either absent of physically indisposed. Other attempts were made to reach them but without avail.

It was therefore necessary for Major Wright and his son to raise the capital from some other source, and change their plans besides. They didn't waiver. They decided to abandon the State Bank and Trust Company plan and apply for private banking license. The amount required by the State Banking Department for a charter to do business in Pennsylvania was $156,250. Major Wright sold some of his property. His son Dr. R. R. Wright, Jr. and his second daughter, Lillian — now Mrs. Clayton — got together all they had saved up. He kept at it until the amount of money was in hand and he had complied with every other demand.

In June 1920 an application was filed with the Secretary of Banking and Auditor General of the Commonwealth of Pennsylvania for private banking license. Then came the struggle, the worries, the beaten path to and from Harrisburg, the lying-in-wait to button hole the Governor, the Secretary of Banking, the Banking Commisioners, the Attorney General, legislators and other public officials to obtain a charter. The Governor at first told him he had the legislature on his hands and would be tied up with it for several months, he wouldn't have time to consider the matter. Politicians gave him the run around while they fought the proposition. The banks of Philadelphia were skeptical and non-cooperative. Major Wright however, who had been in many battles before never slept until his charter was granted. With that achieved, he lost no opportunity in publicizing his ability to pay the Commonwealth of Pennsylvania $156,250 for his bank charter.

In the meantime, he had bought an old store on the corner of 19th and South Streets and hired carpenters to fix it up. One afternoon as he sat on the sidewalk watching the carpenters hammer away, he saw an old woman in a shop across the street buying spectacles, Inasmuch as she was a loud speaker, he could hear everything she said about what her madame had told her relative to her 'specks' and cooking over the hot stove. He kept his eyes on her as she, heavy on her feet, crossed the street in his direction scowling up at the building. When she stepped on the sidewalk a few feet from him, she looked at him with pity and discouragement.

"Good evenin'. They tell me you goin' to open a bank."

He rose to his feet with his hat in his hand.

"Yes, Madame, and I want you to be the first depositor in the bank." She shook her head sadly and moved on with the departing words, "I sho' sympathize with you." The next day as he sat almost in the same spot watching the carpenters at work, he saw another Negro woman, an upper crust lady this time, approach him. He had his head up supposedly watching the carpenters at work as she stopped just opposite him, with a scowl on her face.

"Where are you from?" she asked him.

"I'm from Georgia." He rose to his feet.

"Why don't you go back where you came from? Coming up here ruining us; making believe you going to open a bank."

"I have eight children, madame. My wife is coming next month."

"My! my! Why don't you go back and stay. All of those children! You can't make a living up here. A bank in this old store?"

"Yes, madame this bank will be the Citizens and ——. You see, in the first place; it is the Citizens Bank. You are a citizen of Philadelphia, I know."

"Yes, indeed. Both father and mother born right here in Philadelphia."

"Where did your grandfather came from, madame?"

"Philadelphia."

"Well, may I ask where your great grandfather came from°"

"From Virginia."

"Well, this bank — The Citizens and Southern Bank will cater to the citizens first, you see. They come first. Then it will include all of us Southerners next." He continued to show her the esteem he had for the old citizens first, and the leading part he expected them to take in the Citizens and Southern Banking Company.

When his store bank shack, as some of the "dicties" termed it, was completed, he equipped it with the necessary pieces of second-hand oak furniture, cleaned and polished like new. He laid linoleum on the main office floor. He organized a banking company and gave it the name — Citizens and Southern Banking Company —of the banking company in Savannah which had driven him out of its bank. After his election as its President, he sent out a flood of literature. He spoke in the churches. He contacted other groups and individuals and invited the other banks of the city to the great opening on the 15th day of September 1920.

On that day, he opened his banking institution as a partnership. The partners concerned were himself — R. R. Wright, Sr.; R. R. Wright, Jr.; and his daughter Lillian M. Wright. Each had invested to make up the $15,000 capital to open the bank. With the struggles and the cruising against the tide still in his bones and body — no time to sleep it off — he was on hand that morning before 9 o'clock, greeting depositors and visitors and feeling as light as a "basket of chips," he said.

The first depositor with whom he shook hands was the

bespectacled cook who had extended her sympathies to him the day he sat on the sidewalk watching the carpenters. She told him she had saved up $1.50 to make her first deposit in a bank in all of her born days. She had never thought she would live to see the day when she would have money in the bank. He took fifty cents of the $1.50 for deposit to her credit, and advised her to keep the dollar to eat on until she would earn more. She went out singing the praises of the President of the Citizens and Southern Bank. Others — even the skeptical — chimed in until Major Wright was a happy man. He greeted all the citizens who came in that first day and swelled the deposits to more than $10,000.

Despite all the success talk, many curious persons made special trips to 19th and South Streets to see the "store front bank" run by a school teacher and preacher. It was sure to fail. Some of the officials of Philadelphia Banking Institutions gave the old broken down school teacher's bank just six months to stay open. These predictions didn't baffle the Major. He had been in other battles and was always ready to fight. He did fight and at the end of the first year, had more than $100,000 in deposits.

Among his most enthusiastic continued depositors was the bespectacled cook. She came back week after week with her bankbook which she prized, and a few more dollars to deposit until she had $125 in the bank.

"Lord a'might! En!" Everybody in the bank could hear every word she said. She could scarcely recover from the fact of having saved up that much money. She came in so often with her little money, she felt at home; and once in a great while, just couldn't restrain her enthusiasm for President Wright.

"What y'all chillun doing here? Sho' better treat the President of this City Southern Bank right. Cause he done stop me from paying rent. I eats and sleeps, and boards under my own vine an' fig tree." Under Major's guidance, she bought a little home and paid for it. When she passed away, she had on deposit in the Citizens and Southern Bank and Trust Company over two hundred dollars.

Another gratifying incident in the early days of the bank was a letter from the Citizens and Southern Bank of Savannah, Georgia to President Wright. The President of that bank wrote telling President Wright how proud they were of him and his bank with the same name as theirs.

To win the good will and confidence of the Philadelphia bankers with whom he was competing, President Wright had to be very judicious. He said they often came in with a chip on their shoulders, but he didn't notice the chip. When they would snap at him he would say, "Well, you know and I don't know. It's one of the finest things in the world to have you advise me on the best way to do that." He thought with such handling of the people, with integrity, with hustle for business and hard headed judgment in making investments and loans, the bank grew in favor with the people of Philadelphia and leading Negroes of the country. One of the facetious sayings relative to this bank's caution in making loans in its early years was, "If you need $25, Major Wright wants you to leave both eyes, both legs and all the collateral you can muster."

In 1921 he took his son, Emanuel Crogman Wright, into the bank as janitor and assistant bookkeeper. He recalled his youngest daughter, Harriet, now Mrs. Lemon from Radcliffe College, and had her enter Wharton Business College. He said to her and Emanuel, "You know we've got to make new opportunities for ourselves."

During the first few months of the bank's existence a number of persons came in and promised to do much for the institution, but at the same time asked to become the first borrowers. A number of bad loans were made during the first year; all small, but amounting to nearly $1000. To sift out the bad from the good applicants for loans was one of the most difficult problems Major Wright had to face.

The next problem which gave him the most concern was the investment of the funds of the bank in such securities as would give a fair return and be absolutely liquid. He, therefore, decided to select as the bank's financial advisers three of the largest banks in Philadelphia, viz., The Bank of North America, Parsley and Brothers, and Asa S. Wing of the Provident Trust Company.

These institutions and men were constantly consulted on all matters of investments. Busy with their own problems, many suggestions which were made in good faith, lost thousands of dollars in investments for the Citizens and Southern Bank. Major Wright, therefore, decided it was necessary for him to learn at first hand about stocks and bonds, if he intended to run a bank. Accordingly, he registered at the University of Pennsylvania in the Evening School and studied the principles of banking. He was the oldest man in his class. However, the more he learned of this intricate subject the more absorbed and fascinated he became with the field of banking.

He decided to connect his bank with organizations that would give it prestige and dignity. He, therefore, made application for membership in the Pennsylvania Bankers Association in 1922, and in the American Bankers Association in 1923.

In 1924, as a firm believer in the power and influence of organization, he met a group of Negro bankers in special session during their attendance of the National Negro Business League's annual meeting in Cleveland.

In that special session they organized the National Negro Bankers Association with Major R. R. Wright, President, Mr. Wilson Lovett, Secretary and Mr. C. C. Spaulding, President of the Mechanics and Farmers Bank of Durham, North Carolina, Treasurer. At this meeting the next year in Philadelphia, more than thirty banks were represented.

One great service which President Wright felt the National Negro Bankers Association might render at that time would be to act as the nucleus of a cooperative movement throughout the country to induce the ex-service men to save some of the money for which they were filing their applications. His bank also made an appeal to the ministers on this subject. He lectured on it and urged the Negro press to stress it.

His conviction was that if the proper presentation of this whole matter was made to the Negro soldiers, they would save at least part of their bonus. He pointed out that every soldier, every business and household should have a savings account as safety for business or domestic comforts, and as a reserve. Nine-tenths of the business failures he held was due to lack of capital. He went so far as to appeal for some kind of a five-year plan to help the Negro people establish themselves economically. He said with regard to the ex-service men, "From appearances. they need the money. Distressing sight. Crutches indicate many left their legs in France where they worked and fought to make democracy safe. Some are victims of gas." As he heard many of their conversations which indicated they didn't need to spend all of their receipts, he pleaded with them as a man of experience and as the father of three sons to save at least a little of their bonus. Partly as a result, some of them brought their checks to the Citizens and Southern Bank and left on deposit one-third to one-half of their receipts.

Ever on the alert for safe business extension and progress, President Wright turned his attention to the possibilities of a Trust Company. When he was advised that $125,000 capital would be required by the State Banking Department for the launching of such an enterprise, he made up his mind to get out and raise it. He mapped out a plan and immediately began to renew former contacts throughout the South.

In the early autumn of 1925, he left for Florida to sell stock in his proposed Trust Company. In that State alone, he spent one month. Among his "Impressions of Florida" which he jotted down in a rough tablet were, "There is a great development in real estate; 67% of the millionaires of the world own property in Miami; Miami is indeed a magic city; there are colored businesses everywhere."

Following his extensive tour of the South, he returned to Philadelphia. After many ups and downs and careful planning, on the the morning of January 19, 1926, with the weather outside dipping toward zero, he organized the Citizens and Southern Bank and Trust Company by merging the Trust Company with the Citizens and Southern Bank. This new company with a capital of $125,000 and a surplus of $31,250, owned and controlled exclusively by Negroes was hailed throughout the country. Major Wright, praised for his integrity and business sense was elected as its President. The other members of its Board of Directors were: E. W. Thornton, Frank Hopkins, E. Washington Rhodes, W. Sampson Brooks, Edwin B. Maynard, William Newman, J. H. Irvin, R. H. Smirley, Andrew J. Hemmons, J. C. Neely, J. Albert Johnson, W. S. Scarborough, C. G. Collins, R. R. Wright, Jr., J. T. Seth, J. S. Caldwell, W. H. Heard, J. R. Evans.

The Jacksonville Journal, Jacksonville, Florida, carried an article headed, "Wright Heads Trust Concern in Philadelphia." "The President, Major R. R. Wright, is known for his integrity as a business man; and has the proper amount of backbone to demand that those who deal with the Company pay their bills promptly. The fact that Major Wright is a Southern man helped. The citizens of Florida rallied to the support of the institution."

The Philadelphia Tribune came out in an editorial as follows: "When men of integrity and clean business character come together and lead off in an enterprise worthy, the Tribune stands squarely behind them. Major Wright spent a month in Jacksonville last fall, and visited other parts of the State, meeting many business race men who knew him before he went to Philadelphia to live. And knowing the man, many bought stock in his company which has recently opened under such favorable circumstances."

He forged ahead despite odds which were not apparent to the public, and without complaint, or discouragement. Finally, on the 18th of November of that year his Board of Trustees received a communication from the Commonwealth of Pennsylvania, Office of the State Treasurer, "Gentlemen: Enclosed herewith please find draft on the Mellon National Bank, Pittsburgh, Pennsylvania, made payable to the order of your institution in the sum of $10,000 for deposit to the credit of the Commonwealth of Pennsylvania.

General Fund Account."

He smiled as he was reminded of what the confidence and the backing of the Commonwealth of Pennsylvania, though wrung from it, meant to his company at that time; not long economically speaking, before the Depression. Of course, when the Depression struck and knocked into a cocked hat such institutions as the Franklin Trust, Banking Trust, and other Banks of Philadelphia, the interested Negroes in that city trembled with fear for the Citizens and Southern Bank and Trust Company. The doors of the Citizens and Southern Bank and Trust Company, however, never failed to open at the proper time. The Bank examiners continued to report to Major Wright what he facetiously told them they would have to tell somebody else, namely, the Citizens and Southern Bank and Trust Company was the most liquid bank in Philadelphia.

This bank under Major Wright's guidance soon gained the confidence of the Negro people. A seasoned citizen and beautician of Philadelphia — Mrs. Douglas who had a beauty parlor on South Street said to a stranger who dropped into her shop one day and finally inquired about President Wright and his bank, "Honey, I feel like squeezing him every time I see him. He's a master mind and a Christian, too. He don't high hat nobody. Ain't that like Jesus?"

The stranger agreed and said just enough for her to continue.

"Jesus wasn't a hob nobbing with Nicodemus and Zachariah and Zacheus. When he wanted somebody he went and called the lowly fisherman. Major Wright is so plain and simple. Not always seeking the big Niggers. I put a penny or two in his bank when it first opened. I also put some in the Franklin Trust, Sixteen and Market Streets. Bless the Lord, the Franklin Trust which we thought was like the Rock of Gibraltar closed its doors. But the Lord will provide. You see it's like the inlets of the Mediterranean Sea. Shut up them inlets, the sea will dry up. We'se the inlets. Some of 'em don't know they can't flourish if they dry up the inlets."

President Wright with the cooperation of his Board of Directors of the Citizens and Southern Bank and Trust Company catered to every class of depositor. He spoke in the Philadelphia churches and encouraged deposits, where absolutely necessary of scarcely more than ten cents. He asked for the cooperation of the church in all phases of the general welfare of the people — health, education, jobs, thrift, and business.

His reputation and that of the Citizens and Southern

Bank and Trust Company attracted the attention of the leading ciy officials. They, including the Mayor of the city, Mayor Harry A. Mackey, were called upon. The Mayor commended him for his business acumen, integrity, and great courage in the face of odds to which his people were unfortunately heir. He, in turn, presented the Mayor with data relative to the National Negro Bankers Association, and asked his cooperation in welcoming that organization to Philadelphia for its next annual meeting.

In the meantime he welcomed Mayor Mackey as he came down in person and deposited $2000 in the Citizens and Southern Bank and Trust Company. As he did so, Mayor Mackey not only said, "You've got a good bank," but expressed his surprise and pleasure with what he had read of the National Negro Bankers Association, and pledged his hearty support in welcoming it to Philadelphia.

Early in the next month, Major Wright as president of this organization, called upon the Chamber of Commerce and other important bodies to cooperate in promoting its annual meeting to be held in Philadelphia the following September. In making announcements of this meeting to the Negro Press, he called attention to the fact that during the previous year — 1930 — over 1300 banks had closed their doors; and only four of them were Negro banks. He mentioned the consolidation of the three Negro banks in Richmond, Virgina, under the name, The Consolidated Bank and Trust Company, due in large measure to the genius and business management of the late Mrs. Maggie L. Walker.

The other example he pointed out was the Mutual Standard Bank of Louisville, Kentucky. This bank had been organized by the consolidation of two other banks which separately would have been carried down by the failure of a bank which had been trusted with their bank reserves. "Not on your sweet life did they go down;" wrote the President of the National Negro Bankers Association. He exulted in the fact that both presidents of these two separate banks had submerged their personal ambitions and helped to elect a third man as president of the consolidated bank.

He urged his people to foster banks of their own if they are to make the progress which other groups are making. "We cannot forfeit or relinquish," declared he, "the financial part of our economic progress. We must show we can manage money; and we are going to do it."

Representatives of the thirty-one banks in the National Negro Bankers Association, and others interested, came to Philadelphia in larger numbers than even Major Wright had anticipated. At the beginning of the year when he sent out his first release, he had said the bankers were coming to Philadelphia; it mattered not how small the number might be. It would increase with the development of time.

In the first session of this their seventh Annual Convention held at the Catherine Street Y. W. C. A. Building, he struck the keynote — Negro Bank Union and Confidence. No bank, he warned could stand alone. The failure of any bank irrespective of its management was a menace to all banks. Through united effort the Negro banks could restore confidence to the Negro people. Through Negro bank union and stabilized finance there would be opportunities for our young people graduating from schools of accounting and finance.

The following sessions were held at the Union Baptist and other churches in that immediate area. Major Wright was reelected President for the seventh time; Mrs. Maggie L. Walker, Vice President; Mr. C. C. Spaulding, Treasurer; and Mr. M. C. Martin, Cashier of the Danville Savings Bank and Trust Company, Secretary.

As the closing act of their seventh annual convention, the President, other officers and members of that association left Philadelphia at six o'clock in the morning and motored to the Stock Exchange in New York City. Soon after 10 o'clock they were on the floor of the Stock Exchange. From the floor they went into the gallery where they observed the trading for an hour and a half. From the dizziness of Wall Street back to the "What's your hurry?" atmosphere of South Street, Philadelphia, the organizer and manager of money and men went with inspiration to forge ahead through the financial fog.

He organized through the good offices of his daughter, Mrs. Harriet Wright Lemon, as executive secretary, and Mrs. Sue Belle Littlejohn as President, the "Housewives Association." At his suggestion, this Association adopted as its objectives: economy, better home management and boosting Negro business. In line with these goals, it served for the benefit of one of the Negro business organizations, a beautiful luncheon for one hundred and twelve persons at a total cost of five dollars.

At his suggestion, it conducted table setting contests, and studied the budgeting of its members' household allowances or daily hand-outs, as the case might be. Through his influence some of the city's business concerns such as Abbott's Dairy Company and The Philadelphia Electric Company invited its members to their establishments and entertained them free of charge. The latter company presented them with waffle irons for their cooking school. Through his wife, Mrs. R. R. Wright, Senior, one dozen dresses were made for their "Shower" for needy school children, and for their pre-school clothes "Shower."

In addition to these activities, Major Wright encouraged them to open individual savings accounts, although some of them could deposit only ten cents a week at first.

He watched their development and got a thrill out of seeing grown women deposit money in a bank for the first time in their lives; enter night school and open business for themselves.

Through his inspiration and far sightedness, and with Mrs. Lemon's aid, the "Thrift Committee" of the Citizens and Southern Bank and Trust Company was organized. It increased its membership to two hundred and fifty women with each having her own account and with a total in individual monthly deposits of five hundred dollars.

Inspired by these and other ventures even during the days of depression, Major Wright broadcasted a folder in which was listed various departments of the Citizens and Southern Bank and Trust Company. "Open a savings account with $1.00, he urged, "and thereby join the other three thousand nine hundred persons who are glad they have a savings account with the Citizens and Southern Bank and Trust Company. Start a checking account with $50.00. Pay all your bills by check — the best form of receipt and one of the best ways to gain respect and regard, he continued.

Make your family and yourself happy at Christmas time by joining one of the Christmas Club Classes for fifty cents a week to five dollars per week. Travel broadens the individual and gives him new inspiration to do better work. See different parts of the country and the world by joining one of our Vacation Club Classes ranging from $1.00 to $10.00 per week. Rent one of our safe deposit boxes for only three dollars a year — a very small insurance premium on your valuable papers which if destroyed by fire may not be duplicated. Our Trust Department offers advice and counsel on all matters pertaining to estates. Appoint the bank your executor and trustee. Individuals with financial difficulties come to us for assistance. Deposit with the Citizens and Southern Bank and

Trust Company, have security to protect the amount borrowed, and get first preference."

On the back of this folder there were comments by such prominent Philadelphia bankers as Mr. O. Howard Wolfe and Mr. Morton J. Klank. Mr. Wolfe as cashier of the Philadelphia National Bank had already written saying: "Major Wright: I congratulate you upon the liquid position of your bank, which is very commendable and certainly should inspire confidence in your depositors." On the 23rd of February 1932, he received another letter from Mr. Wolfe:

RECONSTRUCTION FINANCE CORPORATION
WASHINGTON

Philadelphia Loan Agency
O. Howard Wolfe
Manager, R. F. C.

Office address:
Federal Reserve Bank
Philadelphia, Pa.

Mr. R. R. Wright, Sr., President
Citizens and Southern Bank and Trust Company,
19th and South Streets, Philadelphia

Dear Major Wright:

I am interested to have your letter of February 20, and commend and congratulate you upon the excellent work you have been doing. I have frequently referred to the meeting which you sponsored last summer and which was conducted with such good results. I could wish there were other bankers as far sighted and as resourceful as you have proved yourself to be.

Your very truly,
(signed) O. Howard Wolfe.

Through the wisdom, resourcefulness and integrity of the President of this bank — the only one then in full operation owned and managed by Negroes north of the

Mason and Dixon line — it became a City, State and Federal depository.

In appreciation of this financial progress on the 10th of April 1933 — Major Wright was presented with a two and one-half-foot Silver Loving Cup by the Citizens of Philadelphia. Later in that year, his great worth and achievement were recognized by Mr. Ellis W. Gimbel of that city; and expressed in the presentation to him of the replica of a model given Amelia Earhart at a banquet shortly after her solo flight across the Atlantic Ocean. This replica of the model given the woman who had earned the Gimbel Award as the most outstanding woman of America in 1932, President Wright was told by Mr. Gimbel, signified the high esteem in which his own achievements were held by the Gimbel Award Committee.

PART II

In the early months of that year — 1933 — as he moved about the historic city of Philadelphia, he was reminded of the fact that the 100th anniversary of the birth of the American Anti-Slavery Society was at hand. Upon further thought he conceived the idea of celebrating this significant anniversary and the 70th year of Negro Emancipation. It was not an easy matter to sell the idea to proud Philadelphia black people who wished to forget their gloomy past. Neither were they credulous of his suggestion to ask the Federal Postal Department to issue a special 70th anniversary stamp with the head of Frederick Douglass on it. Such a request had never been made before, therefore, as they saw it, the utter uselessness of originating it then.

However, with foresight and the words of the late James

Weldon Johnson in his heart, "We have a roll of honor too, of which we are not ashamed," he forged ahead against even the unexpressed desires of his family who feared for his health. He organized a citizens' committee for the promotion of the "70th Anniversary Celebration of Negro Progress." That title he figured would please everybody.

He wrote the Secretary of the Postal Department, the President, and Mrs. Roosevelt with regard to the issuance of this Special Commemorative Stamp. In view of the fact, as stated by the Post Office Department, that numerous other requests preceded this one, it would not be possible to grant it then. Mrs. Roosevelt felt that since a stamp was not issued on the 50th anniversary, it would be more impressive on the 75th or 100th anniversary of Negro Progress. Major Wright not only found comfort in the fact that the application had been made,.and the Negro people of the country would finally press the idea to its consummation, but continued his efforts for its realization.

He rose mornings with the 70th anniversary celebration ideas buzzing in his mind. He left home earlier than usual in his attempts to meet his many engagements and didn't return for luncheon. With still that "keen scent for news," he knew the importance of wide publicity and gave it. As a result of his planning and his tireless efforts the "70th Anniversary Celebration of Negro Progress" was held in Convention Hall under the auspices of the Citizens and Southern Bank and Trust Company the middle of September 1933. It featured the Negro's development in Business, Science, Education, Politics, Art and Religion. It got off to a good start with the great parade of which Mr. Walter C. Beckett, Pennsylvania's Grandmaster of the Masons, was Grand Marshal.

The first day's showing was of such a high order, the Mayor of Philadelphia, Mayor J. Hampton Moore, commended Major Wright in the progress of a speech to a large group which met in his richly furnished reception room in City Hall. On the fifth and closing night of the celebration, Rev. E. D. Caffee, acting editor of the Christian Review of Philadelphia, offered the following resolution:

"That this audience of thousands of citizens here assembled give to Major R. R. Wright, President of the Citizens and Southern Bank and Trust Company, our most hearty commendation for the preparation and rendition of this 70th Anniversary Celebration of Negro Progress. And we pledge him anew our group support in the efficient conduct of the Citizens and Southern Bank and Trust Company with its matchless record of solvency."

The resolution was unanimously adopted by the raising of hands and a viva vote of about 13,000 people crowded into Convention Hall. The thousands of letters of commendation which literally poured into Major's office were too numerous to begin to mention except in so far as businesss, civic, religious, political, professional, fraternal and otherwise leaders emphasized the fact that Major Wright had brought together the largest group of Negroes in one place and at one time they had ever seen. Some said they were taken off their feet at the sight of such a crowd. Others claimed they had lived in Philadelphia over forty years and had never seen before such a crowd of Negroes gathered together in one place. One commentator called attention to the doubters who said it couldn't be done. Another said, it was more than a success; it was marvelous. It had cemented the friendship of the friends of the Citizens and Southern Bank and Trust Company and won other friends for it.

Another achievement of Major Wright and the Citizens and Southern Bank and Trust Company that won friends, was the bank's acceptance into the membership of the American Bankers Association. "This Bank," he had posted on the outside of the bank, "is protected by the William J. Burns International Detective Agency, Inc., for American Bankers." "This Bank is insured against burglary and robbery."

Like the interchange of sunshine and rain, the happiness of his great victories was soon to be mingled with the saddest thing on earth to him — the loss of his wife and companion of fifty-six years. If it had been a loss of money, he thought he might have by hard work and economy retrieved that. If it had been a loss of his own health, he believed he might possibly have prayed as hard as he did before, dieted, slept, used precaution and regained that. No. The only thing left for him to do was to fight like a true soldier just to remain on his feet and keep inching along. Therefore, when he contemplated going on a South American cruise and stopping off at Haiti, his friends warned against it. In their estimation even the four-day voyage to Haiti would be too much for him in his rest broken, worried condition. He accepted their advice with courtesy and grace, but decided to go; and did go.

While he was in Haiti he spent several hours in the Haitian Bond Market and despite its critical condition, bought and traded some with his usual caution. Reinvigorated by such experience with black business men, he returned home and began to lay plans for the exchange of business with the Haitian Government.

At the same time he kept up his fight on behalf of the Commemorative stamp, and the next Negro Progress Celebration. He wrote the President of the United States again and every Governor of the United States requesting their opinion of the celebration of Negro Progress in this country. For example, he wrote Governor Eugene Talmadge of Atlanta, Georgia, on the 25th of July, 1933. In his letter he requested the Governor's opinion on the respect in which he felt Negroes had notably improved in intelligence, education, homes, standards of living, religion, church, as laborers and in their opportunities for employment.

In reply to his letter, Governor Talmadge said the educational progress of Negroes was marked. The heads of most of the educational institutions for Negroes were outstanding he felt, in ability, principle and efficiency. As to Negro homes, he knew many owned their own homes and some of them he noticed were as fine as they could be. They liked nice homes. They had more money and spent it more sensibly. They dressed much better and had more pride in their personal appearance. Great improvement, the Governor noted in every way had been made. When he came to their religion, he said they had always been a religious people, and he didn't know if their religious fervor could have improved. In answering the question of employment, he thought their chances for employment in all lines of work or trade were fine and they often made the most desirable laborers. In the South, he was sure, one would find the preference was for colored labor. He closed with the thought that their progress in every way had been more marked and pronounced than that of any other race or people.

This reply was among the forty-five or more that interested Major Wright the most, because he was born in Georgia and had lived there all of his life. His mention to the Governors of the fact that the Emancipation Proclamation concerned the whole nation, shamed nobody, and therefore, was similar in spirit to the Declaration of Independence, was the least commented upon of all the suggested topics. However, all the letters were so encouraging, Major Wright began to imagine a successful climax to his efforts for the Commemorative stamp.

Despite his aroused hopes, the stamp did not materialize. However, for the celebration of the 71st anniversary of the Emancipation Proclamation and Negro Progress which took place in Convention Hall again and on the 18th of October 1934, the late President Franklin Delano Roosevelt sent the following message of greeting:

Hyde Park, N. Y.

"Mr. R. R. Wright, Sr., Prs.
Citizens and Southern Bank and Trust Co.,
Philadelphia, Pennsylvania.
My dear Mr. Wright:

I count it a privilege to participate, even from a distance, in this meeting assembled to commemorate the noble and far-seeing act of Abraham Lincoln, at once humane and wise, which opened the way to a larger and more responsible share in the life of this nation to millions of Americans. It is altogether fitting that we should hold in grateful remembrance the distinguished acts of our predecessors in the life of this, our country, not only as a means of rendering well merited honor, but also in order that we, ourselves, by contemplation of worthy deeds, may be stimulated to emulate them.

However, while legal freedom has indeed come to all the citizens of the United States, we cannot say that complete liberation abides in this land so long as multitudes of its people lack the economic basis of a well-rounded existence. We cannot count ourselves wholly free until all our neighbors, within and without our borders, attain the opportunity for the fullest development of which they personally are capable. The Emancipation Proclamation is a guide, and not a goal, for all mankind.

Very sincerely yours,
(signed) Franklin D. Roosevelt."

Major Wright appreciated this acknowledgment from the President of the United States so much he printed it on the first half of the second page of his official Souvenir Program. On the second half of that page appeared the following letter from President Stenio Vincent of the Republic of Haiti.

(Translated) Port-au-Prince, Haiti

"Mr. R. R. Wright, Sr., President
Citizens and Southern Bank and Trust Co.
Philadelphia, Pennsylvania.

Dear Mr. Wright:

Neither my government nor the people of Haiti know how to be indifferent to the manifestations commemorating the Emancipation Proclamation of the colored American. I appreciate highly the opportunity which is offered me to express to the Americans of color the part, which, from afar, we are taking in the legitimate joy and the justifiable pride which they symbolize by this grand event.

By their discipline, their solidarity, and their willingness to work, they have demonstrated well that it was not a favor this Emancipation, but the restitution of a right which they have exercised with reserve, with courage, and with a sense of liberty which, truly, they honor.

This guesture of Abraham Lincoln, was not an act strictly American. By his example, by his high humanity, he has acquired a universal radiance. Happy consequence of the ideas springing from the French Revolution, it is with the Proclamation of the Independence of Haiti, the most beautiful example in America of the Triumph of Right, and the Victory of Justice.

Why should we not participate with all our thoughts and soul in your splendid celebration. Interpretative of my personal sentiments, as well as those of my Government and the Haitian people, I send you my cordial congratulations and my entire affiliation in the legitimate and solemn homage which on this day you render to the memory of this citizen of Humanity, the late Abraham Lincoln.

(signed) Steno Vincent.

As a part of the cover design of the Official Souvenir Album, the symbolic Black Boy of Atlanta sat on the Stars and Stripes proclaiming, "Tell 'em we are rising." There were also in the picture of the cover design Haitian peasants picking coffee.

In this souvenir album were printed the Emancipation Address, by Bishop R. C. Ransom of the A.M.E. Church; articles and pictures of the Republic of Liberia; the Republic of Haiti; Abbyssinia and the Virgin Islands. The night of the celebration, twelve thousand Negroes again packed Convention Hall. The wives of the ministers who had cooperated in the celebration plans marched down the center aisle dressed in white, each wearing a red carnation. The O. V. Catto Elks filed in with Military step. Then as Major Wright with military bearing and dignity against a background of full dress and almost snow white hair, marched down the aisle to the platform accompanied by the Haitian delegates and their escorts, all in full dress, the people burst into a thunderous roar of applause and stood until he and his guests were seated. Hall Johnson's choir of five hundred voices sang, and Kenneth Goodman played the great organ. The Lincoln University quartette and choir and the Cheyney Training School singers followed with touching melody. Mr. Finley Wilson, Exalted Ruler of the Elks, introduced Dr. . C. Dorsainvil of Haiti whose message of greetings from the Haitians to the American Negroes was presented in French and then interpreted by Dr. Camille Lherisson. Messrs. Charles Vincent — Brother of President Stenio Vincent, Henry Ch. Rosemond and Albert Blanchet — the other members of the Haitian delegation were introduced. Dr.

George E. Haynes, Secretary of the Race Relations Division of the Federal Council of Churches of Christ in America — who had recently returned from a trip to Africa, brought a message from Native Africans to Negro Americans; and President Leslie Pinckney Hill of Cheyney Training School responded as an American for the Americans. A closing feature of the celebration was a florescent display of a large Haitian coffee pot; and Haitian coffee was sold at the rear of the great auditorium.

After the celebration, Major Wright visited in Florida with his daughter and her husband, Mrs. and Mr. Clayton, Insurance Executive, and then went on a tour of the country for nearly five thousand miles.

As he went he promoted a movement for the importation and sale of Haitian coffee in this country. Already he had imported 10,000 pounds and had received a letter from Haiti stating he could get 40,000 pounds more in a few months.

Impelled by his secret ambition and the necessity for crowding out his great sorrow — the death of Mrs. Wright — he worked like a man compelled to save himself from drowning; but into his life abundance of rain was to fall that year. A second great shock was soon followed by a third of almost equal severity. He lost his son-in-law, Mr. L. B. Thompson, who for years had been a close friend and a Director in the Citizens and Southern Bank and Trust Company. Following his passing, another Director of the Bank, who had been a warm friend of President Wright and his family for some years, was run over by an automobile and killed instantly.

Deeply affected by these irreparable losses, his family saw some of his Indian fire die down, and as they feared, go completely out. Not so. He had already begun to learn as never before something of the solace, the efficacy and the life fuel in new adventure. Accordingly, he tanked up not with Blue Sonoco but with the Haitian Coffee and Trading Products Company's coffee. He sent his youngest son who had become Treasurer of both the Citizens and Southern Bank and Trust Company and the Haitian Coffee and Products Trading Company on a business mission to Haiti with the following letter of introduction:

"Monsieur Marcel Monfils
Directeur du Service de la Production Agricole
et Enseignement Rural
Port-au-Prince, Haiti
Cher Monsieur Monfils:

J'ai le plaisir de vous presenter le porteur de la presente, Monsieur Emanuel Crogman Wright, Tresorier de la Citizens & Southern Bank and Trust Company de Philadelphia, et aussi tresorier de la Haitian Coffee and Products Trading Company. Cette Derniere Compagnie a ete fondee par le pere de Mr. Wright, il y a de cela quelques temps, dans le but de lancer le cafe haitian sur le Marche des Unis.

Le Major Wright, pere de Mr. Emanuel Wright, est mon bon ami. Il est venue en Haiti il y a de cela quelques temps. Je vous serai tres reconnaissant d'accorder a Mr. Wright toute l'assistance qu'il pent desirer relativement a sa mission en Haiti.

Avec mes sinceres remerciments, je vous prie d'agreer, cher Monsieur monfils, mes salutations empressees.

Vice President & Directeur."

In his son's brief absence, President Wright planned a campaign for New Depositors. One of the methods employed in this campaign was to display replicas of a poster on all the Philadelphia billboards. "Now is the time to Deposit in the Citizens and Southern Bank and Trust

Company, 19th and South Streets. It's safe. Ask 5,000 Satisfied Depositors. City and State Depository, member of the National Credit Association, No. 1 of the third Federal Reserve District." Through his unceasing activities and wisdom, his bank had at the close of this campaign resources in excess of four hundred thousand dollars.

When one of the bank's participants in a campaign failed to turn in the money collected for the bank, President Wright became furious, "Bring that money down right now," he commanded. When that participant attempted to out duel him by lining up with a young city employee thirty years old and weighing about one hundred and sixty-five pounds, President Wright became more enraged. One day as he — seventy years old and weighing one hundred and thirty-five pounds — drove through the streets of Philadelphia and saw this young city employee, he jumped out of his car and approached him.

"I've got a good mind to thresh you with my cane." When one of the leading Negro weeklies — "The Afro American" of Baltimore — mistakenly printed a falsehood circulated by these two opponents of the bank saying, "Citizens and Southern Bank and Trust Company is to close its doors," President Wright sued that paper for $100,000.00. Yet, this same weekly carried in its September 21st, 1940 edition a full page photograph — suitable for framing — of Major Wright, with the inscription, "At 85, he's the No. 1 Banker in the United States."

Cognizant of the current financial and economic situation of the country and of what the failure of any bank, especially a Negro bank would mean to his own bank, and concerned about the economic progress of his people, when the Keystone Co-operative Banking Association of Philadelphia closed its doors, Major Wright did his utmost to save the situation. In the face of feverish anxiety among its depositors, and other difficulties, he undertook the liquidation of that bank. He instructed each employee to keep his nerve and be so well acquainted with the liquidity of the bank he could face any problem that might arise.

After one year's time, the situation was satisfactorily taken care of and the two banks merged into one with combined assets amounting to $496,00. That merger, The Citizens and Southern Bank and Trust Company, continued to build up its investments account to such an extent that it acquired the reputation of being one of the most liquid banks in Philadelphia. During the Christmas holidays when it completed the payment of the Christmas Club fund of nearly $50,000 and the payment of $25,000 to the foster mothers of the Bureau of Colored Children, there was nobody happier than Major Wright.

He came to the conclusion as the bank approached its sixteenth anniversary, that its two major objectives should be to increase its deposits and encourage the Haitian Coffee and Products Trading Company to sell more coffee. The accomplishment of this first aim, in the face of its own higher tax rate imposed by the government, the increased taxation on business which automatically affected the bank, business recession and other economic difficulties, was not an easy matter. Then too, the State Legislature ordered that the capital of the bank be increased from $125,000 to $300,000. In addition to these complications, Major Wright was convinced the building next door to the bank should be purchased by it while the owner was desirous of the cash. That was done and the other extra expenses were met. Still at the close of 1937 the Citizens and Southern Bank and Trust Company was one of the most liquid banks in Pennsylvania.

To accomplish his second aim, encouragement of the Haitian Coffee and Products Trading Company, he purchased a nicely decorated Haitian Coffee truck, Major Wright's Genuine Haitian Coffee Truck, 5293 S.

19th Street, Phone Pen. 9044. He placed it on the streets of Philadephia for the delivery of Haitian Coffee to the doors of all Haitian and would be Haitian Coffee drinkers. He had Haitian Coffee broadcasted over the radio. Through him and with the encouragement of the Citizens and Southern Bank and Trust Company, beginnings of Haitian Coffee branches were established in Philadelphia, Newark, New Jersey; Pittsburgh, St. Louis and Jacksonville, Florida. As a commentator on "Major Wright's Genuine Haitian Coffee," Dr. George Washington Carver of Tuskegee Institute wrote him:

"I pride myself on knowing good coffee, and I consider this you are selling unusually fine. I congratulate you upon this fine brand of coffee." Even the chief chef of the White House in Washington, D. C., and the maid to Mrs. Eleanor Roosevelt — the McDuffies — wrote Major Wright they had not words to express how much they had enjoyed the wonderful Haitian coffee. A representative of the Philadelphia Tribune who had lunch one day in the private office of Banker and Coffee Importer R. R. Wright, accused him of making the best Haitian coffee one can drink. Banker and Coffee Importer, Major Wright himself, found his greatest satisfaction in the fact that Haitian coffee was grown, imported, promoted, roasted, packed and sold by Negroes. He took equal pride in the realization that its sale was encouraged by the Citizens and Southern Bank and Trust Company which had during the past eighteen years, assisted more than one hundred churches, five hundred businesses, and five thousand individuals. It had done this through loans which had helped them out of their financial difficulites or increased their business; in the aggregate amount of $875,-000.00.

His serious concern about economic opportunities for the young people of his race, thrust him into the role of a sponsor of equal opportunities for young Negroes to participate in the United States Government's plan to train 20,000 aviators to be named by President Franklin Delano Roosevelt.

In the furtherance of this cause, he organized a Philadelphia Chamber of Commerce one of whose principal objectives was the promotion of aviation in line with the government's plan for the youth of the country. Moreover, in keeping with President Wright's own example of business possibilities for the Negro, and effort to boost Negro business, he incorporated as the other purposes of this Chamber of Commerce:

To encourage, aid and give support to Negro business in Philadelphia and its vicinity.

To create and maintain commerce between this country and Haiti.

To serve as a clearing house for Negro business.

To collect and classify all important reports, and information concerning the progress of Negro business in the Philadelphia locality.

To investigate and suggest new and profitable business opportunities for Negro youth.

To aid in the preparation of credit reports on individual members of the Chamber of Commerce.

To help co-ordinate the religious, social and civic interest of the Negro along economic lines.

To dramatize its aims, President Wright flew to Richmond, Virginia, and back to Philadelphia on the first leg of a Good Will Tour.

On the second leg of his Good Will Flight, he accompanied his son, Mr. E. C. Wright, and his same pilot, Mr. Anderson, for more than 250 miles. This time they set out as messengers of the Good Will Spirit of the American Negro to the Haitians in Haiti. To give solidarity and meaning to that message, Major Wright sought to use the trip also to increase their export trade in coffee to the

United States. He called upon cities en route to take Haitian coffee in quantities. As a result, the citizens of Norfolk, for example pledged themselves to take 250 pounds. Those of Jacksonville, Florida, with the aid of President Long of Edward Waters College, Mr. A. Lewis, and Attorney S. D. McGill, took 500 pounds. One Negro woman of that city, Miss Sarah White known as a Doctor of Mercy, took 100 pounds. Some other cities also cooperated in a similar manner and thus helped to swell the export of Haitian coffee to the United States since 1933 to more than 10 million pounds.

Subsequently, Major Wright engaged in having a Picture Travelogue made of this round trip flight to Haiti — the first successful foreign flight over water ever made by Negroes.

With little warning, the most heartless war the world has ever witnessed cut off Major Wright's trade with Haiti and checked some of his plans for the youth. "However," he smiled, "it's an ill wind that blows nobody good." That one blew the youth groups from the various churches, from the Thrift Committee, from the homes, from the factories and the shops into the Citizens and Southern Bank and Trust Company with deposits. These deposits and Major Wright's business acumen during those five years increased the resources of this bank from eight hundred thousand dollars — $800,000 — to three million dollars — $3,000,000.

During that period, while the late President Franklin Delano Roosevelt emphasized, and rightly so, the Four Freedoms, Major Wright worked for the One Freedom; and a National Freedom Day to promote good will and harmonious cooperation among the citizens throughout the country.

As President of "National Freedom Day Association" he said, "the adoption of National Freedom Day is based on the principle of National Freedom This principal implies that all men are not only equally entitled to all the freedoms, but some men in seeking to possess and enjoy these freedoms, must realize they cannot obtain them for themselves without sharing them with others. In practice, they must prove that our declaration of freedom includes all men."

Major Wright believed that National Freedom Day should be February 1 — the anniversary of the passage of the Thirteenth Amendment to the Constitution of the United States in 1865. The Thirteenth Amendment, he said, is one of the most important pieces of legislation in our constitution. It not only freed the black man legally, but laid the ground work for the white man's also. In the light of the world's struggle for freedom, we should cultivate this underlying principal — the brotherhood of man — which National Freedom Day promotes. Major Wright asked that National Freedom Day be enacted into law by the United States Congress.

Although this was not done immediately, President Franklin Delano Roosevelt approved the idea and sent him the following message for the 1943 Celebration:

The White House
Washington

Dear Major Wright:

I am happy to send you my greetings on this significant anniversary. Freedom is a word which, in these days of war and struggle, means more to all Americans than it has ever meant before. It is freedom that we are defending on seas and continents all over the world; it is freedom that we are striving to win for the prostrate nations who are already in bondage to the slave-masters of the Axis.

It is a tribute to our maturing democracy that here in America all races, all creeds, are fighting side by side in the righteous crusade to make freedom possible everywhere. And we are giving a good account of ourselves.

On February 1, 1865, President Lincoln approved the Resolution of the Congress which; when acted upon by the sovereign states, wrote the Thirteenth Amendment into our Constitution. Seventy-eight years is only a little longer than the Scriptural span of one man's lifetime. The steady progress of our Negro citizens in that time emphasizes what can be accomplished by free people in a free country. They have come a long way.

As you observe National Freedom Day, I want to express confidence that a race which has achieved so much in so few years will go forward to even greater accomplishments in the years and generations ahead.

Very sincerely yours,

Franklin D. Roosevelt.

Major R. R. Wright, Sr.,
Chairman,
National Freedom Day Committee,
Philadelphia, Pa.

On every succeeding National Freedom Day, Major Wright had the great pleasure of receiving a similar message from the President of the United States. For the February 1947 Celebration, he obtained President Harry S. Truman's message and had it read with his own appreciative emphasis.

The White House
Washington
January 31, 1947

Dear Major Wright:

I am happy indeed to send a message of greeting and encouragement to the group gathered in Philadelphia to celebrate Freedom Day.

When President Lincoln signed the Joint Resolution

proposing the Thirteenth Amendment, he set into motion the machinery which resulted in the abolition of chattel slavery. By this enactment the master and the slave were both liberated; the master from the moral stain, the slave from the yoke of bondage.

The cause of freedom is one we must all work for today and every day. As long as tolerance and bigotry exist, we must work to free intolerant men from the bonds of their own prejudice which are too often heaped upon them.

To help you and to help me in the fight against intolerance, I have recently created the President's Committee on Civil Rights. I know you will give this Commttee full support in its great task; and I know you can count on this Committee to work, as you are working, in the cause of freedom everywhere.

Very sincerely yours,

Harry S. Truman.

Major R. R. Wright, Sr.,
President,
National Freedom Day Association,
Citizens & Southern Bank & Trust Building,
Corner South and 19th Streets,
Philadelphia 46, Pennsylvania.

To his great joy, every year on this occasion, the President of the United States sent a message to him as President of National Freedom Day.

Also the governors of twenty-eight States sent letters or delegates to one of the early celebrations of this occasion. Among the delegates and speakers whom he welcomed were: Dr. Channing H. Tobias of New York, Executive of the Phelps Stokes Fund, D. Rufus E. Clements, President of Atlanta University, Dr. John W. Davis, President of W. Virgina State College, Lij Araya Abebe of Ethiopia, relative of Haile Salassi, Hon. John J. Davis, Senator from Pennsylvania, Hon. Joseph F. Cuffey, U. S. Senator from Pennsylvania, Dr. J. S. Clark, President-Emeritus Southern College, Louisiana, Hon. William C. Bullitt, former Ambassador to Russia and France, Hon. Bernard Samuel, Mayor of Philadelphia, Bishop D. H. Sims, A. M. E. Church, Attorney J. E. Mitchell, appointed by Gov. Saltonstall of Massachusetts, President Charles Wesley of Wilberforce University, President Benjamin F. Hubert of Georgia State College; Professor W. A. Shields and A. L. Holsey of Tuskegee Institute.

He was especially proud of the music as rendered on these occasions by Mme. A. C. Bilbrew of Hollywood. She not only captivated him, with her own compositions: "This is Freedom Day," and "Let's Go America," but Mayor Bernard Samuel and the people of Philadelphia.

In the meantime Major Wright's labors with the individual States for the passage of National Freedom Day legislation never ceased. The first four States to share his faith and pass such a bill were: Pennsylvania, Maine, West Virginia, and Ohio. Through his influence, the State of Pennsylvania appropriated $5,000 annually for the Celebration of National Freedom Day. Honorable Edward Martin — former Governor of Pennsylvania and the first Governor to approve National Freedom Day, and U. S. Senator from Pennsylvania sent the following message on a National Freedom Day.

Philadelphia 7, Pa.

U. S. SENATE
Washington, D. C.

Dear Major Wright:

I regret exceedingly my inability to be with you today. Nothing could give me more pleasure than to join with you and your associates in the celebration of National Freedom Day. You may state that in view of the fact that I secured legislative action and issued a proclamation endorsing National Freedom Day in Pennsylvania that I will do everything I can to see that Congress enacts the joint resolution now pending before the Judiciary Committee, H. J. Res. 94, "a proclamation designating the 1st day of February of each year as National Freedom Day —." Put me down as an ardent supporter of the National Freedom Day celebration in honor of the joint resolution adopted by Congress and signed by Abraham Lincoln February 1st, 1865.

Very sincerely,
Edward Martin

Major R. R. Wright, Sr.
President, Citizens and Southern
Bank Trust Company
1849 South Street
Philadelphia, Pennsylvania

In addition, Major Wright always received a communication from the Mayor of Philadelphia for the occasion. On the 29th day of January 1947, Mayor Bernard Samuel wrote:

Bernard Samuel, Mayor:

PROCLAMATION

FREEDOM DAY

Whereas, the Thirteenth Amendment to the Constitution of the United States, abolishing slavery and enforced servitude, was proposed by the Thirty-eighth Congress on February 1, 1865, and later declared ratified by the Secretary of State: and

Whereas, for several years it has been the custom to observe February 1 as "Freedom Day;" and

Whereas, it is particularly appropriate to observe Freedom Day in February, because of the birth during that month of Abraham Lincoln; and

Whereas, an interesting program has been arranged to mark Freedom Day in Philadelphia, on Saturday, February 1, 1947, including a meeting in Congress Hall at 10 A. M., exercises at Independence Hall at Noon and a luncheon at the Ritz-Carlton Hotel at 2 P. M.; together with a mass meeting to be held at the Academy of Music on Sunday, February 2;

NOW, THEREFORE, I, BERNARD SAMUEL, Mayor of the City of Philadelphia, designate Saturday, February 1, 1947 as FREEDOM DAY in the City of Philadelphia for the observance of the anniversary of an event which, rightfully, was outstanding in American and world history; and

FURTHER, I urge as many of our people as possible to participate in the meetings which have been arranged in connection with Freedom Day.

Given under my hand and the seal of the City of Philadelphia this twenty-ninth day of January, one thousand nine hundred forty-seven

Bernard Samuel.

National Freedom Day, yet to be achieved, and its celebrations are indicative of Major Wright's studiousness, courage, perseverance and genius for pioneering. Although it has not become an actuality, progress has been made, and the bill designating February 1st as National Freedom Day has been signed by President Harry S. Truman and enacted into law by the United States Congress.

"It is these and like qualities of mind and heart that

make a man a pioneer; that make a man immortal, irrespective of race, color or creed." Of Major Wright these words were said by Dr. Alexander Stoddard, Superintendent of the Philadelphia Public Schools. They were spoken to Murrell Dobbins Vocational Technical School on the morning of June 5, 1946. It was on that day "Murrell Dobbins Day," that Major Wright as President of the Citizens and Southern Bank and Trust Company was presented with the "Pioneers of Industry Award" given each year by Murrell Dobbins Vocational-Technical School.

Preparatory to his trip out to Murrell Dobbins School that morning, flanked on the right by his daughter, Mrs. Clayton, and on the left by his son, Mr. E. C. Wright, he descended the stairs of his home somewhat painfully. Dressed in a penciled gray suit, tie and socks to match, neat black shoes looking as though his feet had been poured into them, he moved slowly downward. Just before he stepped down to the floor of the living room he extended his hand to his friend who was there to accompany him and his son to Murrell Dobbins School.

"Madame," he said, "I'm at my lowest ebb this morning."

"But you're looking good Major. I never saw your cheeks filled out like that before."

"Is that a fact?" He perked up, emphasizing every word, and smiled in evident surprise.

He kissed his daughter goodbye and casually remarked in her hearing, "She got me ready to go out this morning." With the assistance of his son and his cane he got into the car. On the way, he expressed a little anxiety lest they be late. "Mr. Wright," he inquired jocularly, "do you think we'll be there by a quarter of nine?"

"Well, if we don't, we won't lack more than a minute of it," replied his son in like jest.

"If you're a minute late getting up to the Pearly Gates, you might miss heaven." They were more like two boys than father and son.

In a few moments, the windows of the car were pulled down. He was not feeling any too well. Two months of illness — pneumonia and an oxygen tent — and one month's recuperation had not been enough to kill him or to rest him from his ninety-one years of ceaseless labors.

The car rolled up to one of the gates of a magnificent light brick building, Murrell Dobbins Vocation-Technical School, which seemed to cover a whole city block. With the assistance of his son, the teacher who came out to welcome him, and his cane, Major Wright entered the building. As he walked in, the bright sunshine pushed its way through the great big glass windows as if to vie with the gladness in the hearts of the Principal, the teachers and students alike. It was a great morning. Major Wright and Philip Snyder, President of the Student Council, were snapped together as they held the 30-pound "Pioneers of Industry Award" plaque up in front of them.

On the way through a long hall to the platform back of the chapel, Major Wright had evidently forgotten all about his cane. With his head up, his shoulders square, both his hands locked behind him, he stepped like a man twenty-one instead of ninety-one. He faced, he confessed, one of the most inspiring audiences of his experience, eighteen hundred students apparently of every nationality, creed and color, eighty-five teachers — some of them distinctly colored — and thirty teachers for the five hundred veterans enrolled in Murrell Dobbins School.

He took his seat on the rostum and watched the Color Guard — four boys and four girls — come down the aisles to the rostrum holding aloft their big flags of old glory. He rose as the audience rose and sang "The Star Spangled Banner." He heard the great tribute paid Murrell Dobbins by Mr. Frank R. Robinson, Principal of

Mastbaum Vocational School, and the history of the Pioneers of Industry Award as follows by Mr. J. Norwood Baker, Principal of Murrell Dobbins School:

"In 1942, the idea was presented to me to give an award each year to an outstanding pioneer in Philadelphia industry. The suggestion came from Mr. J. Wesley Miller, a former coordinator of this school, who further suggested that the recipient should be one who started without any more educational or financial advantages than any one of you here today possesses. Going on from there, the recipient should have builded a business or established an industry through his own initiative and willingness to work.

We took the idea and through the next year developed it. It was agreed that the visible symbol of this award should be a bronze plaque carrying the seal of the school and the words "Pioneer of Industry Award," as well as the name of the recipient. This plaque was to be designed and executed entirely in the drawing rooms and shops of the school.

Our first recipient was Edward G. Budd; the second 1944, Horace P. Liverside, and in 1945, Walter D. Fuller. We have had this year's recipient in mind for the past year. Major Wright's life has been a succession of pioneering efforts stretching through a great period of American History, from the days of slavery (which we would like to forget) down to today and he still carries on for the good of mankind.

Read the story of his life. It should be an inspiration to every one of you."

Before Mr. Baker took his seat, he introduced Mr. Philip Snyder, President of the Student Council, who presented the Award in the following words:

Dr. Wright as President of the Student Association of Murrell Dobbins, I am most happy to present to you our

"Pioneer of Industry Award," this is truly a product of Dobbins, representative of the arts and skill acquired here. It was designed in Commercial Art, drawn and detailed in machine design, pattern made in Pattern Making, cast in Foundry Practice, machined in Machine Shop, mounted by the Cabinet Makers, finished by Painting and Decorating. As a pioneer in Banking, you have our best wishes for continued success.

In accepting this Award, Major Wright complimented the student body on its impressive appearance. Then he expressed grave doubt that he would ever again be so honored. "I shall cherish it as long as I live; and I hope to hand it down to my children and grand children."

In compliance with Custom, he gave a brief outline of his life. The first time he remembered himself was as one of the slave children down by the side of a trough of food. The second time he remembered himself was when his father refused to be whipped by his master, and either ran away or was killed. The next time he remembered himself was when his Master came to their cabin to tell his mother she was free. As they left their cabin home, he picked up an old ax without a handle and carried it along. All he took out of slavery, he said, was that old ax.

As he told them about his first Blue Back Spelling Book, his 200 mile walk to Atlanta, the Box Car School, Atlanta University, his experience as a teacher, organizer, and college President, and with only a faint allusion to himself as a banker, the whole body sat in rapt attention. "My final words are to trust in God and do the right. Love your fellow man. Treat him as you wish to be treated yourself and God who has made this great Nation will make you of great use to mankind."

In summing up what Major Wright and the other speakers had said, as well as adding his own interpretation, Dr. Alexander Stoddard, Superintendent of the Philadelphia Public School, called attention to the fact that Murrell Dobbins was being honored more than anybody else by her recognition of one of Philadelphia's noblest and most valuable sons. Murrell Dobbins, he continued, was not alone in this recognition and tribute, but in it the 250,000 students and 8,000 teachers of Philadelphia. Said he, if he went to a school meeting of great importance to all the citizens, Major Wright was there. If he went to other civic or religious or political meetings of general importance Major Wright was there. Of course, Major Wright did not know why they were honoring him but they knew. Major Wright's span of life, he noted, had embraced the harnessing of electricity, the invention of the telephone, the automobile and other industrial achievements. They are subject to and due to change but the eternal verities — truth, courage, studiousness, perseverance — which Major Wright exemplified and had taught there that morning were lasting and would make life and achievement immortal. That occasion, he concluded, would not only be remembered by those present during their life time, but it had become historic and would, therefore, be commemorated by all future student bodies of Murrell Dobbins and Philadelphia itself.

Like a wise man, the next day, Major Wright rested in bed. The following day, Friday, he spent the entire day at the Citizens and Southern Bank and Trust Company. Much of the day, he reclined in his special chair but was busy practically every minute. "Yes," he held the telephone receiver, "Is that right? Yes, we've bought nearly two million dollars worth of War Bonds. Trying to do a little something." He looked up at the person who sat in the chair facing his and kindly gave him ten minutes to state his case. Others were waiting to see him.

In less than a year, another great tribute was paid Major Wright as a banker, humanitarian, educator, and brother 92 years young planning to fly to Liberia. This occasion was on a warm evening in late May 1947, around his birthday. A testimonial dinner was given him in the Wedgewood Room of the Bellevue-Stratford Hotel in down town Philadelphia by Central City bankers and other friends.

In that elegant setting he stood at the speakers' table on the dais and shook hands warmly with each of the special guests. His hair almost white now; his thin brown face wreathed in smiles; his slight but agile body for his years clad in a fitting dark suit; his mind seemingly as young as it ever was — keen and alert; his behavior that of a genial, modest, great man who had done nothing unusual drew everybody's attention. On the table in front of him was a huge, beautifully decorated, white birthday cake with ninety-two candles.

"Major Wright is a man of good manners and action; not words" emphasized the key note speaker, Mr. William F. Kriebel, Vice President and Treasurer of the Pennsylvania Company, one of the largest State chartered banking institutions in Pennsylvania. "Even in a telephone conversation, he's brief and to the point, he concluded. Major Wright's cooperation with the other bank officials of the city was praised as follows by Mr. A. C. Graff, Vice President of the same Banking Company. "At the start of the last war when the bank presidents were all assembled for a meeting to begin the sale of War Bonds, Major Wright attended the first meeting — a dinner meeting at the Midday Club. As usual, he volunteered and gave his full services from the start. The Pennsylvania Company has no branch of its own in the neighborhood of 19th and South Streets because we have the Citizens and Southern Bank and Trust Company there."

Major's long, pleasant association with Central Pennsylvania National Bank, and his uplifting work both among his own group and others were high lighted by Mr. Elwell Whalen, Vice President of that bank. Major Wright had been known to Mr. John P. Stuhltrager,

President of the Roosevelt Bank, many years as a "very fine gentleman who did a great deal for his people in the section where the Roosevelt Bank is located."

Mr. O. Howard Wolfe, Vice President of the Philadelphia National Bank, organized in 1803, insisted that Major Wright was first of all a leader and educator. Said Mr. Wolfe: "He has often told me he does not expect or even hope to make money as a banker. His aim is to teach 'his people' to be thrifty, to be good business men and respected citizens. Major Wright is truly a great man. I will conclude with what I consider one of the greatest pieces of constructive work I ever saw a banker do — whether white or black —" Here Mr. Wolfe depicted Major Wright's skill in saving the Citizens and Southern Bank and Trust Company during the banking holiday and depression.

Major Wright's next friend to speak that night was Mr. Harris Vennema, Editor and General Manager of "The Pennsylvania Banker." As an indication of Major Wright's eagerness to be informed on every banking subject, he said when "The Pennsylvania Banker" was started in March 1946, Major Wright was the first and only person who sent in a three year subscription. When things looked gloomy that year for his paper, he always recalled Major Wright's faith in the interprise and in him. Major Wright had not only encouraged him but had done a fine job in encouraging thrift among his people.

Major Wright as a banker and distinguished citizen was honored by the presence of Mr. John Clark Simms, Market Street National Bank; Mr. Charles B. Roberts — The Pennsylvania Company; Mr. Stephen F. Sayer — First National Bank of Philadelphia and a representative of the Land Title Bank & Trust Company; The Reverend Mr. W. C. Williamson, Pastor of White Rock Baptist Church and other friends, and out of town guests who were called upon to speak from the floor remembered and emulated Major Wright's good manners in speaking over the telephone.

Therefore, before the hands of the clock pointed to 9:30, Major himself was thanking everybody for coming out and for saying and doing so much in his honor. He would always hold dear that occasion. Then he confessed he didn't know why so much honor was being thrust upon him. He supposed it was because he was planning a trip to West Africa — the region whence his grandmother came. For a long time, he had wanted to go there, but for some reason or other he hadn't gotten around to it. At any rate, that occasion was a grand one. To be so honored by friends he had worked with through the years made him very, very happy. His slight, fittingly attired old body bowed a gracious "Thank you and good night."

He smiled obligingly as friends crowded around him with their programs in their hands for him to autograph. He sat down like a man half his years and began to write in the midst of a last hand shake; a 'Goodbye, Major," a God bless you and keep you, Major." We've had a wonderful evening. See you soon about that, Major."

CHAPTER X

FAMILY MAN

The following Sunday afternoon, in the midst of a family reunion and birthday celebration in his home, he called a New York City friend on the telephone.

"Is this Edgecombe 4-77—?" With a suggestion of lisp in his high pitched voice.

"Yes, Major. How are you? You looked so well the other night. That was a great dinner."

"Was it? I thought so, too. Glad you were there. Just called up to let you in on this family reunion. Hear them? All of my children! My grandchildren! My great grands! My! My! All about me! Yes, and another big birthday cake with ninety-one lighted candles! I'm going to send you a piece of it. Au revoir, Madame!" With the sound of his voice breaking with joy, he hung up the receiver.

In that same house, thirteen years prior to this, that same friend had seen him hurry down the stairs to his telephone on a lovely spring morning about seven o'clock.

As he went, he tied more tightly the sash belt of his wine red and black figured bath robe trimmed in black satin. He sat back in the chair by the telephone table and took up the receiver.

"Give me Alleghany - 3985, Reverend G. W. H. on Girard near Haverford, —— Thank you."

"Reverend, I'm intruding into your privacy this morning." He listened a moment and laughed in a dry fashion.

"Ha, ha, ha. I'm feeling pretty fair, thank you."

"Well, now let's see. All right, I'll be there. Glad to come. How about the meeting this afternoon?"

"Is that all right? Ha, ha, ha."

"I'm extremely anxious to have you. I'm deeply interested in this proposition."

He hung up the receiver and hurried back upstairs to the bath. In a short while he came down again dressed in his navy blue serge suit and white oxfords with black tips, front and back, ready for business. He drank a glass of orange juice, ate a dish of oatmeal into which he emptied a side dish of applesause and poured rich milk. He drank his cup of coffee and asked politely, but as if there was little time to waste, if his chauffeur was out front with the car. He looked around the table at the members of his family and the friend who had suspended conversation, and led off in a resonant voice and reverent spirit with: "The Lord is my shepherd I shall not want."

His daughter, Jule, at his right followed with: "He maketh me to lie down in green pastures." And so the following verses were recited until the last one given was coterminus with the person to his left. He bowed his head reverently and thanked his Heavenly Father for hope, for health, for opportunity to serve, for the young people, for the Churches of the land, and for the ministers embued with the spirit of the Master. He rose, reached for his cane and suggested to the girls that their mother rest in bed until she was ready to come down town for lunch with him. Then after turning to the friend who was to accompany him, he walked out on his front porch, and unaided stepped into his car and was whisked away.

As the car eased along with cautious rapidity, he gave vent to some emotion akin to a sigh. "Mrs. Wright was in perfect health," he said, "until she was in an automobile accident at the age of 77." "We," as he told the story, "had just bought a large car. She drove up in it and called for him one afternoon.

"Honey, I'm going to town."

"All right," he replied, "looks like rain though."

He said he waited in his office until seven o'clock that

evening and then until eight. Finally someone came who hesitated to tell him what had happened. "Go ahead. Don't keep anything back," he urged. Just as he surmised, the car had turned over and injured her and their youngest son. "Yes, that was fourteen years ago," he spoke a bit triumphantly; and then admitted with the deepest regret that her collar bone was broken and she had never been quite well since.

During those years, instead of her waiting on him, he waited on her. He wouldn't allow anyone to wait on him. "You know men are very helpless," said one of his daughters, "but now he's fine." He even insisted that Mrs. Wright have the white meat of the chicken. In previous years, she had always wanted him to have it because he was a delicate eater, and had dieted all his life, according to his son, Dr. Whittier H. Wright.

They were such pals that even after they had been married fifty-seven years, he spoke of her as a great girl without whom he didn't know what he would have done. "She's been my salvation," he reiterated. "We've had eight children, three boys and five girls. Guess we've done something to increase the population." He smiled, and paused as his thoughts turned backward for a moment.

Every year since their children had gotten up from underfoot, he and Mrs. Wright had taken a trip somewhere together, if only to Atlantic City on their wedding anniversary — June the seventh. On their twenty-fifth wedding anniversary they took a trip to Boston. Their children called it going off on their honeymoon once a year. Yes, they celebrated their Golden Wedding Anniversary, too. Thought they might as well do it he said, they had been married so long and brought up such a large family of children; all of whom had done fairly well. Yes, he had tried to do his part to make a pleasant, comfortable home for them; he humbly admitted. Their mother was not only a great girl, he proudly acknowledged, but as the Georgia State boys had often told him she was the greatest mother they had ever seen or read about.

As he paused, the friend called his attention to a letter she had read from one of his Atlanta University professors — Professor Thomas N. Chase — who once visited his home while he was President of the Georgia State College. "Yes, yes." His retentive memory picked up the thread at once. He recalled Professor Chase's letter which said, he would remember his visit to their home always and would think of Mrs. Wright and Essie and Lillian and Whittier Howard and Edwina and Harriett Beecher Stowe and dear little bright eyed Jack.

Yes, he mentioned too the report of his family and home which his former professor attempted to get the Atlanta Constitution to print without charge. He was amused as he told of the mention of the folks in the article for whom his children were named — "Richard R. Wright, Jr., for his illustrious, etc.; Julia Ophelia for her maternal aunt. Esse Ware for President Ware of Atlanta University; Lillian Mathilda for her maternal grandmother who lived to be eighty-four years old; Whittier Howard for the poet — John Greenleaf Whittier who presented Whittier Howard with a wallet on which was embossed the letters J. G. W.; Edwina who was named for his little late son Edmund who had been named for President Edmund Asa Ware; Harriett Beecher Stowe for the author of "Uncle Tom's Cabin," Emanuel Crogman for Dr. Emanuel K. Love — a famous Southern Baptist Minister and Editor-in-Chief of his paper, "The Weekly Sentinel," and also for Professor Crogman, a classmate of his, a distinguished Greek and Latin scholar and President of Clark University in Atlanta."

He laughed. He had so many children when he returned to the Georgia State Industrial College from his summer study every year, he brought back a trunk full of dress patterns, shirt patterns, etc., for them. He took great pride in surprising Mrs. Wright. One Christmas Eve he had three boys bring up a load of parcels from Savannah, five miles away, and quietly pile them on his front porch just before Mrs. Wright attempted to step out on the porch at eight o'clock in the evening ready to go down town to do the shopping.

He and Mrs. Wright, their children say, were always like two sweethearts. She drew his bath water, got out his clothes; and would have eaten for him if she could. Sunday mornings when they remained in bed later than usual, their children hearing them talk like two old cronies, would gather around their bed. He never knew what it was to have her differ with him. And in his own recollection of their fifty-seven years of married life he couldn't recall that she ever uttered one cross word to him. She anticipated his wishes and would change her plans in a minute to suit his.

Once she rode into Savannah with him to see him off on a trip to Boston. There were urgent duties at home for her; but he wanted her to go with him. She changed her plans and called up her eldest daughter from the station and told her she was going to Boston with her father.

He so trained and disciplined his daughters as well as his sons that he and Mrs. Wright could leave home together once in a great while even when the children were quite young. Three of his daughters laugh about their first attendance at any sort of party at night. It was a Candy-Pull at the Georgie State Industrial College. They had a good time; left the party and arrived home just before ten o'clock. Afraid they had overstayed their time, the oldest girl tried to open the door by taking it off the hinges. When his second daughter, now Mrs. Thompson, received her engagement ring after she had studied at Fisk University one year, she showed it to her father. He took it, threw it across the room and told her she should wait five years. She replied saying, he didn't wait five days.

Two of his daughters did something contrary to his wishes one time. He told them he was going to whip them. They slipped into the house and each put on five or six heavy dresses. He cut them around their little skirt tails in an effort to make them cry. After he had cut and cut, they finally through fear he might begin to cut elsewhere began to moan. He charged them and let them go. According to the version of the older sisters and brothers, he whipped them nearly every day. When his younger children came along he spared the rod. His youngest daughter he never whipped; and his youngest son he whipped only once or twice.

As an example of his frugality, one of his daughters recalled with amusement the first funeral she ever attended. It was that of her baby brother, Edmund. She was glad the child had died so she could ride in a carriage, and she couldn't cry at the "grave yard" because she didn't have a handkerchief.

In spite of his exactions and economies, however, his eight children look back over the years and declare he was the best father in all the world — so ambitious for each child, and for the young people of his race; so tireless in his efforts for progress, so broad and so spiritual. He in turn, spoke of them as his greatest achievement and blessing. Under his administration as President of the Georgia State Industrial College, he saw all of them graduate from that institution except one daughter who went to Atlanta University because of her exceptional musical talent.

After the graduation of his eldest son, R. R. Wright, Jr., he put him on a German boat where no English was spoken and sent him to Germany. Subsequent to his son's obtainment of the degree of Bachelor of Divinity and of

Master of Arts at Chicago University, he said to him, "Now get the smallest church in Chicago." With one member his son organized a mission among the poorest immigrant Negroes of Chicago and made a study of them which was published under the caption, "The Negro in Times of Industrial Unrest." In mentioning this study, Major Wright emphasized the fact that it was through this medium that his son came to study conditions among Negroes in Philadelphia; and later entered business with him as President of the Citizens and Southern Building and Loan Association and Vice President of the Citizens and Southern Bank and Trust Company. Like a chip off the old block, this son's preference for educational work and the ministry led him into the Presidency of Wilberforce University and the Bishopric of the A. M. E. Church.

As Major Wright had wished and planned, this son married Miss Charlotte Crogman, daughter of one of Major's Atlanta University classmates, and a distinguished graduate herself of Chicago University. Through this union Major Wright became the grandfather of three fine girls — all University graduates, married, teaching or in business; of one grandson, R. R. Wright III, a teacher with his A. B. and M. A. degrees — and the great grandfather of four children among whom is R. R. Wright IV.

It is no wonder that Major Wright's daughter, Miss Julia O. Wright, was the immediate instigator of his organizing the Citizens and Southern Bank of Philadelphia. For in his affection, Jule as he called her, occupied a warm spot. To him she was not only a quiet business woman, once Postmistress at College Station Georgia, but his invaluable assistant in keeping the home fires burning after his wife's death.

His facetious eyes twinkled as he laughed about the way Mrs. Essie Ware Thompson kept her engagement ring and brought into the family one of his best friends and business associates; as well as two more granddaughters, both University women teachers. Of a third daughter, Mrs. Lillian Mathilda Clayton, he proudly said, "She taught at Tuskegee under Booker Washington; and married one of Dr. Washington's ablest business assistants, C. C. Clayton." Then he thoughtfully told how she became his own secretary and was the first to sign his application for the charter of the Citizens and Southern Bank of Philadelphia. When some of her girlhood recollections were mentioned, he immediately endorsed them. For example, the family meal when only the particular language — French or German — was spoken was often provocative of great laughter. Family devotions too, he also recalled. One child would read from the Greek Bible, another from the German Bible, still another from the Latin Bible, and a fourth from the English Bible. In conclusion, he would offer prayer.

He not only taught his children to pray, but he believed a father might help them to lay an economic foundation which the precarious storms of social and economic change cannot entirely obliterate, because they have learned to "Find a way or make one." Each one of his three boys and five girls not only had his or her daily work assignment but knew it had to be done.

He encouraged his second son, now Dr. Whittier Howard Wright of Philadelphia, to sell Negro Weekly Newspapers and Magazines when the latter was a college student. Among those he suggested and which his son sold were: "The New York Age" of which the Honorable Fred R. Moore was owner; and "The Voice of The Negro," a magazine of which Dr. Max Barber of Philadelphia was editor and Mr. Silas Floyd — one of his Georgia State College Students — was contributing editor. Subsequently, he paved the way for his son to write for the American Press Association page in the Afro American of which Mr. Carl Murphy is owner. Through this son's marriage to the late Miss Gaynell Walker, Major Wright again became the grandfather of a beautiful girl and three fine boys among whom is another R. R. Wright IV.

As an example of Major Wright's family team work, his fourth daughter, Mrs. Edwina Wright Mitchell who has her weekly column in the St. Louis Argus owned by her husband, Mr. J. E. Mitchell, tells the story of her expressed desire to go to Pratt Institute. She spoke to her father about it. He told her he just couldn't see how he could do it. Didn't have the money. She then confided her eagerness to go with her mother, and heard no more about it until her father had borrowed the money from some Insurance Society and arranged for her to go.

His ability to manage his family as well as a college and a bank was ably expressed in the change which he made in the life plans of his two younger children, Mrs. Harriett Wright Lemon and Mr. Emanuel Crogman Wright, to have them enter the bank with him. He had Mrs. Lemon, now treasurer and a director of the Citizens and Southern Bank and Trust Company, after one year's study at Radcliffe College, to enter the American Institute of Banking and Wharton School of Finance.

He took Mr. Emanuel Crogman Wright, now President of the Citizens and Southern Bank and Trust Company and also of National Freedom Day Association — from his study of architecture at the University of Pennsylvania and Drexel Institute, and from his supporting job as a carpenter, and had him enter Wharton School of Finance. From this son's marriage to Miss Dorothy Bell who also attended Wharton, Major Wright has a seventh granddaughter. Like his grandma Lucy and her great, great grandma Lucy who could dance with a tea cup of water on her head, she is interested in ballet dancing. Major Wright brought his children up in an atmosphere of simplicity so far as material things are concerned. His residence today is a plain Philadelphia eight-room, two-story brick cottage with an enclosed porch extending clear across the front. It is just one of the two-story cottages in the block. The furniture and furnishings are good, but plain and practical. Even the electrical refrigerator and radio were gifts from Miss Edwina to mother and father. His one great enjoyment was a new automobile every few years. His first was a Cline, his second was a Chalmers, and after that, he bought a Chrysler more often than not.

Riding in his Chrysler one afternoon, he listened with a humorous smile to Mrs. Mitchell's recital of his courageous humility and simplicity. "Father has no false ideas," said she. Some years ago Alpha Kappa Alpha Sorority of which she is a member, held its Boule in Philadelphia. She, after arranging to entertain the Boule in their home on a Sunday afternoon, attended a reception the day before given by Mrs. Brown of the erstwhile Brown and Stevens Bank of Philadelphia. On every floor of the Brown home there was an Oriental rug. There were silk spreads on the beds, and silk and velvet drapes and hangings. There were vases collected abroad. There were servants. In just the appropriate places there were garlands of smilax and poinsettia. "Ah, lovely, lovely," the guests were all raving over the gorgeous setting for their party. As a grand climax, Mrs. Brown came down dressed in silver cloth. The home, the hostess, the musical entertainment, the sumptuous feast served in elegant sufficiency, took the guests completely off their feet.

Mrs. Mitchell couldn't enjoy any of it for thinking about their humble home in which she was to entertain that same Boule the next day. She went home and told her mother how 'funny' she felt entertaining the Boule in their humble home after such a "blow out" at the Brown's home. Her mother transmitted the message to her father. The next morning her father said to her, "Well, Edwina, I'm sorry our home isn't as beautiful as you would like. But everything is paid for. I never wished for that kind of finery. My children are my riches." He was so calm and sorrowful his daughter begged his pardon without knowing he had already lent Brown and Stevens $4,000 in an attempt to tide them over a financial crash.

His youngest daughter, Mrs. Lemon, also adds her testimony to her father's heroic simplicity by telling of a meeting of the Board of Directors of the Philadelphia Lyceum sponsoring music, lectures, etc., of which she was a member in another beautiful Negro home. She informed her father she wouldn't have that Board of Directors meet in their home, it was too plain. He replied, "I'm sorry, Harriett, our house doesn't suit you. It's comfortable; and I don't owe a dime on it. It'll be right here one hundred years in my name." His bedroom in that house has three window. It's a light, sunny room plainly furnished. It is not only a quiet spot for rest but for work as well. Close up to his double bed on the right side, were a gate leg table with a lower shelf, and his late wife's sewing machine with a flat top. Both of these were loaded with books, a pad and pencil, and a midget radio. Despite the fact that for the past ten years and more he had adopted the habit of resting in bed every Wednesday; and he retired pracitically every night at eight o'clock, his room had evidences of being a veritable, if not a midnight workshop. In it there was a bookcase. There was also a beautiful one in the study upstairs, full of such books as one would expect to find in the library of such a student. These books by his bedside bore testimony of the hours he spent with them.

For example, LaSainte Bible, Ancien Testament Par Louis Segond, 1917, was so thumbed and worn, he had bought a 1933 edition of it. Also, Die Bibel, ober bie ganze Heilige Schristbes Alten und Nuen Testaments nach ber Deuts Chen Uberseburg: Holy Bible containing Old and New Testaments by Bagsver & Sons (limited) was pencil marked and very aged. On the frayed back of the latter he had written no doubt years ago, judging from the fade out of the ink, and in his own careful, distinct penmanship, "Richard Robert Wright!" There were also a compendious German and English Dictionary; a Grammar of the French Language, Part 1, for Beginners: a Dictionnaire Des Langues Anglaise Et Francaise; French Conversational Lessons: Berlitz French, With or Without A Master; Le Matin-Portau-Prince, Haiti, which he took as a daily; Elwell's Dictionary-Kurzgesabter Grammatsher; The Complete Works of William Shakespeare, elderly and worn, and Essentials in History, Essentials in American History by Albert Bushnell Hart.

Among his other old friends on that table and that machine were: a Novel of Balzac, The Saturday Evening Post, Brazil: Past, Present and Future; The Unemployment Problem: Black Souls with a foreword by Dr. John Haynes Holmes; Better Health through Internal Cleanliness; Battle Creek Sanitarium News — Heart Disease, Wehman's Spanish Without a Teacher; The Meistershaft System with a Quotation from the New York World and an editorial on the study of modern languages "Can't speak and write after years of study;" Financial Section of the New York Times, Sunday edition, July 24, 1938; United States News, July 19, 1938; Moody's Bond Record, and Moody's Investors Service: Talks, January 1938, The National Educational Outlook Among Negroes, Daily Edition, and the Christian Recorder; Think, May 1948, and Nerve Force.

On the table by his bedside there were also telegrams. One read, "Love and greetings on Father's Day to one who deserves more than I can ever repay." Another said, "To the dearest dad in all the world we want you to know how much we love you. We are thinking of you now as always. Many hearty congratulations on the wonderful address you made in Wilberforce. We are all well. Hope you are all well. Write to us. Your children." Near these and other telegrams was a little book — The Bantu are Coming — on the fly leaf of which was the inscription, "To my father from his eldest son on Christmas Day '37. Just a small reminder of the great task of Christian Evangelization yet so incomplete."

The Bantu are coming. In other words, the people are coming. Or in the words of the Black Boy of Atlanta, "Tell 'em we are rising." Yet, so incomplete is the great task of Christian civilization. President Wright, ten years later, in his ninety-second year, a little worn physically after a ninety-year battle with a weak constitution; and pneumonia and an oxygen tent in his ninety-first year, but vigorous and happy, mentally and spiritually, together with his eight children, eleven grandchildren, five great grandchildren, and his many foster sons and daughters continued his work here, and his preparation for an important flight to Africa.

As a part of that preparation, and as a votary of thorough preparedness, for every occasion, he entered the Jefferson Hospital for a physical check-up. The examination was surprisingly revealing. An operation might possibly or not save his life, if he were strong enough to survive it. He, a man of profound wisdom, a man of many battles and few losses, shook his head — "No." He couldn't stand that now. As one friend put it, "God had given him long life because He had so much for him to do." He had done his work; done it well; and was now ready to hand his mantle over to younger shoulders.

He sank rapidly, as if to clear the way and go on, possibly to his second reward. In keeping with that spirit, Dr. Hobart A. Reimann, Professor of Medicine, the Jefferson Medical College of Philadelphia where he spent his last days said, "Major Wright was a very pleasant patient to take care of. He never complained." Throughout his long life, he had been a worker and a fighter for the rights and opportunities of others, not a complainer. Likewise, his last words uttered July 2nd, 1947, were "National Freedom Day."

Shortly after the news of his passing was flashed over the country, telegrams and other messages began to pour in. They came from the President of the United States, the Honorable Harry S. Truman, from Congressmen, from college presidents, faculty and students, from Churchmen of all denominations, from Mr. Ralph McGill, editor of the Atlanta Constitution, from fraternal orders, from bankers, from women's organizations, and from lowly hired hands and washer women. One of these which seemed to embody the thought and spirit of all the rest said, "The passing of Major Wright calls not so much for sympathy and sorrow as it does for appreciation and enrichment upon the part of millions of Americans who share with the Wright family this legacy of manhood, freedom, self confidence and initiative bequeathed to us who are his legitimate heirs. Major Wright belongs to history. May God help this generation to begin where he left off, by holding up the banner he so bravely carried for more than ninety years."

The last rites in honor of Major Wright were held in St. Matthews A. M. E. Church, Philadelphia. Every speaker — including three Bishops, five ministers, the President of Atlanta University, and a young man in his teens, stressed in his own way the heritage Major Wright had bequeathed to those of us left to carry on, irrespective of race, religion, or creed. The Southernaires of whom he was particularly fond sang in conclusion his favorite spiritual — "Steal Away To Jesus."

His remains, followed and surrounded by his family and friends, were taken to Mount Lawn Cemetery and laid to rest on high ground, in the midst of green grass, lovely flowers, branching trees and singing birds.

THE JOURNAL
OF
NEGRO HISTORY

EDITED BY

CARTER G. WOODSON

VOL. VIII., No. 4 OCTOBER, 1923

PUBLISHED QUARTERLY

CONTENTS

THE ASSOCIATION FOR THE STUDY OF NEGRO LIFE AND HISTORY, INCORPORATED

PRICE AND LEMON STREETS, LANCASTER, PA.
1538 NINTH STREET, N.W., WASHINGTON, D.C.

$2.00 A YEAR **60 CENTS A COPY**

FOREIGN SUBSCRIPTIONS, 25 CENTS EXTRA

BOUND VOLUMES, $3.00 by Mail

Entered as second-class matter January 1, 1916, at the Post Office at Lancaster, Pennsylvania, under the Act of March 3, 1879

NEGROES IN DOMESTIC SERVICE IN THE UNITED STATES *

Introduction

The term *Domestic Service* as used in this study will include those persons performing household duties for pay. In early colonial history indentured servants performed household duties without pay. They were usually imported convicts, assigned to labor for a term on some estate, receiving only their living and stipulated benefits at the termination of their service.[1] In modern use the word "servant" denotes a domestic or menial helper and implies little or no discretionary power and responsibility in the mode of performing duty.[2]

In this discussion of Negroes in domestic service in the United States the facts presented disclose the part Negroes have had in the changes and developments of domestic service in the United States during the past thirty years.[3] They also show to some extent the relation of Negro domestic

* This thesis was submitted in 1923 in partial fulfillment of the requirements for the degree of Master of Arts in the Faculty of Political Science of Columbia University.

1 Bruce, *Economic History of Virginia in the 17th Century,* Vol. I, p. 573.

2 *Century Dictionary and Cyclopedia.*

3 The following works were found helpful in preparing this dissertation: W. A. Crossland, *Industrial Conditions Among Negroes in St. Louis* (*Studies in Social Economics,* Washington Univ., Vol. I, No. 1, St. Louis, 1914); Isabel Eaton, *Special Report on Domestic Service* in The Philadelphia Negro by W. E. B. DuBois (Philadelphia, 1899); George E. Haynes, *The Negro at Work in New York City* (New York, 1912); Frances A. Kellor, *Out of Work; Knickerbocker Press* (New York, 1904); W. I. King, *Employment, Hours and Earnings in the United States, 1920–1922;* Asa E. Martin, *Our Negro Population* (Kansas City, 1913); *Monthly Labor Review* (U. S. Bureau of Labor Statistics, 1919–1920); Ruth Reed, *The Negro Women of Gainsville, Georgia* (1921—A Master's Essay—Phelps Stokes Fund Scholarship); *Report of U. S. Industrial Commission, Domestic Service,* Vol. XIV; I. M. Rubinow, *Depth and Breadth of the Servant Problem* (McClures Magazine, Vol. 34, 1909–1910); Lucy M. Salmon, *Domestic Service* (New York, 1901).

workers to white workers and to some of the larger problems in this field of employment.

The primary data used here were gathered in three ways. First, the writer was a dollar-a-year worker of the Woman in Industry Service, United States Department of Labor, in 1919; and while visiting cities in this work obtained from employment agencies some data on domestic service. Secondly, as domestice service Employment Secretary, United States Employment Service, Washington, District of Columbia, from January 1920 to May 1922, the writer kept careful record of pertinent facts with a view to further study and analysis of this information at a later time.

Three different record cards were used at this office. One was for the employer with name, address, telephone number, kind of help desired, work to be done, whether to "sleep in" or "sleep out," afternoons off, breakfast and dinner hour, size of family, wages, etc. Another card was kept for the employee with name, address, birthplace, age, marital condition, number of dependents, grade at leaving school, kind of work desired, minimum wages applicant would accept, names of three recent former employers and their addresses. On the back of this card were written the name of the employer engaging the worker, the date, and kind of work. There was also a card of introduction for the applicant which the employer mailed back to the office.

A personal canvass of eleven employment agencies in New York City and one in Brooklyn was also made in 1923. The records of only two of these agencies were used, because more time could not be given to securing material in this way.

In the third place, in 1923 a general schedule asking questions relating to number, sex, age, marital condition, turnover, efficiency, wages, hours, specific occupations, living conditions and health was sent by mail to employment secretaries in twelve cities North, South, East, and West, with whom contacts had been established through acquaintances and friends. Responses were received from ten of these cities with data for 1,771 domestic and personal service workers.

I. NUMBER AND SEX OF NEGROES IN DOMESTIC AND PERSONAL SERVICE

Because of the difficulties inherent in the classification of occupations the United States Census Bureau has classified all domestic and personal service occupations in one group. It has not been possible, therefore, to ascertain the exact number of workers engaged exclusively in domestic service. For example, the domestic and personal service classification includes indiscriminately barbers, hairdressers, manicurists, midwives, hotel keepers, policemen, cooks, servants, waiters, bootblacks, and the like.

Fifty years ago there were in the United States 2,311,820 persons ten years of age and over engaged in domestic and personal service, 42.1 per cent of whom were males and 57.9 per cent females. During the succeeding thirty years there was an average increase for males and females combined of 108,961 a year. So that in 1900, persons ten years of age and over engaged in domestic and personal service numbered 5,580,657. As far as distinction from domestic service occupations can be made, the number engaged in personal service has continued to increase since 1900. By contrast, during the decade from 1900 to 1910 and from 1910 to 1920 there was a rather steady decline in the number of those engaged in domestic service. However, the two groups of domestic and personal service occupations combined showed that the number ten years of age and over by 1910 had decreased 1,808,098, and by 1920 had further decreased 367,667. Males constituted 6.4 per cent of the decrease from 1910 to 1920 and females 93.6 per cent. The number of children from 10 to 15 years of age engaged in domestic and personal service in 1910 were 112,171. In 1920 the number had decreased to 54,006.

The trend of the number of Negroes in domestic and personal service occupations compared with the general trend of the total number is indicative of the relation of Negroes and Caucasians in these occupations. We may, therefore, discuss the number and sex of Negroes ten years of age and over engaged in these occupations.

In 1900 there were in the United States 1,317,859 Negroes ten years of age and over gainfully employed in domestic and personal service: 681,926 females and 635,933 males. In 1910 the number of females had increased to 861,497 and the males had decreased to 496,100. In 1890 the total number of Negroes ten years of age and over gainfully employed in domestic and personal service constituted 20.7 per cent of the total number so employed and held third place among all nationalities so employed. Negro men held first place among men thus employed and constituted 40.8 per cent of the total number of male domestic workers.[4] This proportion does not take into account the fact that there were about eight white persons to one Negro in the total population. At that time one in every 5.6 Negroes ten years of age and over gainfully employed was in domestic and personal service. In 1900 Negro women domestic workers occupied second place in point of numbers among the total number and outnumbered the Negro male domestic workers 3 to 1, while the white female domestic workers outnumbered the white male domestic workers about 7 to 1.

The census figures dealing with servants and waiters for 1910 and 1920 in five Southern States where Negroes perform practically all of the domestic service and in five Northern States where conditions are quite different indicate the similarity in the trend of the numbers for both races in domestic service. Although the number of waiters increased by 40,693 between 1910 and 1920, the number of other domestic servants so decreased that we have the following figures for waiters and other domestic workers.

[4] *Report of the U. S. Industrial Commission,* Vol. XIV. DOMESTIC SERVICE, p. 745.

Servants and Waiters 10 years of age and over, in selected States, 1901–1920

TABLE I State	1910		1920	
	Male	Female	Male	Female
Georgia	8,719	38,165	7,752	38,165
N. Carolina	5,553	28,555	4,855	21,321
Louisiana	7,112	30,982	6,761	28,306
Maryland	8,125	32,292	6,859	26,305
Virginia	9,535	42,797	3,144	33,781
Massachusetts	16,969	71,853	16,574	51,941
Ohio	11,695	64,408	15,170	50,232
Minnesota	6,581	37,207	6,134	26,939
Pennsylvania	24,103	134,374	22,173	98,798
New York	63,395	198,970	69,869	151,455

The figures show a decided decrease of domestic servants in both Southern and Northern States between 1910 and 1920, except male servants in Ohio and New York and female servants in Georgia.

The increase in male servants in Ohio and New York may be accounted for by the large increase of waiters in those States. There is no apparent explanation for the lack of change in the figures of female domestic workers in Georgia. It may be said, however, that Georgia has not suffered an actual decrease in its Negro population during the past ten years as have Mississippi, with a 7.4 per cent decrease, Kentucky with a 9.8 per cent decrease, Louisiana with a 1.8 per cent decrease, Alabama with 0.8 per cent decrease, Delaware with a 2.7 per cent decrease, and Tennessee with a 4.5 per cent decrease. This decrease in the Southern States has been due to the migration of Negroes to Northern industrial centers.

For example, the Negro population of Chicago increased from 44,103 in 1910 to 109,456 in 1920; that of New York City increased from 91,709 to 152,467. The number of Negroes in domestic and personal service in these and other Northern industrial centers has increased during the past ten years because the Negroes who have migrated North could enter domestic and personal service more easily than they could other fields of employment.

Since the total number of Negroes in domestic service

has decreased while the total Negro population has increased, the question arises as to why the number of domestic and personal service workers has not kept pace with the growth of the Negro population. In twenty years between 1890 and 1910 Negroes in the United States gainfully employed increased about 65 per cent in agriculture, about 66.6 per cent in trade and transportation, about 129.5 per cent in manufacturing and mechanical pursuits, and about 65.3 per cent in domestic and personal service.

The Census of 1920 shows that of the gainfully employed 4,824,151 Negroes ten years of age and over, 45.2 per cent were in agriculture, forestry, and animal husbandry; 22.1 per cent were in domestic and personal service; 18.4 per cent were in manufacturing and mechanical pursuits; 9.4 per cent were in trade and transportation; 1.7 per cent were in professional service; 0.8 per cent were in clerical occupations; 1.0 per cent were in public service; and 1.5 per cent were engaged in the extraction of minerals. This increase in occupations other than agriculture and domestic and personal service is largely due to conditions incident to the World War. Because of the 3 per cent immigration restriction, Negroes are being attracted to the North in large numbers and are entering industrial pursuits. For several years at least, this movement will most probably continue.

II. Age and Marital Condition of Negroes in Domestic and Personal Service

In 1900, 53.4 per cent of all the women sixteen years of age and over engaged in domestic and personal service were from 16 to 24 years of age. Of the Negro women 16 years of age and over engaged in domestic and personal service, 35.1 per cent, or more than one-third, were between the ages of 16 and 24. The percentage in the other age groups of the total number of women 16 years of age and over engaged in domestic and personal service decreased by classes. That of Negro women 16 years of age and over engaged in domestic and personal service decreased by classes until those 55 years of age and over constituted only 9.6 per cent of the total number of Negro women so employed. The modal age of Negro male domestic workers like that of white male domestic workers was from 25 to 44 years. The age distribution of domestic and personal service workers for 1920 is about the same as that for 1900. Because of the incompleteness of the age data obtained from the general schedule sent to employment agencies, they were not used for this study. The average ages of the 9,976 male and female Negro domestic and personal service workers of Washington, D. C., were: 30.5 years for the males and 28.1 years for the females.

In 1900, among Negro women the percentage of breadwinners did not show such a marked decline after marriage as among white women. Of the Negro female breadwinners 32.5 per cent were married, while only 9.0 per cent of the female breadwinners of all the races were married. The percentage of married Negro male domestic and personal service workers is higher than that of married female workers, while the number of widowed and divorced is three and one-half times as great among female as among male domestic and personal service workers. In 1920, 29.4 per cent of all the female domestic and personal service workers 15 years of age and over were married, while 70.6 per cent were classed as single, widowed, divorced, and unknown.

The significance of age grouping and marital condition of Negro domestic workers in their relation to employers is borne out by the testimony of experienced employment agents in New York City, Philadelphia, Baltimore, Washington, D. C., Chicago, and Detroit. Women domestic workers between the ages of 20 and 25 are the most sought after by employers. Those between 25 and 35 years of age are next in favor. All of the agents testified to the unpopularity of the young girl domestic worker. She is employed principally because of the tight domestic labor market. Employers apparently feel that a majority of the women beyond the ages of 45 and 50 have become too set in their ways, somewhat cranky, and largely unable to do general housework. The most frequent objections of employers to young girl domestic workers are: They are untrained and inexperienced; they are unwilling to sleep in; they are saucy; and their interest in men company causes them to neglect their work.

The older Negro women in domestic service, realizing that with their advancing years their possibilities for employment become less, often hesitate and even fail to give their correct ages when applying at employment agencies for positions. For example, a New York City agency registered a woman who gave her age as 34, but whose written references, yellowed with age, showed that she had worked for different members in one family for fifty years. Frequently an older woman registrant when asked her age hesitates and ends by saying "just say 'settled woman.'"

In addition to the age situation of Negroes engaged in domestic service, the marital condition of female domestic workers furnishes a perplexing problem for both their employers and themselves. The testimony of employment agents relative to employers' most commonly registered objections to hiring married women for domestic service is: Married women take away food for the support of their families; married women have so many responsibilities and problems in their own homes they oftener than not go out to work with a weary body and a disturbed mind; married women find it difficult to live and sleep on employers' premises.

Besides these problems there is apparently a still more perplexing one for the Negro domestic workers with children of their own or other dependents, namely, how to provide proper care and protection for their dependents while they are away from home at work, especially if the hours are long. Day nurseries are often mentioned as a possible solution for this particular problem, but they exist for Negroes in very few cities of the South. Even in the District of Columbia with a population of servants and waiters—servants largely Negroes—totaling 21,444, there is not one day nursery for Negro children. The other alternative is to get some elderly woman to take care of a child. The usual charge made by such a woman for a limited number of hours during the day is from $5 to $6 a week, the mother furnishing food for the child. With these two items and carfare deducted from a mother's weekly wage of $9 there is little left for other necessities.

The problem of dependents manifests itself also among widowed and divorced Negro women engaged in domestic service. The U. S. Employment Office, Washington, D. C., registered 9,774 Negro women 15 years of age and over for domestic service from January, 1920, to May, 1922. Of this number 5,124 were single, 2,579 were married, 2,071 were widowed or divorced. Of the widowed or divorced 2,056 had from 1 to 5 dependents; 79 had from 6 to 10 dependents. Although no record was made of the number of breadwinners in each of these families, many of these widows expressed their weight of responsibilities by referring to the high cost of living when their children had no one to look to for support but themselves.

Divorced domestic workers and also unmarried mothers constitute marital groups that are not all together negligible. Three of the divorced women sent from the Washington office had the added problem of finding their husbands at their respective places of employment after absences of 5, 2, and 2 years respectively. Among the 5,124 single registered at the Washington office there were reported 9 unmarried mothers.

In the District of Columbia there is a Training School for delinquent Negro girls, a large number of whom go into domestic service when they are paroled. They are better trained than the average domestic employee, but since the Training School requires them to keep their young babies with them, it is difficult to place them in homes. If they take a room and attempt to do day work they have the difficult problem of getting someone to take care of their children.

The marital condition of 471 new applicants for domestic positions in Indianapolis, Indiana, for 1922, is given in the following table:

Showing marital condition of 471 women seeking work as domestic servants—
TABLE II *Indianapolis, Ind., 1922*

Widows	63
Separated from husbands	50
Married and living with husbands	238
Divorced	34
Single	85
Unmarried mothers	1

The large proportion of married persons in the table may be accounted for, in part, by the fact that 51 per cent of the total number had recently come into Indianapolis from the adjoining States of Kentucky and Tennessee.

III. TURNOVER, TRAINING, AND EFFICIENCY OF NEGRO DOMESTIC AND PERSONAL SERVICE WORKERS

The increase of 13,738,354, or 14.9 per cent, in the total population of the United States during the last decade, and a decrease of 367,667 in the domestic and personal service occupations population increases the possibilities of turnover. In 1890, the average tenure of service of a domestic worker in the United States was less than one and one-half years.[5] Ten years later the average length of service of a Negro domestic worker in the seventh ward of Philadelphia was five years less than one month.[6] Many of these workers perhaps had been for a long time in the older families of Philadelphia. Figures for a three-year period, from 1906 to 1908, show that the modal period of service of the New York Negro domestic worker was at that time from six to eleven months.[7] In 1914, among 104 unskilled Ne-

5 Salmon, Lucy M., *Domestic Service*, p. 109.

6 Eaton, Isabel, *Special Report on Domestic Service* in THE PHILADELPHIA NEGRO, by W. E. B. DuBois, Philadelphia, 1889, p. 480.

7 Haynes, George E., *The Negro at Work in New York City*, New York, 1918, p. 85.

gro workers of St. Louis—cooks, laundresses, porters, chambermaids, waiters, scrubwomen, manual laborers, and the like—the greatest frequency for length of service among the men was from one to three months, and among the women from three to six months.[8] Six years later the largest proportion of Negro domestic workers of Gainesville, Georgia, showed a disposition to remain in one position less than three months, while the next largest proportion remained in one position from three to six months.[9]

Some concrete illustrations of the frequency of turnover may be referred to as further evidence. Nearly two hundred different women were sent out from the Springfield, Massachusetts, office for day work in 1915. Two years later over 500 different workers were sent out from that office, about 200 of whom were Negro women. Of these 167 white women and 124 Negro women were placed with employers less than ten times in 1917; 2 white and 4 Negro women were sent out from 41 to 50 times; 3 white and 1 Negro woman were placed fifty times during 1917. In 1918, the Springfield office reported as having filled 4,000 places with 1,000 women.[10]

In 1920 the United States Employment Office, Washington, D. C., placed 1,488 different women for day work, all of whom were Negroes except one. Of these, 458, after being given permanent positions for every day in the week, were referred again not over twelve times; 23 of them were sent out over fifty times, and 5 of them over one hundred times during the year. General housework was so unpopular during that year that few would take it. Although the turnover in day work was greater than that in any other specific employment handled by the domestic service section of that office, the 164 cooks remained in one position on an average of about three months.

There was, however, in the District of Columbia during

[8] Crossland, W. A., *Industrial Conditions among Negroes in St. Louis*. St. Louis, 1914, p. 30.

[9] Reed, Ruth, *The Negro Women of Gainesville, Georgia*, 1921, p. 25.

[10] *Massachusetts Bureau of Statistics, Springfield Report*, 1915–1918.

the fall and winter of 1920 a decrease in the rate and volume of turnover for Negro day workers and hotel workers consequent upon the minimum wage law which became effective for hotels and restaurants in the spring of 1920. Many Negro women displaced in the hotels turned to day work. For this reason added to the normal increase during the first half of 1921, the number of day workers increased to 3,115. White workers did not have to apply for day work because they could secure positions in hotels and restaurants.

During an unemployment period which extended over the latter half of 1921 and the first half of 1922, when so many men were thrown out of work, the day workers increased to 4,615. There were more day workers than there were positions for them. Consequently the turnover in day work decidedly decreased, but it increased in general housework. Many who could not get a sufficient number of days' work to make ends meet were forced to turn to general housework.

The difficulty of keeping an accurate record of the turnover in general housework makes the value of figures on turnover in general housework seem very questionable. However, the length of service of 1,000 general houseworkers sent out from the Washington office for the latter half of 1921 and the first few months of 1922 gives a fairly accurate picture of the situation at that time.

Length of Service of 1,000 General Houseworkers, Washington, D. C., 1921–22

TABLE III

317 remained in one position 1 week or less.
582 remained in one position from one to three months.
101 remained in one position 4 months and over.

Some of the conditions of the turnover at that time are illustrated by typical cases. One employer advertised for a general houseworker without laundry, with the privilege of going at night, and with hours off. Eleven domestic workers answered the advertisement in person, and no two met at the house at the same time. The employer engaged every one of them, to return to work the next morning. Every one of them gave assurance of being there, but not one of them came. Another employer with only two in family, very desirous of securing a general houseworker, called up six different employment agencies, each of which sent her a worker. Among the number there was one man. The employer put every one of them to work, each in a different room, with the idea of choosing the two best ones at the end of the day and engaging them for permanent work—thus assuring herself of securing one worker. She managed her plan, as she thought, very successfully, but the next morning she did not have a single worker.

Employers' statements on reference blanks, and reports from employment agencies indicate that the reasons generally given by domestic workers for leaving positions are that they wish a change, or the hours are too long, or the work is too hard, or the employer is too particular, or they have no time off. Time off for domestic employees is no doubt greatly limited. Negro domestic workers, however, proverbially take Christmas Day and the Fourth of July off, giving such various excuses for their absence as death in the family, automobile accidents, and the like. Just after these two holidays, large employment agencies handling Negro help are for the most part swamped with applicants.

To some extent turnover in domestic service is linked up with lack of training and efficiency of domestic workers. Because of their great need of domestic help, employers frequently engage persons who are so utterly untrained that they cannot be retained. There is a tendency on the part of employers to propose to a domestic worker that each take the other on a week's trial. Domestic workers are inclined to refuse such offers on the ground that they are looking for permanent employment. This suggestion of trying out domestic workers leads logically to the question of training and efficiency in domestic service.

Training of White Domestic and Personal Service Workers

Some facts relative to the special opportunities for the training of white household workers in England and in the United States may throw some light on the problem of efficiency. In England, following the World War and under the ministry of reconstruction, there was created a women's advisory committee to study the domestic service problem. Each of the four sub-committees appointed made a report. Among the advisory committee's final recommendations for getting the work of the nation's homes done satisfactorily and reducing waste, were technical training for domestic help and fixed standards of qualifications for them. This committee reported that in 1914 there were only ten domestic service schools in England and Wales, and four of these were in the London area. During the year of 1922 courses of three months' duration were given at some technical institutions in England in all branches of household work and management. This training enabled women to take the better posts in daily or residential work. Training in cooking and catering could be had at any technical college for three or more months as required.

To help meet the serious unemployment situation the Central Committee on Women's Training and Employment in cooperation with the Ministry of Labor set up homecraft training centers in districts where unemployment was most noticeable. At these centers a course of training was given for about three months, such as would enable women to take posts in domestic service at the end of the course. These classes were most successful. By August, 1922, about 10,000 women had received the training and the courses were still continued. These courses were given to women and girls between the ages of 16 and 35 upon their signing an agreement to be punctual in attendance, to do their best in making the classes successful, and stating their willingness to enter domestic service after receiving their training.

In the United States, in 1900, there were more illiterate

persons in domestic and personal service than in any other field of employment except agriculture. The number of agricultural colleges in the different States for the purpose of developing improved farming and farmers has increased since that time, and the Federal Government farm demonstration agents are actually teaching the citizens on the plantations where they live and work. Facilities for the training of domestic help, however, have received little attention from State or Federal Government, and private enterprise in this field has been very limited.

Just twenty years ago the Home Economics Committee of the Association of Collegiate Alumnae of the United States, through the inspiration of Mrs. Alice Freeman Palmer and Mrs. Ellen H. Richards, undertook an experiment for studying at first hand the problems of household labor. Among the disabilities in domestic service regarded as fundamental causes of the disfavor in which it was held, was the low grade of intelligence and skill available among domestic service workers. This household aid company committee opened a training center and applied educational tests to its candidates and undertook to give a course of six weeks' training to each aid before she was sent out to work. The number of aids taking the training was small. Mainly because of a lack of funds, however, the experiment was given up after a trial of two years. Prior to that time the civic club of Philadelphia attempted to standardize the work and wages of domestic workers in that city.

Nearly twenty years later, a committee on household assistants was organized in New York City by the United States Employment Service. The committee succeeded in planning a household occupations course to be given at the Washington Irving High School, and made efforts to advertise the course; but since no one registered for it the committee concluded that the matter would have to be taken up and pushed by employers before it could succeed.[11]

Some of these efforts, however, have met with a meas-

[11] U. S. Department of Labor, *Monthly Labor Review*, Aug., 1919, p. 206.

ure of success. The Bureau of Household Occupations of the Housewives' League of Providence, R. I., organized in November, 1918, has conducted very successful training classes for domestic workers. No meals or lodging are to be furnished the household attendants of the Bureau. The Bureau of Occupations under the auspices of the Housewives' League of Hartford, Connecticut, has given its training courses through the generosity of some of its members. One member taught cooking, another taught waiting table, another laundry work. Classes were taught in the homes of some of the members with much success.

Training of Negro Domestic Workers

Available data shows that opportunities for the special training of Negro domestic workers have been even less than those for white domestic workers. During the latter quarter of the 19th century Mrs. L. J. Coppin, of Philadelphia, maintained a small home for the training of the Negro domestic workers of Philadelphia. In the comparatively few social settlements for Negroes there is meagre opportunity for training in domestic service. The Domestic Efficiency Association of Baltimore, Maryland, an organization of employers, has announced its plans for opening a training school for white and Negro domestic workers. This Association maintained in 1921 and 1922 a training school for Negro domestic help, in which special lessons could be given or general training for one month or more. A rate of $5 a week for board, lodging, and training was charged. If an applicant had no money the Domestic Efficiency Association advanced it on her signing an agreement to secure her position through the Association when ready for it, and to repay the debt out of her wages at the rate of at least $2.50 a week.

The domestic science training given in the public schools may be a small factor in the efficiency of Negro domestic workers, but most of the permanent domestic workers do not go beyond the fifth grade in school and thus do not go far enough to get an appreciable amount of domestic science training. Negro workers who go through the high or normal schools do not enter permanently into domestic service. This statement is based on the data indicated by the permanent occupations of 606 Negro graduates of the Sumner High School, St. Louis, Missouri, of 305 graduates of Miner Normal School, Washington, in the District of Columbia, of 15 graduates of the Gainesville, Georgia, public schools 1917–1919;[12] and on data for students applying at the Washington, in the District of Columbia, and the Indianapolis Employment Agencies. Tables IV and V below set forth these facts.

Occupations of 606 Negro High School Graduates, Sumner High School, St. Louis, Mo., 1895–1911 [13]

TABLE IV

Occupation	Number
Those engaged in, or prepared for, teaching	288
Entered college	49
Clerical work	43
Postoffice clerks	30
Entered business	4
Mechanics	17
Women at home or married	120
Miscellaneous	32
Unknown	23

Although Tables IV and V direct one's attention to the limited fields of employment for Negro high school graduates, especially so since clerical and mechanical work, business and professional service, must be engaged in almost wholly among Negroes, yet few if any of the 911 graduates have entered domestic service. The young women graduates of the Gainesville, Georgia, schools 1917–19, with the exception of three, entered higher institutions of learning.

In Washington, in the District of Columbia, during the academic year 1920–22 there were among the 9,976 applicants for domestic work, 17 male and 159 female students who had attended or were attending high school; 75 female

[12] Reed, Ruth, *op. cit.*, p. 44.
[13] Crossland, William A., *op. cit.*, p. 93.

normal school students; 13 male and 126 female college students. Also in Indianapolis, in 1922, 73 female high school students and 12 female college students applied for domestic service. These large numbers of high school, normal school, and college students seek domestic service mainly for after-school hours, Saturdays, Sundays, summer months, and temporarily for earning money to continue their education, or until they can find other employment.

Occupations of 305 Negro Graduates of Miner Normal School, Washington, D. C., 1913–1922

TABLE V

Occupation	Number
Teaching in Washington, D. C.:	
Elementary	207
Kindergarten	50
Domestic Science	4
Domestic Art	3
Manual Arts	1
Drawing	1
Music	1
Ungraded	1
Teaching in Maryland	8
Teaching in Virginia	2
Teaching in North Carolina	1
Teaching in South Carolina	1
Teaching in New York	1
Substitute teachers in Washington, D. C.	2
Students	5
Government Service	7
Housekeepers	5
Printers	1
Private Music Teachers	1
Physicians	1
Insurance	1
Y. W. C. A.	1

Table VI shows the grades on leaving school of 8,147 Negro domestic workers—men and women—of the Washington, D. C., office; and Table VII shows grades on leaving school of 471 Negro domestic workers, not separated by sex, of an Indianapolis Employment Office conducted by Flanner House in that city. Each of these workers was personally interviewed by the agent at each respective office. The reported grade of each on leaving school was placed on an application card which was filed for reference. The application cards were filled out solely on the testimony of the applicants. The agent in the Washington office handling the women did not ordinarily register men except as man and wife applied at the same time, or a woman sent her husband to the agent, or a special employer asked the agent to select male help, or teachers in the Negro schools sent boys and men who were in search of work. Therefore, the number of men from the Washington office for whom grades are given is comparatively small.

In examining Tables VI and VII below one must take into consideration several factors. In the first place, 81.2 per cent of the Washington applicants and 73.9 per cent of the Indianapolis applicants were born in the South where the standard is not so high as in the North; and many of these applicants attended school in the rural districts of the South where the schools were not standardized, and only a few schools had any domestic science instruction. Then, too, a large proportion of them left school some years ago when all of the grades or groups of a school were taught by one teacher in one room.

Those persons who could not read or write seemed to feel their illiteracy very keenly. Many of them offered excuses by saying that the "white folks raised" them; or their parents died and they had to help the other children; or they were "sickly," and the like. Those who had never been to school but could read and write a little were listed as being in the first grade. One applicant said that she had never been through any grade but she could read and write and go anywhere in the city she wished to go. Another one, an elderly woman, expressed her regrets because she never had a chance to go to school, but she had learned to read and write so that she could sign her name instead of simply "touching the pen" when she was transacting her business.

Grades on Leaving School of 7,975 Female and 172 Male Negro Domestic Workers from the U. S. Employment Service, Washington, D. C., 1920–1922

TABLE VI

	Male	Female
Illiterate	8	418
1st Grade	5	244
2d Grade	7	436
3d Grade	9	842
4th Grade	17	1,073
5th Grade	31	1,417
6th Grade	28	1,237
7th Grade	25	998
8th Grade	42	1,310

Grades on Leaving School of 387 Negro Domestic Workers, Irrespective of Sex, Indianapolis, Ind., 1922

TABLE VII

Illiterate	1st Gr.	2d Gr.	3d Gr.	4th Gr.	5th Gr.	6th Gr.	7th Gr.	8th Gr.
21	7	11	22	44	63	51	47	120

The figures show that of a total of 7,975 female applicants for domestic work in Washington, D. C., 4,430, or 55.5 per cent, had received school training in the sixth grade or below; leaving only 29.9 per cent who had seventh or eighth grade training. Of the 387 applicants for domestic service in Indianapolis, 168, or 43.3 per cent, had received school training up to the fifth grade or below; and 219, or 56.7 per cent, had been to the sixth grade or below, leaving 43.3 per cent who had been in the seventh or eighth grade. The larger proportions of those from higher grades in Indianapolis may be accounted for by the lesser opportunity in other occupations as compared with Washington, and by the smaller number of applicants involved. In short, domestic service as a regular occupation does not attract and hold Negro workers of the higher grades of educational training and intelligence.

In order to understand exactly what is meant by saying that consideration of certain factors must be taken into account in any attempt to formulate some idea of the educational status of the rank and file domestic worker reckoned by his grade when he left school, some letters, typical of the educational equipment among the 9,774 domestic workers (applicants), should be read. These letters were written to the agent in the Washington, D. C., office by 5th grade domestic workers.[14]

Many of these domestic workers also showed their lack of training by their inability to figure out their weekly wages at the rate of $40, 45, or $50 per month. Such inability often caused them to feel and say that their employers were "cheaters." To a considerable number of them, $40 a month meant $10 a week, and vice versa; $45 a month meant $11.25 a week, and $50 a month meant $12.50 a week. They generally secured their pay twice a month—the first and the fifteenth. However, such an arrangement did not seem to clarify matters, since they thought of four weeks as making a month.

Then comes the question of the efficiency of Negro domestic workers. In Philadelphia, Baltimore, Detroit, Indianapolis, and Washington, D. C., agents find that employers of domestic labor, like other employers, do not like

[14] THREE SAMPLE LETTERS OF THE 5TH GRADE DOMESTIC WORKERS OF WASHINGTON, D. C.

Miss X (The agent)

Dear Friend i am sorry to any that i am confind to bed this week but hope to see you again some day i taken sick last friday but i full fill that other place all right but could not go out saturday.

Daisy

Daer Mrs. X (The agent) daer Madam can you get my husban are job in are lunch room cafe boarding or apt. house he is are well exspierence sheref cook we both would like are job together if could get me are dash (dish) wash place please maggie.

Letter from Bell Jones

Dear Mrs. X (the agent) i am writing you a fue lines to let you here from me i am the lady you got me a home with Mrs. Jones at Smithburg, Md I have a little boy with me you know by the name of Bell Jones i dont want to stay up here much longer and i want you to get me a good home down in Washington for me and my little boy with some good white people with no children and a room in the house for me and my little boy my little boy is a mighty good little boy he is not noisy i want to leave sept. 4 i am tired of this place because there is no cullard people up here they are all white i have not been off the lot since i have been out here please get me a good home dont let it be out of town.

Yours Bell Jones

to write down their grievances, but many of them do make complaints to the agents over the telephone about the inefficiency of domestic help. Agents in Detroit and Indianapolis state that Negro domestic workers from the South—many of them from the farms and untrained, unaccustomed to Northern methods of domestic work—find it difficult to give satisfaction. The consensus of opinion of eleven white and Negro agents in New York City was that with respect to efficiency there are three distinct types of domestic workers in New York City. In the first place, comes the West Indian, who is unaccustomed to domestic work, and therefore unable to convince himself that he is on that plane. He makes a more or less inefficient domestic worker. Then there is the New York Negro who has difficulty in adjusting himself to domestic duties. The southern Negro, however, a decidedly different sort of laborer, makes a more efficient domestic worker than either of the other two types.

Opinions elsewhere also vary. There was a migration of Negro women domestic workers from Georgia to Springfield, Massachusetts, in 1916–1917. Many of these women were very satisfactory employees and compared favorably with northern born Negro women domestic workers of that locality, according to the *11th Annual Report of the Massachusetts Bureau of Statistics.* In the United States Employment Office, Washington, D. C., where all sorts and conditions of domestic workers were handled, reports from employers on the efficiency of the new workers from the South indicated that they were unaccustomed to modern methods of housework and were less efficient than northern born workers.

In any attempt to rate the efficiency of Negro domestic workers by verbal testimonials and written references from their employers or by wages received or length of service period of the workers, due consideration must be given to factors beyond the workers' control. Some of these factors are differences in the standards of efficiency in the many homes and the temperament of employers together with the attitude of some employers toward Negroes generally. For example, occasionally, a former employer, in sympathy with the struggles of Negroes and not wishing to hinder an unsatisfactory worker from securing another position, writes for her a letter of recommendation. Sometimes another employer, because of misunderstanding of some sort between her and the worker, refuses to give any reference whatever.

In 1890, 57 per cent of 1,005 housekeepers representing the whole United States found more or less difficulty in securing efficient help. This probably was an underestimate of the true condition.[15] In 1901, out of 1,106 domestic workers from all sections of the United States, 34 per cent were rated excellent; 37.4 per cent good; 24.8 per cent fair; 3.8 per cent poor. Although these figures indicate that 96.2 per cent of the total were between excellent and fair, the Commission's report in summing up the matter states that according to the testimony of employers of domestic labor and of employment agents, the character of the service rendered by domestic laborers is in a large proportion of cases unsatisfactory. It further states that the quality of men's work is about the same as that of women's work.[16]

In New York City, employment agencies send reference blanks to former employers of domestic workers to be filled out and returned.[17] These references are kept on file as a

15 Salmon, Lucy M., *Domestic Service*, p. 124.

16 U. S. Industrial Commission Report, *op. cit.*, p. 751.

17 THREE SAMPLE REFERENCES FOR DOMESTIC WORKERS, NEW YORK CITY

Winchester Ave., Bronx, N. Y. July 14, 1921.

To Whom it may Concern:

Doris X has been in my employ and performed her duties satisfactory. She is honest and capable.

Signed ——

The following person had two reference blanks containing the same questions filled out by her former employers. She had been a child's nurse in the first position and nurse-maid in the second.

record of the domestic worker's capability, sobriety and honesty. From 1906 to 1909 efficiency ratings taken from such blanks for 902 Negro domestic and personal service workers were as follows: 25.6 per cent very capable; 10.2 per cent fairly capable; 2.2 per cent inefficient, and 2.0 per cent not stated.[18] One employment agency in this city made 304 placements of Negro women domestic workers during January, 1923. According to those workers' references from their former employers 93.3 per cent were capable or fairly capable and honest. This high degree of efficiency among domestic workers from this one office is due probably to the fact that this office with its limited staff of secretaries makes no attempt to handle the evidently inexperienced workers. The other employment agencies in New York and Brooklyn visited in 1923 spoke favorably of the quality of service rendered by domestic workers in these cities, according to their reports from employers.

Opinions of employers are not conclusive evidence of the efficiency or inefficiency of workers, but they throw considerable light upon the question. Written references are more or less held in disfavor by the Washington, D. C., employers of domestic labor because they feel that domestic workers sometimes write their own references. This is true to a limited extent. Many of the workers come from small towns and rural sections where the employers of domestic labor do not use elegant stationery, the best Eng-

	First Blank. January 27, 1923.	*Second Blank.* Jan. 30, 1923.
Is she honest?	Exceptionally so	Yes
Is she temperate?	Yes	Yes
Is she neat?	Yes	Yes
What of her disposition?	Best I have ever seen	Wonderful
Does she thoroughly understand her work? ..	Yes	Yes
Why did she leave?	Presumably to be near her husband	Because she was tired of permanence and had a chance to go to the states with our friend

Remarks—Her services with our family for five years have always been most satisfactory.

[18] Haynes, George E., *op. cit.*, p. 87.

27

lish, and the most correct spelling in writing references for domestic workers who leave for the cities. Such references do domestic workers coming to Washington, D. C., more harm than good.

However, domestic workers are more and more seeking written references on leaving their places of employment because they are beginning to realize that such are generally required by employers. Often a former employer has moved away from the city, is in Europe, or has died, when the domestic worker needs most to refer to her. A prospective employer usually doubts that such an excuse, if given, is true. Of course, some workers do try to take advantage in this way, but most of them are not so unwise.

Types of written and oral testimonials of employers of domestic labor in Washington, D. C., are also informing.[19]

[19] FIVE SAMPLE REFERENCES FOR DOMESTIC WORKERS AND ONE LETTER FROM AN EMPLOYER, WASHINGTON, D. C.

Woodford Land, Va.

Lillie worked for me for a long time and she is a nice worker and a fine cook and she worked for Mrs. —— three years going on four, and she got married there with them and she worked for Mrs. —— and she nursed Mrs. ——'s three children.

From Mrs. ——

The following reference is for Fannie B.—who, evidently half crazy, changed her name after registering at the Washington office because she said she had so many ''Enemons'' (enemies).

To Whom in May Concern:

This is to certify that Fannie B has been a trustworthy maid. As to her honesty none come no better. She is very capable and in general very satisfactory.

Mrs. ——

To Whom it May Concern:

This is to say that Sarah — has been in my employ 8 months and that she is a good cook, tries hard to please, and has been nice always to the children.

She has been honest and reliable and likes to try new or fancy dishes.

Signed——Mrs. E. M.

(The foregoing Mrs. E. M.'s name and telephone number were given to another lady who had interviewed Sarah relative to offering her a position, Mrs. E. M. told the second lady that Sarah once stole things but she had had a

In cases where three or more employers testified to the efficiency or inefficiency of a worker, the word "efficient," "inefficient," or "poor" was written across the bottom of his application card. The following table in some measure represents in detail the character of service reported to the United States Employment Service, Domestic Section.

Summary of Testimonials of Former Employers of 9,976 Wage Earners Engaged in Domestic Personal Service, Washington, D. C., January 1920–May 1922

TABLE VIII	Efficient		Fairly Efficient		Inefficient	
	No.	Per ct.	No.	Per ct.	No.	Per ct.
Male	90	44.6	94	46.5	11	19.4
Female	3,008	30.8	4,543	46.5	1,892	.05
Total	3,098	37.7	4,637	46.5	1,903	9.7

No Report

	No.	Per Cent.
Male	7	.03
Female	331	.03
Total	338	.03

good lesson so she thought she would not steal any more. She also said that Sarah was none too clean, and that she gave the girl the above reference because she thought she had improved greatly.)

Sarah Jackson held a domestic worker's certificate bearing the golden seal of a Washington, D. C., Federation of Women's Club.

The X Federation of Women's Clubs awards this certificate to Sarah Jackson for 13 years faithful service in the employ of ——

Signed,

Mrs. —— President,
Mrs. —— Chairman Home Economics Dept.

Robert and wife, each about 40 years of age, bring this written reference from a southern town:

This is to certify that I have known "Shine" and his wife for about a year, during which time he has been running a shoe shine establishment in this town. "Shine" is a steady, alert, energetic boy and I feel sure he will please his employer in the work in which he is given a trial.

Signed, H. C. L.

(Letter to the Employment Agent from an Employer.)

My dear Mrs. X.

I fear you think I am very hard to please but having had a butler for 38

In this table 44.6 per cent of the males as over against 30.8 per cent of the females are reported as being efficient, while 19.4 per cent of the females and only 0.05 per cent of the males are listed as inefficient. This should not lead to the conclusion that the male Negro domestic workers of Washington, D. C., were more efficient than the female Negro domestic workers of that city, since the 202 male domestic workers do not represent the rank and file. They represent men of family responsibilities, and students working their way through high school and college. Both of these groups had a more or less definite responsibility and aim in doing domestic work and therefore were more willing, at least for a time, to accommodate themselves to conditions obtaining in it. The office received no report concerning .03 per cent of the workers. Occasionally both employer and employee were so well pleased with each other that neither was heard from unless the office in its follow-up work discovered the happy situation.

The opinion of employers that 19.4 per cent of 9,773 Negro female domestic workers of Washington, D. C., were reported inefficient does not, without other data, justify this as a scientific conclusion. Some typical examples of their inefficiency are interesting.[20] The inefficiency is due

years, since dead, a maid and a cook 32 years, since married, it cannot seem that I am, when I once get the right one.

The last girl you sent me Anna by name disliked very much being directed or being spoken to. I am giving her up for she has a most violent temper, the most impertinent person I have ever seen. In a way I am sorry for her. None of us think she is all there. Will you try again for me?

20 TYPICAL EXAMPLES OF INEFFICIENCY AMONG WASHINGTON, D. C., DOMESTIC APPLICANTS

(1) A day worker—laundress—not knowing how to cut off the current and unscrew the wringer on an electric washing machine, when a garment wrapped around the cogs, ruined the cogs by trying to cut the garment from between them.

(2) A day worker—one of the best laundresses—hurrying to finish her work placed her hands on a revolving electric machine tub, both arms were carried beneath the tub and had not the current been speedily cut, her arms would have been crushed. As it was the tubs had to be cut in order to extricate her arms. After that she was afraid to use an electric washing machine.

in large measure to pure ignorance which for the most part is the sequel to lack of opportunity and training. For example, the older type cook, who cannot read and write, finds it difficult, if not impossible, to carry all the different modern salad and dessert combinations in her memory and cannot supplement her instructions by the use of literature on domestic science.

Employment agencies in Chicago in 1923, moreover, have hardly told the whole truth in giving the following figures on the efficiency of 200 female domestic workers and 200 male domestic workers: *Women,* satisfactory 175, or 87.5 per cent; unsatisfactory 10, or 5.0 per cent; neither satisfactory nor wholly unsatisfactory 15, or 7.5 per cent. *Men,* satisfactory 125, or 62.5 per cent; unsatisfactory 45, or 22.5 per cent; neither 30, or 15 per cent.

Efficient domestic workers apparently regret that they are in an occupational group representing such a high degree of ignorance and inefficiency. They sometimes take

(3) To ask at the office in a group of from 200 to 250 women for a first class laundress—one who knew how to fold the clothes just so after they were ironed as well as wash them out according to rule—and not find one who felt that she could do the work properly was a common occurrence.

(4) A young woman sent out to do general housework and cooking cut the bone out of a 3½ pound sirloin steak which she fried up into such bits that it was not recognized by her employer. When she was questioned about it, she said "that is every bit of that steak. You did not expect me to cook bone and all, did you?"

(5) A young girl sent out to do general housework and cooking when questioned by her employer about the kinds of dessert she could make, said she sure could make jello but was not so good at making other desserts.

(6) The rank and file of general houseworkers looked upon making salad dressing and salads as an art belonging to fine cooks. Many said they had never tried to make bread of any kind.

(7) An elderly cook who had been at the business for 50 years wished cooking and cooking only. Her price was $75 per month. That's what she "ingenally" got. When she was asked if she could read or write she said she could not. She had never been to school a day in her life, but she realized that cooking is tedious work. "Everything I does, I does by my head; its all brain work, you see I has a good 'eal to remember," said she. However, she felt confident that she could cook anything that was put before her to cook.

(8) A young woman sent out to do cleaning left the print of her hand greasy with furniture oil in a freshly papered wall.

pride in saying that they have never worked for poor people. Such a class of workers is represented by a Washington, D. C., domestic worker who gave as her former employers Mrs. John Hays Hammond, Mrs. Arthur Glasgow, Senator Beveridge, Senator Guggenheim, and President Wilson. She took pride in the fact that she could even show anyone a piece of the president's wedding cake.

Honesty in domestic service is so closely associated with efficiency that practically no reference for a domestic worker is complete without some statement about this qualification. In 1890 Miss Salmon raised a serious question with regard to the honesty of Negro domestic workers in the South. Her question was based on answers received from schedules sent to employers of that section.[21] In 1901, 92.6 per cent of 583 domestic labor employers representing the whole United States testified that their employees were honest and responsible. Most employment bureaus were also agreed upon the general honesty of domestic workers.[22] In 1899 the Philadelphia Negro domestic worker of the Seventh Ward was described as purloining food left from the table but as having the balance in his favor in regard to honesty.[23] In 1906 opinions of former employers of 902 Negro wage-earners in domestic and personal service in New York City were that 91.3 per cent were honest; 7.1 per cent were either honest or fairly so; 0.6 per cent were dishonest, and no statement was given for 1.0 per cent.[24]

Out of 9,638 Negro domestic workers reported upon for Washington, D. C., between the years of 1920–1922, only .2 per cent were rated by their former employers with assurance as being dishonest; 90.4 per cent were listed as being honest. There were various answers for the 9.4 per cent. Some did not remain long enough to have judgment passed upon them. Others were in a doubtful class but with no

21 Salmon, Lucy M., *op. cit.*, p. 123.

22 *Industrial Commission Report*, *op. cit.*, p. 1901.

23 Eaton, Isabel, *op. cit.*, p. 486.

24 Haynes, G. E., *op. cit.*, p. 87.

proof against them, and the like. This low percentage of dishonesty eliminates the tradition of taking food except in seven cases. The seven cases of food taking are included because they were directly reported and regarded by the employers as dishonest. Some employers, according to their own statement of the case, do not regard taking food left from the table as stealing, although such is against the will of the employer. According to the southern tradition of a low wage and taking food to piece it out, domestic workers are still virtually expected to follow this custom.

200 women and 200 men domestic workers of Chicago have the following record for honesty: *Women,* honest, 199, or 99.5 per cent; dishonest, 1, or 0.5 per cent; *men,* honest, 197, or 98.5 per cent; dishonest, 3, or 1.5 per cent.

Employment agents in other leading cities already mentioned have very little complaint against the honesty of Negro domestic workers except in the matter of taking food. Their explanation of the psychology of such dishonesty is as given above.

IV. WAGES, HOURS, AND SPECIFIC OCCUPATIONS

While wages and efficiency are in some degree related in domestic service, there is the custom of paying the "going wage" for specific occupations, irrespective of efficiency. Wages vary, of course, in different sections of the country and in different localities. Occasionally attempts are made to grade such laborers. One employment bureau, in Indianapolis, for example, divides its day workers into grades A and B with respective wages of 30 cents and 25 cents an hour for each grade.

Two other questions current in the problem of wages in domestic service, both of which seem to be slowly lending themselves to adjustment, are the payment of weekly wages instead of bi-weekly or monthly wages, and equal pay for equal work irrespective of whether a man or a woman, a Negro or a white employee, does the work. Bi-monthly payment in domestic service has come to be the custom due largely to the convenience of the employer, and to the possibility of weekly wages increasing the turnover. A domestic worker often leaves unceremoniously as soon as he gets his first pay. However, workers claim that the custom of bi-weekly or monthly pay inconveniences them since they cannot arrange to pay their rent, or purchase clothing and other necessities on that basis.

The question of equal pay for Negro domestic workers does not enter the domestic service wage problem of the South because Negroes pre-empt this field in that section. Although the scarcity of domestic labor seems to be settling this matter in other sections of the country, it still persists in some measure. Twenty-five years ago Miss Eaton discovered that Negro butlers on Rittenhouse Square, Philadelphia, received on an average $36.90 a month, while white butlers were getting from $40 to $45 a month.[25]

In the fall of 1921, during the period of labor depression, eleven of the Washington, D. C., clubs and expensive boarding houses attempted to make a change from Negro to white chambermaid-waitresses at an increase of $10 a month for each worker. The four clubs that succeeded in making the change discharged their white chambermaid-waitresses after one week each and re-employed Negroes at the old wage of $35 a month. One of the successful employers felt that, inasmuch as the white servants were no more satisfactory than the Negro workers, she had just as well keep the Negroes and pay them less.

When the minimum wage law for women and minors of Washington, D. C., recently declared unconstitutional by the United States Supreme Court, went into effect, practically all of the hotels and restaurants in that city immediately discharged Negro workers and took on white ones. Some of the managers told the agent at the United States Employment Bureau that they were making the change because white servants were more efficient than Negro workers. Other managers, some of whom had used Negro

[25] Eaton, Isabel, *op. cit.*, p. 449.

labor for more than fifteen years, simply said that $16.50 a week was too much to pay Negroes, and, therefore, wished white workers instead. The few hotels and restaurants that retained Negroes as a rule put them on a much shorter working week than 48 hours, thus reducing their pay.

Boarding houses and institutions such as private schools, sanatoria, and the like, that offer excuses and fail to pay workers should be mentioned in this connection. The manager of one such boarding house in Washington, D. C., was sued by a worker who won her case because other unpaid laborers testified against the manager. The superintendent of a small private school in that city—also among such paymasters—had repeatedly been reported to the Minimum Wage Board which forced her to pay the Negro women day workers. After a few months of such experience she changed her help and began to employ men, over whom the Minimum Wage Board had no jurisdiction.

The wages of Negro domestic workers today are considerably higher than they were in past decades, as is shown by a comparison of figures in past periods for the Continental United States and for selected cities with figures in 1920–1923. For the twenty-five years prior to the World War there had been only a slight wage increase in domestic and personal service. During the World War there was a considerable increase in wages for both male and female domestic workers, the increase for the latter being larger than that for the former. Since the World War wages for such workers have fallen to some extent but not anywhere near the pre-war level.

The following tables, with one exception, show the wage changes at different ten-year periods over a range of 30 years. In Table IX the figures from the Boston Employment Bureau illustrate the fact that the average weekly wages for female domestic workers of Boston were decidedly higher than elsewhere in the country. This table also makes clear the fact that wages for men were considerably higher than those for women.

Average Daily and Weekly Wages in Selected Domestic Service Occupations, 1889–1890 [26]

TABLE IX

Occupation	Weekly Wages for the United States	Weekly Wages for Boston, Mass.
Women		
Cooks	$3.72	$4.45
Cooks and laundresses	3.39	
Chambermaids	3.39	3.86
Waitresses	3.19	3.7
Second girls	3.16	3.7
Chambermaids and waitresses	3.10	
Parlor maids		3
General servants	2.91	3
Men		
Coachmen	$7.84	
Coachmen and gardeners	6.54	
Butlers	6.11	
Cooks	6.08	
Women	Daily Wages	
Laundresses	.82	
Seamstresses	1.01	
Men		
Gardeners	1.33	
Chore-men	.87	

Table X below gives average wages for selected domestic service occupations in the United States for a decade

Average Weekly Wages for Selected Domestic Service Occupations in the United States, 1900 [27]

TABLE X

Occupation	Average Weekly Wage
Women	
General houseworkers	$3.28
Cooks	3.95
Waitresses	3.43
Other specialists	3.54
Men	
For all domestic service occupations	6.03
Women	
For all domestic service occupations	3.51

later than the figures of Table IX. The slight variation in the figures of Table X from those of Table IX may be

[26] Salmon, Lucy, *Domestic Service*, p. 90.

due to probable error incident to the collection of the data or to some other factor. The indications of these two tables, however, with ten years intervening between the compilation of the data, are that wages probably had changed very little, if any.

In comparison with the two preceding tables, Table XI below gives wages for domestic service in Philadelphia for about the same period. The weekly wages range higher than for the country as a whole. The lower wages in the southern border and middle sections of the United States have reduced the average for the country below that for this eastern city in which also special conditions may have operated to bring such wages above the general level.

Average Weekly Wages of Negro Domestic Workers of Philadelphia, 1896–1897 [27]

TABLE XI

Occupation	Average Weekly Wage
Women	
General worker	$3.24
Janitress	4.06
Chambermaid-laundress	3.58
Cook-laundress	4.00
Laundress	4.04
Lady's maid	3.63
Chambermaid and waitress	3.17
Waitress	3.31
Women	
Chambermaid	3.17
Child's nurse	3.35
Errand girl	2.00
Cook	4.02
Men	
General worker	5.38
Valet	8.00
Cook	6.17
Waiter	6.14
Coachman	8.58
Butler	8.24
Bellboy	2.61

Table XII which follows is drawn from *The Negro at Work in New York City,* and shows the modal wage groups

[27] Eaton, Isabel, *op. cit.*, pp. 447–449.

for specific occupations in domestic and personal service, New York City, 1906–1909. Although data for New York City are not typical of the entire country, these are the only available figures for this period, and they may indicate the trend of wages in domestic personal service in that section. In comparison with the preceding Table of Wages in Philadelphia, the increase in wages in New York City may be due to differences of conditions in the two cities rather than to any general increase or decrease in wages.

Modal Wage Groups for Selected Occupations, 1906–1909 [28]

[28] Haynes, George E., *op. cit.*, p. 81.

TABRE XII

Occupation	Rangh of Model Wage
Female	
Switchboard operator	$4.00–4.99
Chambermaid	4.00–4.99
Chambermaid-cook	5.00–5.99
Chambermaid-laundress	5.00–5.99
Chambermaid-waitress	4.00–4.99
Kitchenmaid	4.00–4.99
Cook	5.00–5.99
Cook and general worker	5.00–5.99
Cook-waitress	4.00–4.99
Cook-laundress	5.00–5.99
Errand girl	Less than 4.00
General houseworker	4.00–4.99
Laundress	4.00–4.99
Lady's maid	4.00–4.99
Parlor maid	4.00–4.99
Nurse	Less than 3.00
Pantry girl	4.00–4.99
Waitress	4.00–4.99
Dishwasher	4.00–4.99
Male	
Bellman	Less than 4.00
Butler-cook	5.00–5.99
Waiter	5.00–5.99
Butler	5.00–5.99
Coachman	5.00–5.99
Cook	5.00–5.99
Elevator operator	5.00–5.99
Furnaceman	5.00–5.99
Gardener	4.00–4.99
Hallman and doorman	4.00–4.99
Houseman	5.00–5.99
Janitor	5.00–5.99

The last decade embraces the World War when wages in domestic and personal service were at their maximum. The following tables for selected cities present graphically the increase in wages for male and female domestic workers and the slight increase in wages of females over that of males. These tables also show how wages vary in different sections of the country. Although these figures are for 1920, and the first quarter of 1921, the decline in wages generally did not begin until the fourth quarter of 1920, and it was not so pronounced in domestic and personal service as in many other occupational groups, and was scarcely appreciable in domestic service until the middle of 1921.

Tables XIII, XIV, XV, XVI, and XVII indicate that although wages in domestic and personal service among Negroes have fallen somewhat, they are still far above those of pre-war times. They also show that since the War there has been considerable decline in rates paid men for day work in New York City and Washington, D. C., but very little decrease in the rates for women day workers in either of the two cities.

Any analysis of these tables must take into consideration that female day workers in the cities included in the tables receive their carfare and at least one meal; cooks, general houseworkers, waiters and waitresses, housemen, mothers' helpers, some kitchen help, part-time workers and nurses receive their meals and, in many instances, their quarters.

In this table wages for clerical workers, factory workers, laborers, truckers, butchers, etc., are given in comparison with the wages of domestic and personal service workers. For example: a stenographer receives $18 a week, while a cook receives from $18 to $25 a week and board; a factory girl receives from 25 cents to 30 cents an hour, while a day worker in domestic service receives $22 a week, and a cook receives $25 a week and board.

Weekly Wages of 118 Negro Men in Domestic Service by Specified Occupations, New York City, 1920–1921 [29]

TABLE XIII

Occupations	Number Employed		Weekly Wages
Cleaners	3		$ .50 per hour
	5		3.00 per day
Cooks	2		15.00–17.99
	3		18.00–19.99
	3		25.00 or more
Dishwashers	2		10.00–12.99
	4		13.00–14.99 and meals
	1		15.00–17.99
	11		18.00–21.99
	1		26.00
Doormen	1		38.50 and meals
	3	(monthly)	40.00–79.00
Elevator operators (apt. house)	1	under	10.00
	1		10.00–12.99
	11		15.00–17.99
	1		18.00–21.99
Elevator and switchboard operators	6		14.00
	6		17.00
	1		18.00
Firemen (apt. house)	1		3.00 per day
	1		20.00–24.99
	1		20.00 and board
	1		30.00
Janitors (apt. house)	1	(monthly)	20.00 and apartment
	1	(monthly)	30.00 and keep
	1	(monthly)	40.00 and keep
	1	(monthly)	60.00 and keep
Assistant janitors (apt. house)	1		10.00–12.99
	1		15.00 and room
Porters-apartment houses	1		16.00
	6		18.00–20.99
Waiters	3	under	10.00
	18	(exclusive of tips)	15.00–17.99
	6		18.00–20.99
	7		10.00–11.99

[29] Haynes, George E., *unpublished data.*

Range of Weekly Wages of 754 Negro Women in Domestic and Personal Service, Specified by Occupations, New York City, 1920–1921 [30]

TABLE XIV

Occupations	Number Employed		Wages
General houseworkers	5	under	$ 9.00
	706		10.00–18.00
Chambermaids	1	under	9.00
Chambermaids-waitresses	7		12.00–18.00
Cooks	6		15.00–21.00
Kitchen helpers	8		12.00–17.00
	2	under	9.00
Mothers' helpers and Nurses	9		10.00–15.00
Nurses (practical)	3		15.00–21.00
Waitresses	5		12.00–14.00

Range of Daily and Weekly Wages of 1,565 Male and Female Negro Domestic and Personal Service Workers, Washington, D. C., 1920

TABLE XV

Occupations	Number Employed	Daily Wages	Weekly Wages
Male			
Butlers	7		12.00–15.00
Chauffeurs	3		14.00–15.00
Chauffeur-butler	13		14.00–15.00
Elevator operator	6		9.00–10.00
Janitors and housemen	34		10.00–12.00
Cooks	21		18.00–20.00
Furnace and yardman	10		7.00– 8.00
Waiters	11		9.00–10.00
Dishwashers	12		9.00–12.00
Day workers	6	4.00	
Female			
General houseworkers	49		10.00–12.00
Cooks	83		10.00–20.00
Maids	86		9.00–10.00
Waitresses	112		9.00–10.00
Personal maids	5		10.00–12.00
Kitchen maids	40		8.00– 9.00
Mothers helpers	75		5.00– 7.00
Pantry maids	62		10.00–12.00
Permanent laundresses	3		12.00–14.00
Cook-laundresses	81		10.00–12.00
Chambermaid-waitresses	240		9.00–10.00
Janitress	7		9.00–10.00
Elevator operator	82		8.00– 9.00
Parlor maids	21		9.00–10.00
Day workers	362	2.50–3.00	
Nurse maid	91		8.00– 9.00
Part-time workers	51		6.00– 7.00

[30] Haynes, George E., *unpublished data.*

Weekly Wages of 200 Male and 200 Female Negro Domestic Workers of Chicago by Occupations, 1923

TABLE XVI

Occupations	Number Enrolled		Weekly Wages
Male			
Factory	15		22.00
Waiter	8		15.00 and board
Bus Boys	6		10.00 and board
Elevator	1		14.00
Cook	10		25.00 and board
Cleaning	11	(per hour)	.50
Wringer	2		20.00
Fireman	2		24.00
Shoe shiners	3	(per day)	2.00 and tips
Butchers	6	(per hour)	.47 and up
Houseman	4	(per month)	70.00 room and board
Dishwasher	43		17.00 and board
Porter	10		20.00–25.00
Trucker	25		22.00
Laborers	54	(per hour)	.45–.60

Average Daily and Weekly Wage of Negro Domestic Workers by Occupation for Selected Cities, 1923

TABLE XVII

	Average Wage by Occupation							
	Day Workers	General House Workers	Cooks	Maids	Waitresses	Part-time Workers	Mothers' Helpers	Child Nurses
New York	$3.80	$13.85	$16.50	$13.00	$7 and tips	$8.00	$11.00	$11.00
Philadelphia	2.75	12.50	13.50	9.50	7 and tips	7.50	8.25	8.25
Baltimore	2.75	9.50	11.00	8.50	7 and tips	6.00	5.50	6.00
Washington, D. C.	2.00	9.25	10.75	8.50	8 and tips	7.50	8.00	8.00
Detroit	3.35	9.50	11.00	9.00	7 and tips	9.50	9.50	10.00
Indianapolis	2.25	10.00	13.50	9.00	7 and tips		8.00	13.50
Boston	3.00	12.00	12.50	10.50	10.50			
Los Angeles	3.80		15.00	11.50	8.00			
Montgomery	1.75	7.00		6.50				
Nashville	1.75	7.00		6.50				

Male	Day laborers	Chauffeurs	Cooks	Janitors	Dishwashers	Bell men	Waiters	Porters	Elevator operators
New York	$3.00	$25.00	$20.00	$ 9.50	$12.00	$ 9.50	$10.00	$15.00	15.00
Boston	4.00	25.00	22.50	20.00	12.00	13.50	12.00	15.00	15.00
Philadelphia	3.80	25.00	20.00	15.00	9.50	6.50	7.00	15.00	15.00
Baltimore	3.50	18.00	21.00	15.00	9.50	7.87	9.30	15.00	9.30-15.00

The table above shows that wages in the specified occupations in different sections of the country, for the most part, do not vary very much. Wages for males are given for only four cities because the wages for males in the other cities mentioned, with two exceptions, are about the same as in these four cities. In addition to money wages received for day work, women get their carfare and often one or two meals, while men receive only the money wages. Elevator operators in Baltimore hotels are paid from $40 to $50 a month instead of $15 a week as in apartment houses because more tips are given in hotels.

Although in consideration of the present rate of wages the total annual wage paid for domestic and personal service in the homes of the United States must be large, there seems to be no available data on this point. However, an estimate has been made of the total quarterly wages for 1920 and 1921 and the first quarter of 1922 paid domestic and personal service employees in the hotels and similar institutions of Continental United States. The range of quarterly wages in such institutions for 1920 was 666 to 700 millions of dollars; for 1921, 660 to 678 millions of dollars; and for 1922, 643 millions of dollars. The maximum cyclical decline in the wages of such workers for that period of time was 8.15 per cent.

Even though seven other groups of occupations had a smaller percentage cyclical decline in wages following the war than public domestic and personal service and twelve other groups of occupations had a larger cyclical decline, the average earnings an hour for each domestic and personal service worker are less than that for any other occupation or industry except agriculture. The average earnings in cents an hour for each employee in domestic and personal service were for the first quarter of 1920, 34 cents; for the first quarter of 1921, 34 cents; and for the first quarter of 1922, 33 cents.[31]

[31] King, W. I., *Employment, Hours and Earnings in the United States, 1920–1922*, Chap. V, pp. 5, 19; Chap. IV, p. 3.

28

Hours of Negro Domestic Workers

Although during the past thirty years there has been considerable advance made in the matter of hours for domestic and personal service workers, the change in this particular has not kept pace throughout the United States with the increase in wages in domestic and personal service occupations. Thirty years ago 38 per cent of 1,434 female domestic employees from all sections of the United States were actually working ten hours a day, 6 per cent of them were working eleven hours a day, 31 per cent were working twelve hours or more a day, and 25 per cent of them were working less than ten hours a day.[32]

In recent years the hours and wages of female domestic and personal service workers in several states of the union have been standardized by the enactment of state minimum wage laws. Utah, which has an eight hour day and a 48 hour week for female workers generally, lists any regular employer of female labor under those occupations covered by law. This would include domestic service for women. The minimum wage rate in this State for experienced women is $1.25 per day. Wisconsin, which has a ten hour day and a 55 hour week for females and minors, includes under its minimum wage law every person in receipt of, or entitled to, any compensation for labor performed for any employer. Domestic workers must be included in this number. Colorado includes under its minimum wage law any occupation which embraces "any and every vocation, trade, pursuit and industry." Since domestic service is a pursuit or vocation, it must come under the minimum wage law of Colorado. The state of Washington has an eight hour day and a 56 hour week and a wage of $18 a week and $3 a day for females engaged in public housekeeping, but not for private domestic workers. North Dakota publicly excludes domestic service and agriculture from its occupations or industries covered by the minimum wage law. Although the other seven State minimum wage laws do not

[32] Salmon, Lucy M., *op. cit.*

openly exclude domestic service, it is not included as yet among occupations and industries. Two attempts were recently made in California to secure through legislation a ten hour day for domestic workers. The first bill was defeated. The second bill passed both houses but received a pocket veto.[33] In States where there is no minimum wage legislation the working hours for day workers and part-time workers are standardized on an eight hour basis.

The extensive use of day workers came into popularity largely through necessity during the World War. At that time such a large proportion of the permanent domestic employees found openings in other lines of work that housewives supplemented their own labor by hiring day workers. The large demand for such workers gave them the leverage of establishing for themselves an eight hour day and a wage commensurate with that in many lines of industry. Day workers have retained since the World War both the eight hour day and the advanced wages.

The part-time workers, too, have definite hours. Many of them do cooking and general housework but for only specified hours. Some of them work four or five hours or less in the mornings, especially when the work is largely cleaning. Not a few of them begin in the afternoon and do general housework and prepare dinner and serve it. But the hours are fixed hours. Some part-time workers have a regular place of employment for mornings and another such place for afternoons. Their hours are definite and their wages are thus very good. Frequently the part-time worker has every Sunday off.

The hours for the other domestic service workers generally do not seem to be so well standardized as yet. Three Washington, D. C., employers wished their general houseworkers to come on duty at seven o'clock in the morning, with the promise that the workers could leave when they finished. Although 75.3 per cent of one thousand domestic workers, exclusive of day workers and part-time

[33] *Monthly Labor Review,* U. S. Bureau of Labor Statistics, August, 1920, p. 212.

workers, in the private families and boarding houses of Washington, D. C., were on duty ten hours or over, this would show that the three employers mentioned above were not typical. Three other employers in the same mentioned city maintained an eight hour day for their help by having an extra worker prepare the dinners and serve them.

Apparently no attempt has been made to compare the hours of the private domestic and personal service workers with those of the workers in other industries. An estimate made of the full-time hours a week during 1920 and 1921 for the average employee in all enterprises of whatever size in the Continental United States discloses the fact that the average full-time hours a week for public domestic and personal service workers were from 56.6 to 57.1, while the average for workers in all industries including domestic and personal service was 50.3 to 51.3 hours a week. In New York City, according to employment agents, the practice of an eight to nine hour day for domestic workers generally obtains.

Specific Occupations of Negro Domestic Workers

The chief employment of the day workers in more than three-fourths of the States is laundry work and cleaning. It is significant that in twenty-one States for which the 1920 advanced occupational census sheets have been obtained, where the Negro population is negligible, there is no principal occupation given as that of launderer and laundress "not in laundries." In all of the States for which there are reports given in the cities of those States where the Negro population is large there is such a principal occupation. However, this occupation in spite of the increased popularity of day work during the World War is decreasing in numbers as the following table will indicate. Whether this decrease is due to the "wet wash" laundry system and to the increased facilities in hand laundries we have no data to prove.

Table XVIII given below represents the States so far

as the 1920 census reports go, which have the principal occupation of launderer and laundress "not in laundries." In all of the States except Vermont, the Negro population is quite appreciable. Just why Vermont is not among the 21 States which have a negligible Negro population and no such principal occupation accessible data did not disclose. The reason why the 21 States have no such principal occupation is probably due to the fact that laundry work is so laborious that white domestic workers are averse to it, and those able to have the work done send it to a steam laundry.

The Number of Launderers and Laundresses in 14 States in 1910–1920

TABLE XVIII State	Male		Female	
	1910	1920	1910	1920
Louisiana	406	389	23,051	17,034
Georgia	832	667	44,710	36,775
No. Carolina	387	296	23,192	15,185
Florida	394	342	14,844	16,552
Dist. of Columbia	121	93	7,920	6,095
Maryland	448	253	16,189	12,418
Delaware	20	26	1,665	1,110
Indiana	300	245	10,130	7,238
Vermont	34	21	1,256	684
Kansas	210	163	4,814	3,760
New Jersey	452	322	11,171	7,626
New Mexico	71	51	1,678	1,299
Oklahoma	154	124	5,349	4,350
West Virginia	140	84	3,923	2,505

A general houseworker has come to be thought of by the public as a maid of all work, and sometimes she is; but in many homes she is relieved of doing the laundry work. In some cities general housework does not always include cooking. For example, in New York City and Brooklyn it may not include cooking unless specified by the terms cooking and general housework. In New York and some other cities men have been tried as general workers.

According to employment agencies, butlers are not used in such large numbers as they were before the World War. During the war it was difficult to secure them because men were needed for war work. Since then wages have been such that employers have largely used chambermaid-waitresses or chauffeur-butlers instead of regular butlers. Among the 779 Negro men in domestic and personal service (New York City, 1921, Table XI), there is not one butler. This does not mean that there are no Negro butlers in New York City, but it indicates their scarcity and shows that employers living in apartment houses can do without them. Negro cooks, however, are yet an important factor in the domestic and personal service groups.

There are still Negro personal maids who make provision for the special comfort and well being of their employers as well as do their little mending, and the like. And there are Negro pantry maids whose first duty it is to make salads. Chambermaid-waitresses and parlor maids to do such as to answer the door bell are also still used. The tendency, however, is in the direction of having but the one general maid, together with a laundress to come in by the day. Mothers' helpers or young girls to assist in all the work of the house and with the children are also being employed quite extensively, and at less wages than would be paid to an older general houseworker.

These different occupations for the most part call for different types of workers. A butler or a chambermaid-waitress who is tall and comely may have access to a larger number and to better places than one who is short. Especially is this true of cooks for apartment or for a general houseworker where there are stairs to climb. These are much more frequently chosen from among the medium-sized women than from the stout women. The reason for the latter choice is apparent. In the case of the butler or chambermaid-waitress, the basis of choice is apparently appearance and custom.

V. LIVING CONDITIONS, HEALTH, SOCIAL LIFE, ORGANIZATIONS OF NEGRO DOMESTIC WORKERS, AND THEIR RELATION TO EMPLOYMENT AGENCIES

Living conditions here refer only to those on employers' premises. The general living conditions of Negro domestic workers in different parts of the country, or even in different localities of the same section, vary so widely that the subject cannot be treated here. For example, in the South laundresses for the most part take bundle wash to their small homes, and do large "washes" there. Such a situation makes it difficult for southern Negro laundresses to live comfortably and healthfully. Laundresses in the North are relieved of this problem by going to the homes of employers, but, on the other hand, are affected by the excessive rents and the overcrowding in their own homes.

Living conditions on employers' premises for domestic workers vary to some extent in different homes of the same city but to a larger extent in the different sections of the country and in different cities of the same section. In Montgomery, Alabama, for example, out of two hundred Negro female domestic workers interviewed, 54 or about 27 per cent were living in a two-room detached frame house on the rear of the employers' premises. The remaining 73 per cent did not "sleep in" or live on their employers' premises. In Philadelphia, living conditions on employers' premises are reported as being good. They consist, in the main, of a third floor room. Very few basement rooms are offered as living quarters for domestic workers in that city. In Indianapolis, about 50 per cent of those working by the week among the 471 domestic workers go home nights. Living conditions for those "sleeping in" are fair as a rule. Some have basement rooms but a majority of them have rooms either on the third floor or in the attic or over a garage. A small percentage of the homes have a bath room for the maid.

Employment agencies in Boston, New York City, Brooklyn, Philadelphia, Detroit, Chicago, and Los Angeles give favorable reports on the living conditions of domestic workers who "sleep in." While the reports from Baltimore are not as conclusively favorable as for the above-named cities, one fact stands out prominently, namely: that in the main, only apartment houses in that city offer basement rooms as living quarters for domestic workers. Employment agencies in all of the cities mentioned state that there are far more calls for workers to "sleep in" than there are workers who are willing to do so.

Out of 500 domestic workers in Washington, D. C., selected at random from 3,000 permanent employees for the year 1921–22, about 64.1 per cent were requested to "sleep in." Out of an equal number of employers requesting workers to "sleep in," selected in the same manner, about 83 per cent provided basement rooms as sleeping quarters for such workers; about 10 per cent either provided first floor or third floor rooms—some of them with baths; about 7 per cent either offered attics or they failed to furnish a statement as to the location of the rooms. Occasionally an employer would like to have the worker "sleep in" but because of having only a basement room to offer, she would forego her wish in the interest of the health of the employee. Two of the workers sent out from this office were partially incapacitated by the poor living and working conditions. One of the problems, however, involved in housing domestic employees is the frequency of the turnover which necessarily brings in different kinds of workers, varying in degrees of personal cleanliness and health.

Closely connected with the living conditions, too, are the working conditions of domestic employees. In fact, one of the strains of such service often is the lack of break between the place of work and of living, which makes for resulting monotony and much loneliness. Much of a domestic worker's life is spent in the kitchen, in the laundry or on the premises of his employer. The only available accurate data on this point have come from Indianapolis, Ind. This was secured in response to a questionnaire sent to the employers who were patrons of the employment office at Flanner House. The following table gives a summary of the replies as to the appliances employers had in their homes for use of Negro domestic workers.

Replies from 523 Employers Showing the Appliances in the Homes for Doing Laundry Work, in Indianapolis, Ind., April, 1922

TABLE XVIII

		Per Cent
Number having electric machines	**249**	**47.6**
Number having water power machines	2	.4
Number having hand power machines	5	.9
Number not having machines of any kind	267	51.1
		100.0
Number having electric irons	479	91.6
Number having gas irons	5	.9
Number having mangles—ironing machine	31	5.9
Number having stationary tubs	202	38.6
Number having driers	3	.6

According to this record about 48.9 per cent of the 523 employers had washing machines of some kind and about 51.1 per cent had none at all; about 38.6 per cent had installed stationary tubs and 0.6 per cent had driers. To one who is conversant with the old way of doing laundry work with heavy portable wooden tubs, and with the lighter weight zinc tubs, into which water was lifted for washing and from which it was lifted after washing, and then placed upon either a dry goods box or a wash bench of uncertain height, this table shows marvelous improvement in working conditions of Negro laundresses in Indianapolis and indicates unusual possibilities there and elsewhere. However, unless there were, in each of the homes having washing machines, a stationary tub, or a rubber tube for draining the water out of the washing machine, there still would be that lifting of water, and possibly undue exertion because of the uncertain height of the portable tub. The principle of having the tub set at the right height involves relief from straining the back, an important item in relation to good health. There were about 98.4 per cent of the 523 employers who had either electric or gas irons or mangles. Such appliances facilitate ironing as well as enable a laundress to do better work. Washing machines and mangles make it possible to do the bed linen at home instead of sending it to a steam laundry. Driers are particularly serviceable in winter when drying out of doors is difficult as well being hard on the laundress because of the cold weather.

The employment agency that sent out the questionnaire congratulated the employers on the marked improvement made in appliances for laundering, and added that like improvements will in time be made in the type and conditions of work rooms in which laundresses must labor.

The Health of Negro Domestic Workers

Although the health of domestic workers is an extremely important matter because of the nature of their work and the homes into which they go, and because their support depends so largely upon their physical ability to work, no records apparently are kept by the various employment agencies relative to the health of the workers. In 1899 out of 152 male and 395 female domestic workers in Philadelphia, 80 per cent of the men had not been ill during the year, and 74 per cent of the women had not been ill during the year. This per cent of good health excluded colds. The most prevalent disabilities among them were: consumption, lagrippe, quinsy, sore throat, rheumatism, neuralgia, chills and fever, and dyspepsia.[34] That there is much opportunity for danger from infection incident to the ill-health of domestic workers cannot be denied.[35]

Very careful note was taken for one week in March, 1922, of the health of women domestic workers reporting at the United States Employment Agency, Washington, D. C. It was not a typical week because of the fact that it followed an epidemic of lagrippe. However, out of 1,043 domestic workers, only 325 or about 31 per cent had not been ill during that winter and had no complaint whatever. Lagrippe, surgical operations, indigestion, heart trouble, weak back, and neuralgia were the illnesses of which they most commonly complained.

There were among the number above, five evident cases of mental disturbance, one of which was taken to St. Elizabeth's Hospital for observation and treatment. Another

[34] Eaton, Isabel, *op. cit.*, p. 495.

[35] Reed, Ruth, *op. cit.*, p. 35.

from the number had been discharged from the same hospital after treatment for mental trouble. This fact was not known by the Agency until an officer from the hospital visited the woman at her place of work to see how she was getting along. Three cases that were suspected of having tuberculosis were referred as waitresses at different times to a public hospital, at some risk of course to the reputation of the office, largely to see what the reaction of the nurse in charge would be. In each case the nurse reported that she could not use such a person about the food. Yet such persons were taken into some of the most desirable homes in Washington as household employees.

Social Life of Negro Domestic Workers

The social life of the older domestic Negro workers centers largely in their church and secret order society connections. From 1916 to 1920 seven out of every eleven Negroes in the United States were enrolled in churches. Many of them are willing to accept a place at a much lower wage than another if it gives them their Sundays off so that they may attend their churches.

It is important then to see the scope of such organizations in Negro city life. Kansas City, Missouri, with a Negro population in 1910 of 23,566, had 19 Negro churches and 16 Negro missions in 1913, with a total membership of 7,156. In this city there were 135 different lodges, or households (women's chapters), with a total membership of 8,055, 4,226 men and 3,829 women. The average initiation fee in the men's orders was $11.50 and in the women's $4.51 with additional monthly dues of 50 cents and 25 cents respectively. Endowment insurance policies of these lodges for which there is an annual fee from $2 to $4 are for the most part optional. These 8,055 members pay into their lodges annually $55,411.40. Their property in Kansas City is valued at $46,100. Each of the 135 orders has sick benefits ranging from $2.50 to $4.50 a week and all of them, with

[36] Haynes, George E., *unpublished data*, 1921.

one exception, pay burial expenses in case of death.[37] In Harlem, New York, with a Negro population of about 90,000 in 1920 there are 25 Negro churches and about 16 missions. There are in this densely populated section six moving picture theatres which cater largely to Negro patronage.[38] Gainesville, Georgia, with a Negro population in 1910 of 1,629 had a Negro church membership of 1,023. Five of the Negro lodges in that city admit women, some of whom are members of several lodges.[39] In the lodges composed as they are very largely of the masses of the Negro people with a few of the more intelligent leaders as officers, there are many possibilities for improving the efficiency of the domestic workers.

Just what is the social life of the younger Negro domestic workers, many of whom are away from their own families, is a question. Of the 471 Negro domestic workers registered at the Indianapolis office, about 44.5 per cent were rooming and only about 2.3 per cent were living with parents or relatives. As possible attractions for such workers there are the moving picture and low vaudeville theatres, usually located in Negro neighborhoods, the pool and billiard rooms, cabarets and questionable dance halls.

Dr. Rubinow says that of 2,300 domestic white workers, a large majority of whom were under 30 years of age, interviewed by the Michigan Bureau of Labor, only 51 belonged to fraternal societies of any kind. Of 230 questioned by the Domestic Relation Reform League, 20 belonged to clubs and 15 to classes of some kind, and 118 entertained no men callers. A domestic worker, he says, not only loses caste among other groups of workers, but she loses at the hands of her employers even her family name. She lives a life of loneliness, "in a family but not of it." [40]

[37] Martin, Asa E., *Our Negro Population*, Kansas City, 1913, pp. 180, 143.

[38] Haynes, Geo. E., *unpublished data*, 1921.

[39] Reed, Ruth, *op. cit.*, p. 51.

[40] Rubinow, I. M., *Depth and Breadth of the Servant Problem*, *McClure's Magazine*, Vol. 34, p. 576, 1909–1910.

Organization of Domestic Workers

In order to show concretely what domestic workers themselves have attempted to do to improve their conditions, some discussion of their organizations as an expression of that attempt is in place here. It is not certain how many of these organizations are still active nor how many have Negro members. Some of them have such members, no doubt. However, three of them are composed entirely of Negroes.

In Los Angeles, California, the "Progressive Household Club" with a membership of 75 domestic workers is still active. This club was organized primarily for the purpose of furnishing a cheerful and welcome home for a domestic worker taking a rest or not employed for a time. It has a self-supporting home which will accommodate twenty-five girls. Their recreational and educational features are not startling, as the secretary writes, but they enable the girls to pass some cheerful hours out of their "humdrum" lives. This club was among the 15 other domestic workers' clubs organized in 1919 and 1920. In 1919 a Domestic Workers' Alliance with a membership of over 200, affiliated with the Hotel Waitresses under the American Federation of Labor, was granted a charter. During that year, the secretary of Hotel and Restaurant Employees of the International Alliance and International League of America reported that this organization had established a domestic workers' union in each of the following cities: Mobile, Alabama; Fort Worth, Texas; and Lawton, Oklahoma. A union of domestic workers was also organized in Tulsa, Oklahoma, in 1919. The following March a charter was granted to a domestic workers' union in Richmond, Virginia.[41] In 1920 there were 10 unions of domestic workers affiliated with the American Federation of Labor. These unions were located in the following cities: Los Angeles and San Diego, California; Brunswick, Georgia;

[41] *Monthly Labor Review*, U. S. Bureau of Labor Statistics, Aug., 1919, p. 212, May, 1920, p. 116.

Chicago and Glencoe, Illinois; New Orleans, Louisiana; Beaver Valley, Pennsylvania; Denison, Harrisburg, and Houston, Texas. The New Orleans Union, a Negro organization, was composed of about 200 members. All of these organizations have now ceased to be affiliated with the American Federation of Labor. There is, however, one union of domestic workers in Arecibo, Porto Rico, affiliated with the American Federation of Labor.

Relation of Negro Domestic Service to Employment Agencies

In view of the volume and extent of turn-over in domestic service, employment agencies, especially in the North, East, and West, have a close relationship to both employers and workers. A person in need of domestic help secures it either by advertising in the help wanted section of the newspapers, by applying to one or more employment agencies, by means of inquiries among friends and acquaintances who may have been a former employer of some available laborer, by accepting some one who may by chance apply in person or by hiring a former worker.

In some of the southern cities where there is no local employment agency, domestic workers are secured in all other of the above-mentioned ways. For example, this condition prevails in Montgomery, Alabama. Although the United States Employment Service, the Department of Labor, and the Municipal Employment offices of Birmingham and Mobile, Alabama, are co-operating, there is no State license applying to local employment agencies except those soliciting laborers to go outside of the State, according to a recent statement from the Alabama Tax Commission. A like condition exists in the State of Louisiana. Georgia, however, issues licenses to employment agencies for domestic positions. In this State as in some others, there is no law regulating the fee which an agency may charge either employer or employee for service rendered. Neither Ohio, Pennsylvania, California, nor Maryland, and several other States have such a fee regulated by law. However, in Pennsylvania, every employment agent must file with the commissioner for his approval a schedule of fees, proposed to be charged for any service rendered to employer or employee, and these may be changed only with the approval of the commissioner. Every employment agent in this State is required to give a receipt to any applicant for any money which the applicant pays him; and if an applicant fails through no fault of his to secure a position to which he is referred, the entire amount paid by such a person to the agent is to be refunded. Such a law obtains in some other States.

In Baltimore there are 50 employment agencies, mainly of a domestic nature. The usual fee charged an employer, though not regulated by law, is $2. An agency ordinarily agrees to supply an employer with help for at least 30 days without additional cost.

New York State issued in 1918, 674 licenses to employment agencies engaged in various kinds of employment business. In 1919, 719 employment agency licenses were issued; in 1920, 728 and in 1921, 788. The law stipulates that the fees charged domestic work applicants by employment agencies shall not in any case exceed ten per cent of the first month's wages. If a domestic worker does not accept a position to which he is referred or fails to obtain employment, the full amount which he paid the agency is to be refunded after three days allowed for obtaining facts. If an employee fails to remain one week in a position, the agency is required to furnish the employer with a new employee, or return 3.6 of the fee paid in by the employer, provided the employer notifies the agency within thirty days of the failure of the worker to accept the position or of the employee's discharge for cause. If the employee is discharged within one week without his fault, another position is furnished him or 3.5 of the fee returned.

Employment agencies in New York State must also give receipts for money paid them. Day workers receiving a rate of $3.60 to $4.00 per day each pay an initial fee of 50 cents to the agency furnishing them with work. Employers of domestic labor pay the agency for one month's service a flat rate of from $6 to $10 for general houseworkers and from $3 to $5 for part-time workers. For a temporary laborer, employers pay a fee of $1 and for a day worker they pay a fee of 50 cents. For commercial and industrial placements an employee pays to the agency 5 per cent of her first month's wage, but no charge is made for the employer furnishing the work.

The laws of Massachusetts regulating employment agencies of a domestic nature are almost similar to those of New York State, the difference in the main being in the size of the fees. In Massachusetts an intelligence office keeper is entitled to receive from an applicant, employer or employee, a fee of 25 per cent of the first week's wages; and in case of day work a fee of 10 per cent of a day's pay. The Michigan domestic employment agency fees for employee and employer are about the same as that for New York State.

In the District of Columbia, a domestic employment agency is entitled to receive in advance from an employer $2 for each employee for at least 30 days service, and from an applicant for work $1. One-half of this fee is to be returned on demand if such applicant does not have a fair opportunity of employment within 15 days from date of payment. When an applicant actually receives employment at a wage of $25 a month or more he pays the agency an additional $1. However, it is a common practice among Washington employment agencies to have applicants pay $2 in advance of securing a place for work. In the light of the total amount of money paid in wages of domestic and personal service, especially with such a heavy turnover, the fees paid to employment agencies by both employers and employees evidently amount to quite a considerable sum.

Thirty years ago Miss Salmon in her study of domestic

service pointed out, not only the exorbitant fees charged by employment agencies, but the vice and crime nurtured by them.[42] In 1915 investigations of Miss Kellor in Baltimore, Philadelphia, New York, Boston and other cities brought out some more striking facts. In Philadelphia 84 per cent of the employment agencies were in private residences and 3 per cent of them were in business buildings. In New York 85 per cent of these agencies were conducted in very close contact with the families of the agents. In Chicago 81 per cent of them were in buildings occupied by families. In Boston 73 per cent of the agencies were in business buildings and only 27 per cent were in residences. The poor business methods of many private intelligence offices, surrounded by gambling dens, fortune tellers, palmists and midwives, and their frauds are insignificant as compared with their conscious, deliberate immorality. Miss Kellor says that many Negro intelligence offices are hopelessly immoral but that some city authorities often argue that since they do not affect the whites there is no reason for disturbing them.[43]

The Third Biennial Report of the Department of Labor and Industry of Maine for the year 1915–1916 contains a warning against employment agencies collecting fees in excess of the law. This report recommends that the important economic task of employment be taken out of the hands of the agents and placed under management of the State. A similar note was voiced by one of the committees of President Harding's conference on unemployment.

The large experience with both municipal and State offices and with the United States Employment Service has given unmistakable evidence that the recruiting and placement of labor is a public necessity and a general benefit to the whole community. It can therefore well become a matter conducted under public supervision and at public expense. Domestic service, especially in large cities and particularly because of the absence of organization and

[42] Salmon, Lucy M., *op. cit.*, p. 115.

[43] Kellor, Frances A., *Out of Work*, pp. 197, 222, 225, 229.

group connection of the workers, is especially in need of such public direction.

SUMMARY AND CONCLUSIONS

From 1870 to 1900 there was an increase in the total number of persons engaged in domestic and personal service in the United States. Since that time there has been a steady decrease in the number so engaged. Although Negroes have followed the general trend of increase and decline, in proportion to their population, they furnish a larger percentage of domestic workers than any other group in the United States, the female workers outnumbering the male.

The fact is also evident that Negroes are gradually entering trade and transportation and manufacturing and mechanical pursuits. With the existing conditions following the World War, and the present restriction on immigration, the opportunities in these fields of labor are enlarging and domestic and personal service workers are, therefore, correspondingly decreasing.

The ranks of the domestic service workers are being recruited to some appreciable extent from the younger Negro women, between the ages of 16 and 24 years. The very young women and the old women are not the most sought after by employers because of their inexperience on the one hand, and on the other, their inability to do domestic work. The problems of married women in domestic service are increasing because of their family responsibilities and cares which make demands upon their earnings and energy.

The domestic labor turnover has increased the past thirty years. During and since the World War, it has been so greatly accentuated that the modal period of service is from 3 to 6 months. The length of the period of service will perhaps become still shorter because of the increasing opportunities in trade and transportation and in manufacturing and mechanical pursuits.

Provision for the training of domestic workers generally has been meager, and in the case of Negro domestic workers it has been less than that for them as a group. Since the World War greater attempts have been made to extend training to domestic workers both in England and the United States, the government in each of these countries taking a small part in this extension of education. Training especially for Negro domestic workers has been undertaken. Employment agencies under government supervision, with the co-operation of domestic service employers, offer possibilities for such training and for the standardization of private household work. However, Negroes with any appreciable degree of intelligence are not entering domestic service as a permanent employment. This field in the United States is being left largely to the untrained and inefficient.

During the twenty years preceding the World War, very little advance was made in the wages of domestic workers, but during the war their wages increased about 150 per cent. Since the war, according to Dr. King, while the decline in public domestic service wages has not been as great as that in many other fields of employment, the average earnings an hour in money wages of public domestic service workers are still below those in a majority of the industries. Although there has been an increase in wages of domestic service workers, their working hours are longer than those of any other group of laborers.

In some cities living conditions on employers' premises for domestic workers are good, in others there is need of great improvement along this line. However, with the increasing disinclination on the part of the domestic workers to "sleep in" and the slowly growing public interest in standardizing house work, this problem will in time be solved. There has been much improvement in the working conditions of domestic employees, but there is still need of much more.

The indications are that little attention is paid to the

health and the social life of domestic workers. This neglect, especially of the health of domestic workers, is no doubt fraught with dangerous consequences, not only for themselves but for the homes and welfare of the nation.

That the social life of the older Negro domestic workers is supplied at least to some extent in their churches is proved by the fact that about seven out of every eleven Negroes in the United States are enrolled as members of churches. Their interest in secret orders is also shown by the number of members and the money spent in such organizations. As social attractions for the younger domestic employees, there are such places as dance halls, moving pictures, pool and billiard rooms, and the like. The social stigma attached to domestic service bars young domestic workers from many of the entertainments of real value and benefit.

Domestic workers in ten or more cities of the United States have attempted to better their conditions by means of organized effort. The organization in California is rendering real service to its members through its home. With the present large percentage of domestic workers who are rooming in the various cities, and the conditions obtaining in many rooming houses connected with employment agencies, there is urgent need of establishing clubs or homes for domestic workers.

Many private employment agencies in their relation to the homes of the United States act as brokers. The fees charged both the employer and the employee are generally exorbitant. The service rendered by them is on the whole poor. The harm inflicted upon society by many of them is irreparable. Public control of employment agencies has great possibilities for social betterment.

ELIZABETH ROSS HAYNES

DOCUMENTS

Documents and Comments on Benefit of Clergy as Applied to Slaves

The following transcripts from the records of the Superior Court of Richmond County, North Carolina, illustrate the application of benefit of clergy to slaves charged with and found guilty of crimes punishable with death.*

Fall Term 1828

State vs George (A Slave) } Burglary { Pleads "Not Guilty" The following Jury empaneled therein (Viz) (1) Cyrus Bennet

(2) Alen Shaw
(3) Try McFarland
(4) Wade LeGrand
(5) George Wright
(6) James Covington
(7) William Crowson
(8) Thos. B. Blewett
(9) Israel Watkins
(10) Risdon Nichols
(11) Lenard Webb
(12) Hampton Covington—

Who find the Prisoner "not Guilty" of Burglary in manner and Form as charged in the Bill of Ind't'm't But guilty of Grand Larceny . . .

The Prisoner appeared at the Bar and being asked by the Court If he had any thing to say why Sentence of Death should not be pronounced against him, Answered by Council praying the benefit of his Clergy. Which was allowed him by the Court & adjudged that he receive *THIRTY NINE* lashes on his Bare Back & stand committed till his Master enter into recognisance of $200 for his good behavior for the Space of Twelve months & pay cost of Prosecution. . . . Sentence to be Carried into effect on Tomorrow at 4 Oclock P. M.

* These documents were collected by Prof. Wm. K. Boyd, of Trinity College, Durham, North Carolina.

ABOUT THE AUTHORS

Henry Louis Gates, Jr., is the W. E. B. Du Bois Professor of the Humanities, Chair of the Afro-American Studies Department, and Director of the W. E. B. Du Bois Institute for Afro-American Research at Harvard University. One of the leading scholars of African-American literature and culture, he is the author of *Words, Signs, and the Racial Self* (1987), *The Signifying Monkey: A Theory of Afro-American Literary Criticism* (1988), *Loose Canons: Notes on the Culture Wars* (1992), and the memoir *Colored People* (1994).

Jennifer Burton is in the Ph.D. program in English Language and Literature at Harvard University. She is the volume editor of *The Prize Plays and Other One-Acts* in this series. She is a contributor to *The Oxford Companion to African-American Literature* and to *Great Lives from History: American Women*. With her mother and sister she coauthored two one-act plays, *Rita's Haircut* and *Litany of the Clothes*. Her fiction and personal essays have appeared in *Sun Dog, There and Back*, and *Buffalo*, the Sunday magazine of the *Buffalo News*.

Francille Rusan Wilson is Assistant Professor of Afro-American Studies at the University of Maryland at College Park. She is currently completing a book entitled *The Segregated Scholars: Black Social Scientists and the Development of Black Labor Studies, 1890–1950*, one of the first collective biographies of twentieth-century black intellectuals. Her article "'This Past Was Waiting for Me When I Came': The Contextualization of Black Women's History" was published in 1996 in *Feminist Studies*.